Publications in Librarianship Number 68

Not Just Where to Click

Teaching Students How to Think about Information

Edited by Troy A. Swanson and Heather Jagman

D1082102

2015

Association of College and Research Libraries
A division of the American Library Association
Chicago, Illinois 2015

The paper used in this publication meets the minimum requirements of American National Standard for Information Sciences–Permanence of Paper for Printed Library Materials, ANSI Z39.48-1992. ∞

Library of Congress Cataloging-in-Publication Data

Not just where to click : teaching students how to think about information / edited by Troy A. Swanson and Heather Jagman.
    pages cm. -- (Publications in librarianship ; #68)
  Includes bibliographical references and index.
  ISBN 978-0-8389-8716-2 (pbk. : alk. paper) -- ISBN 978-0-8389-8717-9 (pdf) -- ISBN 978-0-8389-8718-6 (ePub) -- ISBN 978-0-8389-8719-3 (Kindle)
  1. Information literacy--Study and teaching (Higher)--United States. 2. Research--Methodology--Study and teaching (Higher)--United States. 3. Library orientation for college students--United States. 4. Media literacy--Study and teaching (Higher)--United States. 5. Academic libraries--Relations with faculty and curriculum--United States. 6. Knowledge, Theory of. 7. Library science--Philosophy. 8. Academic libraries--United States--Case studies. I. Swanson, Troy A., editor. II. Jagman, Heather, editor.
  ZA3075.N68 2014
  028.7071173--dc23
                              2014045103

Table of Contents

2.3 Interpreting the World

Introduction:
More than Just Where to Click

Troy A. Swanson and Heather Jagman

We are part of a generation of librarians who entered the profession in the mid-to-late 1990s at the cusp of the digital revolution. As undergraduates, we lived in a primarily print-based world with shelves of indices, cabinets of microfilm, and cutting-edge CD towers for retrieving articles. Books dominated. DVDs had not even hit the scene. Random cassette tapes and boxes of vinyl LPs could still be found in most library collections. But by the time we were in library school and immediately after graduation, everything had changed. The graphical interface to the Internet, the World Wide Web, had not only arrived but was starting to be recognized as the great disruptor it would become. Yes, it was still the time dominated by AOL, Alta Vista, and Yahoo!, but with the first free e-mail services via the web, the first chat room, and the first search engine results page, we knew that things were different.

We were in library school at a time when people, including faculty members, were asking whether libraries would survive the decade. The web brought an avalanche of inexpensive and easy-to-access information directly into homes, offices, and classrooms. Would people still need libraries? Or, more precisely, *in an age of information abundance, would libraries be relevant?* It was one of the central questions driving our education and early careers. Since that time, our profession has answered this question many times over by evolving, growing, and remaining vital to the communities we serve.

The advent of the web commingled many different kinds of sources, and thus placed the burden of decision making on the shoulders of the searcher, but it did not fundamentally alter the epistemological stances or understanding of authority. The nature of methodologies, expertise, documentation, scholarship, and investigative journalism remains fundamentally unchanged. Today it seems that digitally delivered information has come to dominate, but this digital dominance is not a paradigm shift regarding *how* we know things.[1] Perhaps we may find a new form of authority in crowdsourced documents like *Wikipedia*, but this innovation, with its own strengths and weaknesses, has not signaled an upheaval of our epistemological approaches to information. Over a decade ago Edward L. Ayers and Charles M. Grisham noted,

> The form in which scholarship appears has barely changed, despite all the revolutions in computing. Across almost every field, researchers, no matter how sophisticated the technology they use in discovery, translate those discoveries into simple word-processed documents. Sure, we sometimes add JPEG images and other simple illustrations, and in the sciences, pre-prints rush around the world long before the articles appear in print journals, but merely putting scholarly discourse into HTML and PDF formats has not changed scholarship in any significant manner. The nature of argument has remained remarkably resistant to innovation in rhetoric or form in every field of scholarly endeavor.[2]

In an age of information abundance, the web makes epistemological understandings more important by removing the filters of scarcity, but it does not greatly alter those understandings. The most common concerns and frustrations about the web result from the ways that information is shared, not from epistemological crises. Students do not recognize the differences between sources and bring assumptions with regards to what research looks like and how it works. **Ashley Cole, Trenia Napier, and Brad Marcum** (in Chapter 5, "Generation Z: Information Facts and Fictions," of this book) examine common assumptions held by students during the research process. They suggest that social psychological theories on learning that emphasize reflection can move students toward deeper understandings of information.

Similarly, **Rob Morrison** and **Deana Greenfield** (Chapter 8, "Towards an Assumption Responsive Information Literacy Curriculum: Lessons from Student Qualitative Data") utilize reflective journals and Brookfield's critical incident questionnaire to understand student experiences. They redesigned their curriculum to heighten student awareness of interactions connected with research and learning. **Alison Hicks** (Chapter 10, "Knowledge Societies: Learning for a Diverse World") addresses the need for a more reflective stance on the global nature of the information ecosystem. She also used reflective surveys as prompts to inform both teaching and learning. **Julie Obst and Joe Eshleman** (Chapter 14, "Librarians and Students: Making the Connections") encourage students to explore their own motivations through the use of reflection. They challenge librarians, and by extension the students themselves, to build deeper understandings of the drivers behind the research process.

Andrew D. Asher (Chapter 6, "Search Epistemology: Teaching Students about Information Discovery") reports that the search environment itself may discourage reflection by students. He notes that discovery tools and more effective search platforms (such as Google Scholar) "can reinforce unreflective search habits" by conditioning students to expect simple searches. **Barbara Fister** (Chapter 4, "The Social Life of Knowledge: Faculty Epistemologies") reminds us that students do not start out with the subject expertise or experience that faculty, as subject matter experts, already possess and that students find it challenging to make good choices. **William B. Badke** (Chapter 9, "Expertise and Authority in an Age of Crowdsourcing") explains how our perceptions of expertise have evolved and explores the variety of challenges students face in identifying appropriate expertise and authority. He calls us to more intentionally teach students how to recognize and appreciate appropriate scholarship. **MaryBeth Meszaros and Alison M. Lewis** (Chapter 3, "Librarianspeak: Metaphors That Reflect [and Shape] the Ethos and Practice of Academic Librarianship") present mixed findings about how librarians conceptualize their own work around information literacy. They note that the metaphors used by librarians suggest approaches that encourage surface-level learning, not the deep learning that impacts students' understandings of information. They call for a move toward fostering "reflective judgment" in students and ask librarians to work to develop "mature and nuanced personal epistemologies in emerging adults." **Patricia Brown** (Chapter 7, "Studying Sources: Truth, Method, and Teaching Bibliography") suggests that the metaliteracy needs of today's students can be enhanced by teaching students to appreciate the nature of sources through the creation of bibliographies.

Students have not had as many opportunities as faculty and librarians to examine how information is situated in context. **Jessica Critten, Anne C. Barnhart, and Craig Schroer** (Chapter 16, "Logical Fallacies and Sleight of Mind: Rhetorical Analysis as a Tool for Teaching Critical Thinking") note that "the reshaping of mental maps and examination of previously unexamined beliefs is an outcome that, ideally, should be a positive sign of maturation and acquisition of higher-level critical thinking skills." Ideally, these skills will enhance students' abilities to recognize the value in diversity of thought. Online communities and social networks tend to breed selective perception and reduce participants' awareness of the diversity of ideas, contributing to the ultra-polarization of public discourse. This echo chamber effect brings together like-minded individuals who repeat and reinforce ideas, undergirding preexisting beliefs without providing opportunities for exposure to opposing viewpoints. Online echo chambers form around political, religious, lifestyle, and other beliefs. Consequently, participants do not carefully weigh evidence in an effort at reaching toward observable reality but reinforce existing beliefs and ensure the continuation of the group's philosophies.[3]

Echo chambers can also breed skeptics for better and for worse. Critical thinking is, of course, essential. However, as Michael Roth, president of Wesleyan University puts it, "Fetishizing disbelief as a sign of intelligence has contributed to depleting our cultural resources."[4] Farhad Manjoo has called this the "photoshopification of society."[5] Manjoo's concern is the default approach to new information one encounters is that of extreme skepticism. After we have seen countless photos that have been faked, we assume that all photos have undergone the Photoshop treatment. The fear is that extreme skepticism, in the end, leaves the individual open to confirmation bias because there is no mechanism by which to judge external information sources.

David Weinberger challenges us to consider whether we are entering a post-fact information ecosystem. In the networked environment, each fact seems to have a counter-fact a click away.[6] For instance, data demonstrating the coming impact of climate change is one Google search removed from sources arguing that this data is inaccurate. Weinberger notes that the scientific endeavor has always assumed that with the same data, our collective efforts could reveal truth. But his fear is that the Internet has taught us all data is suspect of hidden agendas, corporate tampering, and political motives. Furthermore, as **Laura**

Saunders (Chapter 19, "Witnessing the World: Journalism, Skepticism, and Information Literacy") notes, misinformation, once absorbed, can be difficult to correct. She describes a number of ways that librarians and faculty can (and should) integrate news sources into their instruction, providing opportunities for students to evaluate information and develop their sense of skepticism, decreasing their vulnerability to media bias. **Willie Miller** (Chapter 15, "Fragmented Stories: Uncovering News Bias through Information Literacy Instruction") demonstrates how political news coverage can be used teach students how to uncover evidence of bias.

At some level, the "new" concerns above are not that new. They have been with us for quite some time; however, the Internet has made them feel more intense and widespread. Weinberger notes that the world has always been "too big to know" but that the limits of the print-based world helped hide this reality.[7] It may be more disconcerting that the easy access to fact, counter-fact, and counter-counter-fact distorts our perception of consensus on many topics. Patricia King notes that we often struggle with ill-structured problems that do not have clear right or wrong answers.[8] For instance, should we increase the minimum wage, cut the corporate tax rate, or legalize marijuana? These questions do not have clear answers. Their answers may incorporate data, research, and outside sources, but they are also deeply wrapped up in the ways that we view the world. Our beliefs about how the world works will have a significant impact on our answers. **Stephen A. Sanders** (Chapter 13, "Through a Mirror Darkly: A Postmodern Approach to Teaching Expertise, Authority, and Bias"), in his overview of postmodern thinking as it relates to current library practice, reminds us how ideologies (our own and others') influence the way we create and interpret information.

When considering ill-structured problems, there are often two overriding factors that come into play when addressing these problems. First, beliefs often come first and then evidence is found to support these beliefs.[9] With something like increasing the minimum wage, a student may find a plethora of economic, employment, socioeconomic, and other data to support an argument for or against an increase, but political belief and beliefs about free markets may have a stronger influence than data.

Second, when considering ill-structured problems, confirmation bias conditions us to ignore data that may contradict our existing beliefs and cling to data that supports these beliefs. In this way, our beliefs become self-reinforcing and difficult to change. Not only do our beliefs remain in place, but they become more ingrained in our worldview.[10]

Teaching students *about* information crosses many of the traditional disciplinary lines, and references work across fields, especially psychology, philosophy, sociology, and behavioral economics to just name a few. Library and information science has also made a notable contribution to teaching students *about* information with Patrick Wilson's work on *cognitive authority*. For Wilson, cognitive authority is a type of authority that is granted by the listener, not something that is determined by an outside, objective set of criteria. People construct knowledge based on their firsthand interactions with the world and based on secondhand information from other people. Individuals use several criteria (personal beliefs, educational background, familiarity with the subject, etc.) to find others whom they trust. They give away authority in the form of trust in the knowledge of others.[11]

Another perspective on teaching students *about* information comes from social psychology in the line of research around *personal epistemology*. This line of inquiry is "a field that examines what individuals believe about how knowing occurs, what counts as knowledge and where it resides, and how knowledge is constructed and evaluated."[12] Researchers dealing with personal epistemology are seeking ways to move students from dualistic thinking toward reflective judgments where students recognize that knowledge is contextual and that their own beliefs play a role in building that context.[13] **Brian W. Young and Daniel Von Holten** (Chapter 11, "Student Author[ity]: Engaging Students in Scholarship") show how students can begin to build this context for themselves. When students are given an assignment to study local concerns for which little secondary research is available, students rise to the occasion and begin to see themselves as novice researchers participating in a knowledge-building community, instead of just passive compilers of information. In a related way, **Lucy Mulroney and Patrick Williams** (Chapter 18, "Doing It Yourself: Special Collections as a Springboard for Personal, Critical Approaches to Information") illustrate how they were able to create opportunities for students to first deeply engage with zines held in their library's special collections, and then use that experience as a springboard to explore their own passions through the creation of a new, unique zine. Concerned that students were not engaging with their topics or the research process, **Rebecca Halpern and Lisa Lepore** (Chapter 17, "Scholarly Storytelling: Using Stories as a Roadmap to Authentic and Creative Library Research") wondered if students might be better able to identify as storytellers and decided to reframe research as a narrative process. In all of these cases, students find new ways to establish their authority and see themselves as active participants in the knowledge-sharing process.

A separate but still fruitful area of research relating to information literacy has been the application of critical pedagogy to teaching research. Critical library instruction or critical information literacy draws on the work of Paulo Freire and others to examine power structures relating to information. From this perspective, information literacy can become a form of empowerment where students consider whose voices are privileged in society, who has access to knowledge, and who participates in its creation. When teaching students *about* information, critical pedagogical perspectives provide an avenue to explore power dynamics and access.[14] **Hicks** (Chapter 10) takes a critical approach to information literacy in her chapter, exploring how foreign language information literacy instruction can be employed to develop students' "linguistic and transcultural competence" as they explore the information landscape in support of their Spanish language research assignments. Students begin to understand that not all topics are given the same level of coverage (for a variety of social and economic reasons) and that access to information is not always so simple. Being forced to consider the value and relevance of information outside of the usual familiar databases and academic journals helps students develop their own strategies for assessment and evaluation. **Beth McDonough** (Chapter 2, "Beyond Tools and Skills: Putting Information Back into Information Literacy") applied critical information literacy as a way to move beyond teaching tools. As part of this approach, the librarian gives up her or his authoritative stance in the classroom in order to approach the student on a more equal footing.

Through these perspectives a more complex view of the research process emerges. It becomes an interaction between the worldview of the student, his or her understanding of what counts as knowledge, the context for his or her learning, and (last but not least) information sources that the student may discover. From this vantage, sources are no longer neutral, information containers. "Facts" are not immutable statements about reality but are measurements based on predefined parameters. All sources have a perspective and are value laden. All researchers approach the research process from their own perspective with value-laden expectations for how the world works. And, perhaps, "information literate" may actually mean possessing a reflective capacity where one understands the beliefs and interpretations used in the research process. **Nicole Walls and Amy Pajewski** (Chapter 12, "From Counting Sources to Sources That Count: Reframing Authority and Accountability in First-Year Composition") report that students seem to view information and sources obtained via personal interviews very differently from information gleaned from research articles discovered via library research. They argue that librarians and composition instructors benefit from intentional and deliberate collaboration. They recommend both parties work together to repeatedly examine, assess, and revise what is being taught in order to identify the assumptions each makes with regards to what students should be taught and what they actually learn.

Our profession is moving toward a deeper understanding of information literacy. This is especially important for librarians working within the curriculum because we are challenged to reflect on our own practice. **Lane Wilkinson** (Chapter 1, "Theories of Knowledge in Library and Information Science") asks us, in a sense, to know ourselves. He navigates a "third way" for librarians in terms of epistemological stance. He lays claim to the ground between the strictness of positivism (only observable reality is to be trusted) and the unmoored feeling of social constructionism (*all* meaning is constructed within social contexts). **McDonough** (Chapter 2) follows this direction but takes us deeper into the classroom. She encourages librarians to "to relinquish expertise and efficiency" and recast the information ecosystem as a place where "singular truth" does not exist. **Mezaros and Lewis** (Chapter 3) examine the very language that librarianship uses to discuss information literacy. They recommend our profession create "an environment that challenges students and encourages them to question not only the ideas of others but their own as well." Interestingly, they note that librarian-faculty relationship is a complex one where faculty members are often cast as "both an adversary to be conquered as well as a heathen to be converted." **Fister** (Chapter 4) pushes us to take the faculty perspective when she notes that in order to successfully evolve information literacy in meaningful ways, librarians "need to understand how faculty conceptualize knowledge and how their research processes and habits may influence their expectations of students."

Taken as a whole, this collection answers a challenge made over a decade ago. In 2002, Brad Marcum offered a critique of information literacy practice within higher education. He noted that it both overreached by claiming to be an all-encompassing learning construct that required "competency with tools, resources, the research process, emerging technologies, critical thinking, and an understanding of the publishing industry and social structures that produce information products" while at the same time it under-reached by being "too grounded in text, and overly concerned with conveying basic skills."[15] Marcum called for a greater vision of information literacy that moved beyond the rote, show-and-tell mechanics emphasized by bibliographic instruction. The chapters within this book move beyond clicking and focus on thinking. As Marcum stated in 2002, "It is learning rather than information, and sociotechnical fluency rather than literacy that comprise the agenda for tomorrow."[16]

This book answers Marcum's challenge, but as these chapters were being written, our profession as a whole worked to offer an additional answer to his challenge. A task force charged by the Association of College and Research Libraries (ACRL) released drafts the *Framework for Information Literacy for Higher Education*.[17] The release of the various *Framework* drafts offered a context for conversations within this collection. Specifically, the new *Framework* offered a broader definition of information literacy that moved beyond the outcomes-based emphasis of ACRL's previous *Information Literacy Competency Standards for Higher Education*.[18] The new definition of information literacy emphasizes "flexible engagement with the information ecosystem, underpinned by critical self-reflection."[19] This emphasis is shared by the chapters in this collection. Information literacy is bound up in self-reflection and worldview. We cannot escape ourselves as we interact with the information ecosystem. In the end, the charge we must face as information literate individuals is the charge given to the philosophers at Delphi, "Know thyself."

Notes

1. John V. Pavlik, *Media in the Digital Age* (New York: Columbia University Press, 2008).
2. Edward L. Ayers and Charles M. Grisham, "Why IT Has Not Paid Off as We Hoped (yet)," *EDUCAUSE Review*, 38 (2003): 42.
3. Brendan Nyhan, "Why the 'Death Panel' Myth Wouldn't Die: Misinformation in the Health Care Reform Debate," *Forum* 8 (2010); Kathleen Hall Jamieson and Joseph N. Cappella, *Echo Chamber: Rush Limbaugh and the Conservative Media Establishment* (Oxford: Oxford University Press, 2008); Aaron Smith, "The Internet's Role in Campaign 2008: The Internet as Source of Political News and Information," Pew Research Internet Project, April 15, 2009, accessed July 16, 2014, http://www.pewinternet.org/2009/04/15/the-internet-as-a-source-of-political-news-and-information/.
4. Michael S. Roth, "Young Minds in Critical Condition," *Opinionator: The Stone* (blog), *New York Times,* May 10, 2014, http://opinionator.blogs.nytimes.com/2014/05/10/young-minds-in-critical-condition/?_php=true&_type=blogs&_r=0.
5. "The Convenient Untruths," *On the Media,* April 4, 2008, radio broadcast transcript, accessed July 16, 2014, http://www.onthemedia.org/story/129992-the-convenient-untruths/transcript/; Farhad Manjoo, *True Enough: Learning to Live in a Post-Fact Society* (Hoboken, NJ: Wiley, 2008).

6.   David Weinberger, *Too Big to Know: Rethinking Knowledge Now That the Facts Aren't the Facts, Experts Are Everywhere, and the Smartest Person in the Room Is the Room* (New York: Basic Books, 2012).

7.   Ibid.

8.   Patricia King, "How Do We Know? Why Do We Believe? Learning to Make Reflective Judgments," *Liberal Education* 78 (1992): 2–9.

9.   Michael Shermer, *The Believing Brain: From Ghosts and Gods to Politics and Conspiracies—How We Construct Beliefs and Reinforce Them as Truths* (New York: Times Books, 2011).

10.   Christopher Chabris and Daniel J. Simons, *The Invisible Gorilla and Other Ways Our Intuitions Deceive Us (New York: Crown, 2010); M. Frank Pajares, "Teachers' Beliefs and Educational Research: Cleaning Up a Messy Construct," Review of Educational Research* 62 (1992): 307–32.

11.   Patrick Wilson, *Second-Hand Knowledge: An Inquiry into Cognitive Authority* (Westport, CT: Greenwood Press, 1983).

12.   Barbara K. Hofer, "Introduction: Paradigmatic Approaches to Personal Epistemology," *Educational Psychologist* 39 (2004): 1.

13.   King, "How Do We Know?."

14.   James Elmborg, "Critical Information Literacy: Implications for Instructional Practice," *Journal of Academic Librarianship* 32 (2006): 192–99; Troy A. Swanson, "A Radical Step: Implementing a Critical Information Literacy Model," *Portal: Libraries and the Academy* 4 (2004): 259–73; Maria Accardi, Emily Drabinski, and Alana Kumbier, *Critical Library Instruction Theories and Methods* (Duluth, MN: Library Juice Press, 2010).

15.   James Marcum, "Rethinking Information Literacy," *Library Quarterly* 72 (2002): 20.

16.   Ibid., 21.

17.   Association of College and Research Libraries, *Framework for Information Literacy for Higher Education*, accessed July 16, 2014, http://acrl.ala.org/ilstandards/wp-content/uploads/2014/02/Framework-for-IL-for-HE-Draft-2.pdf.

18.   Association of College and Research Libraries, *Information Literacy Competency Standards for Higher Education*, http://www.ala.org/acrl/sites/ala.org.acrl/files/content/standards/standards.pdf.

19.   See lines 63 and 64 of Association of College and Research Libraries, *Framework for Information Literacy for Higher Education*.

PART 1

Bridging the Gap between Librarians, Students, and Faculty: Conceptualizing Information

1.1 Librarian and Faculty Epistemologies and Beliefs

CHAPTER 1

Theories of Knowledge in Library and Information Science

Lane Wilkinson

Prior to the introduction of the measles-mumps-rubella (MMR) vaccine in 1988, seasonal outbreaks caused over 1.4 million reported cases of measles each year in the United Kingdom alone.[1] By 1994, due to widespread adoption of the vaccine, measles was effectively eliminated in the UK: The MMR vaccine worked.[2] Yet, since 2006, hospitalized cases of measles have returned to pre-immunization levels in parts of Wales and England and measles—eradicated for more than a decade—is now endemic in the UK.[3] Though epidemiologists frequently struggle to identify the causes of such outbreaks of infectious diseases, in the case of measles the culprit is clear: Many parents believe that the MMR vaccine is linked to childhood autism, and they choose not to vaccinate their children.[4] Of course, these parents do not *merely* believe that the MMR vaccine is linked to autism, they claim to *know* that it does: As one vaccination-averse pediatrician in the United States exclaimed before the

National Institutes of Health, "We know that autism is immunological...why don't *you* know this?"[5]

While it is uncontroversial that they *believe* it, is it the case that the members of the anti-vaccination movement *know* that the MMR vaccine is linked to autism? When pressed, critics of the MMR vaccine allude to a range of information sources: personal experience, peer agreement, websites alleging pharmaceutical malfeasance, and—most importantly—a now retracted paper by Andrew Wakefield and 12 others that purported to establish a causal connection between the thimerosal in early MMR preparations and an increased prevalence of autism-spectrum disorders.[6] Clearly there is a great deal of information supporting the link between vaccinations and autism, but is this evidence enough to confer knowledge? Especially in light of the retraction of the Wakefield paper and the numerous studies confirming that the MMR vaccination has no causal connection to autism, it would seem as though there is an equally substantial body of information suggesting a different conclusion: The MMR vaccine is not linked to autism.[7] Who is right? Whose purported knowledge about the MMR vaccination should take precedence, if anyone's?

How information contributes to knowledge should be of the utmost concern for librarians. After all, librarians have deep-rooted affinities for both information and knowledge-creation. We librarians collect information, organize it, make it accessible, and advocate for information literacy in our communities, all with the hope that our patrons will use those resources in the pursuit of knowledge. Indeed, as Abraham Kaplan argued, library science "has thrust upon it, as its appropriate domain, the whole of knowledge, the whole of culture."[8] And library patrons? They come to libraries seeking information that will help to create knowledge. Patrons do not want misinformation or disinformation; they do not want to be deceived. Quoting Don Fallis, patrons seek out information "in order to bring about good epistemic outcomes. That is, they want to acquire knowledge, true beliefs, justified beliefs, understanding, etc."[9] Through the provision of information, libraries can certainly help patrons acquire knowledge, but, unfortunately, this is a task easier said than done in large part because librarians do not exactly agree as to what knowledge even is.

To wit, the controversy over the MMR vaccination is a controversy precisely because scientists and concerned parents have different conceptions of what constitutes acceptable grounds for knowledge. Caught in the middle are librarians. Should the information librarians provide favor one side of the debate, or should we strive for equal representation? Is information alone sufficient to create knowledge, or does the quality of that information play a role? Is there a fact of the matter? These and related questions suggest that epistemology—the branch of philosophy concerned with the study of knowledge—is an area of pressing importance in librarianship.

This chapter has three aims. First, I intend to provide an overview of the classical conception of knowledge as justified, true belief. The second part of this chapter will explore three major schools of thought in library and information science (LIS)—epistemic realism, social constructionism, and hermeneutics—with the intent of discovering the predominant ways in which librarians conceive of knowledge and information. Finally, I will suggest that librarians consider social epistemology as the optimal theory of knowledge in the profession. As a bridge between the social contexts that motivate constructionism and the commitment to objectivity that motivates realism, social epistemology is fruitful ground for any future library epistemology.

The Classical Conception of Knowledge

When we say that a critic of the MMR vaccine believes that the MMR vaccine is causally connected to autism-spectrum disorders, we are ascribing to that person a particular mental state. To believe that the MMR vaccine can cause autism is simply to have a mental representation of the world such that the concepts of *MMR vaccine*, *causation*, and *autism* stand in a particular relationship that can be expressed by the following proposition:

The MMR vaccine can cause autism.

In fact, all of our beliefs can be formulated as propositions in just this way, and when combined, this set of propositions constitutes the "language of thought" through which we understand our world and our experiences.[10] Moreover, when coupled with other mental states like desire, our beliefs about the world both motivate us to act and provide reasons for our behavior.[11] Beliefs, understood as mental representations of how we take the world to be, are thus indispensable. As D. M. Armstrong put it, beliefs are the "maps by which we steer."[12]

However, belief comes in degrees. Some of our beliefs are tentative, and we would have no objection to modifying them. Though I believe that my oldest child received his first dose of MMR vaccine in June, I could be mistaken; maybe it was in July. Other beliefs, however, are far less susceptible to revision: I not only believe my oldest child was born on May 22, I claim that I *know* it. Likewise, my beliefs that measles is caused by a virus, that the sum of two and three is five, or that as of 2014 Detroit is the most populous city in Michigan are similarly unshakeable. So it goes, no doubt, for the person who believes that the MMR vaccination can cause autism: That person may be willing to amend their belief, or they may be steadfast in their resolve. In ordinary language, these unshakeable beliefs are typically what we mean when we talk about knowledge. To know is to have a belief about which you are not willing to change, a belief about which you are certain.

But, is believing enough? If you claim to know that the MMR vaccine causes autism and I claim to know that there is no causal connection between vaccinations and autism, are these contradictory beliefs both knowledge? Most epistemologists and (I presume) most people would say that one or the other of us is wrong about vaccinations and though we both *think* that we know, only one of us *actually* knows. This distinction suggests the first criterion for knowledge: To know is to have a *true belief*; false beliefs simply do not fit our ordinary use of the term knowledge. As Duncan Pritchard explains, "To ascribe knowledge to someone is to credit that person with the achievement of having got things right."[13]

There are many competing theories about what it means to "get things right," but the most widely held position is some version of the so-called *correspondence theory of truth* according to which a belief is true just in case it corresponds to the way the world is. To the correspondence theorist, a true belief is a mental representation that accurately represents some *fact* about the world. So, the belief that the MMR vaccine causes autism can only be true if the MMR vaccine is, in fact, causally connected to autism. Likewise, the belief that measles is caused by a virus can only be true if it is a fact that measles is caused by a virus. Again, truth is correspondence with the facts. Though this definition of truth is fairly simple and intuitive, there are substantive disagreements over what types of phenomena can be represented in the mind, over the extent to which our representations can be considered accurate, and especially over the nature of facts. We will return to these disagreements in the next section.

Even if a person has a true belief, it is not yet certain that the person has knowledge. When we ascribe knowledge to an individual, we want to rule out the possibility that the belief is held accidentally; we want to rule out lucky guesses. For example, suppose the library catalog goes down and a patron desperately needs a book about vaccines. As a librarian you may have a rough estimate of where to find the book in the Library of Congress Classification—either Q for Science or R for Medicine. Not being sure, you flip a coin: Q it is. Of course, there is an awful lot of science books in the library, and you really like the letter R, so you figure the call number ought to start with QR to help narrow it down. As for the classification number, you have no idea so you pick the number of the bus you took to the library: 189. Putting it together, you tell the patron to head to shelving location QR189 for books on vaccines. Clearly, this is bad librarianship, but, as it turns out, books about vaccines actually *are* classified from QR189 to QR189.5! Now the question: Did you *know* that books about vaccines can be found at QR189? Despite the fact that you came to a true belief, the hunches and random choices that got you there seem to amount to more of a lucky guess, not knowledge. These sorts of lucky guesses and accidental true beliefs are covered by the final criterion for knowledge: justification.

To say that a belief is justified is just to say that the person holding that belief has good reasons for holding it. In a very rough sense, to have justification it to be able to answer the question, "How do you know that?" In the case of the anti-vaccination movement, this criterion allows us to ask not just whether their belief is true, but also whether they have good reasons for accepting that belief: We want *evidence*. For example, my belief that measles is caused by a virus is supported by evidence including statements in textbooks, an article on *Wikipedia*, common knowledge, and reports about the success of the measles vaccine. The vaccination-averse parent will also undoubtedly appeal to evidence found in websites, books, journal articles, and personal experience. Other possible reasons for belief abound: personal experience, religious tradition, scientific experiment, sensory perception, logical deduction, cultural tradition, and so on. As we will see shortly, there are important disagreements about whether some forms of justification are better than others, but there is general agreement that whether a true belief can be considered knowledge ultimately depends on whether that belief is backed up by reasons, evidence, or justification.

At this point we have a working definition: *Knowledge is justified, true belief.* Using the standard schema, a subject *S* knows some proposition *p* just in case

1. *p* is true,
2. *S* believes that *p*, and
3. *S* is justified in believing that *p*.[14]

While these conditions may not be jointly sufficient as a definition, the general consensus among philosophers is that these three conditions are at least necessary conditions for claiming knowledge.[15] For example, if I claim to know that measles is caused by a virus, then at the very least (1) it must be true that measles is caused by a virus, (2) I must believe that measles is caused by a virus, and (3) I must have good reasons for believing that measles is caused by a virus. This is knowledge, and though epistemologists further distinguish each condition according to a range of technical considerations, when broadly construed the concept of justified true belief is well established enough to provide the grounds for epistemology in librarianship.

Current Trends in Library Epistemology

Though to know is to have a justified true belief, there are several competing conceptions of truth and justification. In LIS these conceptions can be grouped into two general categories: positivism and social constructionism. To the positivist, a justified true belief involves an objective fact about the world that we come to believe through direct perception, reason, experiment, or similar "scientific" means of justification. Positivism is committed to a sort of epistemological optimism: We can, in fact, acquire objective, universal knowledge about the world. In contrast, the social constructionist believes that a justified true belief involves an intersubjective agreement about the world that we come to believe through social processes such as negotiation or conversation. Social constructionism is committed to a sort of epistemological ambivalence: No facts are objective, and all claims to knowledge are characterized by hidden biases and sociocultural constraints. Distinctions between these approaches tend to arise out of positions that Archie L. Dick has described as the neutral and normative conceptions of library science.[16] The neutral conception of library science values neutrality, objectivity, and a generally scientific worldview.[17] In contrast, normative conceptions of library science seek to replace neutrality and objectivity with a "conscious partiality" that places greater emphasis on the intersubjective and social forces that ultimately construct knowledge.[18] Accordingly, positivism aligns with a neutral conception of LIS; social constructionism aligns with a normative conception. We will look at each LIS epistemology in turn.

Neutrality, Positivism, and Realism in LIS

The neutral approach to LIS generally holds that LIS is akin to an empirical science. Also known as *scientism*, Michael H. Harris explains that it involves a commitment to four general beliefs: (1) "the methodological procedures of natural science are applicable to library science;" (2) "the library must be viewed as a complex of facts governed by general laws;" (3) those general laws allow librarians to "explain, predict, and control" the flow of information; and (4) the librarian can and should maintain "value-neutrality."[19] These beliefs are most clearly evident in the profession's commitment to neutrality in collection development and reference services as well as in the organization of information according to law-like classification schemes and ontologies. By following these scientific principles of neutrality and organization, librarians tacitly accept the closely related position known as *positivism*.

Positivism has its roots in the scientific revolution and, particularly, in the writings of Enlightenment philosopher August Comte. Originally proposed as a rejection of religious and metaphysical thinking, Comte's positivism advocated that the scientific worldview and scientific methodologies such as reason, observation, and experiment are the ideal paths to knowledge.[20] In other words, scientism is not merely one choice among many competing ways of viewing the world—it is the only acceptable way; positivism expressly denies that religion, tradition, or similar social and cultural systems of belief are reliable means of attaining knowledge. In the early half of the 20th century, the theory of *logical positivism* attempted to strengthen Comte's positivism through the introduction of a principle of verification: The only statements we can actually know are those that can be conclusively verified to be true.[21] However, by mid-century, it became clear that conclusive verification of any belief is virtually impossible and logical positivism was largely abandoned. In its place, so-called *post-positivists* like Thomas Kuhn and Karl Popper ushered in a new way of thinking about positivism. Popper, in particular, introduced the criterion of *falsifiability*: An acceptable belief must, at least in principle, be able to be refuted by experience.[22] Though no belief can ever be conclusively verified, false beliefs can and are routinely discarded. Through a rigorous process of experiment and replication, new claims to knowledge are developed, published, tested, and in this way human knowledge grows. Popper's post-positivism is now the dominant way of understanding scientific inquiry.

Post-positivism admits many variations, but when it comes to knowledge, most post-positivists are united in support of *epistemological realism*. The epistemological realist, as Paul Boghossian explains, is committed to the view that "the world which we seek to understand and know about is what it is largely independently of us and our beliefs about it."[23] Moreover, the realist believes that we are capable of discovering objective facts about the external world: We are capable of accurately forming and communicating beliefs about reality. Regarding justification, the objective position is simply that some reasons for belief (such as scientific experiment) are better than others (such as religious tradition). Objectivist theorists disagree on precisely why some forms of reasoning are superior to others, but one of the more robust theories in favor of giving preference to logic and empirical evidence is known as *reliabilism*. Briefly, reliabilism holds that the justification of a belief-forming process "is a function of the reliability of the process or processes that caused it" where "reliability consists in the tendency of a process to produce beliefs that are true rather than false."[24] Since empirical evidence, observation, logical deduction, and similarly "scientific" methods tend to uncover facts more reliably than processes like tradition or social convention, these means of justification are to be preferred. In sum, the realist attitude towards knowledge is that there are mind-independent facts about the world, and some ways of coming to know those facts are more reliable than others.

Taken together, reliabilism, realism, positivism, and scientism unite to create a general theory of the flow of knowledge in LIS. On this view, libraries are places where librarians do their best to collect, organize, and provide access to information in a meaningful yet value-neutral way. Through the judicious application of reliable critical thinking and reasoning methods—of which librarians are willing and able to instruct patrons—patrons can navigate through the information ecosystem identifying truth from falsity and acquiring the justified, true beliefs that constitute knowledge.

Though it is difficult to find librarians or other LIS practitioners who explicitly admit to following a neutral or positivist approach to LIS, there is no doubt that positivism is a major influence on library thinking. The American Library Association Code of Ethics calls for reference responses to be "accurate" and "unbiased" and urges us to "distinguish between our personal convictions and professional duties."[25] Evidence-based library and information practice has become prominent in LIS as librarians turn to quantitative studies and assessment methods to promote information literacy and library use.[26] Even the core Library Bill of Rights is saturated with language suggesting a commitment to neutrality: Materials should not be excluded on account of their "origin, background, or views of those contributing to their creation," materials should not be censored "because of partisan or doctrinal disapproval," and so on.[27]

At this point it may be worth considering the role of information in the positivist conception of library science. One of the more common means of understanding the relationship between information and knowledge is by way of the so-called *DIKW pyramid*. Popularized by Russell L. Ackoff, the DIKW pyramid posits a hierarchical relationship between data (D), information (I), knowledge (K), and wisdom (W), such that information is defined in terms of data, knowledge in terms of information, and wisdom in terms of knowledge.[28] More precisely, data are "symbols that represent properties of objects, events, and their environments" and, especially, data are unorganized, unprocessed, and lacking in meaning or value.[29] When we process and ascribe meaning or value to data, we gain information. Though information is a notoriously polysemous term, with most definitions referring "only to the subset of information as studied in that particular discipline," Luciano Floridi offers a general definition of information that should be broad enough for our purposes: Information is well formed, meaningful data.[30] So, whereas each reported case of measles in the US in 2011 may be considered an individual datum, we can process and derive meaning from the set of all measles data to arrive at information: There were 222 reported cases of measles in the United States in 2011.[31]

It goes without saying that information can be expressed in a variety of ways, from text to sound to visual artifacts and more. When we encounter true information and choose to believe it on the basis of some rational grounds (i.e., justification), information is transformed to knowledge. This is the point that should be of most interest to librarians: the conversion of information to knowledge. How we organize information, how we evaluate it, and how we teach others to do the same all have a direct effect on the creation of knowledge. If, for example, we adopt "you can believe the truth of anything you find in a library" as our principle of justification, then our understanding of knowledge will be quite broad and all interactions with the library would result in knowledge. On the other hand, if we adopt the narrower principle that "libraries provide access to both information and misinformation and cannot vouch for the truth of any particular datum," then we embrace a narrower account of knowledge. Importantly, the methods and principles we advocate in pursuit of information literacy are directly tied to identifying truth and establishing justification. Even a well-worn information literacy concept such as the "CRAAP Test" (currency, relevance, authority, accuracy, purpose) is ultimately aimed at the transition from information to knowledge: If a piece of information passes through the CRAAP Test without raising any red flags, then we are justified in believing that information to be true—we gain knowledge.

In sum, the positivist conception of knowledge and information in LIS is invoked every time we differentiate between true beliefs we hold on the basis of evidence or reason and beliefs we merely take to be true due to tradition or social convention. Likewise, when we draw (or attempt to draw) a clear dividing line between true, factual information and misinformation or disinformation, we are tacitly accepting not only that to be informative is to be true but also that factual information is somehow preferable and should be sought above all else. To the positivist librarian, there is a single, objective world "out there" that we can come to know through the information collected and organized by a library. Granted, libraries collect a great deal of false information; librarians are fallible. But, even if some errors persist in the library collection, it is in striving to create a library collection that faithfully represents reality—and in promoting information literacy skills that allow patrons to distinguish between truth and falsity—that the positivist conception of librarianship finds its home.

Normativity, Social Constructionism, and Intersubjectivity in LIS

To many librarians, the preceding account of knowledge will seem intuitive: The truth is out there, and it is our job to seek it out. Yet, many other librarians—especially of late—are hesitant to adopt realism or positivism in LIS. Why should this be? What is the problem with seeking truth and absolute knowledge? After all, the old chestnuts about "speaking truth to power" or "the truth shall set you free" seem to privilege truth above mere opinion or belief. In response, those librarians pursuing a *social constructionist* epistemology will respond, "Yes…but *whose* truth?" Drawing on mid- to late-20th-century social theory, social constructionists argue that the very ideas of absolute truth and objectivity are chimerical at best, oppressive at worst. As an epistemological position, social constructionism argues that *every* belief we have—no matter how certain that belief seems—is the by-product of the social and cultural forces that have shaped our minds. On this account, privileged access to an external "truth" or objective reality is impossible: Every belief we have about the world is constructed through our interactions with other people. Following Dick's characterization of the "normative" approach to LIS, the social constructionist in LIS seeks to move away from an idealized pursuit of absolute truth and, instead, looks to how knowledge is shaped and directed by external social forces. Social constructionism is not about finding the best path to knowledge—that would be positivist. Instead, social constructionism is about deconstructing and understanding the social structures and processes that determine what we, as a society, have agreed to accept as knowledge.

The idea that we are unable to escape our social structures is not a particularly new idea. Indeed, Plato attributed the idea to the pre-Socratic sophist Protagoras, whose doctrine Plato summarized in the *Theaetetus* as that "man is the measure of all things" (152a).[32] However, constructionist epistemology did not come to preeminence until the middle of the 20th century, thanks to a number of unprecedented developments in science and sociology. On the scientific front, the early 20th century saw the upheaval of many long-held theories such as Newtonian mechanics. Understood to be immutable laws of nature for some 250 years, Newton's observations—that an object at rest stays at rest, that force is mass times acceleration, and that for every action there is an equal and opposite reaction—fell apart in the wake of special relativity, quantum mechanics, and other scientific developments. Sure, Newton's laws provide approximations of reality, but at sufficiently high speeds or sufficiently small sizes, these "facts" about the world break down. Looking at the history of science, post-positivist Kuhn developed the now popular theory of *paradigm shifts*, explaining that Newtonian mechanics is but one worldview held by the scientific community.

As with all scientific worldviews, classical mechanics was long beset with anomalies it could not answer—for example, deviations in Mercury's orbit or the dual wave/particle nature of light. As is the case with any worldview, Kuhn argues, these anomalies compound over time and reach a critical mass, at which time scientists are forced to abandon the "truth" of their theories and develop a wholly new worldview. These paradigm shifts are recurrent and obvious: the transition from a geocentric model of the universe to a heliocentric model, the adoption of Darwinian evolution over theories of spontaneous generation, and the adoption of plate tectonics to explain geologic processes, just to name a few. Kuhn's key insight came in asking whether we should consider Aristotle, Galileo, or Newton lesser scientists for subscribing to theories we now know to be false. The answer, Kuhn argued, was no. The work of our scientific predecessors was important, groundbreaking, and absolutely true *within the context of the relevant paradigm*. "Scientific knowledge…is intrinsically the common property of a group or else nothing at all. To understand it we shall need to know the special characteristics of the groups that create and use it."[33] By situating scientific theories within the context of paradigms, Kuhn has effectively moved the foundations from an external "reality" to a socially constructed set of agreements. Scientists do not study reality, Kuhn argues: They study the dominant paradigm, and after becoming sufficiently acquainted with the official account of reality, a scientist joins other scientists "who learned the bases of their field from the same concrete models" and who are "committed to the same rules and standards for scientific practice."[34] In other words, what counts as true or as an accepted means for justification is constructed by the community of researchers working within a particular paradigm. Under another paradigm, truth and justification may be constructed quite differently.

Kuhn was not alone in noticing the socially constructed reality behind our claims to truth and knowledge. In the wake of the Second World War and the rapid decolonization of subjugated peoples, many social theorists began to question the colonial-era wisdom that subjugated peoples stood to benefit from "superior" Western science and culture. Is it the case that Western science and culture are truly superior to other worldviews, or is the Western worldview merely one of many equally valid ways of describing the world? Similarly, feminists began to question whether paradigmatic values of objectivity and universalism held true for women, people of color, and other oppressed groups who, traditionally, were not part of the mainstream scientific community of practice. Indeed, objectivity and universalism are frequently employed as tools of oppression.[35] Various "standpoint" epistemologies arose to tackle issues of truth and justification specific to these underrepresented and ignored communities, perhaps the most familiar epistemology being the "constructed knowledge" described by Mary Field Belenky et al.: All knowledge is relative to a subjective frame of reference and knowers can construct and reconstruct frameworks however they see fit.[36] Finally, drawing on Freudian theories of unconscious bias, Marxist theories of power and oppression, and "post-structuralist" linguistic theories, so-called *critical theory* was developed in the 1970s to provide a means of situating putative knowledge-claims within their appropriate historical and cultural contexts. To the critical theorist, all beliefs (including justified true beliefs) must be understood as both culturally contingent and as the products of often unseen social and cultural forces. The task of the critical theorist, then, is to question all claims to knowledge and seek the hidden biases and power structures that guide the social construction of "truth."

In the context of LIS, social constructionism has gained appreciable footing. LIS constructionists have argued that the traditional library values of objectivity, neutrality, and order are, in effect, values passed down from a particular worldview propagated by a predominantly white, Western, male community with roots in 18th-century Enlightenment, and as many have argued, "When one discourse takes up a dominant position in relation to others it potentially means that marginalized groups within, for example, an organization are forced to use tools that have been created to further the interests of other more 'powerful' groups."[37] Thus, to the social constructionist, the emphasis on science and rationality to the exclusion of other ways of knowing has the effect of silencing voices in the community at best and contributing to systematic oppression at worst. Moreover, a commitment to positivism carries with it a certain elitism that tends to valorize order and control. The objectivity-obsessed librarian may hold up freedom of expression, neutrality, or privacy as virtues of the profession, but in doing so, Gary P. Radford argues, positivism "renders the library an emotionless, cold, and mechanistic place."[38]

At this point, social constructionism has not been precisely defined, if only because the theory admits of so many variations. To tease out the role of social constructionism in LIS, it may help to analyze a representative theory. In his popular *Atlas of New Librarianship*, R. David Lankes advocates for an approach to librarianship rooted in *conversation theory*, which holds that "knowledge is a set of agreements in relation to one another through a memory that is derived from language exchange between conversants."[39] In slightly less technical language, Lankes' theory is that we acquire knowledge through conversations (and any exchange of information—from talking to reading to viewing a film and so on—is a conversation), and if two or more conversants agrees on an idea, then the idea is justified. For example, the anti-vaccination community has, through many conversations, come to the agreement that the MMR vaccine causes autism. So, in their community, it is true that the vaccine causes autism because they have agreed that it is true; they are justified in believing that vaccines cause autism because they have had a conversation about it, and, therefore, they have a justified, true belief (i.e., knowledge). Of course, the scientific community has its own conversations—typically carried out through scholarly publishing—and scientists have agreed that there is no causal link between vaccines and autism (i.e., the scientific community has *different* knowledge). In both cases, knowledge is constructed, rather than discovered "out there" in the world as the positivists would prefer. Importantly, conversation theory, like all social constructionist theories, allows multiple, contradictory beliefs to count as knowledge. So, both the anti-vaccination community and the scientific community really do know what they claim to know. Knowledge is constructed through social processes, and there is no independent (nonsocial) means of adjudicating "good" from "bad" knowledge. There is only *different* knowledge.

At first blush, social constructionism shows a lot of promise for librarianship. Consider that libraries collect and make available a wide and incredibly divergent set of claims and beliefs about the world. If LIS truly embraced positivism, social constructionists argue, we would be forced to go through our collections and eliminate whatever information does not fit the scientifically accepted consensus. Robert V. Labaree and Ross Scimeca helpfully explain that positivism's relentless focus on absolute truth is a danger and that librarians should instead suspend the notion of absolute truth in favor of a constructionist account of truth. They argue, "Without this suspension of truth in librarianship, the accumulation of past and present knowledge could be compromised. This compromise can take various forms, such as eliminating whole collections or suppressing information that does not share the present majority view, be that view scientific, religious, or political."[40]

Lankes, Labaree, Scimeca, and other constructionist theorists in LIS tend to agree on this point: Unless we adopt the understanding that truth is relative to individual communities, we run the real risk of eliminating or suppressing information. Moreover, as Bernd Frohmann has argued, by ignoring the social nature of knowledge, positivist epistemologies fail to account for inequality, oppression, and social justice; positivism in LIS ends up reifying the status quo of treating "information as a commodity, and persons as surveyable information consumers, within market economy conditions.[41] Surely, librarians should avoid any epistemological system that perpetuates oppression and injustice.

Positivism and Social Constructionism

The two dominant theories of knowledge in LIS both admit of many variations. However, their core differences are almost universal. Both theories accept that knowledge is justified, true belief, though they differ as to the nature of truth and as to what constitutes appropriate justification. Whereas the positivist sees truth as a correspondence between our beliefs and the world, the social constructionist sees truth as a matter of social acceptance. Whereas the positivist understands justification in terms of evidence and reason, the social constructionist argues that justification is conferred through social processes such as conversation. So far we have looked at social constructionism as a critical response to positivism, but is social constructionism truly an improvement? Before abandoning positivism it may be worth considering some common criticisms of social constructionism: Constructionism is self-refuting, it impedes learning, and it disenfranchises minority voices.

First, a logical problem with social constructionism: Isn't the claim "there are no objective facts" an objective statement? It seems as though if it truly is the case that all facts and knowledge are contingent on social processes, then it would have to be the case that social constructionism is contingent on social processes. In denying the existence of objective facts, constructionism has the unfortunate side effect of reducing everything we believe into propositions "that we can neither express nor understand."[42] For example, Lankes's conversation theory asks librarians to think of knowledge as a set of agreements between conversants. So, the claim "the MMR vaccine is not causally connected to autism" is to be interpreted as "according to the agreement we have reached, the MMR vaccine is not causally connected to autism." But, this is now an objective statement about our agreement; to remove the objectivity we have to reword it: "According to the agreement we have reached, there is an agreement that the MMR vaccine is not causally connected to autism." Unfortunately, this is still a categorical statement, so another rewording is in order: "According to an agreement we have reached, there is an agreement we have reached according to which there is an agreement that the MMR vaccine is not causally connected to autism." The infinite regress is unavoidable; at some point there simply have to be mind-independent, objective facts. Any theory that is based in acceptance, agreement, or assent as the foundation for truth will fail in this respect.

Second, and more seriously, social constructionism runs the risk of impeding learning. This is especially paradoxical because social constructionism is often touted as a boon to education. Consider a patron who visits a library reference desk inquiring after books or articles that prove that vaccines cause autism. Assume that this patron is very active in the anti-vaccination community and rarely associates with people outside of that community. If we adopt social constructionism, then we must accept that this patron *knows* that vaccines cause autism. However, if the patron already *knows* that vaccines cause autism, then providing any materials other than those that validate the patron's beliefs would be a disservice. Rather than being a place for learning and the creation of new knowledge, social constructionism entails that libraries must instead focus on validating preexisting beliefs. After all, if a patron's preexisting, community-derived beliefs already constitute knowledge, there seems to be no compelling reason to seek to change those beliefs.

Perhaps more seriously, social constructionism runs the real risk of disenfranchising oppressed and minority voices. Whereas a positivist makes a distinction between "is true" and "is *believed* to be true," the social constructionist has no such option, and hence, the knowledge claims of any given community are true. Extended to all discursive communities, it quickly becomes clear that even two radically opposed communities can both be secure in what they take to be knowledge. So, both the anti-vaccination community as well as the medical community can truly say that they possess knowledge. Likewise, in seeking to protect oppressed minority communities from the hegemony of a more powerful group, social constructionism seeks to give power to minority voices by leveling the playing field, but ends up making it impossible to criticize the powerful. As Boghossian explains, "If the powerful can't criticize the oppressed, because the central epistemological categories are inexorably tied to particular perspectives, it also follows that the oppressed can't criticize the powerful."[43] Far from a liberatory epistemology, social constructionism allows the powerful to place their beliefs beyond criticism.

Despite the many problems, constructionist epistemologies are an improvement over positivist epistemology in at least one important respect: Positivism fails to account for the unique role of the social in knowledge creation. Traditional positivist epistemology has almost exclusively focused on the knower in isolation, placing great importance on idealized notions of rationality, experience, and introspection. Traditional positivist epistemology valorizes the lone researcher working deep into the night, the brilliant scientist tinkering away in a secluded lab, and the Cartesian thinker postulating grand truths about the world from a comfortable armchair. But, especially in the increasingly interconnected digital world, positivism fails to account for the interpersonal and institutional contexts where most knowledge is actually acquired; positivism has little to say about the way both knowledge and ignorance propagate through social interactions. Somewhere, between the sterile individualism of positivism and the haphazard relativism of social constructionism, there must be a balanced means of approaching the problem of knowledge. Thankfully, there is a third path: social epistemology.

Social Epistemology and LIS

In 1952, librarians Margaret E. Egan and Jesse H. Shera sought to bring a more robust sense of epistemology to library science. Noting that "epistemology has always revolved about the intellectual processes of the *individual*," Egan and Shera proposed the new field of "social epistemology" as a means of "lift[ing] the discipline from the intellectual life of the individual to that of the society, nation, or culture."[44] The proposed epistemological position would focus on analyzing "the production, distribution, and utilization of intellectual products," which is something for which librarians are perfectly suited.[45] Unfortunately, though Egan and Shera proposed this shift in epistemology, they did not necessarily pursue social epistemology in any robust sense, preferring to rely on more straightforward social constructionism.[46] As such, though the *idea* of a social epistemology that analyzed collective knowledge and the distribution of "intellectual products" was proposed in library science, this approach to knowledge only truly flourished in philosophical circles and has only recently returned to the LIS literature.

Alvin I. Goldman, one of the leading proponents of social epistemology, frames contemporary social epistemology in terms of a singular quest: the quest for truth. Whether pursuing academic research concerning the risks of vaccination or simply listening to the morning weather report, "what we seek in all such cases is true or accurate information, not misinformation."[47] Nowhere is this pursuit of truth more obvious than in libraries; as Fallis explains, patrons seek information "in order to bring about good epistemic outcomes. That is, they want to acquire knowledge, true beliefs, justified beliefs, understanding, etc."[48] Identifying these good epistemic outcomes and understanding how information contributes to them is the goal of an epistemologically informed librarianship. In distinguishing between information and misinformation, or between truth and error, social epistemology is clearly aligned more with positivism than social constructionism, and it is certainly the case that social epistemology accepts the existence of objectivity and facticity. Yet, even though social epistemology is heavily indebted to a realist conception of truth, it still accommodates certain insights found in social constructionism, chief among these being the fact that the vast majority of things we believe are believed solely on the basis of our social and cultural interactions. Specifically, most of what we claim to know is believed purely on the basis of *testimony*.

Though social epistemology is a well developed field with myriad philosophical rabbit holes, the philosophical problem of testimony is perhaps the most salient area of inquiry for library science and information literacy. Put simply, the problem of testimony asks whether, and if so to what degree, we are justified in believing the assertions (i.e., testimony) made by other people. Classical epistemology, with its focus on pure reason and direct experience, has little to say about when and how we can come to trust the things we hear about or read about secondhand. For example, though I claim that I *know* my date of birth is May 14, this sort of fact seems curiously distant from logic, reason, and certainly direct experience. Instead, I know my date of birth strictly through the testimony of other people: My family wishes me well on May 14, and my birth certificate indicates I was born on May 14. I claim to *know* with absolute certainty that I was born on May 14, and all I have to serve as justification is the testimony of my family, the hospital, and assorted government agencies. Far from being the exception, testimonial-based beliefs tend to be the rule. From the things we read in books to the scholarly articles we use in our research to the prosaic stories we share between friends, coworkers, and family, most of what we claim to know has its basis in testimony, and classical epistemology has difficulty accounting for how some of our most important and valued claims to knowledge can be justified in the absence of pure reason and direct experience.

Of course, this is not a new problem by any means. Enlightenment philosopher David Hume argued that "there is no species of reasoning more common, more useful, and even necessary to human life, than that which is derived from the testimony of men and the reports of eye-witnesses and spectators," yet he too struggled to make sense of how we should evaluate testimony.[49] Hume's solution was to adopt a *reductionist* approach to testimony: Testimony is only *truly* acceptable to the extent that it can be supported by more positivist means such as reason, perception, and, importantly, induction. According to the Humean position, "Hearers must observe a constant and regular conjunction between the reports of speakers and the corresponding facts" in order to accept testimonial evidence as a source of justification.[50] For example, to determine whether the *Wikipedia* article on the MMR vaccine is a credible source to justify my beliefs about vaccinations, I must first obtain independent, inductive evidence that *Wikipedia* is a consistently reliable source for factual information, that the authors of the *Wikipedia* article in question consistently report facts, and so on. On the reductionist approach, information evaluation reduces to evaluating how reliable the information provider is at reporting facts over time. From a library instruction perspective, this makes a certain amount of sense, as we privilege "reliable" sources, like *The New York*

Times, over "unreliable" sources, such as *The National Enquirer,* because we have inductive evidence that *The New York Times* is far more reliable when it comes to accurately reporting facts. As James Van Cleve summarizes the reductionist position, "testimony gives us justified belief and reflective knowledge not because it shines by its own light, but because it has often enough been revealed true by our other lights."[51]

Yet, reductionism about testimony is beset with difficulties. As C.A.J. Coady points out,

> Many of us have never seen a baby born, nor have most of us examined the circulation of the blood nor the actual geography of the world nor any fair sample of the laws of the land, nor have we made the observations that lie behind our knowledge that the lights in the sky are heavenly bodies immensely distant nor a vast number of other observations that [reductionism] would seem to require.[52]

The point being that we more often than not lack the sorts of independent evidence for reliability that reductionism requires. For example, most, if not all, of us have not read every issue of *The New York Times* to assess its reliability. Likewise, we have not independently established the veracity of every fact reported in *The New York Times*. Put simply, it is too much of a burden to require that we back up *everything* we read or hear with independent evidence that it is true. This problem, among others, leads many social epistemologists to endorse an *anti-reductionist* approach to testimony. First articulated by Thomas Reid, one of Hume's contemporaries of the Scottish Enlightenment, the anti-reductionist position treats testimony as a properly basic source for justified beliefs, on a par with reason, memory, direct experience, induction, and the like (rather than being reducible to one of these basic sources as per reductionism). To the anti-reductionist, we are justified in accepting the testimony of others without having to appeal to these other types of justification, provided there is no reason to believe that the speaker or author is or may be untrustworthy. Thus, anti-reductionism entails that we can trust the credibility of an information source so long as there are no "red flags" warning us that the source might be untrustworthy. Leslie Stevenson explains,

Our acceptance of testimony is just as intellectually re-
spectable as our inductive inferences. Admittedly, both
need to be moderated by experience—each person finds
out as he goes through life that certain kinds of testimo-
nies are unreliable, and that some observed correlations
are merely accidental. But Reid's position is that any assertion is creditworthy until shown otherwise; whereas
Hume implies that specific evidence for its reliability is
needed.[53]

For librarians, this distinction manifests in a clear dividing line: Do
we believe (and teach) that information sources should be approached with
skepticism until independent confirmation of their credibility is found, or do
we believe (and teach) that we ought to accept the credibility of information
sources provided there are no obvious warning signs? Social epistemologists
debate these positions, some going so far as to attempt compelling (though
technical) hybrid third-path theories (e.g., Jennifer Lackey). However, all social
epistemologists are united on at least one thing: Understanding the way we learn
and acquire knowledge from the testimony of other knowers is of the utmost
importance. Librarians would, no doubt, agree.

Outside of issues surrounding testimony, several other aspects of social
epistemology are relevant to librarianship. For example, Goldman points out
that with the rise of the Internet the information ecosystem "is an increasingly
complex and changing affair, which can no longer be handled exclusively by
the traditional print-dominated library," and one social epistemic goal is to
provide "a clearer…picture of how communication can enhance knowledge."[54]
Goldman outlines two goals for social epistemology on the Internet. First,
social epistemology can help us make sense of how knowledge communities
can help regulate the quality of information found online.[55] Second, the
interactivity inherent in most online media (especially social media) allows
knowledge communities to create "extended argumentative discourses" aimed
at uncovering truth.[56] In a certain respect, these goals are reminiscent of the
social constructionist's focus on discourse as a means of constructing beliefs
about the world. The key difference is that, on the social constructionist account,
there is no independent fact of the matter when communities debate, argue, or
otherwise share ideas—all are just different perspectives, and there are no facts
independent from the contingent social forces that created them. In contrast,

the social epistemologist sees such argumentative discourses as essentially truth oriented and chooses instead to focus on how objectivity and truth spread through online communities. Whereas the social constructionist must treat the anti-vaccination online community as possessing knowledge—they actually know that the MMR vaccine causes autism because they have agreed that it does—the social epistemologist is more concerned with understanding how that community came to their belief, how that belief propagates through other communities, and, importantly, how to help others distinguish credible information about vaccinations from the passionately held but demonstrably false beliefs of the anti-vaccination crowd.

As a third (and for this chapter, final) example of social epistemology in practice, Goldman argues that social epistemology allows us to make greater sense of the so-called marketplace of ideas that libraries both champion and reside in. There are two distinct senses of this marketplace of ideas. On one hand, there is the metaphorical marketplace understood as the sociocultural world of free expression. On the other hand, there is the actual commercial marketplace where information products are regulated and traded as economic objects. Social epistemology addresses both of these marketplaces in a way that other epistemological positions do not.

On the metaphorical level, social epistemology is concerned with the marketplace of ideas insofar as "the best way for a community to discover truth is to ensure that a wide range of diverse views vigorously compete with one another in the public arena through critical examination."[57] This concern lends itself to opposing censorship and promoting diversity. On the more literal level, social epistemology focuses on the way information is treated as an economic good subjected to varying degrees of regulation and a host of what Goldman calls *gatekeepers*: those who control the otherwise free flow of information, including editors, referees, publishers, censors, and so on. Though we may have a nominal right to express ourselves and share whatever information we choose, in practice free expression is governed by these economic regulations and information gatekeepers who "control the production of speech or affect the dissemination of messages to possible audiences."[58] Whether metaphorical or literal, the key insight is that information—hence, knowledge—is profoundly affected by social forces. Knowledge benefits from cooperation, dissent, debate, and diversity just as much as knowledge benefits from economic systems that facilitate equitable access to information and discourage monopolistic gatekeepers.

In sum, social epistemology represents a viable "third way" between the overly rigid strictures of positivism and the ambivalence of social constructionism. From positivism, social epistemology inherits an orientation towards truth and objectivity. From social constructionism, social epistemology inherits a sensitivity to the ways in which social processes affect the flow of information and the credibility of information sources. As a theory of knowledge born in library science and honed in philosophy, the time is right to consider social epistemology as a foundation for LIS. In the introduction to a special information-science-themed issue of the journal *Social Epistemology*, Fallis wrote,

> Most of our knowledge is acquired through communication with other members of society rather than through direct observation of the world. Much of this socially acquired knowledge is transmitted via recorded information (books, journals, websites, etc.). Libraries and other information services facilitate knowledge acquisition by collecting, organizing, and providing access to this recorded knowledge … [but now], with an explosion in the amount of recorded (especially digital) information, it is increasingly difficult to manage information so as to facilitate knowledge acquisition. As a result, social epistemology is needed more than ever as a theoretical foundation for information science.[59]

Whatever epistemological position ultimately informs library practice, it is important to understand the way in which epistemology affects how we approach information and how we teach others to navigate the world of information.

Notes

1.   Mary E. Ramsay, "Measles: The Legacy of Low Vaccine Coverage," *Archives of Disease in Childhood* 98 (2013): 752.

2.   Ibid.

3.   Michael J. Goldacre and Jenny J. Maisonneuve, "Hospital Admission Rates for Measles and Mumps in England: Historical Perspective," *The Lancet* 389, no. 9889 (2013): 308.

4.   Zsuzsanna Jakab and David M. Salisbury, "Back to Basics: The Miracle and Tragedy of Measles Vaccine," *The Lancet* 381, no. 9876 (2013): 1433.

5.   Michael Goldberg as quoted in David Kirby, *Evidence of Harm: Mercury in Vaccines and the Autism Epidemic; A Medical Controversy* (New York: St. Martin's Press, 2005), 104 (emphasis in original text).

6.   "Retraction—Ileal-lymphoid-nodular Hyperplasia, Non-Specific Colitis, and Pervasive Developmental Disorder in Children," *The Lancet* 375, no. 9713 (2010): 445; Andrew Wakefield et al., "Ileal-lymphoid-nodular Hyperplasia, Non-Specific Colitis, and Pervasive Developmental Disorder in Children," *The Lancet* 351, no. 9103 (1998): 640.

7.   Tom Jefferson et al., "Unintended Events Following Immunization with MMR: A Systematic Review," *Vaccine* 21, no. 25-26 (2003): 3954–60.

8.   Abraham Kaplan, "The Age of the Symbol," *Library Quarterly* 34, no. 4 (1964): 304.

9.   Don Fallis, "Epistemic Value Theory and Social Epistemology," *Episteme* 2, no. 3 (2006): 177.

10.   Jerry Fodor, *The Language of Thought* (Cambridge, MA: Harvard University Press, 1975).

11.   Fred Dretske, *Explaining Behavior* (Cambridge, MA: MIT Press, 1988), 109.

12.   D. M. Armstrong, *Belief, Truth, and Knowledge* (Cambridge, UK: Cambridge University Press, 1973), 4.

13.   Duncan Pritchard, *What Is This Thing Called Knowledge?* (New York: Routledge, 2006), 5.

14.   Edmund Gettier, "Is Justified True Belief Knowledge?" *Analysis* 23, no. 6 (1963): 121.

15.   Ibid.

16.   Archie L. Dick, "Library and Information Science as a Social Science: Neutral and Normative Conceptions," *Library Quarterly* 65, no. 2 (1995): 217.

17.   Ibid., 221.

18.   Ibid., 226.

19.   Michael H. Harris, "The Dialectic of Defeat: Antinomies in Research in Library and Information Science," *Library Trends* 34, no. 3 (1986): 518.

20.   Auguste Comte, *The Positive Philosophy of Auguste Comte*, trans. Harriet Martineau (New York: Calvin Blanchard, 1858).

21.   Moritz Schlick, "Positivismus und Realismus," *Erkenntnis* 3 (1932/1933): 1–31.

22.   Karl Popper, *The Logic of Scientific Discovery* (New York: Basic Books, 1959), 6.

23.   Paul Boghossian, *Fear of Knowledge: Against Relativism and Constructivism* (Oxford: Oxford University Press, 2006), 22.

24.   Alvin I. Goldman, "What Is Justified Belief?" in *Justification and Knowledge*, ed. George Pappas (Dordrecht, Holland: Reidel, 1979), 10.

25.   American Library Association. "Code of Ethics of the American Library Association." Accessed September 30, 2014. http://www.ala.org/advocacy/proethics/codeofethics/codeethics.

26.   Jonathan Eldredge, "Evidence-Based Librarianship: The EBL Process," *Library Hi Tech* 24, no. 3 (2006): 341–54.

27.   "Library Bill of Rights," American Library Association, accessed April 30, 2014, http://www.ala.org/advocacy/intfreedom/librarybill.

28.   Russell L. Ackoff, "From Data to Wisdom," *Journal of Applied Systems Analysis* 16 (1989): 3.

29.   Ibid., 3; Jennifer Rowley, "The Wisdom Hierarchy: Representations of the DIKW Hierarchy," *Journal of Information Science* 33, no. 2 (2007): 171.

30.   Robert M. Losee, "A Discipline Independent Definition of Information," *Journal of the American Society for Information Science* 48 (1997): 254; Luciano Floridi, "Is Information Mean-

ingful Data?" *Philosophy and Phenomenological Research* 70, no. 2 (2005): 351–70.

31.   Centers for Disease Control, "Measles-United States 2011," *Morbidity and Mortality Weekly Report* 61, no. 15 (2012): 253.

32.   Plato, "Theaetetus," trans. F. M. Cornford, in *The Collected Dialogues of Plato*, ed. Edith Hamilton and Huntington Cairns (Princeton, NJ: Princeton University Press, 1961), 856.

33.   Thomas Kuhn, *The Structure of Scientific Revolutions* (Chicago: University of Chicago Press, 1970), 210.

34.   Ibid., 11

35.   Catharine MacKinnon, *Feminism Unmodified* (Cambridge, MA: Harvard University Press, 1987), 50.

36.   Mary Field Belenky et al., *Women's Ways of Knowing* (New York: Basic Books, 1986), 138–139.

37.   Olof Sundin and Jenny Johannisson, "Pragmatism, Neopragmatism, and Sociocultural Theory: Communicative Participation as a Perspective in LIS," *Journal of Documentation* 61, no. 1 (2005): 35.

38.   Gary P. Radford, "Flaubert, Foucault, and the Bibliotheque Fantastique: Toward a Postmodern Epistemology for Library Science," *Library Trends* 46, no. 4 (1998): 621.

39.   R. David Lankes, *The Atlas of New Librarianship* (Cambridge, MA: MIT Press, 2011), 32.

40.   Robert V. Labaree and Ross Scimeca, "The Philosophical Problem of Truth in Librarianship," *The Library Quarterly* 78, no. 1 (2008): 63.

41.   Bernd Frohmann, "The Power of Images: A Discourse Analysis of the Cognitive Viewpoint," *Journal of Documentation* 48, no. 4 (1992): 365.

42.   Boghossian, *Fear of Knowledge*, 56.

43.   Ibid., 130.

44.   Margaret E. Egan and Jesse H. Shera, "Foundations of a Theory of Bibliography," *Library Quarterly* 22, no. 2 (1952): 132.

45.   Ibid., 133–34.

46.   John M. Budd, "Academic Libraries and Knowledge: A Social Epistemology Framework," *The Journal of Academic Librarianship* 30, no. 5 (2004): 362.

47.   Alvin I. Goldman, *Knowledge in a Social World* (Oxford: Oxford University Press, 1999), 3.

48.   Fallis, "Epistemic Value Theory and Social Epistemology," 177.

49.   David Hume, An Enquiry Concerning Human Understanding, ed. Eric Steinberg (1748; Indianapolis, IN: Hackett, 1993), 74.

50.   Jennifer Lackey, *Learning from Words* (New York: Oxford University Press, 2008), 143.

51.   James Van Cleve, "Reid on the Credit of Human Testimony," in *The Epistemology of Testimony*, ed. Jennifer Lackey and Ernest Sosa (Oxford: Oxford University Press), 64.

52.   C. A. J. Coady, *Testimony: A Philosophical Study* (New York: Oxford University Press, 1992), 82.

53.   Leslie Stevenson, "Why Believe What People Say?" *Synthese* 94 (1994): 433.

54.   Ibid., 163.

55.   Ibid., 166.

56.   Ibid., 170.

57.   Ibid., 209.

58.   Ibid., 189.

59.   Don Fallis, "Introduction: Social Epistemology and Information Science," *Social Epistemology* 16, no. 1 (2002): 1.

CHAPTER 2

Beyond Tools and Skills:
Putting Information Back into Information Literacy

Beth McDonough

For the past 18 years, I have taught information literacy in a variety of educational settings, including P–12, community college, and, for the past six years, a library serving a regional, comprehensive university. My situation is similar to most teaching librarians: Sometimes I teach graduate students or present multiple information literacy sessions to the same class in the same semester, and the typical venue for my instruction is a single 50–75 minute session (known as a one-shot) for students enrolled in an undergraduate course. As a guest instructor, my time with students is limited, and I have little control over the research assignments my instruction is designed to support.

Over time, I became dissatisfied with my inability to accomplish more with my instruction. Despite my best efforts, most students resisted looking beyond the surface of the information they were required to use for research projects; only a few students became passionate about research; and based on comments from a wide range of teaching faculty in multiple disciplines, the resulting research papers and projects typically failed to synthesize information to the degree that course instructors and librarians desired. A few years ago, I radically changed my teaching style. I was weary of presenting the very best sources and search strategies for students to use for a given assignment, only to observe them typing poorly constructed searches into Google five minutes later. I realized that my approach of modeling information expertise and expecting the students to mimic it was at odds with my desire to empower them to find, evaluate, and use information to solve problems. By simply offering students the *right* tools and techniques to conduct research, I was denying them the opportunity to build upon their prior knowledge to gain new understanding.

I began to experiment with ceding control in the classroom by adopting a less prescriptive, more inductive approach. The results have astounded me. When I give students control and begin with their own experiences, they are much more willing to dialogue with me about information contexts and uses. Together we critically examine their information strategies and the resulting sources. We all learn from each other, and I find that when the students are allowed to have a voice in the process, they are much more willing to listen.

Despite this newfound willingness to take risks in the classroom, I had much to learn. One day when working with a freshman English class, I offered the students 10–15 minutes of time at the start of class to free search using any means they preferred—an activity that has come to be my go-to when working with beginning students because it honors their prior knowledge and usually teaches me as much as it teaches them. This session was no exception. When I asked for a volunteer to come to the front and demonstrate what he or she had found, a young student showed us the website http://www.epilepsy.com. Despite my best intentions, my librarian's heart surged with anticipation of the possibility of delivering a pat lecture about the dubious quality of .com sites.

Thankfully, I held my tongue. It turned out that the site had a listing of recently published journal articles, albeit without links to full text. Following the student's lead, I was able to guide the class to recognize that the listing referred to journal articles by helping them recognize the obvious clues such as title of the journal and volume numbers. Then together we were able to locate the full text of the articles using the library interface. The student went on to explain that she had epilepsy, and she and her mother often used the site not only for medical information but to communicate in forums with other families in similar situations. Clearly it was a valuable resource to her, and I was grateful that I knew enough at that point to withhold my ill-informed value judgments and use the opportunity to spark questions rather than deliver answers.

Eventually, I discovered a body of library literature dedicated to the concept of *critical information literacy,* a teaching perspective that does not focus on student "acquisition of skills" but rather encourages a critical and discursive approach to information.[1] Just as I had found in my own classes, critical information literacy is not about teaching the *right* way to do things, an approach that is bound to be off-putting to young adults. Instead, critical information literacy encourages students "to think of research not as a task of collecting information, but instead as a task of constructing meaning."[2]

As I began a three-year period of working on my dissertation, I became engaged in a formal, systematic study of the literature with the intent of uncovering best practices, while experimenting in the classroom with my own pedagogy. This dual role of practitioner and scholar challenged me to continually take risks, reflect, revise, and, most of all, inquire of my colleagues through the literature. The experience did not leave me with a perfect recipe for effective information literacy instruction, but it did leave me with some interesting and worthwhile ideas for teaching librarians to consider as we embark a new era guided by the new *Framework for Information Literacy for Higher Education.*[3]

Traditional Information Literacy vs. Critical Information Literacy

For my dissertation's literature review, I identified 128 studies related to critical information literacy and selected 42 to comprise the actual sample for the study.[4] As the review was intended to be configurative, the studies for the sample were selected on the basis of their potential to contribute to the best practices of teaching librarians. Almost all of the studies critiqued or criticized traditional approaches to information literacy. Critical information literacy advocates agreed that traditional information literacy overly focuses on tools and skills. Traditional information literacy also presents an overly simplistic model of the research process that is out of sync with the reality that research is a nonsequential, iterative, and messy process. Most called the Association of College and Research Libraries' *Information Literacy Competency Standards for Higher Education* and other definitions of information literacy to account for overemphasis on tools-and-skills-based approaches. Some also held accountable the design and focus of traditional research paper assignments. Various voices from the literature negatively described traditional approaches to information literacy as technical, mechanical, behavioral, strategic, and skills-based, while positively describing critical approaches to information literacy as critical, problem-posing, multidimensional, creative, intellectual, process-based, and supportive of student agency. Figures 2.1 and 2.2 are word clouds that I created to contrast terms from the literature used to negatively and positively describe information literacy.

Figure 2.1. Word Cloud 1
Negative descriptions of traditional approaches to teaching information literacy. Critical information literacy proponents negatively described traditional approaches to teaching information literacy as technical, mechanical, behavioral, strategic, and skills-based. Larger words represent words that were used more frequently than smaller words in the quotations used to create this word cloud.

Figure 2.2. Word Cloud 2
Positive descriptions of critical approaches to teaching information literacy. Critical information literacy proponents positively described critical approaches to teaching information literacy as critical, problem-posing, multidimensional, creative, intellectual, process-based, and supportive of student agency. Larger words represent words that were used more frequently than smaller words in the quotations used to create this word cloud.

Relinquish Expertise and Efficiency

One of the most striking findings of my study was the idea that librarians must somewhat counterintuitively relinquish their role as efficient information experts in the classroom in order to create an environment where all learners find space to share and act upon their own ideas about information and the knowledge that it represents. There are a number of justifications for this shift in how librarians think about their role in the classroom. For one, the attempt to simply model or transfer information expertise to students is unlikely to be successful with most learners—though you can always reach a small group of ambitious students, the rest are likely to be bored. This is especially true of beginning undergraduate students, who come to today's information literacy classroom with little academic disciplinary knowledge but with a tremendous amount of experience finding and using information. Teaching librarians' knowledge about finding and using information is undoubtedly superior to that of students', but that's a hard selling point given the brief amount of time most have to spend with students.

Perhaps unsurprisingly, given librarian stereotypes, most librarians are introverts.[5] It may be impractical for many to cede authority and expertise to students in favor of interaction with students. It is possible that authority and expertise shield introverted librarians from the very interaction that critical pedagogy is designed to promote. Elizabeth Peterson observed,

> [A] side effect of this lecture-demonstration, cram-it-all-in approach is distance. When I teach this way, I don't have to engage with the students beyond a superficial level. It's all show and tell on my part with no discussion or active reflection with the group. I am the expert at the podium in the front of the classroom and the students are the passive receptacles.[6]

On one hand it may be difficult for many librarians to change their approach in the classroom by ceding efficiency and expertise, but on the other, it is a readily obtainable goal that can be accomplished by an individual gradually through self-reflection and without the need for outside resources. For librarians who seek to increase student engagement, such a goal seems worthwhile, for as Daniel Coffey and Karen Lawson suggest, it is desirable for "successful librarians… [to]…shed their 'expertness' (not expertise, but the attitude of expertise) in order to truly serve, and not alienate, their clientele."[7]

Teach about Information

A second finding of my study is seemingly at odds with the first: Many scholars and practitioners who contributed to the literature of critical information literacy believe that librarians should spend more time teaching about the nature of information itself, rather than, as is common, teaching about specific tools and skills. They feel that students needed instruction about how information is created and organized and that such instruction provides a useful introduction to academia. In view of these two findings—that librarians should relinquish efficiency and expertise about information in the classroom and that librarians should teach more about information—it is fair to question how these two things might be accomplished at the same time. Fortunately, the literature revealed several practical steps for accomplishing these two seemingly disparate goals.

The overarching message from the literature of critical information literacy instruction is that teaching librarians must strive to be reflective practitioners and reexamine taken-for-granted perspectives. One such perspective is best described as the deficit approach to student instruction. If the assumption that students come to our classrooms knowing little to nothing about finding and using information was ever valid, it is certainly much less likely to be valid in the current environment of the almost ubiquitous access current college and university students' have had to information throughout their lives.

Several scholars and practitioners argued this point in the literature and urged teaching librarians to use students' existing knowledge about information sources that are familiar to them as the basis for helping them understand the unfamiliar scholarly information sources that they are expected to use for their coursework. While students' approaches to information differ from librarians', these differences can be celebrated and serve as the basis for rich discussion in the classroom—so long as the discussion starts with honoring the students' prior experiences. Several authors described their positive experiences with this approach. For example, one team of teaching librarians described their experiences integrating critical information literacy into a first-year experience course—experiences that mirrored my own:

> Fighting our urge to deposit knowledge, we are astounded by the quality of student-generated ideas when we allow them to expand in an open-ended, nonjudgmental discussion.… Despite our initial skepticism, after taking a leap of faith and testing out the student-led activity,

we were thrilled to observe students transforming into eager mini-experts who have a great deal to say about searching with variant tools, investigating an author or source, limiting searches and developing new keywords. Indeed the students began to build methods of critical evaluation arriving at precisely the conclusions we previously had attempted to drive home through our woefully inauthentic methods.[8]

Start Where They Are

Along with ceding expertise and building upon students' knowledge about information, another tactic that critical information literacy scholars and practitioners found helpful was to begin by teaching about sources students are already familiar with to form a bridge between their personal lives and academia. Necessarily this involves librarians putting aside cherished value judgments about the quality of sources—value judgments that have been traditionally based on format. Several teaching librarians richly described successful information literacy instruction that embraced sources like *Wikipedia* and Google Scholar—not as examples of poor sources, but as a gateway to discussions with students about the differences between types of sources (not formats) and their purposes. For example, a few teaching librarians found the discussion pages behind each *Wikipedia* article, explaining edits made and why, as fertile ground for helping students understand how knowledge is negotiated through dialogue in our society. Others found discussion with students about how familiar tools functioned to be a great way to help them distinguish similarities and differences when compared to more scholarly tools.

Some scholars and practitioners of critical information literacy pointed out that teaching students to unquestioningly accept peer-reviewed journal articles and other library resources as authoritative, while rejecting outright the sources they are more familiar with using, insults their intelligence and the culture that they live in. In today's world, blanket categorizations of sources by format are overly simplistic. One team of teaching librarians pointed out, "As librarians, we know the situation is much more complex and we have a responsibility to incorporate this murkier landscape into our instruction."[9] Another team envisioned that information literacy should "move away from the demonstration of technical search processes and simplistic claims that certain sources are *authoritative* because authorizers have decided they are."[10]

Heidi L.M. Jacobs described her use of *Wikipedia* for information literacy instruction and explained her teaching rational:

> Telling students not to use *Wikipedia* and to accept our judgments unquestioningly does not model or encourage the kinds of critical thinking we want our students to learn and practice. This is not to say that librarians and professors need to encourage or allow the use of *Wikipedia.* Rather we need to allow room in our classes and curriculum for critical inquiry into our information sources be they subscription databases, university press monographs, librarian-selected websites or *Wikipedia.*... Whether we like it or not *Wikipedia* is here to stay... many of our students know they will need to negotiate questions related to *Wikipedia* and other similar resources in their lives outside of school. We are doing them a disservice if we ignore the complexities of *Wikipedia*... Further, we need to think about the message we sent to students when we banish, forbid, or ignore a resource in our classes that is firmly of their generation in favor of promoting resources of previous generations.[11]

Jacobs raises a great point: What message *is* sent by librarians who discount the vast range of sources available to today's college student? It is certainly tidy to be able to say that Internet sources are less accurate, but is such a general statement even true? Obviously it would depend on the information landscape for the topic being researched and students' purposes for conducting the research. I wonder how many college professors could make sense of an unfamiliar subject in an unrelated discipline solely on the basis of peer-reviewed journal articles? Yet, that is the charge that is often delivered to students, even beginning college students, in the form of research paper assignments. It can be argued that librarians often have little control over such assignments, but in reality we do wield some influence with course instructors and certainly much influence about discussions with students that take place during library instruction.

Another librarian commented on the harm librarians can unwittingly inflict when they do not honor student experiences:

> Our patrons have been searching online for years, so to assume they know nothing about information seeking is offensive and naïve. Giving these patrons detailed instructions that directly contradict what they have been doing for years is not going to help them or our image. Rather, we must encourage and acknowledge the benefits of experimentation with library tools and demonstrate our appreciation for learning from our patrons' approaches to searching.[12]

Most of my teaching colleagues, both within and outside of the library, have expressed resistance to the idea of not limiting students to academic sources for their research assignments. The general reaction seems to be wariness on the part of instructors that students will run amok, and their assignments will reflect less critical thinking and poorer quality sources. Consider that the opposite may be true. Critical information literacy practitioners who have tried this approach argue that source limitations undermine student criticality. One team of teaching librarians explained their approach:

> We want students to be aware of their information agency and to understand the impact of source selections, but we avoid making value judgments about the sources students select in the activity. Issues of academic authority are often brought up in discussion, and while we encourage these topics, we try to remain neutral. We do not advocate a blind preference for peer-reviewed publications, nor do we dismiss the value of popular sources. We want students to become critically sensitive to issues of legitimacy and power within information systems and environments. Imposing traditional evaluation criteria or norms of authority would contradict our intention to advance students' critical examination of information.[13]

Librarians are likely to find it difficult to resist the urge to help students find quick, neat, and tidy answers to their information questions in the form of library resources. Pamela N. Martin described the tendency of librarians "to direct people away from chaos and toward our subject-specific databases, our lovingly maintained reference collections, and our carefully crafted catalogs."[14] She pointed out,

> While this can no doubt help patrons, especially with their academic research, guiding students away from chaos and to tools to which they will not have lifelong access contradicts the goals of information literacy and undermines mastery of important skills in patrons' lives. Library instruction should help students develop life-long information literacy skills. Knowing how to use databases will not make you information literate, and avoiding chaos does not help you harness the power of information. Instead of guiding patrons in an open-ended exploration through the universe of information, too often the library plays the part of the overprotective parent.[15]

To me, this seems the one of the greatest challenges to the profession. Librarians are by nature helpers—perhaps programmed to jump in and *fix* things, rather than stand back and empower others to find their own solutions. I have heard librarians say that helping patrons to find the *right* answers is what they most enjoy about their jobs. Despite the stereotype of librarians as meek and mild, it's a heady business being the keeper of the *right* answers.

Teach about Information in Terms of Purposes, Not Format

One pitfall that can be easily avoided is the categorization of sources by their physical formats, rather than by what they are intended to accomplish and how the student might use them in support of whatever argument they are trying to make. Joel M. Burkholder commented,

As part of the information literacy initiative, librarians teach students how to develop a critical awareness of the sources used in their research. Unfortunately, we seem to ignore this particular advice in our current definition of sources. What are *sources?*...

For reasons that appear to be born out of convenience and expedience, most attempts to define sources do so by describing aspects of their physical natures. Due to our increasingly digital environment, these kinds of definitions are becoming much more difficult to defend.... The larger problem with definitions that focus on sources as mere objects is that they neglect their significance as communicative acts.[16]

Troy Swanson argued in a similar vein when he cautioned against defining sources by their physical formats:

> Librarians need to present them [students] with the information landscape and give them the ability to make judgments about particular pieces of information and about appropriate information tools. This model must reflect the ways in which information is created in society. In order to meet these needs, librarians and instructors need to present students with a model of the information world that focuses on the type of information rather than the format (book, website, periodical, etc.).[17]

In an earlier study, he offered this example:

> An article from *Newsweek* may exist in print, it may be on the *Newsweek* website, and it may appear in a subscription database... it is the same article in all three formats, for all intents and purposes. For a searcher, the concern should be that this is a news article, and the fact that it is news tells us something about the credibility of the information. This information would be different than information found in a scholarly publication, in a professional/trade publication, or on a personal website.[18]

From a practical perspective, traditional scholarly sources simply may not be the most effective and appropriate information to answer the students' research questions. Librarians (and course instructors) place themselves in an inauthentic situation when they prohibit students from using sources that may be of value to their development of new knowledge. For example, recently, following a flurry of hastily enacted legislation regarding public education and other issues in North Carolina, a freshman English student chose North Carolina public education funding as his topic and asked for my help. While the blogosphere was buzzing and several state and national newspapers picked up on the topic, traditional peer-reviewed journal articles and monographs had not yet been published. Fortunately, in this case, the course instructor was flexible about the types of sources students used. But sometimes, instructors (and librarians) are not. Ruth Mirtz argues that the practice of redirecting students' topic selections in order to conform to source requirements is a critical missed opportunity for teaching librarians. Using the example of a student interested in extreme sports, she argued,

> Whenever students have to eliminate topics of primary interest to them or adapt topics to fit what they can find literature on (such as switching from the topic of deer baiting to bovine tuberculosis) instead of pointing students to other professional sources of information (such as Department of Natural Resources reports on stakeholders' meetings about deer hunting regulation changes), the library has missed the chance to intermediate with users in a critically supportive way. The search process then fails to engage a citizen in a collective process or in ethical questions that could alter the status quo. The library hasn't encouraged or provided a challenge to disintermediation, but encouraged failure…The library has thus, in this situation, failed to help the students negotiate the movement between scholarly, individual, and public spheres, nor to create a conversation among the data created by researchers, the values a student brings from home, and the potential to enact change in the world. [19]

Challenges Moving Forward

While these seem simple enough perspectives—to relinquish expertise and efficiency, to build upon students' prior knowledge, to teach about information in terms of purposes and types rather than formats, and to teach about all types of information, rather than privileging library sources—such viewpoints are antithetical to traditional approaches. Since its inception, bibliographic instruction has been about teaching students *how to use the library*. And though the reframing of bibliographic instruction as information literacy was intended to broaden those horizons, many think that effort has fallen short of its goals—hence the endless debate over the meaning of information literacy and the recent development of the *Framework for Information Literacy for Higher Education*.[20] While it is much easier to teach students where to point and click than to teach them about the nature of scholarly communication itself, clearly the former approach is no longer sufficient.

Also, there is the problem of librarians' own views about information. Having embraced the *science* aspect of information science, perhaps cherishing it more than the *literacy* aspect of information literacy, many librarians cling to world where information needs can be matched to distinct and correct sources of singular truth—a world where truth is uncontested, one-size-fits-all, and, most of all, neutral. Those that urge a critical information literacy approach reject these notions in favor of teaching about information as scholarly dialogue, truth as evolving, and information sources as having a non-neutral purpose both in their publication and in how the reader might use them to create new knowledge. Certainly the latter presents a challenge to the profession and one that begins with examining and perhaps deconstructing one's own views about a subject that is near and dear to librarians' self-identity.

One of the more promising findings from the literature is that librarians may be able to employ critical pedagogy to ease students' transition into academia. Increasingly, higher education is being called to account for student retention, especially state run institutions. In response, libraries have successfully sought methods to demonstrate the value of library programs and services to student attainment. If, as the literature suggests, taking a critical approach to information literacy instruction can ease student transition into academia, then there is substantial motivation for teaching librarians to experiment with the pedagogies called for by such an approach.

Perhaps most alarming is the idea from the literature that tools-and-skills-based, traditional information literacy instruction may actually discourage student criticality by stripping information from its context. Much energy is expended by well-meaning librarians who have the goal of helping students become critical consumers of information. The possibility that such efforts might be counterproductive is reason enough for teaching librarians to reexamine their pedagogy to determine which methods they employ in the classroom are actually supporting the long-term goals of information literacy beyond student acquisition of tools and skills and which may be hindering those goals. Certainly, the calls from the literature for greater reflection on teaching practice and continuing discussion among teaching librarians are well grounded and hold promise for the profession.

Notes

1. Michelle Holschuh Simmons, "Librarians as Disciplinary Discourse Mediators: Using Genre Theory to Move toward Critical Information Literacy," *Portal: Libraries and the Academy* 5, no. 3 (2005): 299.

2. Ibid.

3. Association of College and Research Libraries, *Framework for Information Literacy for Higher Education*, accessed June 13, 2014, http://acrl.ala.org/ilstandards/wp-content/up-loads/2014/02/Framework-for-IL-for-HE-Draft-2.pdf.

4. Beth Allsopp McDonough, "Critical Information Literacy in Practice: An Interpretive Review" (EdD diss., Western Carolina University, 2014), http://wncln.wncln.org/re-cord=b5404335.

5. Mary Jane Scherdin, "How Well Do We Fit? Librarians and Faculty in the Academic Setting," *Portal: Libraries and the Academy* 2, no. 2 (2002): 237–53.

6. Elizabeth Peterson, "Problem-Based Learning as Teaching Strategy," in *Critical Library Instruction,* ed. Marie T. Accardi, Emily Drabinski, and Alana Kumbier (Duluth, MN: Library Juice Press, 2010), 71.

7. Daniel Coffey and Karen Lawson, "Managing Meaning: Language and Technology in Academic Libraries," *College and Research Libraries* 63, no. 2 (2002): 159.

8. Caroline Sinkinson and Mary Caton Lingold, "Re-Visioning the Library Seminar through a Lens of Critical Pedagogy," in *Critical Library Instruction,* ed. Marie T. Accardi, Emily Drabinski, and Alana Kumbier (Duluth, MN: Library Juice Press, 2010), 87.

9. Scott Warren and Kim Duckett, "Why Does Google Scholar Sometimes Ask for Money?" *Journal of Library Administration* 50, no. 4 (2010): 151.

10. Jonathan Cope, "Information Literacy and Social Power," in *Critical Library Instruction,* ed. Marie T. Accardi, Emily Drabinski, and Alana Kumbier (Duluth, MN: Library Juice Press, 2010), 25 (emphasis in original).

11. Heidi L.M. Jacobs, "Posing the Wikipedia 'Problem:' Information Literacy and the Praxis of Problem-Posing in Library Instruction," in *Critical Library Instruction,* ed. Marie T. Accardi, Emily Drabinski, and Alana Kumbier (Duluth, MN: Library Juice Press, 2010), 193.

12. Pamela N. Martin, "Societal Transformation and Reference Services in the Academic Library: Theoretical Foundations for Re-envisioning Reference," *Library Philosophy and Practice*

11, no. 1 (2009): 5.

13. Sinkinson and Lingold, "Re-Visioning the Library Seminar," 86.

14. Martin, "Societal Transformation and Reference Services," 6.

15. Ibid., 6.

16. Joel M. Burkholder, "Redefining Sources as Social Acts," *Library Philosophy and Practice* 12, no. 2 (2010): 2.

17. Troy Swanson, "Teaching Students about Information: Information Literacy and Cognitive Authority," *Research Strategies* 12, no. 4 (2007): 324.

18. Troy A. Swanson, "A Radical Step: Implementing a Critical Information Literacy Model," *Portal: Libraries and the Academy* 4, no. 2 (2004): 262–63.

19. Ruth Mirtz, "Disintermediation and Resistance: Giroux and Radical Praxis in the Library," in *Critical Library Instruction*, ed. Marie T. Accardi, Emily Drabinski, and Alana Kumbier (Duluth, MN: Library Juice Press, 2010), 301–02.

20. Association of College and Research Libraries, *Framework for Information Literacy.*

CHAPTER 3

Librarianspeak:
Metaphors that Reflect (and Shape) the Ethos and Practice of Academic Librarianship

MaryBeth Meszaros and Alison M. Lewis

Although librarians write extensively about student information literacy, faculty-librarian collaboration, and the role librarians play in the fostering of information literacy, little attention has been paid to linguistic features of librarian discourse, features that could reveal underlying attitudes of librarians towards their two primary client groups—faculty and students. One reason for this neglect is the nature of librarian discourse itself: By and large, scholarly communication in the field aspires to the condition of discourse in the social sciences—straightforward and, by humanistic standards, "dry," that is, devoid of colorful, figurative language. Similes, metaphors, and other literary devices are generally (and understandably) eschewed. However, as with other discourse communities, librarians frequently do invoke what are known as "conventional metaphors." An examination of these types of metaphors via a technique known as "corpus analysis" can reveal librarian sentiments toward faculty and students.

1.1 Librarian and Faculty Epistemologies and Beliefs

The consensus among librarians as expressed in librarian professional literature is that information literacy is a skill that must be acquired by students in order that they may become "lifelong learners." The literature of information literacy has, as Cushla Kapitzke points out, "a sense of urgency about ensuring that learners are 'information literate.'"[1] This article of faith is so compelling for librarians that they see information literacy as a meta-skill, one that consequently equals or even trumps traditional academic disciplines.[2] Put another way, librarians perceive themselves as teaching the whole student, whereas faculty educate the student merely within the specific discipline. When faculty resist or ignore the mandate to prioritize information literacy, librarians have sometimes responded by invoking a discourse of warfare: "Faculty inattention to IL" is "a competition that must be tamed, turf that must be claimed, or …a battle that must be won."[3] Katherine Beaty Chiste, Andrea Glover, and Glenna Westwood's "Infiltration and Entrenchment: Capturing and Securing Information Literacy Territory in Academe" and Ken Kempcke's "The Art of War for Librarians: Academic Culture, Curricular Reform, and Wisdom from Sun Tzu" offer particularly straightforward and compelling examples of the adoption by librarians of a rhetoric of warfare.[4] Kempcke makes the point that his article is grounded in a tradition of librarian war talk: "The library literature on instruction is surprisingly (perhaps) scattered with warlike analogies."[5] (As will become evident, there is nothing surprising about the discourse's implementation of such "analogies.") However, Kempcke's point requires interrogation: While our initial goal was to measure the intensity and prevalence of military rhetoric within the librarian discourse community, we remained open to the emergence of additional, alternative metaphors. These did indeed materialize as we began to analyze our data. In fact, these alternative metaphors proved more pervasive.

While much has been written on librarian-faculty relationships, a curious silence reigns on the subject of librarian-student affective relationships, this despite the fact that librarian professional discourse focuses persistently on student learning. Thus, another purpose of this study is to address this lack and also to offer a comparison between what librarian conventional metaphors reveal about librarian-student relationships and what they reveal about librarian-faculty relationships.

Librarian perceptions and attitudes can negatively or positively affect the dynamics of both faculty-librarian and student-librarian relationships, yet building and maintaining good relationships are critical to the delivery of effective academic library service, particularly in the context of information literary instruction. This study of the discursive practices of academic librarians offers a window into the underlying mental constructs that academic librarians reflexively bring to bear as they interact with faculty and students.

Conceptual Metaphor Theory and Corpus Analysis: An Overview

Metaphors are usually understood as highly figurative language, the hallmark of poetry and other imaginative literature. However, "in the cognitive linguistic view, metaphor is defined as understanding one conceptual domain in terms of another conceptual domain…. Examples of this include when we talk and think about life as a journey … about arguments in terms of war."[6] One need not be a poet to employ metaphor; in fact, metaphor-making and metaphor usage are endemic qualities of human thought. Highly original metaphors, over the passage of time, can become clichés; they are indeed metaphors nonetheless. Metaphors of this type are said to be conventional metaphors. The discourse of any given profession or social group will be replete with a variety of conventional metaphors that members of that discourse community will instantly recognize and widely employ.

Metaphors—both the highly original (i.e., "creative") and the conventional—function by mapping a relatively abstract concept onto a comparatively concrete, physical target. When there is no mapping, the language is said to be literal (i.e., nonmetaphorical). Thus, for example, the employment of military metaphors in the context of a battlefield description is likely to be literal; their use in a nonmilitary context is likely to be metaphorical. Context is crucial.

According to Jonathan Charteris-Black, the usefulness of metaphor analysis lies in the fact that metaphors, especially conventional metaphors, "tap into an accepted communal system of values."[7] Put another way, "critical analysis of metaphors can provide insight into the beliefs, attitudes, and feelings of the discourse community in which they occur."[8] Thus, the tacit communal values of librarians as a discourse community can be explored by examining the patterns of metaphors that commonly emerge in the profession's discourse.

However, metaphors not only reflect a discourse community's shared values, they also shape them. Metaphor theorists, such as Charteris-Black,

Alice Deignan, and Lynn Cameron, argue that metaphors serve a rhetorical function, that is, they have the "underlying purpose of influencing opinions and judgments by persuasion."[9] Cameron puts the case quite forcefully: Metaphor operates by "systematically pervading our language and thinking, and even at its strongest, controlling our minds and actions."[10] Initiates of a group become socialized into the group by learning (and using) the group's conventionalized metaphors: "Metaphor contributes to 'membershipping' people into a group and developing the shared discourse of a group."[11] In short, metaphors are never ideologically neutral.

While a discourse community's shared conventionalized metaphors serve to bind it together, at the same time they also present a potentially insidious feature. As metaphor theorists point out, any conventional metaphor within any discourse community can become so ingrained and inscribed within the group's shared narrative, that, as Veronika Koller puts it, it is seen as "an unproblematic picture of reality"—the conventional metaphor is "stripped of its ideology and rendered uncontested 'common sense.'"[12] Thus, metaphors can be implicated in the phenomenon of group-think. In short, conventional metaphors can squelch unconventional, critical thinking.

As Jill J. McMillan and George Cheney observe, "Metaphors bear watching and listening."[13] Charteris-Black goes so far as to claim that metaphor "is a potent and potentially powerful weapon."[14] Metaphors can mask and obscure one set of meanings while simultaneously crystallizing and throwing into relief another set. (A good example is the word "target." On the one hand, we are invited to visualize an audience towards which a speaker or writer directs a message. On the other hand, the militaristic overtone of the firing of a weapon is simultaneously and inescapably present.) Some observers have noted that because of their nonliteral nature, the manner in which meaning is implied rather than stated, metaphors offer a "hedging" function for speakers and writers.[15] Put plainly, "speakers can hide behind metaphoric language."[16]

This "potent and potentially powerful weapon" (Charteris-Black is here using a metaphor to describe the action of metaphors) can be deployed defensively or offensively.[17] George Lakoff, the pioneer theorist of conceptual metaphor theory, underscores the latent lethality of metaphor: "Metaphorical thought, in itself, is neither good nor bad; it is simply commonplace and inescapable," yet, he adds, "Metaphors can kill."[18] Critical linguistics seeks to deconstruct conventional metaphors as they surface in texts in order to question and problematize the "picture of reality" they present.[19] Critical linguistics recognizes that power and social domination are inescapably registered in language. Finally, critical linguistics analysis "attempts to demonstrate how particular discursive practices reflect sociopolitical power structures and, by implication, to modify practices to the benefit of those whom they currently disadvantage."[20]

One way to study the use of metaphor within and by a specific discourse community is through "corpus linguistics." A corpus is defined as "any collection of spoken or written texts."[21] Corpora can be either "ready-made," that is, one that has been "compiled by groups of academic or commercial researchers," or they can be specifically compiled for a particular project by the individual researchers.[22] The corpora used for this study belong to the second category. Specifically compiled corpora are relatively small, and they are especially well suited to the study of metaphor: "Small corpora can allow for an in-depth analysis of metaphor in its discoursal and social contexts."[23]

Once the corpus or corpora are assembled, the researcher begins by compiling, with the aid of special software, a list of lemmas. A lemma **is** a "head word" or a word-stem. For example, "run" would be a lemma encompassing a number of lexemes (variant forms) such as *ran, running, runs, to run,* for example. A lexical field (sometimes referred to as a semantic field) consists of a set of interrelated lemmas that "belong to a defined area of meaning (e.g., education)."[24] A simple example would be color terms, which would include lemmas such as *red, blue, white,* etc. The lexical field of warfare might include lemmas such as *muster, challenge, charge, arm, target, launch,* etc. All of the lexemes of each lemma would also be included, for example, *arms, arming, armed, to arm.* The lemma *run,* for example, might be identified as belonging both to the lexical fields of sports and politics. In fact, many lemmas can be assigned to more than one lexical field. This quality of multiple assignability allows metaphors to generate complex connotations beyond the most obvious, overt meaning toward which the writer or speaker gestures.

There is no standard, approved way to derive lexical fields from any given corpus: "There is no set of agreed upon criteria for establishing semantic fields."[25] Ultimately, the individual researcher depends on his or her own "linguistic knowledge:" The use of a concordance program simply "brings patterns to the researcher's attention."[26] Based on Kempcke's hypothesis, we provisionally expected to find conventional metaphors related to the lexical field military science. We were surprised to find that while this lexical field is indeed present, it is not as dominant as the other lexical fields that emerged.

Review of Literature: Applied Linguistics, Metaphor, and Librarian Discourse

Metaphors have long been used by library professionals to describe the pur-pose(s) and nature of libraries, the types of work performed by librarians, and the roles of librarians themselves. A well-known example of this type of meta-phor use in librarian professional discourse is that of the library as the "heart of the university." This particular metaphor has been repeated so often that it is now almost a conventional metaphor. Even so, it has gained renewed life in recent years as academic librarians struggle to find ways to either retain this cen-tral position in their institutions or find new ways to define themselves and their worth.[27] These works are representative of the most common type of metaphor analysis within the literature of library and information science—studies or opinion pieces that recognize the power of metaphor within librarian discourse and seek to leverage it to some purpose.[28]

It should be noted that these types of articles do not exploit metaphor as a means of discovering librarian conceptual models of, attitudes toward, and beliefs about their two primary user groups—faculty and students. None of them undertake to extrapolate librarian views of their patrons, none attend to librarians as a distinct discourse community *per se*, and none make use of more formal linguistic analysis. Such studies are exceedingly rare, but there are a few that do invoke a linguistic framework.

A pioneering discussion of the use of conceptual metaphors to describe academic libraries and librarians is provided by Danuta Nitecki, who created a corpus comprised of letters and opinions published in *The Chronicle of Higher Education* between 1989 and 1992.[29] Like the authors of the present study, Nitecki endorses the premise that "people's conceptual models are reflected in their communications."[30] Her "totally unobtrusive study" concludes that two academic groups, higher education administrators and librarians, "shared three metaphors—library as partner, library as activist, library as economic model."[31] Nitecki offers a corpus-based analysis of librarians' own perceptions of the role of the library and the nature of librarianship. The "metaphoric stories" that librarians might be telling about faculty and students is outside the scope of her investigation, but in discussing the limitations of her own study, she does lay the groundwork for other methodologies of data collection: "The findings about metaphors used by librarians, might, for example, be collaborated [*sic*] by a similar analysis of expressions in their own professional publications such as *College and Research Libraries* or the *Journal of Academic Librarianship.*[32]

Taking her cue from Nitecki, Joan Giesecke consults librarian professional literature to examine "set[s] of metaphors" that librarians use to describe both the library and themselves.[33] Her study is also unobtrusive, but not as robust in that it gleans various conceptual metaphors from a very small body of works—only a dozen or so articles and books. She discusses, for example, Stephen Bell's notion of the librarian as "gate opener" and others' metaphors of library as "heart," "conversation," "place," and "ecosystem."[34] In terms of some of the findings of the present study, she also notes the emergence of a new metaphor—the library as "academic living room:" "We do seem to be running a bed and breakfast for some students, a social gathering place, and a snack and study zone for others."[35]

An equally unobtrusive but much more robust methodology is utilized by Heidi Julien and Lisa M. Given.[36] This study, like the present one, is intensely concerned with librarian attitudes toward faculty. The methodology—content analysis (a research methodology used in linguistics)—is used to analyze librarians' "unscripted" postings to the premier listserv devoted to information literacy librarianship: BI-L (which became ILI-L in 2002).[37] Postings for a seven-year period (1995–2002) were analyzed and coded, the authors focusing solely on postings related to librarian-faculty relationships. The authors do not investigate metaphorical language in the postings *per se*, but this study does inform the present one in that it is, unlike the Nitecki and Giesecke studies, a sustained linguistic exploration of articulated views of librarian attitudes toward instructional faculty. They conclude that many listserv posters expressed disrespect or even hostility toward faculty clients. Moreover, they contend that some librarians go so far as to focus on the student client base to the exclusion of faculty: "Many librarians on the BI-L/ILI-L list made clear that they generally do not consider faculty members to be their clients—only those faculty members' students."[38]

This study points out the inherent incongruity between, on the one hand, a need to collaborate and partner with faculty, and, on the other, the stance of faculty distrust that some librarians maintain. One of the goals of the present study is to compare the findings of the Julien and Given study to conceptual models of faculty that librarians disclose via the more oblique language of metaphor.

Review of Literature: Conceptual Metaphors and Other Discourse Communities

Not surprisingly, the flexibility, adaptability, and scalability of conceptual metaphor theory make it quite attractive as a methodology of discourse analysis. Thus, one can find it deployed in fields as disparate as, for example, fine arts criticism, software engineering, information technology, higher education, and psychology.[39]

Most useful in terms of the present study is Koller's *Metaphor and Gender in Business Media Discourse*. Koller utilizes quantitative and qualitative corpus analysis in order to study the kinds of metaphors that most frequently surface in business periodicals such as *The Economist* and *Fortune*. She concludes that "the conceptual metaphor MARKETING IS WAR is highly entrenched."[40] In a related study, Koller turns her attention to a corpus comprised of business mergers and acquisitions discourse, discovering that marriage and courtship conceptual metaphors coexist with military and martial metaphors.[41] Koller's observations are useful given that a fair amount of librarian discourse vis-à-vis both faculty and students is concerned with marketing: the marketing of library services and in particular the marketing of information literacy. William B. Badke's description of the two seemingly incompatible roles played by librarians—librarian as "tactician" and librarian as "friendship evangelist" tally well with Koller's discussion of marketing as a simultaneous wooing and waging of war.[42] The tactician and friendship evangelist are simply two sides of the same metaphorical coin.

Methodology

The authors of this study undertook to explore conceptual models about faculty and students espoused by academic librarians as expressed in two publications: *LOEX Conference Proceedings* and *College and Research Library News*. Like Nitecki and Given and Julien, we concluded that an unobtrusive method of data collection would be preferable, given the sensitive nature of the topic and especially given the fact that librarian discourse in general expresses an "asymmetrical disconnection" between faculty and librarians, a disconnect occasionally shading into downright hostility.[43] We wished to subject anecdotal evidence—

subjective impressions gleaned from an informal survey of professional librarian discourse—to quantitative and qualitative linguistic analysis. To furnish comparison and/or contrast, we also opted to include analysis of metaphorical language used by librarians in their discussions of students, especially undergraduates. These particular titles were chosen for analysis because of their status as relatively informal professional communication. We believed that their content would be more likely to be indicative of how librarians actually talk to each other, rather than communication mediated through the more formal conventions of scholarly discourse.[44]

Accordingly, two corpora of machine-readable text were compiled. One is comprised of all articles (164 articles) published in *LOEX Conference Proceedings* (*LOEX*) between 2005 and 2009, the most recent issue available at the time of this writing. The second corpus consists of all articles published in *College and Research Library News* (386 articles) between January 2004 and August 2011. The *College and Research Library News* (*C&RL News*) corpus was also prepared by removing all extraneous materials such as classified advertising and the "departments" section (e.g., reviews, news items).

With the aid of a concordance software program, each corpus was analyzed first in terms of frequency of references to faculty as compared to frequency of references to students and frequency of references to librarians themselves. (A stop list consisting of *a*, *an*, and *the* was utilized). Table 3.1 demonstrates that in both corpora, references to *student(s)* occur far more frequently than do references to *faculty*.

Table 3.1. Frequencies of Terms Student(s), Faculty, Librarian(s) in Corpora

	LOEX 2005–2009	LOEX 2005–2009	C&RL News	C&RL News
Student, Students	Rank: 6	Frequency: 6,185	Rank: 14	Frequency: 4,911
Faculty	Rank: 38	Frequency: 1,287	Rank: 34	Frequency: 1,977
Librarian, Librarians	Rank: 19	Frequency: 2,365	Rank: 19	Frequency: 3,261

In the *LOEX* corpus, the lemma *student* occurs approximately 4.8 times as often as the lemma *faculty*. In fact, overall, *student* ranks as the sixth most frequently used lemma in this corpus. In the *C&RL News* corpus, references to *student(s)* occur 2.48 times as often as references to *faculty*. In fact, in both corpora, references to *librarian(s)* occur more frequently than do references to *faculty*; that is, librarians are more likely to reference themselves than faculty. This finding seems to bear out Caitlin Tillman's contention that "our professional literature concentrates more on the librarian's undergraduate constituency than it does on professors, transient patrons at the expense of the permanent."[45]

The next phase of the process was the determination of lexical fields (i.e., lexical field analysis). In order to explore the corpora's lexical fields, the lemma lists of each corpus were manually scrutinized. As Koller points out, "Computer-generated results require quite extensive manual reworking."[46] We subjected our corpora to qualitative analysis, searching for patterns. Candidate metaphors from the software-generated word lists needed to be examined in the context of textual passages to verify that the lemma was indeed being used as metaphor, rather than as literal expression.

Our initial working hypothesis was that Badke's notion, discussed earlier, of the librarian as both "tactician" and "friendship evangelist" implies a vision of faculty as both an adversary to be conquered as well as a heathen to be converted. For us, as for Koller, "anecdotal evidence" drawn from the professional discourse at large "served as the starting point."[47] We provisionally accepted Koller's notion of marketing as veiled warfare, and accordingly we began by searching for lemmas drawn from the field of military science. In so doing, we discovered a significant number of lemmas drawn from other lexical fields. Although a number of lexical fields emerged, we chose the four most dominant for close analysis and discussion: (1) military science, (2) romance-marriage-courtship, (3) guesthood-entertainment, and (4) barriers-gaps/bridges-convergences. Throughout the data-gathering process, the *Oxford English Dictionary* (*OED*) was consulted so as to determine word origins, derivation, and various definitions and to verify a lemma's membership in lexical field domains.

Results and Discussion: Lexical Field— Military Science

We began with the lexical field military science since our initial premise, following Kempcke's and Koller's lead, was that "war talk" would readily surface in our corpora. This lexical field did indeed prove to be robust; however, as will become evident, metaphors belonging to the other three lexical fields were discovered to be more numerous. It should be noted that all of the lemmas pertaining to the lexical field "military science" are "attenuated" expressions of warfare.[48] In other words, the metaphors invoked by these corpus writers are usually not related to the actual concussive aspects of warfare, but rather the devices and schemes one uses to advance a cause or conquer a rival (i.e., military strategy)(table 3.2).

Table 3.2. Top Ten Lemmas in the Lexical Field of Military Science

LOEX Lemmas in Descending Order with Frequency		*C&RL News* Lemmas in Descending Order with Frequency	
Engage	469	1. Strategy	451
Strategy	416	2. Challenge	379
Challenge	297	3. Engage	342
Position	137	4. Position	340
Advance, Embed	108	5. Mission	193
Target	89	6. Force	159
Mission	69	7. Advance	141
Liaison	67	8. Embed	126
One-shot	64	9. Recruit	123
Capture	58	10. Charge	106

Note: The lemmas engage, strategy, challenge, position, advance, embed, and mission are dominant in both corpora.

The language of combat overtly pervades librarian discourse in the context of faculty relationships as Badke has noted and as one of our corpus writers has expressed: "Much of the literature that focuses on integrating IL student outcomes into campus-wide curricular programs characterizes the process in warlike battle stages where librarians find themselves pitted against faculty and administrators who have other programmatic and territorial agenda issues."[49] This orientation held true for our corpora as well. Faculty are to be "ambushed" or "recruited." Librarians are advised to seek faculty "champions," that is, those who fight "on behalf of another, or on behalf of any cause" and to develop "strategic partnerships" even though faculty "can become territorial at times."[50] A particularly interesting "mixed metaphor" occurs in the following passage: "The next foray into collaboration involved an activity common to writing centers and composition programs." Although the ostensible focus is collaboration, the terminology in which that collaboration is rendered is militaristic: A "foray" is "a hostile or predatory incursion or inroad, a raid."[51]

The lemma *embed* deserves particular attention. Until quite recently, the term was defined thus: "to fix firmly in a surrounding mass of some solid material" or "to enclose firmly."[52] As such, this lemma seems more properly to belong to the lexical field "barriers-gaps/bridges-convergences," in the sense that the librarian entity simply merges with a course or program unit. However, a draft addition to the *OED* entry "embed," dated 1996, adds the US Military definition: "to attach (a journalist) to a military unit to report on a conflict."[53] Embedded librarians are likened to war correspondents attached to a military unit. The librarian is simultaneously an insider and outsider, while the activity in which the unit is engaged is implicitly compared to a military conflict. This metaphor is quite useful in that it situates the librarian as associated with yet not truly part of the ongoing fray. If we draw out the extended metaphor, we infer that it is faculty, not the librarian, who send the student "troops" into battle.

Instances of militaristic metaphors vis-à-vis faculty were expected. More surprising, however, were occurrences of military metaphors in the context of librarian-student relationships. Librarians position themselves as adversaries of student anxiety, student boredom, and student misunderstanding, all of which they must "combat:" "No matter how energetic, upbeat, intelligent and entertaining this librarian is, she will have an uphill battle on her hands. How will she get through to these students?" To be sure, it is not students themselves who are the objects of these tactical maneuvers but problematic student behaviors and attitudes. Student attention and interest must be "captured." Getting students to utilize scholarly sources is like fighting "the war of the roses." Even the widely accepted sobriquet "one-shot" carries militaristic overtones: A "shot" is defined as "the action of shooting with the bow, catapult, or firearms; the mechanical discharge of arrows or other projectiles as a means of attack; shots or discharges of missiles collectively."[54] One librarian unabashedly describes her one-shot session as a "surgical strike," that is, "a swift, precise military attack."[55] Another is pleased to report that the library's subject guides "packed a powerful punch."

These conventional metaphors drawn from the lexical field of military science in the context of librarian-student relationships are initially puzzling until we bring to bear an understanding that information literacy as conceptualized by many librarians is a public good that needs to be vigorously marketed. The student is positioned much as the consumer is positioned in any marketing campaign: as "the static object of dynamic marketing activities."[56] And, as we have already noted, marketing discourse is often couched in militaristic terms. Thus, there are no qualms when students are rendered as "captive audiences" or recipients of "targeted" messages: "I was interested to learn of such aggressive marketing to a more or less captive student audience." The lexical field of warfare and battle evoked by these conventional metaphors passes unnoticed, as "uncontested common sense."

Our data corroborates that military metaphors do indeed pervade much librarian discourse in the context of both faculty-librarian and faculty-student relationships. This stance is disadvantageous, given that mutually respectful relationships with faculty are essential in conveying to students a high regard for erudition and cognitive authority. Worse still, a tacit misconstruction of students as "static objects" fails to recognize that undergraduates are, or should be, engaged in the dynamic and arduous process of testing and discarding lower-order epistemic beliefs. In short, the library marketing imperative is a distraction that runs counter to the goal of fostering mature epistemologies in students.

Results and Discussion: Lexical Field— Romance-Marriage-Courtship

In stark contrast to the lexical field of military strategy is the lexical field romance-marriage-courtship. To our surprise, we discovered in our corpora that the lemmas clustered in this field significantly outnumbered those drawn from the lexical field military strategy, thus establishing a distinct and significant presence. As with Koller's study of marketing discourse, we found that military metaphors and marriage metaphors are not the strange bedfellows they appear to be—these two lexical fields can readily coexist (table 3.3).

Lemmas in this lexical field appear to celebrate the possibility of librarian-faculty and librarian-student connection and partnership. We also discovered that in terms of this lexical field, the librarian-student relationship received much more attention from the corpora writers than did the faculty-librarian relationship.

For many writers in our corpora, faculty are envisioned as prospective collaborators and partners, sometimes even in terms that suggest an "affective bond." Many librarians welcome opportunities to "form close relationships with students and faculty beyond classroom contact." For one writer, it is "the faculty

Table 3.3. Top Ten Lemmas in the Lexical Field of Romance-Marriage-Courtship

LOEX Lemmas in Descending Order with Frequency		C&RL News Lemmas in Descending Order with Frequency	
Engage	469	1. Support	879
Support	382	2. Share	582
Share	342	3. Contact	570
Partner	234	4. Partner	383
Connect	197	5. Engage	342
Relationship	158	6. Relationship	266
Contact	119	7. Connect	137
Familiar	84	8. Join	133
Desire	69	9. Proposal	130
Liaise	67	10. Excite	110

Note: The lemmas engage, support, share, partner, connect, relationship and contact are dominant in both corpora.

contact who makes the first move" in a "dance" in which librarian and instructor take turns in leading or following. Yet another writer advises librarians not to play the shy maiden but rather to "make the initial relationship-building move." More boldly, this corpus writer recommends that fellow librarians "lure in" teaching assistants. Such courtship metaphors move beyond "friendship evangelism."

However, faculty-librarian relationships are more often portrayed as needing to be "forged," the intimation being that such relationships must be hammered out, beaten into shape, with a fair amount of force exerted. "Building rapport" may help "the buy-in process" but some faculty will "put up extra resistance." The path to faculty-librarian union is beset with many barriers, a point to which we will return.

The lemma *engage*, which appears in the overall top ten lemmas in both corpora (ranking second in *LOEX* and sixth in *C&RL News*), merits extended discussion by reason of its ubiquity in both corpora and also because it straddles multiple lexical fields. It can allude to betrothal, military encounter, engrossment, fascination, and interlinkage, thus spanning all four lexical fields we have identified. However, in the discourse of librarianship, the lexical field most often invoked by this word is romance-marriage-courtship. The *OED* definitions most relevant are (1) "to gain, win over, as an adherent" and (2) "to attach by pleasing qualities; to attract, charm, fascinate."[57] Although *engagement* is often used to designate a desired state of attentiveness and interest among students, the lemma is freighted with overtones of power assertion, be they ever so benign in intent. Some of our corpora writers unconsciously convey the unsettling association of entrapment and allurement: "The Academic Center initiated a program… to capture and engage the students." Student engagement is always posited as a desideratum in librarian discourse probably because the military connotations of the word are suppressed and because the end (information literacy) justifies the means. Here is one writer who actively ponders variant definitions of the word and concludes that "passion" is very much the point:

> We often speak of engaging our students…. However, what actually happens when students and teachers are engaged? Recently, in musing on this question, I began to make a distinction between a verb of action, how we engage others, and a verb of being, what happens with us or with them when we or they are engaged. What is embedded in this verb of being? If we can discover this, then perhaps we can assess student engagement not only by the skills students master but also by the passion and behavior they demonstrate in the mastery.

Although lemmas belonging to this lexical field certainly do occur in the context of librarian-faculty relationships they tend to figure more prominently in the context of librarian-student relationships. If faculty are more apt to be "recruited" and "ambushed," students are more likely to be wooed.

We conclude that descriptions of student-librarian relationships frequently elicit romance and courtship metaphors in librarian discourse. Librarians are urged to "spice up library instruction" to "entice, intrigue, and seduce learners." They should "embrace" millennials and devise attractions that will "draw" them in. Given enough inducements, students will become willing to be "bewitched by a brief video about research habits."

As in the case of military science lemmas, one ostensible purpose is to enhance student motivation and learning. Another sought after outcome is effective library marketing. In other cases, however, the courtship of students seems directed at the transformation of student-librarian relationships as a goal unto itself. This writer sees these three objectives as intertwined: "When Facebook launched in 2004, I, like many librarians, thought it would revolutionize the way I communicated with and related to students. I saw possibilities for promotion and outreach and quickly created a Facebook profile in hopes that students would be drawn to my smiling profile picture and would respond in droves to my offers of research help in my "information" section."

No matter what the rationale, however, the goal for this corpus writer is affective—a bonding of student with librarian: "We really became shameless in asking our current students to 'talk us up' to other students." Librarians bemoan the ubiquity of the one-shot for many reasons, one of which is that it is less likely to generate "an atmosphere of trust where students feel safe enough to share their comments with their peers and instructor." One writer who felt successful in creating a close student-librarian bond put it thus: "I felt myself replying with heartfelt smiley faces to six word library memoirs." An elegiac undercurrent in librarian discourse is a longing for personal relationships with students. Many share the sentiments of this librarian who sees such relationships as essential to overall job satisfaction: "My work has allowed for deeper, more personal ongoing contact with students…. I often get e-mails asking for assistance with other classes, advice on job-hunting etc…. Students tell me that… they find me approachable and friendly." The personal connection between librarian and student is envisaged as "a perfect match." Beyond personal job satisfaction, some corpus writers go so far as to perceive a warm, affective librarian-student relationship as crucial to the practice of the profession: "Some will not be comfortable inviting users to sit next to them on their side of the desk. Establishing rapport requires a certain amount of emotional energy and a greater level of personal involvement. Not everyone is willing to give that."

Whether achieved via Facebook friending or by the simple placement of side-by-side seating, the intent is that librarians meet students "where they are:" "Proximity and familiarity do make a difference in student comfort level." There is no possibility of the librarian playing the role of "friendship evangelist" when it comes to students because such a role would position the librarian as superior to students. The profession's discourse places the librarian side-by-side with students. The profession's discourse is also at pains to distance itself from the image of librarian as shushing sourpuss.

As with the military stance, the stance of wooer can be somewhat problematic when it comes to challenging student biases and epistemological beliefs. On the one hand, it can be argued, and has been argued, that a close, friendly working relationship with students produces the hospitable climate in which that sort of intellectual labor can occur. On the other hand, the posture of courtship can become self-limiting, as one commentator has observed: "The only real lesson we are concerned with imparting is that the library is a friendly place and librarians are approachable people. I learned from some of my mentors early on that if the only message that stuck with students after one of our brief information literacy sessions was to ask a librarian when they need help, we should be satisfied."[58] Ultimately, the profession needs to reevaluate its overemphasis on student enthrallment and the frequent enjoinder to "embrace" students. Here is a writer who suggests that the words we use do matter: "We should understand what it means to use, and even embrace, such terms as 'value,' 'accountability,' and 'standards.'"[59] Librarians also need to understand what it means to embrace such terms as "embrace," a word that connotes uncritical buy-in, a posture anathema to highly sophisticated reflective thinking.

Results and Discussion: Lexical Field— Guesthood-Entertainment

Closely allied with the lexical field romance-marriage-courtship is the lexical field guesthood-entertainment. In fact, many of the lemmas in this field can readily be cross-assigned to the lexical field romance-marriage-courtship. The library as "host" or "academic living room" is the metaphor of library as place that best fits this lexical field. If the lexical field romance-marriage-courtship is skewed toward the librarian-student relationship, this lexical field is completely dominated by it: It is students, not faculty, who are the party guests. In other words, faculty receptions are comparatively rare; fun-filled, prize-strewn, and candy-stocked student orientations are pervasive (table 3.4).

Whereas the lexical field romance-courtship-marriage delineates the librarian-student relationship in terms of charm and allure, the lexical field guesthood-entertainment shifts the emphasis to student relaxation, amusement, and comfort. This corpus writer is very clear about what library instruction and library visitation is *not* supposed to be: "Sometimes our quest to guide students to knowledge… can feel… more like a forced family road trip. You know the kind: leave before dawn, no stopping, no candy, no fighting in the back seat." A vivid, clever, and colorful metaphor, it nonetheless regrettably reduces the emerging adult student to adolescent or child. Even more unfortunately, it presents the academic project as innately dull, oppressive, and joyless; students, like the

Table 3.4. Top Ten Lemmas in the Lexical Field of Guesthood-Entertainment

LOEX Lemmas in Descending Order		C&RL News Lemmas in Descending Order	
Game	365	Interest	634
Interest	305	Encourage	337
Interact	289	Play	292
Play	242	Interact	256
Encourage	174	Serve	253
Serve	105	Friend	189
Invite	93	Game	138
Comfort	81	Host	131
Friend	77	Invite	125
Fun	68	Comfort	123

Note: With the exception of the lemmas fun and host, the same lemmas appear in each corpus.

kids in the back seat, are, in their natural, unmediated state, bored, alienated, and unhappy. As another writer puts it, "As I look around the room, I see many stricken and uncomfortable expressions. This is why I hasten to reassure them."

Given this widely shared view among librarians, it is to be expected that librarian discourse often portrays librarians as soothers and libraries as stress-free zones in contrast to other campus geographies and "the pressures of classroom performance." Librarians are exhorted to "establish a friendly and welcoming atmosphere where students can feel relaxed and at ease." This ambiance is partially achieved via the provision of physical creature comforts— cozy upholstered seating or a library café, for example. Moreover, the librarian, as host or hostess, is expected to persuade students to see the library "as a familiar and nurturing space on campus." The goal is for students to "warm to the library as a social gathering place." Not surprisingly, librarians are urged to employ "icebreakers" and provide "comic relief." Smiles, "banter, and playful behavior" are the recommended modes of relating to students.

Not only are students to be reassured and set at ease, they should also be energized and entertained. Lemmas in this category often evoke parties, games, carnivals, prizes, contests, skits, and stand-up comedy, ostensibly to alleviate student boredom or frustration, as this writer observes: "Educational games and other forms of competition that do not promote a pressure to win may also stimulate student engagement." Millennials are perceived as having "a low threshold for boredom," the remedy for which is "fun, silliness, experiential activities, exposure to positive people, personal interactions, and rewards."

However, as we have already observed, and as this corpus writer divines, a critical goal is to market library services: "While most libraries may not have quite the glitz and glamour of a three-ring circus, we do offer invaluable services that many students will want to learn about, especially if we market to them in an appealing way." This writer is even more direct: "Embrace your inner marketer…. Come up with snazzy [workshop] titles since they will spark curiosity and interest."

Although the lemma *game* figures prominently in both corpora, manual analysis revealed that it tends to be used literally rather than metaphorically—"bibliography bingo" or a "catalog race," to name but two. In other words, library instruction is less likely to be represented as game-like but rather reconfigured as a literal game. However, both corpora are replete with lemmas drawn from the lexical fields of sports and specific games; many of these are indeed employed metaphorically. The librarian is cast as a "metacognitive coach" who regularly "fields questions." On the subject of one-shots, one writer laments that "a library instruction session is 'a difficult horse to bridle.'" Assessment is a "playing field" that needs to be "leveled." The one-shot session is a "race to beat the clock." Hands-on research can be a "building block, much like hitting the tackling dummy or juggling a soccer ball." Today's students are characterized as "team players" and librarians "slam home the point that authoritative library sources are better than the free web."

The lemma *serve*, which surfaces in both corpora, is particularly multifaceted because it references librarianship as a genuine service profession but also alludes to the consumer marketing that we have previously noted. To *serve* is to "minister to the comfort" of another, to "supply with food at a meal," to supply a customer "with a commodity," or "to start play by striking a ball" in games such as tennis.[60] However, on a more general level, the word can refer to assistance rendered in any matter. It can therefore be said that librarians do indeed serve the intellectual needs of library patrons, but the lemma *serve* also hints that information and intellectual service can all too readily be commoditized.

The reasons for this state of affairs are complicated. On the one hand, librarians often have such restricted contact with students that they frequently must devote disproportionate energy to the elicitation of student attention. Another contributing factor may be student expectations. Nancy Fried Foster in *Studying Students: The Undergraduate Research Project at the University of Rochester* argues that undergraduates in particular expect a "Mommy Model of Service:" "If they have a need, they want it filled. If they want a need filled, they want to go to a font of all sorts of service…. In other words, they want Mommy …a Mommy who is the provider of everything to the infant."[61]

Regardless of causality, librarians often settle for crowd-pleasing and mothering. Our corpus analysis indicates that this narrow goal is not much bemoaned; in fact, the through line is cheerful acceptance: "Librarians should foster a sense of play in the work that they do. Being playful promotes a fun and welcoming environment for students." These corpus writers are even more adamant: "Be off the wall—make it fun." Although the context is often the planning and delivery of freshman orientation activities, it also includes direct classroom instruction.

The real shortcoming with this stance is that the development of reflective judgment requires deep processing—immersion in difficult, myriad texts; the synthesis of multiple, conflicting points of view. As Troy Swanson points out, "It is in the synthesizing process where knowledge construction occurs."[62] Many students understandably find this task to be onerous and uncomfortable. (Another reason that the games approach to instruction is problematic is that the nature of scholarship remains "rhetorical" and print-based, regardless of the vehicle by which those texts are accessed.[63]) Instruction rendered as game may indeed garner student attention, and it can lend itself to the solving of well-structured problems. However, it is poorly suited to the negotiation of ill-structured problems, the sorts of problems that promote the development of reflective judgment.[64] The unspoken assumption among librarians may be that it is instructional faculty, not librarians, who should do the heavy lifting—the yeoman's work of motivating students to grapple with off-putting, challenging material. In fact, many librarians may intuit that these two agendas can and often do conflict: Those who undertake the unglamorous job of pushing and coaxing students out of their comfort zones do run the risk of alienating those whom they most wish to bond with and please. They run the risk of losing the customer base they obviously most value.

Results and Discussion: Lexical Field— Barriers-Gaps/Bridges-Convergences

Thus far, our analysis of three lexical fields presents a somewhat unflattering portrait in terms of librarian attitudes toward and beliefs about faculty and students. The final (and most extensive) lexical field to be discussed herein—barriers-gaps/bridges-convergences—offers a contrasting perspective. These "convergence" metaphors convey themes of access, unity, and the negotiation of impediments—the "brambles, rocks, and obstacles" that prevent connection and partnership (table 3.5).

Table 3.5. Top Ten Lemmas in the Lexical Field of Barriers-Gaps/Bridges-Convergences

LOEX Lemmas in Descending Order		C&RL News Lemmas in Descending Order	
1. Collaborate	663	1. Open	842
2. Engage	469	2. Collaborate	683
3. Team	345	3. Separate	582
4. Share	342	4. Partner	383
5. Integrate	297	5. Team	366
6. Partner	234	6. Engage	342
7. Link	202	7. Link	294
8. Connect	198	8. Outreach	282
9. Open	197	9. Integrate	253
10. Reach	145	10. Gather	152

Note: Although some of the same lemmas appear in each corpus, there is more variation than in the other three lexical fields. Significantly, these lemmas (with the notable exception of *separate*) focus on convergences rather than barriers and gaps.

Many of our corpus writers articulate a sense of isolation from other campus constituencies (particularly instructional faculty) as this writer observes: "Unfortunately, institutions of higher learning are very stratified, and real power and status differences are deeply rooted." Thus, for this particular writer, the barriers between faculty and librarians are systemic. Other writers identify faculty attitudes and faculty culture as posing the most formidable roadblocks, nonetheless urging librarians to surmount them. This writer is quite blunt about the disconnect, positioning the professoriate itself as the principal impediment: "Even if we think we're figured it out, there is another significant obstacle: the professors themselves." Librarians and faculty are likened to "ships passing in the night …using different language to describe their desired outcomes." This "different language" suggests that librarian discourse bears little similarity to faculty discourse and even intimates that the "desired outcomes" of librarians and faculty may be dissimilar as well: The ships passing in the night are likely bound for separate destinations. However, we discovered a corpus writer who sees librarians themselves as obstructionist in that they are unwilling to engage with faculty discourse: "Few academic librarian bloggers ever mention posts written by faculty. It's almost as if an invisible barrier separated our two blogoverses." Regardless of which party offers the more formidable impediment, the conclusion drawn by most librarians is that there are "hurdles to overcome."

Nevertheless, while some librarians find this separation galling and frustrating, many of our corpus writers speak positively in terms of bridging the gaps, reducing the barriers, and working toward establishing themselves as mediators and the library as the "hub to all campus activities," a "lynchpin connecting faculty and students." A metaphor often pressed into service in this context is the conventional metaphor of the bridge, a lemma that appears 50 times in the *C&RL News* corpus, with 32 instances in the *LOEX* corpus. The bridge as metaphor is quite apt in that it conveys both connection and disconnection. An alternative metaphor sometimes invoked is the threshold or boundary, spatial markers that librarians are urged to ignore or cross.

Convergence metaphors tell a hopeful metaphorical story about librarian-faculty relationships. The lemmas most frequently introduced in this context are *partner* and *collaborate*. Although these two tend to be used interchangeably, there are subtle differences between them. The lemma *partner* can be assigned to the lexical field guesthood-entertainment as well as romance-courtship-marriage—one can speak of tennis partners, dancing partners, or marriage partners, for example. *Partner* simply establishes a pairing of individuals engaged in a common activity. *Collaboration*, on the other hand, is more specific: Not only is there partnership, there is a definitive outcome of the endeavor—"to work in conjunction with another or others, esp. in a literary or artistic production or the like."[65] Our corpus writers strongly prefer to collaborate rather than merely partner. *Collaborate* ranks first and second respectively in our two corpora whereas *partner* ranks fourth and sixth respectively. The difference is a subtle one, but it suggests that librarians regard the product of their labor much as if it were a creative artifact. The process of providing information literacy instruction becomes a creative endeavor in which, ideally, faculty and librarians work in tandem.

Although some librarians regard their potential faculty partners as needing to be strong-armed—"brought on board"—others envision that partnership in more egalitarian terms: "The need is critical to collaborate with faculty… to share the library's vision with faculty, and to find ways to let faculty share their vision with library staff." Sustained collaboration can reveal that faculty and librarians have "more in common than not." The stance of these writers is less sententious, more open-minded, less likely to relegate faculty to the status of mere "gateway" to students. This corpus writer expresses definite solidarity with instructional faculty: "We hope it's not too bold to claim that… librarians support faculty."

Barriers and gaps are positioned quite differently in contexts that focus on students. We often found that librarians typically situate the perceived gap as occurring between students and academic attainment. This corpus writer envisions the student's journey from information illiteracy to information fluency as beset by a host of blockades: "Their paths wind through a variety of information environments, some hostile, all evolving rapidly even as the students pass through. The trail often circles back on itself, showing the same landmarks from different angles, and often there are obstacles, barriers, to access or understanding."

These "barriers" are variously construed and interpreted. For example, some corpus writers identify these "conceptual gaps" as emanating from academic unpreparedness: "It is in the gap between students' experience and the tacit requirements of college work where librarians must insinuate our expertise." Other corpus writers see students' tendency toward expedience as the source of the derailment: "Many library instruction sessions contain an inherent disconnect between goals and motivations: The instructor is attempting to build information-seeking skills while the learner is focused on the act of finding material." For some corpus writers, students can be variously characterized as "overwhelmed," "apathetic," or simply recalcitrant. On the other hand, another corpus writer argues that the textual straitjacket of the traditional research paper itself poses a stumbling block to the development of student information literacy: "Students might be better served by learning how to communicate outside the constraints of the research paper, or, without the necessity to explicitly state ideas through copious amounts of text."

To move the student "over the hump," to overcome the learning "bottleneck," librarians have employed many of the strategies we have already noted—the entertainment ploy, for example. However, a study of convergence lemmas suggests that some, if not many librarians, address the gap by utilizing pedagogical strategies that emphasize an intermeshing of disciplinary course content with information literacy goals and objectives and, in some cases, those that entail higher-order thinking. Librarians are advised to "create a seamless integration of research-based skills and course content." This corpus writer makes a similar argument: "The tasks and assignments that develop information fluency can simultaneously assist the students in acquiring primary subject content, thereby reducing resistance to learning about information literacy." Another writer insists that information literacy instruction should not be "isolated from the overall curriculum, causing research to be treated as separate from the learning and writing processes."

Ultimately, unlike the other lexical fields we have previously examined, the barriers-gaps/ bridges-convergences field suggests that librarians can play a significant supportive role in the development of reflective judgment in students. Librarians who focus on finding "common ground" with faculty, as revealed through their use of convergence metaphors, are pursuing a shared, rather than a competing agenda. This shared agenda has less to do with teaching students how to find "stuff" for their papers and more to do with initiating novices into the academic discourse community (and, by implication, the particular conventions of a disciplinary discourse community). As Barbara Fister points out, "Most of our systems don't retrieve information, they retrieve texts."[66] This rhetorical notion of information literacy is well expressed by Michelle Holschuh Simmons: "If students want to become members of a particular discourse community, they need to learn the conventions of the discipline's communications."[67] She goes on to argue that "because the written word is central to academic discourse, this understanding of the assumptions, practices, and the conventions of a particular field's *writing* is integral to the study of any discipline" (emphasis added).[68] The ability to analyze, synthesize, and critique sources depends on the students' level of print literacy. Thus, librarians who interpret information literacy as a matter of mastering a new language and a disciplinary epistemology (rather than generic "skills" acquisition) are better poised to become the collaborators they clearly yearn to be.

Librarians who conceive of themselves as merger-makers and gap-menders are more likely to function well as "discourse mediators," occupying an "in-between position," serving as a bridge between student and faculty, between student and academic field of study.[69] Patricia M. King and Karen Strohm Kitchener argue that "individuals in many roles foster reflective thinking in students.... The term 'teacher' and 'educator' do not refer exclusively to those who serve in faculty roles."[70] In fact, this "monumental task" cannot be accomplished by "faculty members alone"—it takes an academic village.[71]

Clearly, librarians can contribute to the intellectual maturation of students, "nurturing better reading and more authentic writing."[72]

Conclusions, Limitations, and Suggestions for Further Research

Our corpus analysis of librarians as a discourse community reveals a mixed picture of librarian attitudes toward both faculty and students. For example, the use of military metaphors suggests an oppositional affective relationship to the academic librarians' client base. The lexical fields of romance-marriage-courtship as well as guesthood-entertainment seem to indicate that academic librarians' relationship to faculty tends to be exclusionary while the relationship to students is colored deeply by the marketing imperative and a construction of students as consumers. However, the lexical field of barriers-gaps/ bridges-convergences does go some way toward contradicting these unhelpful sentiments.

We return here to the mandate of critical linguistics, that is, to question and "problematize" the "picture of reality" that academic librarians as a community accept as "uncontested 'common sense.'"[73] Along with Simmons, we believe that the profession benefits from self-critique: "While it is useful for our profession to be critiqued from the outside … it is equally important—if not more so—to critique our practices from within the profession so as to push the field to more thoughtful and carefully considered positions."[74]

One of the positions we would like to set forth is to advocate for librarians' understanding of and appreciation for the need to foster student intellectual growth in reflective judgment. Librarians should focus less on student entertainment and more on providing an environment that challenges students and encourages them to question not only the ideas of others but their own as well. The library should be less an "academic living room" and more akin to a well-equipped gymnasium wherein students work out, stretch themselves, and wrestle with ill-structured problems. Librarians can best collaborate with faculty by rejecting the mommy model of service; instead, they should emulate a rigorous personal trainer. Even so, we found that the lemma *rigor* makes a poor showing in our corpora: There are 20 instances in *C&RL News* and only five in the *LOEX* corpus.

We searched our corpora for word clusters (coupled lemmas) that would be readily associated with the development of mature and nuanced personal epistemologies in emerging adults. For example, we searched for the cluster "reflective judgment" and found no instances. (We did find one reference to "reflective analysis" and one mention of "reflective research" in *C&RL News*.) We searched for "personal epistemology" and found no instances in either corpus. We discovered two references to "ill-structured problem(s)" in the *LOEX* corpus, but none in our *C&RL News* corpus. Even the bedrock, foundational cluster "reading comprehension" surfaced only once (in the *LOEX* corpus). Although clusters such as these do appear from time to time in peer-reviewed literature of the profession, their near absence in our corpora suggests that personal epistemology theory has made little inroad into the profession as a whole.[75]

This study has focused only on the informal communication taking place between librarians in the context of two organs of published professional discourse, the *LOEX Conference Proceedings* and *College and Research Library News*. There is room for further linguistic analysis of librarians' discourse through corpus analysis of other informal venues of professional communication such as listservs, blog postings and commentary, and grey literature. It could also be instructive to study the metaphorical content of the scholarly, peer-reviewed literature of the field to determine if the linguistic patterns noticed here are repeated. If they are not, analysis of the differences in the ways that librarians represent themselves and their relationships with students and faculty in different published contexts may yield fresh insights. The ultimate limitation of corpus linguistics is that it can only analyze what we say, not what we do. Despite this limitation, we believe that analysis on this level can reveal underlying assumptions that impact behavior. When these assumptions are brought into conscious awareness and critically reflected upon, librarians can choose to modify the ways they think about and express their relationships with their two major user groups, which can in turn impact librarian professional practices.

We further believe that a corpus-based research approach to the discourse of higher education pedagogy could furnish an interesting, useful comparison and/or contrast to the findings of this study. Venues such as *The Chronicle of Higher Education, Inside Higher Ed,* and the faculty blogosphere (as suggested by one of our corpus writers) could be transformed into corpora and similarly analyzed. Particularly salient could be the discourse community of compositionists, instructional faculty who traditionally have been particularly charged with the responsibility for teaching students to think reflectively. What metaphorical stories do discipline-based faculty tell? How do their stories differ from those of librarians? The answers to these questions could engender not only enhanced librarian-faculty relationships but also information literacy pedagogies that actively promote higher-order epistemic thinking in students.

Notes

1.   Cushla Kapitzke, "Information Literacy: A Positivist Epistemology and a Politics of Outformation," *Educational Theory* 53, no. 1 (2003): 42.

2.   See, for example, Thomas P. Mackey and Trudi E. Jacobson, "Reframing Information Literacy as a Metaliteracy," *College and Research Libraries* 72, no. 1 (2011): 62–78.

3.   Heidi Julien and Lisa M. Given, "Faculty-Librarian Relationships in the Information Literacy Context: A Content Analysis of Librarians' Expressed Attitudes and Experiences," *Canadian Journal of Information and Library Science* 27, no. 3 (2002/03): 69.

4.   Katherine Beaty Chiste, Andrea Glover, and Glenna Westwood, "Infiltration and Entrenchment: Capturing and Securing Information Literacy Territory in Academe," *Journal of Academic Librarianship* 26, no. 3 (2000): 202–08; Ken Kempcke, "The Art of War for Librarians: Academic Culture, Curriculum Reform, and Wisdom from Sun Tzu," *portal: Libraries and the Academy* 2, no. 4 (2002): 529–51.

5.   Kempcke, "The Art of War," 536.

6.   Zoltán Kövecses, *Metaphor: A Practical Introduction* (New York: Oxford University Press, 2002): 4.

7.   Jonathan Charteris-Black, *Corpus Approaches to Critical Metaphor Analysis* (New York: Palgrave Macmillan, 2004), 12.

8.   Ibid., 13.

9.   Charteris-Black, *Corpus Approaches*; Alice Deignan, "Corpus Linguistics and Metaphor," in *The Cambridge Handbook of Metaphor and Thought*, ed. Raymond W. Gibbs Jr. (New York: Cambridge University Press, 2008); Lynn Cameron, *Metaphor in Educational Discourse* (London: Continuum, 2003). See also Lynn Cameron and Graham Low, eds. *Researching and Applying Metaphor* (Cambridge: Cambridge University Press, 1999); Charteris-Black, *Corpus Approaches*, 21.

10.   Cameron, *Metaphor in Educational Discourse*, 22.

11.   Ibid., 110.

12.   Veronika Koller, "'A Shotgun Wedding:' Co-Occurrence of War and Marriage Metaphors in Mergers and Acquisitions Discourse," *Metaphor and Symbol* 17, no. 3 (2002): 183.

13.   Jill J. McMillan and George Cheney, "The Student as Consumer: The Implications and Limitations of a Metaphor," *Communication Education* 45, no. 1 (1996): 1, doi: 10.1080/03634529609379028.

14.   Charteris-Black, *Corpus Approaches*, 23.

15.   See Cameron and Low, *Researching and Applying Metaphor*; Melissa L. Walters-York, "Metaphor in Accounting Discourse," *Accounting, Auditing, and Accountability Journal* 9, no. 5 (1996): 45–70, doi: 10.1108/09513579610367242; Koller, "A Shotgun Wedding."

16.   Veronika Koller, *Metaphor and Gender in Business Media Discourse: A Critical Cognitive*

Study (New York: Palgrave Macmillan, 2004), 4.

17. Charteris-Black, *Corpus Approaches*, 23.

18. George Lakoff, "Metaphor and War: The Metaphor System Used to Justify War in the Gulf (Part 1 of 2)," *Viet Nam Generation Journal and Newsletter* 3, no. 3 (1991), http://www2. iath.virginia.edu/sixties/HTML_docs/Texts/Scholarly/Lakoff_Gulf_Metaphor_1.html.

19. Koller, "A Shotgun Wedding," 183.

20. Charteris-Black, *Corpus Approaches*, 29.

21. Deignan, "Corpus Linguistics and Metaphor," 282.

22. Ibid.

23. Ibid.

24. Howard Jackson and Etienne Zé Amvela, *Words, Meaning, and Vocabulary: An Introduction to Modern English Lexicography* (New York: Cassell, 2000), 92.

25. Ibid., 111.

26. Deignan, "Corpus Linguistics and Metaphor," 284.

27. See, for example, Stuart Basefsky, "Mis-Information at the Heart of the University: Why Administrators Should Take Libraries More Seriously," *Information Outlook* 10, no. 8 (2006): 15–19; Lenora Berendt and Maria Otero-Boisvert, "Future-Proofing the Academic Librarian," in *Defending Professionalism: A Resource for Librarians, Information Specialists, Knowledge Managers, and Archivists*, ed. Bill Crowley (Santa Barbara, CA: Libraries Unlimited, 2012), 75–90; Robert Moropa, "Academic Libraries in Transition: Some Leadership Issues—A Viewpoint," *Library Management* 31, no. 6 (2010): 381–90, doi: 10.1108/01435121011066144.

28. See also Kathleen de la Peña McCook, "The Search for New Metaphors," *Library Trends* 46, no. 1 (1997): 17; Gary Hartzell, "The Metaphor Is the Message," *School Library Journal* 48, no. 6 (2002): 33; Karen Coyle, "Catalogs, Card—and Other Anachronisms," *Journal of Academic Librarianship* 26, no. 3 (2000): 202–08; D. Grant Campbell, "Metadata, Metaphor, and Metonymy," *Cataloging and Classification Quarterly* 40, no. 3-4 (2005): 57–73; Hope A. Olson, "The Ubiquitous Hierarchy: An Army to Overcome the Threat of a Mob," *Library Trends* 52, no. 3 (2004): 604–16.

29. Danuta Nitecki, "Conceptual Models of Libraries Held by Faculty, Administrators, and Librarians: An Exploration of Communications in *The Chronicle of Higher Education*," *Journal of Documentation* 49, no. 3 (1993): 255–77.

30. Ibid., 264.

31. Ibid., 269.

32. Ibid., 273, 269.

33. Joan Giesecke, "Finding the Right Metaphor: Restructuring, Realigning, and Repackaging Today's Research Libraries," *Journal of Library Administration* 51, no. 1 (2010): 59, doi: 10.1080/01930826.2011.531641.

34. Stephen Bell, "From Gatekeepers to Gate Openers," *American Libraries* 40, no. 8-9 (2009): 50, quoted in Giesecke, "Finding the Right Metaphor," 58; 59, 60, 61.

35. Ibid., 63.

36. Heidi Julien and Lisa M. Given, "Faculty-Librarian Relationships in the Information Literacy Context: A Content Analysis of Librarians' Expressed Attitudes and Experiences," *Canadian Journal of Information and Library Sciences* 27, no. 3 (2002): 65–87; Lisa M. Given and Heidi Julien, "Finding Common Ground: An Analysis of Librarians' Expressed Attitudes towards Faculty," *The Reference Librarian* 43, no. 89-90 (2005): 25–38, doi: 10.1300/J120v43n89_05.

37. Julien and Given, "Faculty-Librarian Relationships," 65.

38. Given and Julien, "Finding Common Ground," 36.

39. See, for example, Robert Schweik, "Painting as 'Exploring' and Related Metaphors in

20th-Century Art Commentary," *Metaphor and Symbolic Activity* 11, no. 4 (1996): 285–96; Alan F. Blackwell, "Metaphors We Program by: Space, Action, and Society in Java," in *Proceedings of Psychology of Programming Interest Group* 18, ed. P. Romero et al. (Brighton, UK: University of Sussex, 2006), 7–21, http://www.ppig.org/papers/18th-blackwell.pdf; Richard C. Hicks, Ronald Dattero, and Stuart D. Galup, "A Metaphor for Knowledge Management: Explicit Islands in a Tacit Sea," *Journal of Knowledge Management* 11, no. 1 (2007): 5–16, doi: 10.1108/13673270710728204; McMillan and Cheney, "The Student as Consumer," 1–15; Jonathan Charteris-Black, "Shattering the Bell Jar: Metaphor, Gender, and Depression," *Metaphor and Symbol* 27, no. 3 (2012): 199–216, doi: 10.1080/10926488.2012.665796.

40.   Koller, *Metaphor and Gender*, 72.

41.   Koller, "A Shotgun Wedding," 179–203.

42.   William B. Badke, "Can't Get No Respect: Helping Faculty to Understand the Educational Power of Information Literacy," *Reference Librarian* 43, no. 89-90 (2005): 63–80, doi: 10.1300/J120v43n89_05.

43.   Lars Christiansen, Mindy Stombler, and Lyn Thaxton,"A Report on Librarian-Faculty Relations from a Sociological Perspective," *Journal of Academic Librarianship* 30, no. 2 (2004): 117.

44.   It should be noted that the organizers of the annual LOEX conference choose a central theme metaphor; papers presented sometimes implement the chosen metaphor and extend it. For example, the conference theme for 2006, "Moving Targets: Understanding Our Changing Landscapes," elicited a number of military strategy metaphors from the conference presenters.

45.   Caitlin Tillman, "Library Orientation for Professors: Give a Pitch, Not a Tour," *College and Research Library News* 69, no. 8 (2008): 470.

46.   Koller, *Metaphor and Gender*, 54.

47.   Ibid., 48.

48.   Koller, *Metaphor and Gender*, 56.

49.   We follow the standard practice of corpus linguistics methodology in that we do not identify individual corpus writers by name. Non-corpus writers, however, are identified throughout.

50.   *OED Online*, s.v. "champion," accessed January 30, 2014.

51.   *OED Online*, s.v. "foray," accessed January 30, 2014.

52.   *OED Online*, s.v. "embed, imbed," accessed January 30, 2014.

53.   Ibid.

54.   *OED Online*, s.v. "shot," accessed January 30, 2014.

55.   *OED Online*, s.v. "surgical," accessed January 30, 2014.

56.   Koller, *Metaphor and Gender*, 85.

57.   *OED Online*, s.v. "engage," accessed January 30, 2014.

58.   Mara Thacker, "A Paradigm Shift: Changing Approaches in the Classroom," *College and Research Library News* 73, no. 3 (2012): 148.

59.   Sheril Hook, "Impact? What Three Years of Research Tells Us about Library Instruction," *College and Research Libraries* 73, no. 1 (2012): 8.

60.   *OED Online*, s.v. "serve," accessed January 30, 2014.

61.   Nancy Fried Foster, "The Mommy Model of Service" in *Studying Students: The Undergraduate Research Project at the University of Rochester*, ed. Nancy Fried Foster and Susan Gibbons (Chicago: Association of College and Research Libraries, 2007), 76.

62.   Troy Swanson, "Information Literacy, Personal Epistemology, and Knowledge Construction: Potential and Possibilities," *College and Undergraduate Libraries* 13, no. 3 (2006): 103, doi: 10.1300/J106v13n03_07.

63. Ibid., 98.

64. See Anne M. Fields, "Ill-Structured Problems and the Reference Consultation: The Librarian's Role in Developing Student Expertise," *Reference Services Review* 34, no. 3 (2006): 405–20, doi: 10.1108/00907320610701554. Fields defines ill-structured problems as "problems with indefinite starting points, multiple and arguable solutions, and unclear maps for finding one's way through information. These problems often ask students to deal with complex, multi-focal social and moral issues. Learning to wrestle with them" equips students for lifelong learning. Fields's use of the metaphor "wrestle" suggests that learning can be and often is an agonistic process.

65. *OED Online*, s.v. "collaborate," accessed January 30, 2014.

66. Barbara Fister, "Teaching the Rhetorical Dimensions of Research," *Research Strategies* 11, no. 4 (Fall 1993): http://homepages.gac.edu/~fister/rs.html.

67. Michelle Holschuh Simmons, "Librarians as Disciplinary Discourse Mediators: Using Genre Theory to Move toward Critical Information Literacy," *portal: Libraries and the Academy* 5, no. 3 (2005): 300.

68. Ibid., 303.

69. Ibid., 305.

70. Patricia M. King and Karen Strohm Kitchener, *Developing Reflective Judgment: Understanding and Promoting Intellectual Growth and Critical Thinking in Adolescents and Adults* (San Francisco: Jossey-Bass, 1994), 223.

71. Simmons, "Librarians as Disciplinary Discourse Mediators," 304.

72. Arlene Wilner, "Fostering Critical Literacy: The Art of Assignment Design" in "Identity, Learning, and the Liberal Arts," ed. Ned Scott Laff, special issue, *New Directions for Teaching and Learning* 103 (2005): 24.

73. Koller, "A Shotgun Wedding," 183.

74. Simmons, "Librarians as Disciplinary Discourse Mediators," 301.

75. See, for example, Etheline Whitmire, "Epistemological Beliefs and the Information-Seeking Behavior of Undergraduates," *Library and Information Science Research* 25, no. 2 (2003): 124–42, doi: 10.1016/S0740-8188(03)00003-3; Etheline Whitmire, "The Relationship between Undergraduates' Epistemological Beliefs, Reflective Judgment, and Their Information-Seeking Behavior," *Information Processing and Management* 40, no. 1 (2004): 97–111, doi: 10.1016/S0306-4573(02)00099-7; Swanson, "Information Literacy, Personal Epistemology, and Knowledge Construction;" Fields, "Ill-Structured Problems and the Reference Consultation;" Rebecca Jackson, "Cognitive Development: The Missing Link in Teaching Information Literacy," *Reference and User Services Quarterly* 46, no. 4 (2007): 28–32.

Bibliography

Badke, William B. "Can't Get No Respect: Helping Faculty to Understand the Educational Power of Information Literacy." *Reference Librarian* 43, no. 89-90 (2005): 63–80. doi: 10.1300/J120v43n89_05.

Basefsky, Stuart. "Mis-Information at the Heart of the University: Why Administrators Should Take Libraries More Seriously." *Information Outlook* 10, no. 8 (2006): 15–19.

Berendt, Lenora, and Maria Otero-Boisvert. "Future-Proofing the Academic Librarian." In *Defending Professionalism: A Resource for Librarians, Information Specialists, Knowledge Managers, and Archivists*, edited by Bill Crowley, 75–90. Santa Barbara, CA: Libraries Unlimited, 2012.

Blackwell, Alan F. "Metaphors We Program by: Space, Action, and Society in Java." In *Proceedings of Psychology of Programming Interest Group* 18, edited by P. Romero, J. Good, E. Acosta Chaparro, and S. Bryant, 7–21. Brighton, UK: University of Sussex, 2006. http://www.ppig.org/papers/18th-blackwell.pdf.

Cameron, Lynne. *Metaphor in Educational Discourse*: *Advances in Applied Linguistics*. London: Continuum, 2003.

Cameron, Lynne, and Graham Low, eds. *Researching and Applying Metaphor*. Cambridge: Cambridge University Press, 1999.

Campbell, D. Grant. "Metadata, Metaphor, and Metonymy." *Cataloging and Classification Quarterly* 40, no.3-4 (2005): 57–73. doi: 10.1300/J104v40n03_04.

Charteris-Black, Jonathan. *Corpus Approaches to Critical Metaphor Analysis*. New York: Palgrave Macmillan, 2004.

———. "Shattering the Bell Jar: Metaphor, Gender, and Depression." *Metaphor and Symbol* 27, no. 3 (2012): 199–216. doi: 10.1080/10926488.2012.665796.

Chiste, Katherine Beaty, Andrea Glover, and Glenna Westwood. "Infiltration and Entrenchment: Capturing and Securing Information Literacy Territory in Academe." *Journal of Academic Librarianship*, 26, no. 3 (2000): 202–08.

Christiansen, Lars, Mindy Stombler, and Lyn Thaxton. "A Report on Librarian-Faculty Relations from a Sociological Perspective." *Journal of Academic Librarianship* 30, no. 2 (2004): 116–21.

Coyle, Karen. "Catalogs, Card—and Other Anachronisms." *Journal of Academic Librarianship* 31, no. 1 (2005): 60–62. doi: 10.1016/j.acalib.2004.12.001.

Deignan, Alice. "Corpus Linguistics and Metaphor." In *The Cambridge Handbook of Metaphor and Thought*, edited by Raymond W. Gibbs Jr., 280–94. New York: Cambridge University Press, 2008.

Fields, Anne M. "Ill-Structured Problems and the Reference Consultation: The Librarian's Role in Developing Student Expertise." *Reference Services Review* 34, no. 3 (2006): 405–20. doi: 10.1108/00907320610701554.

Fister, Barbara. "Teaching the Rhetorical Dimensions of Research." *Research Strategies* 11, no. 4 (Fall 1993): 211–19. http://homepages.gac.edu/~fister/rs.html.

Foster, Nancy Fried. "The Mommy Model of Service." In *Studying Students: The Undergraduate Research Project at the University of Rochester,* edited by Nancy Fried Foster and Susan Gibbons, 72–78. Chicago: Association of College and Research Libraries, 2007.

Giesecke, Joan. "Finding the Right Metaphor: Restructuring, Realigning, and Repackaging Today's Research Libraries." *Journal of Library Administration* 51, no. 1 (2010): 54–65. doi: 10.1080/01930826.2011.531641.

Given, Lisa M., and Heidi Julien. "Finding Common Ground: An Analysis of Librarians' Expressed Attitudes towards Faculty." *The Reference Librarian* 43, no. 89-90 (2005): 25–38. doi: 10.1300/J120v43n89_03.

Hartzell, Gary. "The Metaphor is the Message." *School Library Journal* 48, no. 6 (2002): 33.

Hicks, Richard C., Ronald Dattero, and Stuart D. Galup. "A Metaphor for Knowledge Management: Explicit Islands in a Tacit Sea.*" Journal of Knowledge Management* 11, no. 1 (2007): 5–16. doi: 10.1108/13673270710728204.

Hook, Sheril. "Impact? What Three Years of Research Tells Us about Library Instruction." *College *and Research Libraries* 73, no. 1 (2012): 7–10.

Jackson, Howard, and Etienne Zé Amvela. *Words, Meaning, and Vocabulary: An Introduction to Modern English Lexicology.* New York: Cassell, 2000.

Jackson, Rebecca. "Cognitive Development: The Missing Link in Teaching Information Literacy Skills." *Reference and User Services Quarterly* 46, no. 4 (2007): 28–32.

Julien, Heidi, and Lisa M. Given. "Faculty-Librarian Relationships in the Information Literacy Context: A Content Analysis of Librarians' Expressed Attitudes and Experiences." *Canadian Journal of Information and Library Science* 27, no. 3 (2002/03): 65–87.

Kapitzke, Cushla. "Information Literacy: A Positivist Epistemology and a Politics of Outformation." *Educational Theory* 53, no. 1 (2003): 37–53.

Kempcke, Ken. "The Art of War for Librarians: Academic Culture, Curriculum Reform, and Wisdom from Sun Tzu." *portal: Libraries and the Academy* 2, no. 4 (2002): 529–51.

King, Patricia M., and Karen Strohm Kitchener. *Developing Reflective Judgment: Understanding and Promoting Intellectual Growth and Critical Thinking in Adolescents and Adults.* San Francisco: Jossey-Bass, 1994.

Koller, Veronika. "'A Shotgun Wedding:' Co-Occurrence of War and Marriage Metaphors in Mergers and Acquisitions Discourse." *Metaphor and Symbol* 17, no. 3 (2002): 179–203.

———. *Metaphor and Gender in Business Media Discourse: A Critical Cognitive Study.* New York: Palgrave Macmillan, 2004.

Kövecses, Zoltán. *Metaphor: A Practical Introduction.* New York: Oxford University Press, 2002.

Lakoff, George. 1991. "Metaphor and War: The Metaphor System Used to Justify War in the Gulf (Part 1 of 2)." *Viet Nam Generation Journal and Newsletter* 3, no. 3 (1991). http://www2.iath. virginia.edu/sixties/HTML_docs/Texts/Scholarly/Lakoff_Gulf_Metaphor_1.html.

Mackey, Thomas P., and Trudi E. Jacobson. "Reframing Information Literacy as a Metaliteracy." *College and Research Libraries* 72, no. 1 (2011): 62–78.

McCook, Kathleen de la Peña. "The Search for New Metaphors." *Library Trends* 46, no. 1 (1997): 117.

McMillan, Jill J., and George Cheney. "The Student as Consumer: The Implications and Limitations of a Metaphor." *Communication Education* 45, no. 1 (1996): 1–15. doi: 10.1080/03634529609379028.

Moropa, Robert. "Academic Libraries in Transition: Some Leadership Issues–A Viewpoint." *Library Management* 31, no. 6 (2010): 381–90. doi: 10.1108/01435121011066144.

Nitecki, Danuta A. "Conceptual Models of Libraries Held by Faculty, Administrators, and Librarians: An Exploration of Communications in *The Chronicle of Higher Education.*" *Journal of Documentation* 49, no. 3 (1993): 255–77.

Olson, Hope A. "The Ubiquitous Hierarchy: An Army to Overcome the Threat of a Mob." *Library Trends* 52, no. 3 (2004): 604–16.

Schweik, Robert. "Painting as 'Exploring' and Related Metaphors in 20th-Century Art Commentary." *Metaphor and Symbolic Activity* 11, no. 4 (1996): 285–96.

Simmons, Michelle Holschuh. "Librarians as Disciplinary Discourse Mediators: Using Genre Theory to Move toward Critical Information Literacy." *portal: Libraries and the Academy* 5, no. 3 (2005): 297–311. doi: 10.1353/pla.2005.0041.

Swanson, Troy. "Information Literacy, Personal Epistemology, and Knowledge Construction: Potential and Possibilities." *College and Undergraduate Libraries* 13, no. 3 (2006): 93–112.

doi: 10.1300/J106v13n03_07.

Thacker, Mara. "A Paradigm Shift: Changing Approaches in the Classroom." *College and Research Library News* 73, no. 3 (2012): 148–49.

Tillman, Caitlin. "Library Orientation for Professors: Give a Pitch, Not a Tour." *College and Research Library News* 69, no. 8 (2008): 470–75.

Walters-York, L. Melissa. "Metaphor in Accounting Discourse." *Accounting, Auditing and Accountability Journal* 9, no. 5 (1886): 45–70. doi: 10.1108/09513579610367242.

Whitmire, Ethelene. "Epistemological Beliefs and the Information-Seeking Behavior of Undergraduates." *Library and Information Science Research* 25, no. 2 (2003): 127–42. doi: 10.1016/S0740-8188(03)00003-3.

———. "The Relationship between Undergraduates' Epistemological Beliefs, Reflective Judgment, and

Their Information-Seeking Behavior." *Information Processing and Management* 40, no.1 (2004): 97–111. doi: 10.1016/S0306-4573(02)00099-7.

Wilner, Arlene. "Fostering Critical Literacy: The Art of Assignment Design." In "Identity, Learning, and the Liberal Arts," edited by Ned Scott Laff. Special issue, *New Directions for Teaching and Learning* 103 (2005): 23–38. doi: 10.1002/tl.201.

CHAPTER 4

The Social Life of Knowledge:
Faculty Epistemologies

Barbara Fister

When the original *Information Literacy Competency Standards for Higher Education* were first published in January 2000, I was delighted to see the complexity of research articulated. Finally, information literacy wasn't just about using library tools to find sources.[1] It was about articulating questions, making judgments, and creating new things within an ethical and social context. It seemed obvious at last that information literacy could no longer be conceived as a library program. Rather, it was a project so complex that it would have to be embraced by faculty across the disciplines.[2] These standards confirmed my strong feeling that students could not become information literate by more or less randomly scattering library sessions into their classroom experiences. Rather, it was work that would have to be intentionally embedded throughout courses and within entire programs. It seemed to be a document designed to promote collaborations and campus-wide discussion.

A few months after the standards were published, we hosted a weeklong workshop for faculty across the curriculum who wanted to revise or create new courses that would intentionally include a developmental approach to learning and practicing research skills.[3] On the final day of the workshop, our plan called for moving beyond the design of specific courses into a conversation about what our students should be able to do upon graduation. To frame that conversation, we reserved the closing hours of the workshop to discuss ways in which we could move beyond courses and think about how programs could intentionally develop research skills in a sequential, intentional manner. As an introduction to this conversation, we shared the new standards.

Workshop attendees' reaction was not what we expected.

The faculty seemed universally puzzled by the standards and even distressed. "The word 'creativity' doesn't appear anywhere in this document," one faculty member said. Another wondered why all references to original thought were left out. The focus seemed too much on finding and manipulating things rather than working with ideas to create new knowledge. A professor in the economics and management department likened the detailed list of performance indicators and outcomes to a Tayloristic time and motion study, breaking something organic into small mechanical steps. Others protested that a student who did well on each of the steps might still have difficulty writing a coherent paper based on research. Conversely, a student who might fail miserably on many of the listed "performance indicators" might conduct brilliant research. Some faculty confessed *they* would not fare well if tested on many of the outcomes listed in the document. Yet the books and articles they had published provided some evidence that they were demonstrably information literate.

In some ways, it was a dispiriting end to an exhilarating week of collaboration and discovery—our standards failed the test!—but in reality, it was an affirmation that faculty felt a strong sense of ownership of and commitment to the kind of learning we try to promote. If anything, the standards simply didn't go far enough in describing a creative process of using information to create new knowledge.

It also brought home our very different perspectives on what we are talking about when we talk about research. Librarians tend to work more closely with students than with faculty and, as a result, tend to think about research in terms of finding and evaluating information that will be used for a particular short-term task. In academic libraries, that task is most frequently imagined as the completion of an assignment that involves discovering, choosing, and using sources to write a paper or make a presentation. The standards seem to suggest information use is inevitably tied to a need to carry out a particular task. The next steps, after determining that use, are to find information, make choices among the options, and use sources in a "product or performance," without violating rules. This is not at all how faculty in the disciplines do research. It isn't even how librarians do research.[4]

Faculty members' experiences as researchers influence what their learning outcomes are, how they design assignments, and what processes they expect students to engage in as they complete them. In this chapter, we'll explore what those experiences and expectations are.

Disciplines exhibit strong differences among themselves when it comes to methods and publication patterns. However, some of the underlying values and beliefs that seem to apply to faculty in all disciplines are trust in expertise and rigorous professional training, a sense of knowledge being created in and by a community, a strong belief that evidence matters, and a reliance on research methods that differ greatly from one discipline to another but are all rooted in a desire to be rigorous, fair, and open-minded in the search for meaning.

Expertise

The value assigned to expertise is sometimes conveyed in the way faculty refer to their training: "I was trained in…" is a phrase often used to distinguish one's strengths. "I don't have training in…" is frequently used to delineate the boundaries of one's abilities. Expertise is gained primarily through a difficult and extensive apprenticeship in a discipline, encompassing years of study; carrying out extensive original research for a dissertation; becoming an active member in disciplinary organizations, both formal and informal; having a deep and continuing knowledge of the literature of the field; and earning a credential, which is usually a doctoral degree. This training and its credentialing confers upon expert scholars special status as contributors to knowledge and confers on texts produced by experts an assumption of likely validity that is withheld from expertise earned by other means. An art historian's analysis of street art is presumed to be more insightful and valuable than an artist's blog post. A trained historian's article about a historical event or artifact is assumed to be a greater contribution to what we know about the past than an untrained local historian's self-published book. A physicist with post-doc experience at a national laboratory who proposes a novel approach to supersymmetry will get more notice than a citizen-scientist without formal training. A political operative with deep knowledge of the Washington political scene may be an expert, but without training in political science methods and theory, his or her insights will likely become part of what political scientists know only if someone with that training studies it and validates it.

When faculty tell students to use scholarly sources, they do so under the assumption that scholars produce material that is, by virtue of training in a particular way of knowing, superior to and more rigorous than other forms of information. Scholarship is analytical, critical, and bound by certain methodological and ethical conventions that make it trustworthy. Not all scholarship is equally valuable, and sophisticated readers can distinguish work that is groundbreaking from pedestrian, derivative, or shoddy work. But in general, the methods and values inculcated in graduate training and developed over the course of an active scholar's life are valued more highly than the kinds of knowledge-seeking and idea formation practiced by journalists, hobbyists, or members of non-scholarly trades.

Faculty members' implicit faith in scholarly expertise can be at odds with both undergraduate experience and with preparation for lifelong learning. Novice researchers can quickly learn to identify scholarly articles by their surface features, though even these can be confusing. One professor may tell their students that scholarly articles are ones that are at least 15-pages long in publications that have few images and no advertisements, which would exclude most peer-reviewed publications in the sciences. Another will instruct students to reject anything that doesn't have a clearly labeled methodology section, which would exclude most humanities scholarship. To some extent these differences are overcome by database vendors when they use metadata drawn from periodical directories to allow students to limit search results to scholarly or peer-reviewed sources—but even those filters can fail. Sometimes periodicals are mislabeled as scholarly when they are not. They also may fail to distinguish between an editor's introductory essay or a book review and a peer-reviewed research article. A seasoned scholar would recognize those differences instantly, but when undergraduates are focused on externalities, these differences in genres within scholarly publishing are less distinguishable.

A more significant problem is that focusing on the external appearances of scholarly publications oversimplifies the complexity of making choices among thousands of peer-reviewed possibilities and being able to make sense of the scholarly articles chosen for further examination. Undergraduates typically have little or no knowledge to draw on to create the kinds of filters seasoned scholars use—knowing which journals are the most influential and respected ones or even (unless it's obvious from the title) whether a journal is within a particular discipline. To make good choices, students have to interpret clues in the titles and abstracts, which assume knowledge they don't have. Unlike the audience for which these articles were written, students are not well prepared to interpret from these scant clues the content that will be covered, the audience to which it is addressed, and the direction an argument is likely to take.

Reading and making sense of the articles students have chosen can be difficult too. As first-year students interviewed in a Project Information Literacy study reported, students come to college having little or no exposure to scholarly texts.[5] It takes a great deal of time and effort for them to read dense prose full of terminology they don't know, reference to literature they haven't read, and rhetorical conventions that are unlike those used by the texts they are familiar with—magazine articles, textbooks, and books for popular audiences. First-year students also report difficulty grasping the specialized vocabulary that will help them construct an effective search and then comb through a massive number of results to weed out irrelevant articles and find ones that they can use.

So, though faculty put a high value on the expertise represented by scholars' publications, the means by which they discover, make sense of, and make use of these expert texts depends upon work habits and deep background knowledge that helps them discover, select, store, read, and draw on scholarly texts in ways that are not available to nonexperts. One simple means of helping faculty members recognize the challenges their students face is to ask them to find five high-quality scholarly sources on an unfamiliar topic in a field entirely foreign to them and to do it quickly. This exercise can reveal the tacit knowledge faculty depend on when doing their own research and demonstrates that expertise, while valuable, often sets up barriers that it is difficult for nonexperts to overcome.

The Conversational Nature of Knowledge

Librarians, as disciplinary outsiders, often unconsciously approach the management and discovery of knowledge in terms of *things* that are about *subjects*. A source that contains knowledge about a topic is bounded by the shape of its container. If it is a book, it will be on a shelf, in a collection of e-books, or available from another library, its location identified through WorldCat or another union catalog. If it is an article, it will be part of a journal located in a database or (if the specifics of the container are known) retrieved through a link resolver. As disciplinary outsiders, we tend to discover these containers through catalogs, databases, and discovery layers, using likely subject terms (rather than known authors or publications), refining our search language along the way as we encounter more precise terminology, applying additional subjects to narrow a search down, and using other limiters to hone the results of a search. In short, we search for knowledge in things, relying primarily on tools that connect us to published containers.

Faculty, as insiders, see knowledge in social and conversational terms. Sources are written by people and are addressed to groups of people. These people know one another through disciplines, a tribe of experts who engage in long, ongoing conversations of common interest. Each publication is documentation of a contribution to that conversation, one that locates itself within the conversation by naming previous contributors. A literature review is both a way to mark which conversation this new contribution belongs to and to demonstrate in what ways this publication contributes something new to it. For a contribution to have value, it first must establish that there was a gap in the conversation that needs filling before explaining how it fills that gap, often ending with suggestions about what work still needs to be done. The literature review, itself, is a map of how ideas have taken shape through collaborative work. It argues that knowledge is constructed out of many voices and that those conversations have a meaningful shape: This group of scholars has developed one school of thought; those scholars have gone off to address a related set of questions; another group of scholars has splintered from the dominant group and is proposing a radically different approach. The conversations split, diverge, loop back and over time collectively take many different approaches to questions, adding to and challenging what is collectively agreed-upon knowledge within a disciplinary community.

This has a profound influence on the process scholars use to find things out. Sources aren't containers full of knowledge. They are people with ideas who are developing those ideas over time and within a community. Disciplines are a key category, in that members of a discipline share assumptions about what we know, how we know, and what questions are appropriate to ask. They are further subdivided by interests and theoretical foundations. Members of disciplines develop a tacit grasp of how a discipline divides into subdisciplines and where bridges between disciplines can support interdisciplinary inquiry that may, in time, form disciplines of their own. On any college campus, the boundaries of disciplines are delineated in departments and programs, with programs typically holding a more precarious position when it comes to resource allocation and how many majors they support.

This can, at times, contribute to lack of understanding or false assumptions about other disciplines that does not make it easier for undergraduates, who are forced to cross disciplinary boundaries to meet general education requirements. Students have to distinguish what matters to their instructors in disciplines with different expectations and vocabularies. These differences can be as clear-cut as requirements to use different citation rules. Students may have to format citations according to three or more different style manuals within a single semester. Often the differences are subtler. One instructor may think it wholly inappropriate for a student to use first person in formal writing, while another deducts points for using passive voice. What is called a "primary source" in students' history class is defined differently by a biology teacher insisting that students find and use a "primary article" in their research. It's rare for faculty members to define a term such as "primary" by contrasting it to how other disciplines use it. Their disciplinary conventions are normative and so deeply familiar that they may not realize that their discourse conventions are not universal.

There have been efforts to bridge the differences between disciplines through learning communities, interdisciplinary programs, service and community-based learning and efforts to integrate learning through revised general education curricula. Scholars of composition and rhetoric have effectively probed disciplinary conventions from the perspective of student writers. The Writing Across the Curriculum (WAC) movement has arguably done more than any other pedagogical approach to clarify and articulate the tacit assumptions embedded in discipline-based discourse practices. Librarians interested in helping faculty understand the differences in disciplinary discourses and how they affect undergraduate learning can learn much from the work accomplished by proponents of WAC and from the scholarship of composition and rhetoric.[6]

The notion that "sources are people talking to other people" and that knowledge is advanced through conversation can be a powerful heuristic for undergraduate researchers.[7] Often students begin their college career having expectations that it will proceed along the lines of what Paolo Freire has called "the banking concept of education."[8] Knowledge isn't made by people like them. It is a commodity controlled by other, more powerful people. The students' role is to passively have that knowledge deposited from the experts into their heads. They have no effect on that knowledge, and they have nothing at all to contribute to what we know. When writing research papers, this concept suggests that knowledge is something to be found in authoritative sources. Students have no right to say anything themselves; they need to find a source that can say it for them.

Every academic librarian has had the experience of working with students who either feel they need to drop an interesting topic because they can't find a source that says exactly what they want to say. Others become frustrated that they can't find "the perfect source," the one with the answer to the question they are posing. Somehow, because they have been asked to back up their claims with evidence (preferably found in publications that have every appearance of being scholarly), they get the impression that originality is against the rules. Research becomes a process of visiting the library as a bank of knowledge to withdraw the information they need. They then arrange quotes, quite often lifted directly from their sources, and document them to demonstrate exactly how safely unoriginal their thinking is. Failing to document a source properly is the equivalent of property theft, a crime that carries heavy academic penalties. There is little in this version of research that departs from the banking concept of education.

When students begin to realize that sources are people talking to other people in an unfinished conversation and that they themselves can be part of it, their sense of agency in the making of knowledge can change profoundly. The shift from being a consumer of information to being a creator of knowledge is empowering. It may be one of the most profound changes a college student can go through, and it is a change in identity that is fundamental to lifelong learning. It primes students to become active, involved participants in the world they will graduate into. It is also a significant change in their understanding of how information works, which is a necessary part of intellectual development. No longer is truth something absolute and external; our understanding is socially situated, constructed, and subject to change.

In 1984, Stephen K. Stoan argued that research instruction bore little relationship to library instruction and that librarians "weaken the image of the profession by giving the impression of looking on books and journals as just so much merchandise, so many units of information, to be purchased, accessioned, cataloged, shelved, identified through access tools, circulated, re-shelved, and finally discarded according to some undefinable criterion."[9] Treating research as the retrieval and manipulation of things, in his estimation, misrepresented the true nature of research. Essentially, he argued that librarians' contributions to learning were minimal and that their claims for the importance of what was then called "bibliographic instruction" were wildly overblown.

Two years later, Joan Bechtel, who had higher hopes for the role librarians played in learning, proposed conversation as a paradigm for librarianship. She suggested that we should "begin to think of libraries as centers for conversation and of ourselves as mediators of and participants in the conversations of the world."[10] She criticized the emerging emphasis on information management and delivery as an overly commercialized and unimaginative identity for libraries. Rather, academic libraries serve "to introduce students to the world of scholarly dialogue that spans both space and time and to provide students with the knowledge and skills they need to tap into conversations on an infinite variety of topics and to participate in the critical inquiry and debate on those issues."[11] More recently, R. David Lankes has called on librarians to embrace conversation as a model and to make facilitating that conversation and promoting community knowledge creation for the betterment of society the primary mission of libraries of all kinds.[12]

The use of citations for discovery is one of the ways knowledge manifests itself as an ongoing conversation. Decades ago, Stoan argued that librarians were wrong to characterize the systematic use of library search tools as a research strategy and accused librarians of neglecting the fact that footnotes constitute a highly refined self-indexing function for scholarly literature, providing "greater comprehensiveness, better analytics, and greater precision" than library tools. "Footnotes," he writes, "are, after all, the traditional medium whereby scholars communicate with each other directly." By contrast, library tools are crude in their ability to link related sources together and do little to rank sources in order of significance or relatedness.[13]

Faculty often expect students to naturally adopt a practice that is second nature to them. They are used to decoding citations as they evaluate an argument. It is a natural part of reading a text because it's how a reader can determine if the author adequately acknowledges what is going on in disciplinary conversations, if the author missed something important, and what theoretical framework the author is using. Faculty members can decode a citation and know how to get their hands on cited works. Though the citation network does provide a sense of context and relative value of cited sources, undergraduates often find citations undecipherable and don't know how to go from a citation to a work. Discovery layers are currently not as good at locating specific sources as they are at aggregating sources on a common topic. For many students, a reference list is a collection of broken links. Librarians who want to emphasize the social nature of knowledge could spend less time demonstrating the features of library databases and do more to help students navigate the self-indexing nature of scholarly texts.

The conversation metaphor, while it is a valuable and often overlooked heuristic, does have a significant drawback: It assumes everyone feels equally invited to participate in scholarly conversations. In reality, conversations can be inhospitable to outsiders. All students will, at first, feel marginalized. Some students, including first-generation college students, students with socioeconomic disadvantages, or students who lack welcoming support systems, will feel more excluded than others. Simply pointing out that knowledge is created by people fails to acknowledge genuine inequities. It also may invite students to mimic a certain kind of discourse without enabling students to connect that discourse to their own lives and identities.[14]

Stoan (like many critics of librarians' efforts to provide meaningful learning opportunities to students) felt that librarians exaggerate their instructional mission; that they misrepresent research as a systematic process of using discovery tools; that research is not as essential an undergraduate learning experience as we assume; and that research instruction, if it is needed at all, would be best left to the faculty in the disciplines who, unlike librarians, actually do research and so know what is involved.[15] Michelle Holschuh Simmons takes another approach, arguing that librarians are uniquely positioned to serve as discourse mediators.[16] Faculty assume their discourse conventions are normative, and they forget that they once learned them. Librarians occupy a position that is both inside and outside scholarly discourses and can play an important role in helping faculty understand the tacit knowledge and assumptions they have (which students lack) as well as nudging students toward an understanding that knowledge is constructed, not merely found. The role librarians play, then, isn't as experts so much as translators and cultural informants. Librarians could also take their mission in the direction of fostering faculty conversations within their local communities to seek connections among disciplines and between college experiences and life before and beyond college. Through involvement in first-year programs, librarians are instrumental in introducing students to college-level inquiry.[17] They could play a greater role in promoting students' transition to life after college by helping both students and faculty consider how inquiry skills practiced in college will be used after graduation in nonacademic settings. Two reports published by Project Information Literacy—*Learning the Ropes* and *Learning Curve: How College Graduates Solve Information Problems Once They Join the Workplace*—provide excellent material for such conversations, which librarians, as custodians of the commons, are well suited to host.[18]

Evidence, Methods, and Ethics

In addition to rigorous training and participation in scholarly communities, faculty in all disciplines value rigorous methods and respect reasoning from evidence. Methods differ from one discipline to another, with some disciplines valuing empirical research, others more open to qualitative methods, and many in the humanities focused on close reading of primary texts and the interpretation of culture through theoretical lenses. Though the methods and their assumptions differ, there are some values common to them all.

Whatever method is used to conduct research, it cannot be driven by self-interest. One might question whether objectivity is possible, but it is generally an ideal that guides researchers' behavior. Research begins with a question or hypotheses, not with a foregone conclusion. Evidence matters, but it has to be handled fairly. Cherry-picking material that suits an argument while ignoring evidence that doesn't is conduct unbecoming of a scholar. Research is conversational, but it would be unethical to fail to cite the person who expressed an idea first. Other people's contributions to the conversation must not be misrepresented. Peer review is flawed; it can let bad research slip through, or it can be too conservative, suppressing research that challenges the status quo. Yet because originality is so highly valued among scholars, there are incentives for dissent.[19]

These ethical values are not always made clear to students, at least not in their early forays into research. While evaluating sources is often emphasized in lower-division composition courses, the common checklist approach typically focuses on externalities (whether the source was published in a scholarly journal, how recently it was published) or on qualities that few undergraduates are positioned to assess such as the authority of the author or the reputation of the publisher. Students may not have sufficient background to evaluate the source's use of evidence or the soundness of its methodology. Yet often—in the flurry of work involved in learning how to organize an argument effectively, write in a suitably academic voice, avoid grammatical mistakes, draw on sources without plagiarizing them, and cite them according to Byzantine rules—some of the most fundamental ethical values of research can get lost. In particular, students are often encountering the use of the word "argument" as scholars use it for the first time. Rather than meaning debate or conflict, this kind of argument refers to the development of an idea using examples, evidence, and logic. Students often believe they must assemble quotes from sources to support a position, making tactical choices the ways political candidates do, but they do not realize that research can change the mind of the researcher, that the evidence they encounter might overturn their thesis completely. It's not uncommon for students to ask reference librarians for help finding sources for a paper they've already written. That's an extreme example of misunderstanding the purpose of using sources in writing, but it's hardly uncommon.

In the 1990s, Jennie Nelson studied undergraduate writers, finding that most first-year students gather material and quote it without engaging in the recursive process of reading, writing, and making meaning, with 75 percent simply compiling information, ten percent seeking sources that would confirm what they had already written, and another ten percent coaxing a thesis from a handful of more or less randomly chosen sources. Only five percent engaged in a recursive process of research and discovery.[20] More recent findings of the Citation Project suggest that little has changed. Students tend to draw quotations from sources that they have not demonstrated they have read and understood and engage in "patchwriting" rather than synthesizing information or creating their own understanding.[21]

At the same time, Alison Head's study of freshman research practices suggests that librarians and composition teachers play a significant role in introducing students to scholarly texts and strategies for navigating library resources and making choices amid an overabundance of options. Students in the study reported enjoying the freedom to explore their own topics and develop their own theses but felt anxious about reading scholarly texts that were entirely unfamiliar to them, chosen from among the resources of a library many times larger than any they had used before. These studies suggest that engaging students in research activities at the beginning of their college careers is a valuable introduction to scholarship and its ways, but also suggests that, without guidance, students are likely to believe that research is a process of compiling information from sources, often through harvesting quotes. Librarians, writing instructors, and faculty in the disciplines could fruitfully collaborate on finding ways to introduce students to the ethical values scholars share, even if it comes at the expense of spending time on learning how databases work and how to cite sources accurately.

Differences in Modeling a Process

The underlying values and beliefs scholars hold about epistemology influence the day-to-day practices of researchers who are well versed in their subject matter and will remain immersed in it for far longer than undergraduates will. Because their knowledge base is so familiar to them, they forget how much what they know guides how they approach the tasks they assign their students.

Formulating a research question, for a member of the faculty, grows out of knowing where the gaps in current knowledge are and which gaps are most intriguing and likely to be of interest to others in the discipline. That insider knowledge comes from having organized a personal method for monitoring the regular flow of new information being produced by practitioners in the field. That new information is viewed in the context of an already deep knowledge base, which provides a foundation and a framework into which new information can be situated. Faculty often fail to take into account how much research an undergraduate must do before even being able to determine what research questions are meaningful and manageable.

For faculty, choosing which publications to pay attention to is informed by knowledge of which publishers and journals have the strongest reputations and which authors are well-established experts and which are outliers. Students, who have none of this knowledge, will not find it in library databases.

Faculty often put more faith in footnotes than in subject databases or discovery layers when it comes to reviewing related literature, but students find the process of interpreting citations and getting their hands on cited sources difficult.

Faculty spend little time in the physical library and may only rarely use the library's website to find out what's been published.[22] For faculty, the library's collections and tools are a kind of switching station where they can see if a source is locally available or if it must be obtained by other means. The discovery of what sources they want to pursue is less likely to happen on the library's website or in the library's stacks than it is through their professional networks, the citation network, or announcements of new content in journals they depend on.

Librarians typically guide students through a process that is better suited to novice researchers, who lack the contextual knowledge and the cues that faculty have internalized. However, it can inadvertently encourage a process that pays insufficient attention to the conversational context of research and the network of connections represented through citations. If the emphasis is on finding, evaluating, and using sources, it can suggest that research is primarily about mining quotes from published sources. Collaboration with faculty should include discussing the different perspectives librarians, faculty in the disciplines, and students bring to knowledge, negotiating the most effective ways to help novice researchers navigate the anxiety-producing vastness of an academic library without losing sight of the faculty member's learning goals.

Realpolitik and the Diplomacy of Collaboration

The professional lives of librarians and faculty in the disciplines are significantly different (though one must also admit that there is a great deal of variation among disciplines; the professional life of a faculty member in the performing arts may be just as different from that of chemists or classicists as from librarians). A long-recognized difference between librarian and faculty in general is in social status. Lars Christensen, Mindy Stombler, and Lyn Thaxton analyzed librarian-faculty relationships from a sociological stance, concluding that there is an asymmetrical interest between the two groups; librarians are highly motivated to collaborate, but faculty have little incentive to do so.[23] This situation is at least partially influenced by a differential in status, which is partly related to campus power structures, perceptions of the relative value of the work librarians and faculty do, and gender. The literature on faculty-librarian collaboration, which is voluminous in the literature of librarianship but scant in other disciplines, reinforces this study's findings. A study conducted in Ireland of faculty attitudes toward learning information skills suggests that many faculty evaluate research products rather than teach a process, assume motivated students will figure things out on their own, decide "learning by doing" can suffice rather than formal instruction, and believe failure to complete research successfully can largely be put down to lack of motivation on the part of students.[24] The authors suggest that information literacy is not a high concern for faculty and that librarians should do more to take the case for information literacy out of the library literature and into other disciplinary venues. A more recent survey of faculty at two- and four-year colleges in New Jersey found that nearly all faculty across the disciplines value information literacy, feel it's an important part of what they teach, and make assignments that give students opportunities to practice information literacy skills.[25] However, nearly half of respondents felt students were not adequately prepared on graduation, particularly at the end of two-year programs. A large majority of faculty felt that this kind of learning belongs in the curriculum; a majority (though a smaller one) felt that librarians have a role to play either through instruction sessions or one-on-one consultation. These findings suggests that the level of faculty interest and concern is high and that faculty recognize the value of librarians' contributions to this kind of learning—yet many feel students are not learning enough. Faculty seem interested in making available a more coherent cross-curricular effort to build on what students learn in their courses. Whether faculty will welcome librarians' leadership will largely depend on local campus cultures and the availability of time and funding for initiatives.

A newer distinction between librarians and faculty in the disciplines bears consideration. Though a substantial percentage of academic librarians are faculty, they seem to have largely been spared a trend in many academic departments: to reduce the number of full-time staff by hiring instructors by the course.[26] The fact that three-quarters of the professoriate currently is neither tenure track nor tenured has had a great deal of influence on the lives of emerging scholars, just as the defunding of public education has raised the level of debt graduate students must bear to complete their education.[27] As the number of well-paying academic jobs has dwindled, the demand to stand out with more research publications has increased.[28] The pressure on early career faculty to get grants and produce publications while, in many cases, having difficulty finding secure work that pays a living wage, could have a detrimental and lasting impact on efforts to embed information literacy into courses and programs. For undergraduates, learning how to conduct research well depends on coaching from librarians and apprenticeship to scholars. The programs that most highly value the kinds of research that libraries support are particularly vulnerable to budget cuts and loss of tenured faculty positions. There is also evidence that the positions that support novice researchers—those who teach first-year composition courses, particularly in community colleges—are even more precarious than other faculty positions.[29]

If librarians want to collaborate with faculty to enhance information literacy, they need to understand how faculty conceptualize knowledge and how their research processes and habits may influence their expectations of students. Librarians also need to recognize how to blend library-focused practices and students' practical desire to complete assignments as efficiently as possible with the higher-order learning that can involve students in deeper, more conceptually rich research experiences. Students should be encouraged to see themselves as active contributors to the construction of knowledge, and faculty epistemologies may provide a far richer framework for that kind of discovery than any tool-and-resource-focused model of research. Yet, because the library belongs to all disciplines and librarians are discourse mediators between disciplines and between novices and experts, librarians may be particularly well positioned to provide opportunities for faculty to explore their research practices and how they can enhance undergraduate education. Whether providing faculty development opportunities or simply connecting with faculty who might be interested in collaboration, librarians must also bear in mind the current economic and political status of faculty. In the interests of student learning, librarians should be aware of and be prepared to support faculty as they face stratification between tenured faculty and the contingent majority and confront the serious threats many academic programs face in an age of austerity.[30]

Notes

1.   Association of College and Research Libraries, *Information Literacy Competency Standards for Higher Education,* accessed April 7, 2014, http://www.ala.org/acrl/sites/ala.org.acrl/files/content/standards/standards.pdf. As of this writing, the standards are being thoroughly revised.

2.   In this chapter, I use the term *librarian* to refer to library professionals, regardless of whether they hold faculty status. By *faculty* I mean instructors in all other disciplines, regardless of whether they hold faculty, lecturer, or other titles.

3.   This workshop was part of a two-year IMLS National Leadership Grant project titled Enhancing Developmental Research Skills in the Undergraduate Curriculum. Information about the grant and the faculty workshops is available online at https://gustavus.edu/library/IMLS/.

4.   Nancy Fried Foster, "The Librarian-Student-Faculty Triangle: Conflicting Research Strategies?" (paper, Association of Research Library's Library Assessment Conference, Baltimore, Maryland, October 26, 2010), http://hdl.handle.net/1802/13512.

5.   Alison J. Head, *Learning the Ropes: How Freshmen Conduct Research Once They Enter College,* accessed August 14, 2014, http://projectinfolit.org/images/pdfs/pil_2013_freshmen-study_fullreport.pdf.

6.   A particularly useful examination of the challenges students face as they navigate different discourse conventions can be found in David Bartholomae, "Inventing the University," in *When a Writer Can't Write: Studies in Writer's Block and Other Composing-Process Problems,* ed. Mike Rose (New York: Guildford, 1985), 134–65. A valuable collection of open access texts on Writing Across the Curriculum is available at the WAC Clearinghouse at Colorado State University: http://wac.colostate.edu/. CompPile, an ongoing database of publications on WAC and writing studies, is available online at http://comppile.org/.

7.   I first encountered this insightful phrase in personal communication with Doug Downs, associate professor of English at Montana State University.

8.   Paolo Freire, *Pedagogy of the Oppressed,* trans. Myra Bergman Ramos (New York: Continuum, 1970).

9.   Stephen K. Stoan, "Research and Library Skills: An Analysis and Interpretation," *College and Research Libraries* 45, no. 2 (1984): 108.

10.   Joan M. Bechtel, "Conversation, a New Paradigm for Librarianship?" *College and Research Libraries* 47, no. 3 (1986): 219.

11.   Bechtel, "Conversation," 221.

12.   R. David Lankes, *The Atlas of New Librarianship* (Cambridge, MA: MIT Press, 2011).

13.   Stoan, "Research and Library Skills," 103.

14.   A useful feminist exploration of the differences between mimicking a scholarly identity

and connecting that identity to one's personal life experiences, values, and goals can be found in *Women's Ways of Knowing: The Development of Self, Voice, and Mind* (New York: Basic Books, 1997).

15.   In "Research and Library Skills," Stoan writes, "Research scholars, who may make significant contributions to knowledge, seldom possess library skills. Librarians, who possess library skills, seldom do research. Indeed, they work in a field whose research tradition is universally acknowledged to be weak… From these facts, it must be deduced that research skills and library skills are neither the same thing nor bear any organic relationship to each other" (105).

16.   Michelle Holschuh Simmons, "Librarians as Disciplinary Discourse Mediators: Using Genre Theory to Move toward Critical Information Literacy," *Portal: Libraries and the Academy* 5, no. 3 (2005): 297–311.

17.   Alison J. Head's *Learning the Ropes* study confirms that librarians, along with composition instructors, play a significant role in introducing first-year students to academic discourse conventions and faculty expectations.

18.   Head, *Learning the Ropes*; Alison J. Head, *Learning Curve: How College Graduates Solve Information Problems Once They Join the Workplace,* accessed August 14, 2014, http://projectinfo-lit.org/images/pdfs/pil_fall2012_workplacestudy_fullreport_revised.pdf.

19.   This conflicted negotiation between conservatism and originality is described well by Michael Polanyi in "The Republic of Science: Its Political and Economic Theory," *Minerva* 38, no. 1 (2000): 1–21.

20.   Jennie Nelson, "The Research Paper: A 'Rhetoric of Doing' or a 'Rhetoric of the Finished Word'?" *Composition Studies/Freshman English News* 22, no. 2 (1994): 65–75.

21.   The Citation Project's findings are available online at http://site.citationproject.net/.

22.   Ithaka S+R has documented a trend among faculty to value the purchasing agent role of the library more highly than its role in discovery. See the "Faculty Survey Series," available online at http://www.sr.ithaka.org/research-publications/faculty-survey-series.

23.   Lars Christiansen, Mindy Stombler, and Lyn Thaxton, "A Report on Librarian-Faculty Relations from a Sociological Perspective," *The Journal of Academic Librarianship* 30, no. 2 (2004): 116–21.

24.   Claire McGuinness, "What Faculty Think: Exploring the Barriers to Information Literacy Development in Undergraduate Education," *The Journal of Academic Librarianship* 32, no. 6 (2006): 573–82.

25.   Eleonora Dubicki, "Faculty Perceptions of Students' Information Literacy Skills Competencies," *Journal of Information Literacy 7, no. 2 (December 2013): 87–125, doi: 10.11645/7.2.1852.*

26.   Federal surveys unfortunately track only FTE staff in academic libraries, not the ratio of full-time to part-time staff. One personal account from a library director who has had to deal with staffing patterns that mirror those of faculty in other disciplines can be found in a blog post by Jacob S. Berg, "The Adjunctification of Academic Librarianship," *Beerbrarian* (blog), April 29, 2013, http://beerbrarian.blogspot.com/2013/04/the-adjunctification-of-academic.html.

27.   John W. Curtis and Saranna Thornton, "Here's the News: The Annual Report on the Economic Status of the Profession, 2012–13," *Academe* (March-April 2013): 4–19, http://www.aaup.org/file/2012-13Economic-Status-Report.pdf.

28.   Indeed, a recent Nobel prize winner in physics told a reporter that he would not be considered sufficiently productive to retain an academic position today, criticizing the current emphasis on quantity over the lasting value of scholarship. See Dekk Aitkenhead, "Peter Higgs: I Wouldn't Be Productive Enough for Today's Academic System," *The Guardian,* December 6, 2013, http://www.theguardian.com/science/2013/dec/06/peter-higgs-boson-academic-system.

29.   David Laurence, *Demography of the Faculty: A Statistical Portrait of English and Foreign Languages, Modern Languages Association,* December 10, 2008, accessed April 7, 2014, http://www.mla.org/pdf/demography_fac2.pdf.

30.   Michael Bérubé, "The Humanities Declining? Not According to the Numbers," *Chronicle of Higher Education,* July 1, 2013, https://chronicle.com/article/The-Humanities-Declining-Not/140093/.

CHAPTER 5

Generation Z: Information Facts and Fictions

Ashley Cole, Trenia Napier, and Brad Marcum

Libraries have long embraced service-oriented, user-centered approaches. Consider S.R. Ranganathan's 1931 theory *Five Laws of Library Science,* which includes three clearly user-centered tenants (every reader his or her book, every book its reader, save the time of the reader) and two that arguably hint at a user-centered approach (books are for use, the library is a growing organism). Despite such foundational user-focused theories, early research into information seeking focused not on user needs and behaviors but on "the artifacts and venues of information seeking: books, journals, newspapers, … and the like."[1] This method of investigation persisted through the 1960s, with researchers focusing on the information types, or *what,* users selected, with little to no interest as to *why* users selected particular pieces of information or the assumptions they made about information.[2] In the 1970s, William Perry's scheme of intellectual and ethical development heralded a shift toward user-centered investigations, which were extended by similar theories from Mary Field Belenky et al., Marcia B. Baxter Magolda, and Patricia M. King and Karen Strohm Kitchener. Of particular influence, however, was the work of Brenda Dervin, who challenged ten assumptions that she determined dominated and distracted research concerning information seeking. While Dervin's research focused on adult public library users and their general, everyday information needs, her ten assumptions resonated with academic libraries serving the more formalized information needs of the higher-education student. Dervin's challenges of these flawed assumptions, along with the work of other like-minded researchers and practitioners, illustrates a paradigm shift in library theory and practice, reflected in the literature by research focused on user assumptions about the nature of information and knowledge acquisition.

In recent years, academic library literature, and literature from higher education in general, has heavily focused on generation Y, better known as the millennial generation.[3] As the first generation exposed at an early age to computers and the Internet in their homes and schools, millennials demonstrate a marked increase in familiarity and use of digital technologies when compared to previous generations. This increased use and cognizance of technology, however, does not necessarily translate to a more information-savvy generation, and recent research ascertains many tech-saturated populations possess poor information literacy skills.[4]

Complicating matters further, students coming of age and entering higher education in 2013 differ from the millennials in subtle, yet distinct and powerful ways, due in part to their ubiquitous digital environment. Born in the early to mid-1990s, this newly emerging generation's label has yet to be finalized, although suggestions range from post-gen (referring to its members tendencies to broadcast even the most minute details of their lives via social media) to post-millennials or generation Z (in homage to its predecessor). Although the generations overlap a few years, sharing a common history and somewhat similar experiences with technology, the emerging generation, hereafter referred to in this chapter as generation Z, can be distinguished from the millennial generation in that its members have *never* lived in a disconnected world. In many cases they have been "wired" 24/7 from birth and, as such, seldom differentiate between their "online" and "offline" worlds. Whereas millennials began interacting with technology and the Internet in their early to mid-elementary school years, generation Z entered primary school having experienced a wide range of digital technologies and devices, from PCs to smartphones, allowing them to connect to and consume, modify, and create a wealth of information. The ubiquity of smart mobile devices with direct connections to multitudes of free web authoring services, online social networks, information outlets, and collaborative platforms empowers these students to consume and produce information in ways heretofore unimagined, making them the most information-immersed generation in history. From

SMS, Facebook, YouTube, and Twitter to Google+ Hangouts, FaceTime, and Skype, this generation is developing an instinctive set of behaviors and expectations about the nature of information as well as its access, consumption, and creation.

The authors recognize such highly connected, digitally founded environments inevitably affect our incoming students' assumptions about information. Generation Z's information milieu allows content to be ever-changing, individualized, and personal. Such an environment calls for students to develop and strengthen the critical thinking skills necessary to recognize and accommodate these information characteristics. By examining generation Z through the lens of Dervin's assumptions, we hope to define and challenge the information assumptions of generation Z in order to realize the possible implications of such assumptions on our interactions with these students and the faculty we work with to serve them.

Background

How one comes to know, the beliefs one has about knowing, and one's expectations about the nature of information are developed through learning experiences and shaped by situational factors. Reciprocally, the nature of knowledge and learning, or epistemological beliefs, influences the learning experiences of students. Research suggests that such learning experiences encourage deeper introspection and enable the development of sophisticated beliefs about learning and knowledge.[5] Psychological research into the development of epistemological beliefs and their effect on decision-making began in the early 1950s; since, researchers have become increasingly aware of the effect of students' beliefs about knowledge and learning on academic performance.[6] Inspired by William Perry's scheme of intellectual and ethical development, psychologists have developed theories illustrating how epistemological beliefs develop over time. Four central theories and models of epistemological development address and define linkages in cognition and situational factors as they relate to our assumptions about information and information acquisition. While Dervin's ten assumptions of information and information seeking provide the theoretical framework on which the current study is based, these four theories inform the current study and, as such, are worthy of a brief review.

Review of Epistemological Theories
Scheme of Intellectual and Ethical Development

Psychological research into epistemological beliefs concerning information began with Perry's scheme of intellectual and ethical development. The first to study college undergraduates' beliefs about knowledge, Perry suggests that college students make meaning of their educational experiences through developmental stages based on personal assumptions. Starting in the 1950s, Perry conducted a longitudinal study involving primarily white male undergraduates from Harvard.[7] Through a series of interviews, Perry identified nine epistemological positions, which he grouped into four categories: dualism, multiplicity, relativism, and commitment within relativism. Students move through these developmental positions, responding to new experiences by relying on and adhering to existing personal assumptions (dualism) at one end of the spectrum or critically evaluating and incorporating information according to context and situations (commitment within relativism) at the other end, oftentimes modifying personal assumptions in reaction to new information.

Women's Ways of Knowing

Belenky et al. identified limitations in Perry's study and conducted similar interviews with women to discover how their epistemological beliefs vary in comparison to their male counterparts. Belenky et al. suggested that women possessed five unique perspectives through which they view reality and draw conclusions: (1) silence, in which one feels both mindless and voiceless; (2) received knowledge, in which information is received and reproduced from an all-knowing authority; (3) subjective knowledge, in which truth is personal, private, and subjectively known or intuited; (4) procedural knowledge, in which one engages in a conscious, deliberate, and systematic *analysis* of knowledge and information; and (5) constructed knowledge, in which one "integrate[s] knowledge that [one] felt intuitively was personally important with knowledge [one] had learned from others."[8] These five ways of knowing depict a woman's cognitive development, each dependent on the other to progress.

Epistemological Reflection Model

Baxter Magolda developed her model of epistemological reflection in an attempt to address gender-related differences noted in the work of Perry and Belenky et al. Through a five-year longitudinal study, Baxter Magolda found that college men and women experience four ways of knowing that develop over time: absolute, transitional, independent, and contextual.[9] Absolute knowers assume that knowledge is absolute, and uncertainty is only in relation to the unknown, while those in the transitional knowing stage shift the focus of knowledge from acquiring to understanding.[10] Independent knowing allows the student to begin to question authorities as all-knowing and trust their own opinions about information.[11] Knowers in the final stage, contextual knowing, now have the ability to construct their own perspective by contextually judging evidence. Baxter Magolda determined that patterns of knowing are determined by one's own personal experiences and that personal experiences ultimately assist in cognitive development. Educational experiences strengthen these epistemological beliefs and, as a result, contribute to a higher level of knowing.

Reflective Judgment Model

King and Kitchener's reflective judgment model asserts, "As individuals develop, they become better able to evaluate knowledge claims and to explain and defend their points of view on controversial issues."[12] To illustrate this developmental progression, King and Kitchener used the reflective judgment interview to ask participants to address and describe their position to a problem. The reflective judgment model explains intellectual development through the application of seven stages of development, which are further classified into three broader categories. In this model, individuals transition from believing knowledge is certain (pre-reflective) through acknowledging knowledge is uncertain and that some problems do not have a right or wrong answer (reflective) to finally recognizing that "knowledge is not given but must be understood in relation to the context in which they were generated" (reflective thinking).[13]

Dervin: Information Seeking and Information Use
Sense-Making Theory

Dervin's work identified and challenged information assumptions dominating research on communication and information seeking, ultimately leading to the development of her sense-making theory. Dervin's research focuses on the individual as he or she seeks, finds, and accesses information in different, individualized situations and contexts. These situational and contextual constraints and assumptions about information ultimately establish gaps that impact one's ability to use or apply information in order to "sense-make," or construct an understanding of and apply information to one's own needs.[14]

Ten Information Assumptions or Myths

In relation to her sense-making theory, Dervin identified ten assumptions (which provide the framework for the current study) that affect both the individual's approach to locating, accessing, evaluating, and using information and the methods and systems through which information professionals and institutions address information needs.[15] While others have provided insightful summaries explaining these ten fundamentally flawed assumptions, they are, in brief—

1. Only "objective" information is valuable.
2. More information is always better.
3. Objective information can be transmitted out of context.
4. Information can only be acquired through formal sources.
5. There is relevant information for every need.
6. Every need situation has a solution.
7. It is always possible to make information available or accessible.
8. Functional units of information, such as books or TV programs, always fit the needs of individuals.
9. Time and space—individual situations—can be ignored in addressing information seeking and use.
10. People make easy, conflict-free connections between external information and their internal reality.[16]

Dervin posited that in order to provide the most effective services and resources, we must take such assumptions into consideration in the development of services, resources, and systems of information access, storage, and retrieval.[17]

Purpose of Study

A cursory glance at the literature concerning today's traditional student reveals stark differences in the information environment, practices, and beliefs of these students as compared to the original populations studied by Perry, Belenky et al., Baxter Magolda, King and Kitchener, and Dervin. We can be certain that generation Z's collaborative, individualized, and evolving information environment impacts their information-seeking behaviors and, more importantly, their assumptions about information; however, *how* and *in what ways* remain unexamined. Given this theoretical orientation, the authors propose a pilot study with the purpose of establishing a body of preliminary descriptive, qualitative information exploring the following research questions:

1. Are Dervin's ten information assumptions present in generation Z students?
2. Has technology hampered or assisted generation Z's beliefs about how one finds, accesses, and uses information?
3. How does their collaborative, individualized, evolving information environment affect generation Z's information assumptions?
4. Do the assumptions and expectations of this new generation call for a new approach our services, resources, and/or systems?

Methods and Procedures
Subjects and Setting

With the goal of viewing generation Z through the lens of Dervin's information assumptions, the authors sought to survey generation Z students currently enrolled as freshmen at a higher education institution using a survey instrument designed to explore the assumptions that generation Z makes about information. Eastern Kentucky University's (EKU) Institutional Review Board approved the study and granted permission for EKU to serve as the research site. EKU is a "regional, co-educational, public institution of higher education centrally located in Richmond, Kentucky, offering general and liberal arts programs and pre-professional and professional training at both the undergraduate and graduate levels."[18] EKU's service region extends into eastern and south central Kentucky, an area comprised of mostly rural counties in the Appalachian mountains of Kentucky.[19] Total enrollment in the fall of 2012 was 15,968, including part- and full-time students enrolled at the main Richmond campus, three regional campuses, several educational centers, and online.[20]

Current literature does not agree on any one particular year as a line of demarcation between the millennial generation and generation Z, although most research acknowledges a generational shift occurring in the early to mid 1990s. For the purposes of this study, the authors recognize 1994 as a transitional year and establish a birth date of 1994 for the beginning of generation Z. Using this definition, the first batch of generation Z is coming of age and entering institutions of higher education as freshman in 2013. Since EKU requires all incoming freshman students to enroll in a freshman orientation course during the first semester of freshman year, the authors speculated that freshman orientation courses would most likely provide the highest concentration of students falling within the targeted range of birth dates for generation Z. To facilitate data collection, the authors further narrowed the research population by targeting 12 freshman orientation courses scheduled for both a library orientation/tour and a follow-up bibliographic/library instruction session (most freshman orientation courses receive only the orientation/tour); the rosters of these particular freshman orientation courses included *only* first-time freshman. While the resulting population may not be representative of all generation Z students, the pilot nature of the current study, time constraints connected to the academic calendar, and issues concerning accessibility of a viable student sample necessitated this convenience sampling of students.

Data Collection

As stated, the focus of the study is to examine how the information assumptions of generation Z students adhere to or deviate from Dervin's ten information assumptions, or, as labeled by Donald O. Case, "Dervin's Ten Myths about Information."[21] To test generation Z's information assumptions, the authors created a 24-question survey using Dervin's ten assumptions—or, more specifically, Case's 2002 reimagining of Dervin's assumptions—as a framework. While based on Dervin's work, these questions were not taken directly from Dervin's original research questions. Those questions were uniquely formulated to assess the information-seeking and sense-making behaviors of Dervin's specific study populations and also were too exhaustive for the authors' pilot study. Rather, in the spirit of the experiential nature of the pilot study, the authors formulated the questions based upon their cumulative experiences in relation to Dervin's ten assumptions, modifying based on feedback from institutional library colleagues. The authors propose that the survey questions be revisited following the pilot study to reassess the effectiveness of each question in gauging adherence to or deviation from Dervin's assumptions, which is reflected in the discussion and results section of this paper. Each survey question was presented as a statement about information and/or research, and respondents were asked to indicate the degree to which they agree or disagree with the statements, based on their own assumptions and experiences, using a seven-point Likert scale (see Appendix 5A).

The authors solicited the assistance and approval of the 11 teaching faculty assigned to the targeted 12 freshman orientation courses. The eight teaching faculty who consented to allow their students to participate in the study assisted with the research by distributing a survey packet containing the questionnaire and an informed consent form to students a week prior to the second library visit, with instructions to return the packet during the second library visit. Completion of the research instrument was strictly voluntary and, apart from requesting date-of-birth information from each respondent in order to limit to the authors' definition of generation Z (only students born in or after 1994 were included), the authors collected no personally identifiable information in the context of the study. Further, informed consent forms were separated from surveys before data entry and analysis.

Data Analysis

Data analyses comprised the following steps: collecting the surveys; verifying the entry of the requisite date of birth and completion of each survey to be included in the pool; entering data obtained from the surveys into Excel spreadsheets; using Excel formulas to calculate percentages of students who responded to each question with *totally disagree* (1), *moderately disagree* (2), *slightly disagree* (3), *neither agree nor disagree* (4), *slightly agree* (5), *moderately agree* (6), or *totally agree* (7); and analyzing and drawing conclusions from the data collected. Responses on the Likert scale (1–7) were tabulated and generalized into three categories: *disagree* (1–3), *neutral* (4), and *agree* (5–7), while still preserving the granularity of the individual one through seven responses.

Of the 87 completed surveys, eight were disqualified because the respondents' birthdates were prior to 1994, six were disqualified because the respondents did not list a birthdate, and 73 fell within the delineated age parameters, leaving N=73. Nine respondents failed to fully complete the survey by answering all 24 questions. These surveys were not disqualified, but to preserve the validity of the sample, analysis of the questions left blank was adjusted to take into account this lower number of respondents.

Limitations

Broadly speaking, generation Z is described within this study and in much of the external literature as having lived in an ever hyper-connected world from birth; however, such definitions fail to adequately consider variables such as socioeconomic status, gender, ethnicity, language, education, or cultural or ethnic and religious differences. Due to the experiential, pilot nature of the current study and to accommodate the time constraints and concerns of the faculty and classrooms in which the study was executed, the authors consciously chose to collect and consider only the age of participants and forgo any investigation into mitigating factors beyond age. The authors did not intend to evaluate the survey questions in a quantitative or statistical manner in this initial pilot study. Rather, the authors anticipated seeing recurring generation-based themes emerge in relation to Dervin's Ten Myths about Information and information seeking through a qualitative and descriptive analysis, presenting opportunities for more in-depth research in the future. Given the lack of demographic data beyond birthdates, the diversity inherent in all generational groups, the differences between EKU's demographics in relation to other institutions, and the small sample population, we would be remiss in assuming our findings could be used to make comprehensive generalizations about generation Z. As such, the authors acknowledge the sample population may not be representative of all generation Z students. Regardless of these limitations, however, important findings and themes do arise. While this research is only a sampling into generation Z's assumptions about information, the analyses and recommendations add to the understanding of gen Z students and serve as an entry point for a broader, more diverse conversation.

Discussion and Results

Students' cumulative responses were mapped to Dervin's Ten Myths about Information to determine to what degree, if any, the information assumptions held by this group of generation Z students deviated from each of the ten myths about information and information seeking (see Appendix 5B). The results are discussed in the following sections.

Myth #1: Only "Objective" Information Is Valuable

An information literate student knows how to find information and ascertain if it is credible, accurate, and reliable, all while identifying which sources should be avoided because of inaccurate or simply irrelevant information. Such critical thinking skills also attribute to the ability to understand the significance of sources that do not adhere to objectivity. In fact, many experienced researchers and scholars reject the assumption that *only* objective information is valuable. Recognizing that true objectivity cannot be achieved and that all sources are created under and carry with them certain biases, such sophisticated researchers understand that objective and even seemingly biased information can be of use if carefully evaluated and considered in the proper context, situation, and application. To test this assumption in generation Z students, the authors asked participants to consider statement 18, "Editorials and other opinion-based pieces are useful," and statement one, "Only information based on research is credible." Survey results show that while some generation Z students seem to be transitioning beyond this assumption, the percentage of respondents that adhere to this assumption—or myth—remains substantial. Nearly 51 percent of respondents agree that only information based on research is credible, while roughly 32 percent disagree. Contrarily, 50 percent agree that editorials and other opinion-based pieces are useful.

The authors recognize that gen-Zers may misconstrue the purpose of statement one, answering in a way they presume librarians and faculty want them to, particularly in the context of their experiences with academic assignments (the design of which often stipulates a need for more scholarly, research-based information sources). Even so, statement 18 suggests that generation Z's experiences with blogs and other social media have inculcated a familiarity and confidence in parsing opinion-based sources. This may be leading generation Z to transition to the understanding held by most experienced researchers or scholars: While research-based information is often of higher quality and is generally more reliable, especially when researching and conversing in a scholarly milieu, opinion-based or seemingly biased information can be useful if evaluated and used with a critical eye. Nevertheless, the vast amount of information available to gen-Zers in the digital environment requires constant examination and (re)evaluation; thus, librarians and faculty must not ignore the individual assumptions and skill levels of the students with whom they work. Rather, librarians and faculty should be mindful of this dilemma and provide guidance through formal learning activities, such as instruction in information literacy and research practices that look beyond categorizing information as simply "black and white" to acknowledge those "gray areas," in order to encourage critical thinking.

Myth #2: More Information Is Always Better

Gen-Zers may embrace the abundance of information available in their highly connected, digital world, considering 74 percent of respondents agree with statement ten that "you should keep searching even when the first few sources on a topic seem to answer the question or help complete an assignment," but student responses to related statements suggest they might not know just what to do with all that information once they have it. For example, gen-Zers were divided about how to handle information saturation, with 64 percent disagreeing with statement 17 that "it is sometimes difficult to choose what information to keep and what information to toss" when researching, and 48 percent agreeing with statement 22, "The more information I find, the more overwhelmed I feel." These responses confirm that the "more information is better" assumption is still strong with generation Z, while presenting the troubling conclusion that many students are ill-equipped to cope with the modern day glut of information. The authors acknowledge students might self-report a propensity to search beyond the first few seemingly "correct" sources to please authority figures, such as faculty and librarians, who have reminded them to "look beyond the first few pages of a Google search." Perhaps in reality many students do just that—stop at page one of any search. Regardless, these findings, coupled with gen-Z's self-reported difficulty and anxiety in evaluating and sifting through information, are still quite insightful and should be applied to our reference and instructional services.

For example, assumptions and approaches that advocate a focus on the amount of information fail to recognize the individual need, situation, and context of the user, thus reverting back to approaches that focus on "the artifacts and venues of information seeking" while ignoring *why* and *how* students select and apply information.[22] Most librarians and faculty consider themselves experienced searchers and, likewise, are often much more sophisticated in their search strategies and ability to formulate and manage information-seeking strategies. For such experts, accustomed to the rigor of scholarly research, more information is almost always better as a comprehensive examination of any research topic is optimal. However, such expert searchers should not forget that each student's individual information need must be considered in light of the context and situation of that need as well as each individual student's prior experiences with incorporating information, information-seeking strategies, and the tools and sources available. As such, we must restructure our services, particularly our reference interactions, to investigate and accommodate the unique information needs, contexts, and situations of our students. Training and assistance in search and evaluation strategies to winnow the most important and relevant information sources from the easily obtained mountains of information now available will be of particular benefit to gen-Zers.

Myth #3: Objective Information Can Be Transmitted Out of Context.

Generally speaking, generation Z understands that "information only has meaning in the context of what a person knows, understands, or creates."[23] For example, 74 percent of respondents disagree with statement seven, "As long as the author is a credible expert on a topic, there is no need to read the entire article/book," and 78 percent disagree with statement two in that "when doing research, it's okay to ignore information that contradicts your opinions." These survey responses indicate gen-Zers understand that while there are individual units of information to glean meaning from and that provide a great deal of meaning within, the context of the entire work and, as such, are dependent on this relationship for significance. Nevertheless, respondents are conflicted in regards to statement 23, "It is acceptable to quote facts out of context to make a point," in that only 43 percent of students disagree with this statement, while 20 percent remain neutral and 37 percent are in agreement.

Mass media and our approaches to educating students about it give this particular assumption a greater impact than first realized. News is now acquired through a variety of sources, including collaborative social networks such as Twitter and Facebook. For this reason, our daily news is "unattached and often without meaning," but it is within the context of what a person knows that information establishes meaning, in that without context, information becomes irrelevant. While gen-Zers understand the nature of context and its importance, this does not deter them from isolating facts to make a point. Given the contradictory assertions made in this assumption, librarians and faculty should be conscious of the need to support our students in critical thinking and reinforce these rules and values as early and as often as possible in the future. Encouraging students to evaluate what they encounter in mass media and our educational system further demands an altered approach to instruction, one that goes beyond simply communicating information to ultimately instructing students on how to become informed, critical thinkers.[24]

Myth #4: Information Can Only Be Acquired through Formal Sources

Student responses confirm generation Z no longer assumes that information can only be acquired through formal sources. In fact, when asked to agree or disagree with statement 11, "When researching, it is ok to use information you find on-line," 82 percent agree, while 51 percent disagree with statement 15 that "sources found in the library are all you need to answer your question or complete an assignment," thus reflecting a similar sentiment. Encouragingly, 69 percent of respondents report a healthy skepticism of informal sources by disagreeing with statement 21, "I find friends, family members, and classmates more useful than authors, professors, or scientists," although 61 percent agree with statement 16, "I use Google, *Wikipedia*, blogs, and social media more often than I use library databases, reference books, or other library sources." Such responses indicated that gen-Zers tend to rely on a diverse set of formal and informal information to satisfy their needs; however, survey questions were not designed to calculate how critically students evaluate their sources.

While gen-Zers appear to be moving beyond the assumption that information can be acquired only through formal sources, many faculty and librarians reinforce this assumption in their academic interactions with students. Faced with undergraduate "Google" papers filled with low-quality informal sources, many faculty strictly regulate or forbid the use of informal sources in student papers to ensure a higher level of source quality, and many librarians focus almost exclusively on formal tools and sources (e.g., subscription databases, library catalogs, and scholarly literature and presses) when assisting or teaching students. As our students become more comfortable and immersed in the less formal free web environment, and as the abundance of varying qualities of freely available, easily accessible information increases in such environments, the role of faculty and, particularly, librarians as supporters and facilitators of information literacy becomes progressively critical. Gen-Z's information environment necessitates librarians and faculty to foster in students the skills necessary to evaluate information contextually "in the wild," so to speak, rather than exclusively teaching students to rely on the tools, limiters, and lexicon of academia's formal sources and tools.

Myth #5: There Is Relevant Information for Every Need

To test this assumption, the authors asked participants to consider statement three, "I can always find exactly what I need when searching for information online or in the library." Analysis of the survey question revealed that 60 percent of respondents agree, indicating generation Z students continue to assert the assumption that "there is relevant information for every need" and remain committed to the notion that information is available for *every* problem. This reflects an "amateurish" overconfidence, not informed by experience or, perhaps, informed only by experience researching relatively simple and close-ended topics and augmented by movies and pop culture trumpeting "everything you ever wanted to know is one Google search away," not to mention slick advertising personifying the omnipotence of technology—just ask Siri!

One can speculate that our digitally native, wired gen-Zers might be even more susceptible to this notion than their predecessors, considering the sometimes ambiguous nature and wealth of information available to students in the digital environment. Faculty and librarians are often at ground zero with students during the search process and are well positioned to reinforce that many topics have not been fully explored. It is also important to remember that the capabilities of the faculty member as the expert researcher and the capabilities of the undergraduate as the novice researcher are often at a disjuncture, provided that most gen-Zers have not attained the level of cognitive development required to comfortably deal with the ambiguity of academic research and "do not think in terms of information-seeking strategy, but rather in terms of a coping strategy."[25] The perception that research is simply a means to an end, needed only to complete coursework, contributes to the sanguine feelings of gen-Zers; however, more experienced researchers and scholars understand that research is a method of inquiry and discovery as well. To that end, information professionals must remain mindful of student assumptions as future generation Z students may illustrate an even stronger shift toward this notion as technology continues to saturate their everyday lives, compounding these natural and developmentally common tendencies.

Myth #6: Every Need Situation Has a Solution

The inherent flaw of this assumption is that information alone will not meet every need because *every* need does not have a single clear, established solution; nevertheless, 65 percent of student respondents continue to agree with statement four that "there is an answer to every question—you just have to find it." The magnitude and availability of digital information coaxes students into a false assumption that a resolution can be found with a simple click or swipe of the finger, but students fail to understand that the Internet is becoming so expansive that is it difficult to organize, let alone search. Results from subsequent survey questions illustrate divergence, considering that gen-Zers are torn on the assumption illustrated in statement six, "If I cannot find an answer to my question or sources for an assignment, I must be doing something wrong." Responses are divided almost evenly, with 43 percent disagreeing and nearly 31 percent agreeing with this statement. For this reason, we can assume that our information-rich environment incites doubt in gen-Zers about their ability to find and access information. This indicates that some students may understand that solutions to our problems are not always found in formal systems like the library or the less formal World Wide Web—occasionally, solutions must be carefully crafted by the individual, informed by an arsenal of information, rather than easily and simply plucked directly from an information source. Additionally, librarians and faculty oftentimes also fail to understand that a student's problem cannot always be answered using only conventional resources. Sometimes students are not looking for a solution that comes in a clean, canned response, even though our systems strive to package information as such. As professionals, we must rid ourselves of our own assumptions before we can help students move beyond their assumptions, thus offering our students the freedom necessary to investigate information and seek solutions in and from diverse sources and places while encouraging and supporting them in applying critical thinking skills in crafting their own solutions from the information at hand.

Myth #7: It Is Always Possible to Make Information Available or Accessible

While generation Z is truly a generation of "digital natives" who have never known a world without the Internet, smartphones, and iPads, we do not live in a perfectly ordered universe in which information that is not available or accessible can be made so at whim.[26] Student responses illustrate a divide, in that only half (51 percent) of the respondents agree with statement 12, "I can always find and access information I need" and 62 percent with statement 20, "Any information I could possible need is available locally or online." The majority of generation Z students believe that our digital environment creates an open arena for information, with accessibility easy to institute and maintain at all times; however, while digital resources allude to a plethora of information, the needed information may not always be available. Nevertheless, we can ascertain that generation Z students are beginning to deviate from the foregoing assumption. Results illustrate that some gen-Zers understand that information systems are limited due to our constantly changing needs, given that one-third of responders (29 percent) dispute the assumption of an open, ever-accessible information environment.

While information professionals understand the fault in this assumption, libraries are also inadvertently strengthening student assumptions concerning ubiquitous availability and accessibility through the establishment of "just-in-time" models. For example, patron-driven requests through interlibrary loan have increased accessibility and availability to materials, in turn reinforcing the idea that information is *always* available or accessible. In addition to an awareness of the effect of the free, open web, librarians must also maintain an awareness of the effect interlibrary loan and just-in-time models have on student perceptions of availability and accessibility. Further, they must be prepared to explain why some information is difficult—and sometimes nearly impossible—to access, even with these just-in-time services, whether those reasons are tied up in translation or transcription barriers, journal embargos, or when the answer simply does not exist.

Myth #8: Functional Units of Information, Such as Books or TV Programs, Always Fit the Needs of Individuals

An impressive majority (over 95 percent) of students surveyed agree with statement five, "Sometimes what I need might not exist in one place—I might have to use several sources to answer one question," lending credence to the idea that gen-Zers recognize the flaws inherent in assuming that predetermined information packages set by authors, publishers, vendors, or even libraries always translate easily and cleanly to the individual's information needs. Surprising, then, is the realization that students were more divided in regards to statement 13, "I should be able to find one perfect source to answer any question I might have." While 50 percent of students surveyed disagree with this statement, presenting a similar tone as that set with statement five, the other 50 percent either agree (29 percent) or are unsure or neutral (21 percent) in relation to the idea that "one source should do it all." The relatively high percentage of students demonstrating agreement or uncertainty about statement 13 might give librarians and faculty cause for pause. However, upon further reflection, the authors recognize that statement five might be leading students, as librarians and faculty alike often impress on students to "go beyond the first page of the Google results." It is possible, then, that many students answered in the affirmative to statement five because they knew their authority figure—their classroom instructor and class librarian—would expect them to investigate multiple sources before settling on an answer, rather than because they truly agree with the statement. While the authors cannot say for certain, it is therefore also possible that gen-Zers adhere to the faulty assumption that there exists one (or perhaps a couple?) perfect piece of information for every possible need and that those pieces of information are functional and useful as presented, requiring no additional work or thought on the part of the individual information consumer.

Additional research is necessary to make any definitive statement about student assumptions as they relate to information units, which might also require that the authors revisit and revise the questions used to gauge this particular student assumption. Regardless, librarians and faculty can and should use their instructional platforms and relationships with students to demonstrate the need to evaluate and sift through individual units of information, evaluating what and how to integrate appropriate pieces of larger information units into their own knowledge bases or academic products while simultaneously rethinking the way we create and develop student resources. Further, while intended to gauge student assumptions concerning units of information, statement 13 might also have implications on student assumptions as they relate to Dervin's Myth #5, "There is relevant information for every need," in that it seems to indicate students believe there exists at least one perfect source for every need or question.

Myth #9: Time and Space—Individual Situations—Can Be Ignored in Addressing Information Seeking and Use

The proliferation of and quality enhancements to just-in-time and "at-a-distance" services have alleviated many time and space barriers; however, individual situations, as well as an individual's perception of his or her own situation, shape and define information needs in fundamental ways, and thus must not be ignored. Survey results indicate generation Z students recognize the need to be aware of their own situational constraints, including time and place constraints, in order to meet their information needs: Seventy-eight percent of students surveyed disagree with statement eight, "There is no need to start your research early—any information you might need is freely and readily accessible" (22 percent neutral or agree), while a similar percentage (71 percent) agree with statement 24, "If a book or article is not readily accessible to me, I move on to something I can access now." Similarly, 49 percent of students surveyed disagree with statement number 14, "I accept information that is 'good enough' if it is easily accessible, not necessarily the best information." Yet an alarming percentage of students agree or are uncertain/neutral (33 percent agree, 18 percent neutral). While these results indicate that gen-Zers recognize the need to consider time and space barriers when selecting information, it also suggests that they might resist digging a little deeper or pushing a little harder to find a more suitable, appropriate information source. Librarians and faculty need to be aware of this possibility and encourage students to dig deeper and seek assistance when in doubt.

Additionally, the authors recognize potential flaws with the statements used to gauge student assumptions in this area. First, similar to statement five, it is possible that students responded to statement eight in a way they believe their authority figures would approve of, considering librarians and faculty alike encourage students to "start early" to avoid stress and possible "information roadblocks." Second, the authors again recognize that, while intended to gauge student assumptions concerning time and space and individual situations, statement 24 might have also implications for Dervin's Myth #7, "It is always possible to make information available or accessible," in that it could imply a deviation from this assumption, indicating students realize not all information is readily or easily available and accessible.

Myth #10: People Make Easy, Conflict-Free Connections between External Information and Their Internal Reality

An ordered world in which our personal reality is perfectly aligned to the external information we encounter does not exist. The connections that our students make between external information and their internal realities illustrate how people inform themselves and the conflicts that arise when these two realities differ.[27] Highly connected, technophile gen-Zers may embrace this conflict more frequently than students who are less digitally connected, considering the seamlessness and ease with which transitioning between online and offline worlds exposes them to information contrary to their own beliefs. In fact, student survey responses in this area illustrate that gen-Zers acknowledge the need to weigh and evaluate information, both within the context of what they believe to be true and in relation to additional external information. Seventy-three percent of students surveyed disagree with statement 19, "When I encounter information that differs from what I believe, I immediately feel that the information is wrong and I don't use it," while 59 percent responded in the affirmative to statement 24, "When I encounter information that differs from what I believe, it makes me want to research more," indicating that this new connected generation maintains a healthy skepticism in regards to external information but is also aware of personal assumptions and works to keep these assumptions in check when evaluating new or foreign information.

While the implications are certainly encouraging, suggesting students are moving beyond the assumption that engaging with information is "easy," the data should not be misconstrued as a recommendation that librarians and faculty no longer need to be concerned with assisting students in developing the critical thinking intrinsic in the acquisition and development of information literacy skills. Gen-Zers recognize that conflict may exist between their internal realities and external information; however, it is likely they may still struggle with the application and incorporation of external information into their own internal realities.

Conclusion

Generation Z students have lived their entire lives with instant access to information on nearly any topic imaginable. These students are the most connected and diverse in our history and are using technology in ways never thought possible.

Implications for libraries, universities, and higher education remain to be seen, but we must prepare ourselves for the significant impact generation Z will have on academia. Early research into information seeking and beliefs about information advocated for a user-centered, service-oriented approach to library services. Even so, students and academic faculty and staff continue to look for standard answers from the "right" and "objective" source, believing that, if we only search long enough and wade through enough information, we will discover the proverbial gold at the end of the rainbow; in reality, the search for information is no rainbow and that pot of gold may not be exactly as we hope.[28] An analysis of the survey data reveals gen-Zers deviate from Dervin's ten assumptions of information in significant ways. Nevertheless, students continue to exhibit some of the same fundamentally flawed ideologies of their predecessors. Student information assumptions—as well as librarian and faculty assumptions about student information assumptions—have interfered with our ability to fully focus on the individual information needs, contexts, and situations of our students, a problem with the potential to become ever more prevalent as tech-focused, information-saturated gen-Zers advance into higher education.

Dervin advocated that information professionals, such as librarians, apply sense-making as a methodology, thus bypassing and overcoming the allure of such assumptions by asking neutral, rather than closed or even open, questions. Such questions allow the librarian to see past the user's stated need to the nature of the underlying situations, the possible gaps faced by the user, and the expected uses informing the user's need and information assumptions.[29] The authors agree, believing that such an intentional, focused approach to discovering the underlying information gaps and assumptions of our students is more vital now than ever with the incoming class of tech-focused, information-saturated gen-Zers. Further, the authors recognize that the study's sample size is relatively small in comparison to the larger generation Z population; the study population might be less tech-savvy or information-saturated than its peer populations, especially considering EKU's largely rural service region; and that, beyond age, little is known about the demographics of the study population—all of which impact the generalizability of the results. In response, the authors propose that research into larger, more diverse and digitally immersed populations of gen-Zers could reveal even more drastic deviations from Dervin's Ten Myths about Information, and acknowledge that other factors not addressed in this pilot study—students' educational preparedness, L1/L2 or ESL status, socioeconomic factors, gender differences, etc.—should be considered in order to fully explore adherence to or deviation from Dervin's Myths. Regardless, additional research and attention to the ways generation Z interacts with and develops beliefs about information is necessary to ensure that we do not leave our students behind in terms of information literacy as they move forward in an increasingly connected, ever-changing, information-rich environment.

Acknowledgments

The authors would like to thank the following individuals, without whose contributions and support this would not have been possible: Karen Gilbert, Jeremy Turner, John Hearn, and Eastern Kentucky University's wonderful Learning Community GSD instructors.

Appendix 5A.
Survey Instrument
Generation Z: Information Facts and Fictions

Date of Birth:_____

Below is a list of statements about information and research. Please read each statement carefully and indicate the degree to which you agree or disagree with it. Please respond as honestly and objectively as you can. Use the following scale:

Totally Disagree	Moderately Disagree	Slightly Disagree	Neither Agree nor Disagree	Slightly Agree	Moderately Agree	Totally Agree
1	2	3	4	5	6	7

1.	Only information based on research is credible.	1	2	3	4	5	6	7
2.	When doing research, it's okay to ignore information that contradicts your opinions.	1	2	3	4	5	6	7
3.	I can always find exactly what I need when searching for information online or in the library.	1	2	3	4	5	6	7
4.	There is an answer to every question—you just have to find it.	1	2	3	4	5	6	7
5.	Sometimes what I need might not exist in one place—I might have to use several sources to answer one question.	1	2	3	4	5	6	7
6.	If I cannot find an answer to my question or sources for an assignment, I must be doing something wrong.	1	2	3	4	5	6	7
7.	As long as the author is a credible expert on the topic, there is no need to read an entire book/article.	1	2	3	4	5	6	7
8.	There is no need to start your research extra early—any information you might need is freely and readily accessible.	1	2	3	4	5	6	7
9.	When I encounter information that differs from what I believe, it makes me want to research more.	1	2	3	4	5	6	7
10.	You should keep searching even when the first few sources seem to answer the question or help complete an assignment.	1	2	3	4	5	6	7
11.	When researching, it is okay to use information you find online.	1	2	3	4	5	6	7
12.	I can always find and access the information I need.	1	2	3	4	5	6	7

13.	I should be able to find one perfect source to answer any question I might have.	1 2 3 4 5 6 7
14.	I accept information that is "good enough" if it is easily accessible, not necessarily the best information.	1 2 3 4 5 6 7
15.	Sources found in the library are all you need to answer your question or complete an assignment.	1 2 3 4 5 6 7
16.	I use Google, Wikipedia, blogs, and social media more often than I use library databases, reference books, or other library sources.	1 2 3 4 5 6 7
17.	It is sometimes difficult to choose what information to keep and what information to toss.	1 2 3 4 5 6 7
18.	Editorials and other opinion-based pieces are useful.	1 2 3 4 5 6 7
19.	When I encounter information that differs from what I believe, I immediately feel that the information is wrong and I don't use it.	1 2 3 4 5 6 7
20.	Any information I could possibly need is available locally or online.	1 2 3 4 5 6 7
21.	I find friends, family members, and classmates more useful than authors, professors, or scientists.	1 2 3 4 5 6 7
22.	When searching for information, the more information I find, the more overwhelmed I feel.	1 2 3 4 5 6 7
23.	It is acceptable to quote facts out of context to make a point.	1 2 3 4 5 6 7
24.	If a book or article is not readily available to me, I move on to something I can access now.	1 2 3 4 5 6 7

Appendix 5B.
Survey Questions and Results Mapped to Dervin's Ten Myths about Information
Generation Z: Information Facts and Fictions
Survey Questions and Results Mapped to Dervin's Ten Myths about Information

1. Only "objective" information is valuable.

1. Only information based on research is credible.

	DISAGREE			NEUTRAL	AGREE		
	1	2	3	4	5	6	7
Total	5	7	11	13	23	11	3
Percentage	6.85%	9.59%	15%	17.81%	31.51%	15%	4.11%
		31.51%				50.68%	

18. Editorials and other opinion-based pieces are useful.

	DISAGREE			NEUTRAL	AGREE		
	1	2	3	4	5	6	7
Total	2	2	12	19	25	8	2
Percentage	3%	3%	17%	27%	36%	11%	3%
		23%				50%	

2. More information is always better.

10. You should keep searching even when the first few sources on a topic seem to answer the question or help complete an assignment.

	DISAGREE			NEUTRAL	AGREE		
	1	2	3	4	5	6	7
Total	2	2	4	11	31	17	6
Percentage	3%	3%	5%	15%	42%	23%	8%
		11%				74%	

22. When searching for information, the more information I find, the more overwhelmed I feel.

	DISAGREE			NEUTRAL	AGREE		
	1	2	3	4	5	6	7
Total	4	6	15	13	23	8	4
Percentage	5%	8%	21%	18%	32%	11%	5%
		34%				48%	

17. It is sometimes difficult to choose what information to keep and what information to toss.

	DISAGREE			NEUTRAL	AGREE		
	1	2	3	4	5	6	7
Total	2	0	6	18	28	15	4
Percentage	3%	0%	8%	25%	38%	21%	5%
		11%				64%	

3. Objective information can be transmitted out of context.

7. As long as the author is a credible expert on a topic, there is no need to read the entire article/book.

	DISAGREE			NEUTRAL	AGREE		
	1	2	3	4	5	6	7
Total	7	18	28	10	6	3	0
Percentage	10%	25%	39%	14%	8%	4%	0%
		74%				13%	

2. When doing research, it's okay to ignore information that contradicts your opinions.

	DISAGREE			NEUTRAL	AGREE		
	1	2	3	4	5	6	7
Total	28	19	10	7	6	3	0
Percentage	38.36%	26%	13.70%	9.59%	8.22%	4.11%	0
		78.08%				12.33%	

23. It is acceptable to quote facts out of context to make a point.

	DISAGREE			NEUTRAL	AGREE		
	1	2	3	4	5	6	7
Total	13	9	11	13	11	10	6
Percentage	18%	12%	15%	18%	15%	14%	8%
		45%				37%	

4. Information can only be acquired through formal sources.

11. When researching, it is okay to use information you find online.

	DISAGREE			NEUTRAL	AGREE		
	1	2	3	4	5	6	7
Total	0	2	3	8	17	27	15
Percentage	0%	3%	4%	11%	24%	38%	21%
		7%				82%	

15. Sources found in the library are all you need to answer your question or complete an assignment.

	DISAGREE			NEUTRAL	AGREE		
	1	2	3	4	5	6	7
Total	6	14	17	10	11	4	1
Percentage	8%	19%	24%	14%	15%	6%	1%
		51%				22%	

21. I find friends, family members, and classmates more useful than authors, professors, or scientists.

	DISAGREE			NEUTRAL	AGREE		
	1	2	3	4	5	6	7
Total	15	14	20	12	7	2	1
Percentage	21%	20%	28%	17%	10%	3%	1%
		69%				14%	

16. I use Google, *Wikipedia*, blogs, and social media more often than I use library databases, reference books, or other library sources.

	DISAGREE			NEUTRAL	AGREE		
	1	2	3	4	5	6	7
Total	6	9	6	7	16	11	17
Percentage	8%	13%	8%	10%	22%	15%	24%
		29%				61%	

5. There is relevant information for every need.

3. I can always find exactly what I need when searching for information online or in the library.

	DISAGREE			NEUTRAL	AGREE		
	1	2	3	4	5	6	7
Total	1	5	7	16	20	16	8
Percentage	1.37%	6.85%	9.59%	21.92%	27.40%	21.92%	10.96%
		17.81%				60.27%	

6. Every need situation has a solution.

6. If I cannot find an answer to my question or sources for an assignment, I must be doing something wrong.

	DISAGREE			NEUTRAL	AGREE		
	1	2	3	4	5	6	7
Total	4	13	14	19	15	7	0
Percentage	5.56%	18.06%	19.44%	26%	21%	9.72%	0
		43.06%				30.56%	

4. There is an answer to every question—you just have to find it.

	DISAGREE			NEUTRAL	AGREE		
	1	2	3	4	5	6	7
Total	2	2	12	10	19	14	14
Percentage	2.74%	2.74%	16.44%	14%	26%	19.18%	19.18%
		21.92%				64.38%	

7. It is always possible to make information available or accessible.

12. I can always find and access the information I need.

	DISAGREE			NEUTRAL	AGREE		
	1	2	3	4	5	6	7
Total	2	2	16	14	19	10	6
Percentage	3%	3%	23%	20%	28%	14%	9%
		29%				51%	

20. Any information I could possibly need is available locally or online.

	DISAGREE			NEUTRAL	AGREE		
	1	2	3	4	5	6	7
Total	1	5	7	15	26	11	8
Percentage	1%	7%	10%	21%	36%	15%	11%
		18%				62%	

8. Functional units of information, such as books or TV programs, always fit the needs of individuals.

5. Sometimes what I need might not exist in one place—I might have to use several sources to answer one question.

	DISAGREE			NEUTRAL	AGREE		
	1	2	3	4	5	6	7
Total	0	0	1	2	18	22	30
Percentage	0%	0%	1%	2.74%	24.66%	30.14%	41%
		1%				95.89%	

13. I should be able to find one perfect source to answer any question I might have.

	DISAGREE			NEUTRAL	AGREE		
	1	2	3	4	5	6	7
Total	8	15	13	15	13	5	3
Percentage	11%	21%	18%	21%	18%	7%	4%
		50%				29%	

9. Time and space—individual situations—can be ignored in addressing information seeking and use.

8. There is no need to start your research extra early—any information you might need is freely and readily accessible.

	DISAGREE			NEUTRAL	AGREE		
	1	2	3	4	5	6	7
Total	17	24	16	8	7	1	0
Percentage	23%	33%	22%	11%	10%	1%	0%
		78%				11%	

24. If a book or article is not readily available to me, I move on to something I can access now.

	DISAGREE			NEUTRAL	AGREE		
	1	2	3	4	5	6	7
Total	2	2	6	13	25	16	9
Percentage	3%	3%	8%	18%	34%	22%	12%
		14%				68%	

14. I accept information that is "good enough" if it is easily accessible, not necessarily the best information.

	DISAGREE			NEUTRAL	AGREE		
	1	2	3	4	5	6	7
Total	3	15	17	13	13	6	5
Percentage	4%	21%	24%	18%	18%	8%	7%
		49%				33%	

10. People make easy, conflict-free connections between external information and their internal reality.

19. When I encounter information that differs from what I believe, I immediately feel that the information is wrong and I don't use it.

	DISAGREE			NEUTRAL	AGREE		
	1	2	3	4	5	6	7
Total	16	16	21	11	8	1	0
Percentage	22%	22%	29%	15%	11%	1%	0%
		73%				12%	

9. When I encounter information that differs from what I believe, it makes me want to research more.

	DISAGREE			NEUTRAL	AGREE		
	1	2	3	4	5	6	7
Total	3	5	4	18	25	15	3
Percentage	4%	7%	5%	25%	34%	21%	4%
		16%				59%	

Notes

1. Donald O. Case, *Looking for Information: A Survey of Research on Information Seeking, Needs, and Behavior* (San Diego, CA: Academic Press, 2002), 6.

2. Ibid.

3. Neil Howe and William Strauss, *Millennials Rising: The Next Great Generation* (New York: Vintage Books, 2000), 370; Pew Research Center, *Millennials: A Portrait of Generation Next*, accessed November 18, 2013, http://www.pewsocialtrends.org/files/2010/10/millennials-confident-connected-open-to-change.pdf; Eric H. Greenberg and Karl Weber, *Generation We: How Millennial Youth Are Taking Over America and Changing Our World Forever* (Emeryville, CA: Pachatusan, 2008), http://gen-we.com/sites/default/files/GenWe_EntireBook3.pdf.

4. Graham Coulson, Kathryn Ray, and Linda Banwell, "The Need for a Converged Approach to EIS Provision? Evidence from the JUBILEE Project," *Library Review* 52, no. 9 (2003): 438–43; Educational Testing Service, *2006 ICT Literacy Assessment: Preliminary Findings*, accessed March 14, 2014, http://www.ets.org/Media/Products/ICT_Literacy/pdf/2006_Preliminary_Findings.pdf; David Nicholas, Ian Rowlands, and Paul Huntington, *Information Behaviour of the Researcher of the Future, Executive Summary: A CIBER Briefing Paper*, accessed March 14, 2014, http://www.jisc.ac.uk/media/documents/programmes/reppres/gg_final_keynote_11012008.pdf; Alison J. Head and Michael Eisenberg, *Truth Be Told: How College Students Evaluate and Use Information in the Digital Age*, accessed August 14, 2014, http://projectinfolit.org/images/pdfs/pil_fall2010_survey_fullreport1.pdf; Andrew D. Asher and Lynda M. Duke, "Searching for Answers: Student Research Behavior at Illinois Wesleyan University," in *College Libraries and Student Culture: What We Now Know*, ed. Lynda M. Duke and Andrew D. Asher (Chicago: American Library Association Editions, 2011), 71–85.

5. Lourdes Rodriguez and Francisco Cano, "The Learning Approaches and Epistemological Beliefs of University Students: A Cross-Sectional and Longitudinal Study," *Studies in Higher Education* 32, no. 5 (2007): 647.

6. Michael B. Paulson and Charles T. Wells, "Domain Differences in the Epistemological Beliefs of College Students," *Research in Higher Education* 39, no. 4 (1998): 366.

7. William G. Perry, *Forms of Intellectual and Ethical Development in the College Years: A Scheme* (New York: Holt, Rinehart and Winston, 1970), 16.

8. Mary Field Belenky et al., *Women's Ways of Knowing: the Development of Self, Voice, and Mind* (New York: Basic Books, 1997), 15.

9. Marcia B. Baxter Magolda, *Knowing and Reasoning in College: Gender-Related Patterns in Students' Intellectual Development* (San Francisco: Jossey-Bass, 1992), 70.

10. Barbara K. Hofer and Paul R. Pintrich, "The Development of Epistemological Theories:

Beliefs about Knowledge and Knowing and Their Relation to Learning," *Review of Educational Research* 67, no. 1 (Spring 1997): 98.

11.   Baxter Magolda, *Knowing and Reasoning*, 138.

12.   Patricia M. King and Karen Strohm Kitchener, *Developing Reflective Judgment: Understanding and Promoting Intellectual Growth and Critical Thinking in Adolescents and Adults* (San Francisco: Jossey-Bass Publishers, 1994), 13.

13.   Ibid., 66.

14.   Brenda Dervin, "On Studying Information Seeking Methodologically: The Implications of Connecting Metatheory to Method," *Information Processing and Management* 35, no. 6 (1999).

15.   Brenda Dervin, "Strategies for Dealing with Human Information Needs: Information or Communication?" *Journal of Broadcasting and Electronic Media* 20, no. 3 (1976): 323–33.

16.   Case, *Looking for Information*, 8–9.

17.   Dervin, "Strategies for Dealing with Human Information Needs."

18.   "About EKU," Eastern Kentucky University, accessed November 18, 2013, http://www.eku.edu/about.

19.   "Factbook Report—Enrollment by Kentucky County," Eastern Kentucky University: Office of Institutional Research, accessed November 17, 2013, https://irserver.eku.edu/Reports/Factbook/Files/FB000000011.html.

20.   "Eastern Kentucky University Fast Facts," Eastern Kentucky University: Office of Institutional Research, accessed November 17, 2013, https://irserver.eku.edu/Reports/Factbook/Files/FastFacts/Fall%202012.pdf.

21.   Case, *Looking for Information*, 7.

22.   Case, *Looking for Information*, 6.

23.   Dervin, "Strategies for Dealing with Human Information Needs," 328.

24.   Ibid., 329.

25.   Gloria Leckie, "Desperately Seeking Citations: Uncovering Faculty Assumptions about the Undergraduate Research Process," *The Journal of Academic Librarianship* 22, no. 3 (1996): 203.

26.   Dervin, "Strategies for Dealing with Human Information Needs," 330.

27.   Case, *Looking for Information*, 9.

28.   Dervin, "Strategies for Dealing with Human Information Needs," 324.

29.   Brenda Dervin and Patricia Dewdney, "Neutral Questioning: A New Approach to the Reference Interview," *Research Quarterly* 25, no. 4 (1986): 7.

CHAPTER 6

Search Epistemology: Teaching Students about Information Discovery

Andrew D. Asher

For today's university students, effectively searching for and locating information are critical digital literacy skills. Unfortunately, while students often have a variety of powerful search tools at their disposal, they also regularly lack an understanding of how these tools work and the particular strengths, limitations, and biases these tools might contain. As students work within an information environment that is increasingly open and dynamically changing, searching for the information required to complete research assignments represents a complex and potentially daunting task, and one that is fraught with embedded social and cultural processes and relationships. Because search is such a fundamental component of students' research and writing processes, the various tools and systems students use to complete these searches can also profoundly affect how students acquire information and synthesize knowledge.

This epistemological dimension of search has entwined technological and sociocultural components that together structure and shape how students navigate information environments. Using qualitative and quantitative data collected from over 200 students at six universities, this chapter empirically examines the practices of students as they locate information across a variety of search platforms (including "traditional" library catalogs and research databases, EBSCO Discovery Service, Summon, Google, and Google Scholar) and critically evaluates the potential for bias to be introduced into these processes.[1]

The following chapter will argue that students' experience with Google has structured their expectations for library search tools and that these expectations engender particular search behaviors that privilege the role of the search tool itself in evaluating information quality. In particular, students' tendencies to emphasize the value of highly ranked materials, to rely on the default settings of a search tool, and to iterate search terms rather than refine results, create a situation in which the evaluation of materials is principally performed by search tools' relevancy ranking algorithms. These practices leave students vulnerable to biases embedded within search systems that can affect the types of information they find and utilize in ways that can be directly observed. Unfortunately, very few students are aware of these potential biases and how they might be subtlety structuring their acquisition of knowledge.

Because students typically do not have an adequate conceptual understanding of how information is organized and how search systems work, they often treat their interactions with search tools as "magical" experiences and accept search results uncritically. My goal in this chapter is therefore to move beyond user needs analysis by showing how observations of students' search practices illustrate and contribute to the concept of "algorithmic culture" as well as how librarians might respond to the epistemological implications of search tools.

Search and Algorithmic Culture

Following Ted Striphas, I use the term *algorithmic culture* to describe how many aspects of cultural work, such as "the sorting, classifying, hierarchizing, and curating of people, places, objects, and ideas," are becoming the purview of "machine-based information processing systems."[2] Striphas additionally asserts that "some of our most basic habits of thought, conduct, and expression … are coming to be affected by algorithms, too. It's not only that cultural work is becoming algorithmic; cultural *life* is as well."[3] Here, I am particularly interested in the work that search tools' algorithms do for students as they locate and process information for their research assignments and how, in turn, these search tools influence students' habits of thought and expression within their academic practices.

Because they shape the processes through which information is found and, by extension, becomes known, search algorithms perform an epistemological function. Especially in the case of search, *"algorithmic culture* encourages us to see computational process not as a window onto the world but as an instrument of order and authoritative decision making."[4] By structuring the discovery of information, search algorithms express a form of power that profoundly shapes the way students acquire knowledge and complete their academic work.

Search algorithms are also cultural artifacts themselves and can be understood as embodying a set of socially and culturally embedded negotiations, decisions, judgments, and ideologies. For example, Google's search algorithms use a total of more than 200 "signals" to rank every set of results, including measures related to localization, personalization, timeliness, and quality, each of which represents a specific decision about the relative values of information sources.[5] The most well known of these signals is PageRank, a relevancy ranking algorithm premised on a concept of aggregated social judgment, that is, the assumption that a mathematical calculation, based on the number of links to a website combined with an evaluation of the relative importance of the websites from which those links originate, can be used as a proxy for evaluating the quality of a site.[6] Similarly, web-scale library discovery tools, such as EBSCO Discovery Service (EDS) and Summon, use a variety of factors in ranking their search results, including keyword term matching across various types of metadata and evaluations of the characteristics of specific resources.[7] However, unlike Google, neither system currently uses user-level personalization.

Because of these decisions about how information should be retrieved, organized, displayed, and ordered, it is neither logically nor practically possible to create a neutral search tool, despite claims to the contrary made by search providers. Any search system contains and reflects the collective judgments of its engineers and designers. Since removing these biases is impossible, we should therefore seek to understand their features rather than simply criticize their presence. As Siva Vaidhyanathan points out, "All information technologies favor some content or users over others. One cannot design a neutral system. To use technologies wisely, we need to grasp the nature of biases and adjust expectations to accommodate or correct for them. So a declaration or description of bias is not an indictment of a system or a firm. A bias is not necessarily bad: It is necessary."[8]

This chapter will address how these tacitly embedded biases may affect the experience of student researchers by synthesizing data gathered in two major research projects that examined how undergraduate students search for and utilize information for research assignments. Through a detailed analysis of students' search practices, the results of these studies demonstrate the expression of algorithmic culture within students' everyday academic lives.

About the Studies

The Ethnographic Research in Illinois Academic Libraries (ERIAL) Project, was a 21-month research study conducted in 2008–2010 by a consortium of five university libraries: Northeastern Illinois University (NEIU), DePaul University, Illinois Wesleyan University (IWU), the University of Illinois at Chicago (UIC), and the University of Illinois at Springfield (UIS).[9] By employing a variety of anthropological and ethnographic data collection techniques, the ERIAL Project sought to directly observe what students working in a diverse range of institutional contexts actually did while locating information for their research assignments.[10] Altogether, the ERIAL Project included more than 500 students participating in nine different data collection methods.[11]

In this chapter I will only draw on the methods that specifically addressed search for my analysis: 156 semi-structured ethnographic interviews, in which students were asked to recall and describe in detail a recent research assignment they had completed and to reconstruct searches they had conducted for the assignment, and 60 research process interviews, in which a project anthropologist accompanied and observed students as they searched for and located resources for an assignment they were currently working on.[12]

The Discovery Tools Project, conducted in 2011 with 87 undergraduates at Illinois Wesleyan University and Bucknell University, specifically examined students' usage of web scale library discovery tools.[13] Participants in the project were assigned to one of five test groups depending on the search tool or system they used to complete a set of search tasks—EDS, Summon, Google Scholar, the "conventional" library catalog and research databases—and a "no-tool" group that was allowed to choose any search tool to complete the tasks.[14] With the exception of the no-tool group, students were directed to the initial search page for the tool they were assigned to minimize any effects stemming from differences in the designs of the two libraries' websites. Students in each group were asked to locate two resources that they would use to complete an assignment responding to four separate research prompts similar to those they might be given in a course.[15] After students located these resources, they participated in debriefing interview in which they were shown recordings of their searches and asked to describe how they chose particular resources and their thought processes for evaluating these materials.

All of these methods focus on obtaining a better understanding of "discovery" searches, which along with "recovery" searches broadly compose two principal types of online information seeking.[16] In a discovery search, the searcher is unsure what information will fulfill his or her need, while in a recovery search, the searcher already knows the type of information sought.[17] For example, in an academic context, a recovery search might be locating a known item from a bibliography, while a discovery search might be finding a set of previously unknown articles addressing a particular topic or research question.

Here I will limit my analysis only to discovery searches. Because of the centrality of exercising judgment in determining what is important, relevant, and reliable information in these types of queries, they are especially interesting from an epistemological point of view. Whereas a query for a known item can be evaluated in a relatively straightforward manner—the information either can or cannot be found with a particular search tool or practice—discovery searches are more complex because the quality of the information located and utilized relies on the interplay between the skill and judgment of the searcher and the explicit and implicit mediation of the search tool he or she is using.

Search Patterns

Google's primacy as a search tool is clear, and its place as the preferred starting point for research questions has been demonstrated by many recent studies of students' search habits (including those that found that students do eventually utilize library resources).[18] Google is also by far the most popular general-purpose search engine in the United States. According to the Pew Internet and American Life Project, in 2012 Google was the search engine of choice for 83 percent of search users, up from 47 percent in 2004.[19]

For the students interviewed in ERIAL Project, Google was specifically discussed by 88 percent of the participants—more than three times more frequently than the next most popular search tool (JSTOR). Similarly, in the Discovery Tools Project, about 70 percent of the students who were not assigned a specific tool to use chose to use Google at least once as they answered the search questions.

Google's dominance influences academic search, especially by shaping the expectations of students. The Google search experience has become naturalized for many, if not most, students, and Google's design approaches have become standard expectations for all search tools, including those in the library. In particular, students expect features such as a single search box and relevancy-ranked search results as well as the ability to utilize natural language keyword search.[20]

This is one of the most important expressions of how the algorithmic culture of search is affected by Google: The Google search experience has conditioned students that search should be simple. Academic libraries and information providers have also followed suit in embracing simplicity as a positive value for search, a desire that is reflected in the designs of discovery tools as they provide aggregated results obtained from a single search box from across a library's many platforms, catalogs, and databases.

While discovery tools (as well as nonlibrary search tools like Google and Google Scholar) have probably reduced the "cognitive load" exacted by libraries' various and fragmented catalogs, databases, and interfaces, the practices supported by these tools can reinforce unreflective search habits that diminish the overall quality of the information found and used and, by extension, the synthesis of an academic argument.[21]

These practices were reflected in both the ERIAL and the Discovery Tools Projects. During the 60 research process interviews conducted for the ERIAL Project, the research team observed 128 discovery searches containing 238 sets of search terms.[22] Of these search terms, 85 percent (202) used a "Google-style" simple keyword approach irrespective of the search tool the student chose to use.[23] Students in the Discovery Tools Project also used simple keyword searches 81.5 percent (679/829) of the time across all five search systems.[24]

By relying so heavily on simple keyword searches while simultaneously failing to use features to narrow down or refine search results, students were regularly working with an overabundance of search results and potential resources. Because these results far exceed what a student can effectively evaluate item by item, strategies and heuristics for discerning high quality information are of paramount importance. Unfortunately, students were often unprepared for these evaluation tasks and lacked sufficient conceptual understanding of how information is organized and how to discern scholarly resources. Instead, students relied principally on the relevancy ranking algorithms of the search tools themselves.

Students in both the ERIAL and Discovery Tools Projects rarely evaluated resources to an adequate degree, and students' evaluations of materials were typically based on cursory scans of titles or abstracts rather than a critical reflection on the quality of the materials or their source.[25] When faced with unsatisfactory results, students usually changed their search terms instead of using more advanced search tools to expand or refine the search. In this way, students' search experience tended to be iterative. Students often appeared to believe that if they could only find the magic words or phrase, whatever piece of information they were looking for would be revealed to them and a manageable list of results would be returned. This practice can lead to students using lower quality or less accurate search terms because these terms return fewer results (especially in tools that use full-text search).

When choosing resources, students very rarely investigated sources found after the first page of search results, and 92 percent (598/649) of the resources used by students in the Discovery Tools Project were found on the first page of search results.[26]

Because of this belief that the most credible and highest quality resources should be found on the first page of search results, students often assumed that if they could not quickly locate information then it must not exist. Students rarely concluded that inadequate search results might reflect poorly constructed search terms or an ineffective search strategy. This is another expression of an algorithmic culture that emphasizes speed and ease.[27]

Combined with inadequate source evaluations, the practices of using simple search and utilizing only the first page of results mean that students are *de facto* outsourcing much of the evaluation process to the search algorithm itself by relying on the search tool's relevancy rankings to determine resources' quality.[28] In this way the search tools fill the epistemological role of a "surrogate expert," providing a lay searcher with judgment about which sources of information are likely to be relevant.[29]

User Trust and Search Bias

Relying on search tools in this way leaves students vulnerable to several forms of bias stemming from the design of the search tools as well as their own assumptions about the way they work and the algorithmic culture of the ways they utilize these tools.

Nevertheless, students often reflected on their sense of trust in a favored search tool. This "trust bias" is well documented in the literature on search engines, and search engine users regularly assume that information that is objectively "best" will be ranked first.[30] Through the act of ordering and ranking, search systems' relevancy algorithms impart and reinforce a sense of authority and credibility in the results. Because they hold the power to create a list of results, search engines self-validate the quality of their results. In this recursive loop, users depend solely on their trust in the search algorithms brand, be it Google, EDS, Summon, or something else.

Search tools depend on this trust. Without it, users might conclude that they are being manipulated by the tool they are using and move on to an alternative or competitor.[31] However, because search algorithms are almost always secret, users also have very little information on which to base this trust. Secrecy is therefore a fundamental characteristic of the algorithmic culture expressed by both Google and other discovery tools. While the general parameters search algorithms are known and publicly available, their details are proprietary corporate secrets. One justification for this secrecy is the argument that it helps ensure the efficacy and impartiality of search results by preventing them from being gamed by content providers.[32] In this way, the algorithmic culture established by these search tools ultimately rests on a tension between proprietary knowledge on the part of the corporation and trust on the part of the user.[33]

Somewhat paradoxically, maintaining a trustworthy search algorithm thus requires maintaining its secrecy. If the specifics of a search system were to become known, it would potentially cease to function. Some mystery and ambiguity must be preserved. Furthermore, search algorithms are at some level unknowable—at least from the standpoint of the user—because they are not stable; algorithms are continuously being updated and refined as well as (especially in the case of Google) affected by personalization, localization, and user behavior testing. Additionally, many search algorithms are now so complex that there may be no single person understands them in their entirety. Thus, because search systems cannot be properly interrogated by their users (except, perhaps, by a few with sophisticated technical skills), these users must simply put their faith and trust in the algorithm and the people who designed it. For students who have not yet developed rigorous practices for information evaluation this has concerning implications for the ways they develop knowledge.

Because of students' tendency to utilize resources unreflectively, potential biases built into the design of different search tools can be directly observed in the results of the materials students chose in the Discovery Tools Project.[34] The distribution of material types utilized between the tool groups is shown in Table 6.1.

Table 6.1. Material types chosen by students in the Discovery Tools Project[35]

	Google Scholar	Summon	EDS	Library Catalog/ Databases	No Tool
Academic Journal Articles	55.0%	65.0%	73.8%	49.2%	50.3%
Books	26.5%	13.4%	12.5%	41.3%	15.4%
Newspapers/ Magazines/Trade Journals	2.0%	20.6%	6.3%	3.2%	2.7%
For-Pay Articles	13.3%	0.0%	0.0%	0.0%	1.3%
Websites (including *Wikipedia*)	0.7%	0.0%	0.0%	0.0%	21.5%
Government and Legal Documents	2.7%	0.0%	5.0%	2.1%	2.0%
Other Documents	0.0%	1.0%	2.5%	4.2%	6.7%

The relative percentage of academic journal articles chosen varied widely by the search tool used, ranging from 74 percent of sources chosen by students using EDS to 49 percent by students using the library catalog and databases. The use of non peer-reviewed newspapers, magazines, and trade journals also varied considerably, from just over 20 percent of sources chosen by students using Summon to only two percent for students using Google Scholar (and 6.3 percent for students using EDS). Not surprisingly, books accounted for 49 percent of the sources chosen by students using the library catalog and databases as well as 27 percent by students using Google Scholar, probably due to Google Scholar's integration with Google Books. For-pay articles were only chosen significantly by students using Google Scholar (at 13 percent of sources chosen), whereas websites were only used significantly by students in the no tool assigned group (at 22 percent of sources chosen).[36]

"Judging from these results, it seems that one of the most important—and perhaps the single most important—factor in determining which [materials] students will utilize is the default way in which a particular search tool ranks and returns results."[37] While it is difficult to definitively establish the cause behind this pattern since the ranking algorithms of these tools are secret, it is nevertheless apparent is that students will tend to utilize whichever materials are returned early in the search results.

Conclusions: Evaluating Search Tools and Library Responses

Given that discovery tools all share the inherent problems of embedded biases and the secrecy of their retrieval and relevancy ranking algorithms, how should librarians evaluate a particular system's efficacy? Moreover, how should librarians respond to these evolving systems through instruction and, when possible, through the setup of the systems themselves?

Thomas Simpson suggests three criteria for evaluating a search system: (1) "timeliness," or the measure of the amount of time it takes to locate something; (2) "authority promotion," or the ability of the search system to place relevant and reliable information higher in the search results; and (3) the objectivity of the information provided, defined as how well the "rank ordering represents a defensible judgment about the relative relevance of available online reports."[38] Because users can not readily evaluate the potential biases in the search results, evaluating a search tool's objectivity is problematic, particularly during discovery searches when the searcher does not know the parameters and scope information that will satisfy their information needs. Objectivity in search results is also especially important given users' habit of stopping their evaluation of results on the first page: If any biases affect what is contained in this small handful of results, users will likely not uncover alternate or competing information located on later results pages.[39] Unfortunately, the workings of discovery tools are so opaque that it is difficult even for professional librarians to evaluate their objectivity.

Assuming that from a practical standpoint accurately determining the objectivity of a search is impossible for most users, how should students and librarians therefore evaluate whether they should trust a search tools results? Boaz Miller and Isaac Record apply the epistemological model of "justified belief" as a way of assessing how people utilize search engine results.[40] A belief is considered "justified" when it has been "responsibly formed," that is, when the individual has within practicable bounds made inquiries and evaluations as to the reliability and trustworthiness of the information.[41] In the case of search, Miller and Record argue that the searcher bears responsibility in understanding how search results are generated, how resources are aggregated in search results pages, the representativeness of the database being searched, and the ways search might potentially be manipulated.[42] As we have seen, by failing to adequately evaluate resources or to gain even a conceptual understanding of how search systems work, students are often failing to meet these responsibilities. However, given the secrecy involved in search and discovery tools it may also be technologically impossible to fulfill this responsibility, making the formation of justified beliefs problematic.[43] Nevertheless, these problems do not obviate students from their due diligence, and librarians and teaching faculty also have an epistemic responsibility ensure students are adequately instructed in these algorithmic literacies.[44]

For librarians, these responsibilities can be readily translated into practical responses. First, librarians should explicitly teach students how search systems (Google as well as library resources) work: how sources are indexed, how indexes are queried, how relevancy rankings are determined, and how bias can be introduced at any of these steps. Furthermore, particular emphasis should be placed on the evaluation of materials independent of the search system utilized to locate them.

These algorithmic literacies are critical to educating students to be critical consumers and producers of information; skills that are necessary to the exercise of digital citizenship, especially because most students will likely use the open web and general search engines to fulfill their information needs after completing their degrees. A lack of algorithmic literacy potentially renders students vulnerable to the disciplinary power contained in search systems as well as subjects of, rather than participants in, algorithmic culture.

When implementing discovery and other search tools librarians should also carefully consider the way a tool is set up, particularly when determining its default settings. As this chapter has shown, the default settings are critically important in determining what types of materials and information students will find and use. Librarians might therefore strategically utilize advanced search interfaces as a default setting in order to guide students into making more nuanced and structured queries. "By structuring and ordering the way information is seen and found, any search [system] exerts a form of epistemological power by virtue of its relevancy ranking algorithms. The judgments embedded within these systems are often opaque and unclear for the user, but unfortunately appear to be internalized by many, if not most, students, who routinely trust whatever results a search engine returns."[45]

Key questions for librarians are therefore how to most appropriately exercise this epistemological power and how to participate in the further creation and development of the algorithmic culture of search systems.[46] For example, students could be guided without their knowledge to higher quality academic resources, such as peer-reviewed journal articles, if librarians choose to set up the default search of a discovery tool to exclude materials like newspapers, magazines, and trade journals.[47] However, whether this sort of intervention is desirable should also be carefully considered and debated. Several research studies have suggested that changing the format of display interfaces can affect the evaluation of search results and that some display formats, such as a grid layout, may lead students to rely more on their own evaluation of sources since this approach destabilizes the rank-order format of a list.[48] Librarians must therefore strike a balance between technological solutions aimed at refining library tools and instructing students about the conceptual dimensions of information organization, search, and retrieval.

Librarians also have a responsibility to critically assess the effects of search algorithms that their libraries utilize and to evaluate their potential effects on users' research outcomes. Statistical modeling of usage patterns might be one way to examine these effects as are methods such as point of use surveys and qualitative techniques similar to those discussed in this chapter.[49] Finally, librarians should advocate for additional disclosure and transparency in how discovery tools' relevancy rankings determine the order of search results.[50]

Search algorithms can reveal or conceal information depending on their design and the skills of the user. Unfortunately, the students who participated in the ERIAL Project and the Discovery Tools Project generally did not understand conceptually how search systems work. Although the question was not asked systematically in the two projects, of all the students who were asked how Google works, none could correctly explain how it obtains and organizes results. For most students, search results were returned "as if by magic." Arthur C. Clarke's observation that "any technology, sufficiently advanced, is indistinguishable from magic" has been used in relation to Google perhaps to the point of cliché.[51] However, we should still attend to the reason why search feels like a magical experience. Vaidhyanathan argues that Google seems magical because of its usefulness for helping its users find meaning by providing a managed and ordered set of actionable choices for a query.[52] Coupled with a speed that seems near instantaneous, this experience makes it easy for users to forget that Google and other web scale discovery tools are simply tools, especially since their workings are made intentionally opaque.[53] This secrecy makes it difficult for students to fully understand the embedded decisions and potential biases within how information is organized and retrieved. One challenge for librarians and other educators is to balance facilitating ease of use with a robust understanding of how search works. Search shouldn't be magic; it's only when its processes and algorithmic culture are demystified that our students become empowered to use it effectively.

Notes

1.   Illinois Wesleyan University, Bucknell University, University of Illinois, Springfield, University of Illinois, Chicago, DePaul University, and Northeastern Illinois University.

2.   Ted Striphas, "Who Speaks for Culture?" *The Late Age of Print: Beyond the Book* (blog), September 26, 2011, http://www.thelateageofprint.org/2011/09/26/who-speaks-for-culture.

3.   Striphas, "Who Speaks for Culture?"

4.   Ted Striphas, "Culturomics," *The Late Age of Print: Beyond the Book* (blog), April 5, 2011, http://www.thelateageofprint.org/2011/04/05/culturomics/.

5.   "Google: Our Products and Services," Google, accessed September 4, 2014, http://www.google.com/about/corporate/company/tech.html.

6.   Sergey Brin, and Lawrence Page, "The Anatomy of a Large-Scale Hypertextual Web Search Engine," *Computer Networks and ISDN Systems* 30, no.1 (1998): 107–17; Lawrence Page et al., "The PageRank Citation Ranking: Bringing Order to the Web," Stanford InfoLab (1999), http://ilpubs.stanford.edu:8090/422/1/1999-66.pdf; John Battelle, *The Search: How Google and Its Rivals Rewrote the Rules of Business and Transformed Our Culture* (New York: Penguin, 2005), 75–76.

7.   Summon combines a "dynamic rank," based primarily on matching query terms with metadata fields, with a "static rank," based on the qualities of an item such as publication date, citation counts, and the type of content. See ProQuest, *Relevance Ranking in the Summon Service,* accessed September 4, 2014, http://www.serialssolutions.com/assets/resources/Summon_RelevanceRanking-Datasheet.pdf. EBSCO Discovery System also concentrates first on keyword matching in metadata fields and then on ranking factors based on item characteristics such as currency, resource type, and length. See EBSCO, "EBSCO Discovery Service Relevancy Ranking: Return the Best Possible Search Results," http://www.ebscohost.com/discovery/technology/relevancy-ranking. This keyword-centric approach to search is similar to that of many pre-Google Internet search engines.

8.   Siva Vaidhyanathan, *The Googlization of Everything: (And Why We Should Worry)* (Oakland, CA: University of California Press, 2012), 62.

9.   See *Ethnographic Research in Illinois Academic Libraries (ERIAL)*: http://www.erialproject.org.

10.   Including small and large institutions, residential and commuter campuses, urban and suburban locations, highly selective liberal arts (IWU), public research (UIC), Hispanic-serving institutions (NEIU), religious affiliated institutions (DePaul).

11.   See Lynda M. Duke and Andrew D. Asher, eds. *College Libraries and Student Culture: What We Now Know* (Chicago: American Library Association Editions, 2012).

12.   For additional information on students' research practices and academic assignments, see "ERIAL: Methodology:" http://www.erialproject.org/project-details/methodology/.

13.   Andrew D. Asher, Lynda M. Duke, and Suzanne Wilson, "Paths of Discovery: Comparing the Search Effectiveness of EBSCO Discovery Service, Summon, Google Scholar, and Conventional Library Resources," *College and Research Libraries* 74, no. 5 (2013): 467.

14.   Sirsi at Bucknell and the Voyager VuFind interface at IWU.

15.   The prompts were as follows: (1) You need to give a class presentation that explains general information about the Civil Rights Act of 1964. Find 2 sources that you would use as the basis of your presentation. (2) You need to find information about women's professional baseball in the 1940s. Find 2 sources that would give you this information. (3) You are writing a research paper that argues that increased wealth does not result in increased happiness. Find 2 of the best-quality sources to use. (4) You are writing a research paper on how volcanic eruptions affect the Earth's climate. Your professor has told you to use only peer-reviewed, scholarly articles. Find 2 sources that you might use. See Asher, Duke, and Wilson, "Paths of Discovery," 478.

16.   Battelle, *The Search*, 32.

17.   These types of searches are often labeled differently. For example, Andrei Broder labels recovery searches as "navigational" and discover searches as "informational." See Andrei Broder, "A Taxonomy of Web Search," *SIGIR Forum* 36, no. 2 (2002): 3–10, http://www.cis.upenn.edu/~nenkova/Courses/cis430/p3-broder.pdf.

18.   See Lynn Silipigni Connaway and Thomas Dickey, *The Digital Information Seeker: Report on Findings from Selected OCLC, RIN and JISC User Behaviour Projects,* accessed August 19, 2014, http://www.jisc.ac.uk/media/documents/publications/reports/2010/digitalinformationseekerreport.pdf, 28–29; Alison J. Head and Michael Eisenberg, *How College Students Seek Information in the Digital Age,* accessed August 19, 2014, http://projectinfolit.org/images/pdfs/pil_fall2009_finalv_yr1_12_2009v2.pdf, 15; Cathy De Rosa et al., *College Students' Perceptions of Libraries and Information Resources: A Report to the OCLC Membership,* accessed August 14, 2014, http://www.oclc.org/content/dam/oclc/reports/pdfs/studentperceptions.pdf, 1–7; Chandra Prabha, Lynn Silipigni Connaway, and Timothy J. Dickey, *Sense-making the Information Confluence: The Whys and Hows of College and University User Satisficing of Information Need.: Phase IV Report; Semi-Structured Interview Study* (Columbus, OH: Ohio State University, 2006), 13–14, 16–18; Jillian R. Griffiths and Peter Brophy, "Student Searching Behavior and the Web: Use of Academic Resources and Google," *Trends* 53, no. 4 (2005): 550, 545; Tracy Gabridge, Millicent Gaskell, and Amy Stout, "Information Seeking Through Students' Eyes: The MIT Photo Diary Study," *College and Research Libraries* 69, no. 6 (2008): 516–17; Head and Eisenberg, *How College Students Seek Information*, 3.

19.   Kristin Purcel, Joanna Brenner, and Lee Rainie, *Search Engine Use 2012,* accessed August 14, 2014, http://www.pewinternet.org/files/old-media//Files/Reports/2012/PIP_Search_Engine_Use_2012.pdf.

20.   Stuart Hampton-Reeves et al., *Students' Use of Research Content in Teaching and Learning: A Report for the Joint Information Systems Council (JISC) 2009,* accessed August 19, 2014, http://www.jisc.ac.uk/media/documents/aboutus/workinggroups/studentsuseresearchcon-

tent.pdf, 45. Centre for Information Behaviour and Evaluation of Research (CIBER), *Information Behaviour of the Researcher of the Future: A CIBER Briefing Paper,* accessed August 14, 2014, http://www.jisc.ac.uk/media/documents/programmes/reppres/gg_final_keynote_11012008. pdf, 14.

21.   CIBER, *Information Behaviour of the Researcher of the Future, 30; William Wong et al., JISC User Behaviour Observational Study: User Behaviour in Resource Discovery; Final Report,* accessed August 14, 2014, http://www.jisc.ac.uk/media/documents/publications/pro- gramme/2010/ubirdfinalreport.pdf, 9.

22.   In this study, a search was defined as any time a student opened a new resource to search for information. If the student changed his or her search terms within a resource, it was consid- ered part of the original search, accounting for the difference in searches and search terms.

23.   See also CIBER, *Information Behaviour of the Researcher of the Future,* 14; Hamp- ton-Reeves et. al., *Students' Use of Research Content in Teaching and Learning,* 45.

24.   Asher, Duke, and Wilson, "Paths of Discovery," 473.

25.   This was the case even when subsequent interview questions revealed that the student understood appropriate methods of ascertaining a source's suitability and quality. During the debriefing interviews students described their evaluation practices. See also CIBER, *Information Behaviour of the Researcher of the Future, 10.*

26.   See also Asher and Duke, "Searching for Answers: Student Research Behavior at Illinois Wesleyan University," in *College Libraries and Student Culture: What We Now Know,* ed. Lynda M. Duke and Andrew D. Asher (Chicago: American Library Association Editions, 2012), 80; Bernard J. Jansen and Amanda Spink, "How Are We Searching the World Wide Web? A Compar- ison of Nine Search Engine Transaction Logs," *Information Processing and Management* 42, no. 1 (2006): 257–58; Griffiths and Brophy, "Student Searching Behavior and the Web," 551; CIBER, *Information Behaviour of the Researcher of the Future,* 10; see Asher, Duke, and Wilson, "Paths of Discovery," 474 for a full discussion of these results.

27.   For example, see Urs Heolzle, "The Google Gospel of Speed," Google Think Insights, January 2012, accessed August 14, 2014, http://www.google.com/think/articles/the-google- gospel-of-speed-urs-hoelzle.html.

28.   See also Griffiths and Brophy, "Student Searching Behavior and the Web," 551; Judit Bar-Ilan et al., "Presentation Bias Is Significant in Determining User Preference for Search Results—A User Study," *Journal of the American Society for Information Science and Technology* 60, no. 1 (2009): 135–49; Bing Pan et al., "In Google We Trust: Users' Decisions on Rank, Position, and Relevance," *Journal of Computer-Mediated Communication* 12, no. 3 (2007): 816; Laura A. Granka, Thorsten Joachims, and Geri Gay, "Eye-Tracking Analysis of User Behavior in WWW Search," in *Proceedings of the 27th Annual International ACM SIGIR Conference on Research and Development in Information Retrieval (New York: ACM, 2004), 478–79.*

29.   Thomas W. Simpson, "Evaluating Google as an Epistemic Tool," *Metaphilosophy* 43, no. 4 (2012): 427.

30.   Vaidhyanathan, *The Googlization of Everything,* 59; Eszter Hargittai, "The Social, Polit- ical, Economic, and Cultural Dimensions of Search Engines: An Introduction," *Journal of Com- puter-Mediated Communication* 12, no. 3 (2007): 769–77; Eszter Hargittai et al., "Trust Online: Young Adults' Evaluation of Web Content," *International Journal of Communication 4 (2010):* 27; Pan et al., "In Google We Trust," 801–23; Bernard J. Jansen, Mimi Zhang, and Carsten D. Schultz, "Brand and Its Effect on User Perception of Search Engine Performance," *Journal of the American Society for Information Science and Technology 60, no. 8 (2009): 1572–95.*

31.   Battelle, *The Search,* 183.

32.   For a discussion of Google, see Battelle, *The Search, 159–63.*

33. Ibid.,,183–85.

34. Asher, Duke, and Wilson, "Paths of Discovery," 470–71.

35. Table reproduced from Asher, Duke, and Wilson, "Paths of Discovery," 471.

36. Usually from results linking to Questia or HeinOnline.

37. Asher, Duke, and Wilson, "Paths of Discovery," 471.

38. Simpson, "Evaluating Google as an Epistemic Tool," 432–37.

39. Ibid., 434.

40. Boaz Miller and Isaac Record, "Justified Belief in a Digital Age: On the Epistemic Implications of Secret Internet Technologies," *Episteme* 10, no. 02 (2013): 117–34.

41. Ibid., 118, 122–25.

42. Ibid., 128.

43. Ibid., 128.

44. See Ted Striphas, "Algorithmic Literacies," *The Late Age of Print: Beyond the Book* (blog), October 17, 2011, http://www.thelateageofprint.org/2011/10/17/algorithmic-literacies/; Eli Pariser, *The Filter Bubble: What the Internet Is Hiding from You* (London: Penguin UK, 2011), 227–28.

45. Andrew Asher, "Search Magic: Discovering How Undergraduates Find Information" (paper, Anthropological Association Annual Meeting, Montreal, Canada, November 18, 2011), http://www.andrewasher.net/anthropologyofalgorithms/?p=5; see also Striphas, "Who Speaks for Culture?" http://www.thelateageofprint.org/2011/09/26/who-speaks-for-culture; Ted Striphas, "Culturomics," http://www.thelateageofprint.org/2011/04/05/culturomics/.

46. Asher, Duke, and Wilson, "Paths of Discovery," 477.

47. Ibid.

48. Yvonne Kammerer, and Peter Gerjets, "How the Interface Design Influences Users' Spontaneous Trustworthiness Evaluations of Web Search Results: Comparing a List and a Grid Interface," in *Proceedings of the 2010 Symposium on Eye-Tracking Research and Applications* (New York: ACM, 2010), 299–306. For a review of relevant studies see Yvonne Kammerer and Peter Gerjets, "Search Engine Users' Credibility Assessment of Web Search Results: The Impact of the Search Engine Interface on Credibility Assessments," in *Web Search Engine Research*, ed. Dirk Lewandowski (Bingley, UK: Emerald Publishing Group, 2012), 251–79.

49. For example, see Michael Levine-Clark, John McDonald, and Jason Price, "Discovery or Displacement? A Large Scale Longitudinal Study of the Effect of Discovery Systems on Online Journal Usage" (presentation, Charleston Conference, November 7, 2013), http://www.slideshare.net/MichaelLevineClark/mlc-jdm-jsp-charleston-2013-slideshare-28161600.

50. The National Information Standards Organization has developed a draft of recommended practices for discovery services that addresses potential biases but does not address relevancy ranking: *Open Discovery Initiative: Promoting Transparency in Discovery,* http://www.niso.org/apps/group_public/download.php/11606/rp-19-201x_ODI_draft_for_comments_final.pdf.

51. Arthur C. Clarke, *Profiles of the Future: An Inquiry into the Limits of the Possible,* rev. ed. (New York: Harper and Row, 1973); see Battelle, *The Search,* 129; Vaidhyanathan, *The Googlization of Everything,* 53.

52. Ibid.

53. Ibid., 53–54.

CHAPTER 7

Studying Sources:
Truth, Method, and Teaching Bibliography

Patricia Brown

> "The mechanization of information retrieval poses problems that have still not adequately been solved…. If there ever was a time when society needed constructive action based on valid information it is most certainly now. The problems of our society are mountain-high, they reach to the skies."[1]

> "We regard knowledge as something fine and precious."[2]

In my last year of teaching freshman composition, I discovered that some students literally did not know what "print" is. ("But I printed it off the Internet!") In the digital 21st century, technology has permanently transformed education and libraries, yet it is still far ahead of pedagogy. "After a tremendous start in the 1970s when the first databases were developed, it has become more of a technological information industry than a user-welcoming knowledge base."[3] This chapter will argue, therefore, that in the fluid techno-educational environment of the early 21st century, teaching research as a process along with the structure, production, and use of bibliography should be more than one shot across the bow of the first-year experience.

Library instruction has evolved from orientations and single sessions to encompass online searching techniques, documentation formats, critical thinking about sources, collaborations with classroom faculty, single-discipline research methods courses, and embedded librarianship in combinations of face-to-face teaching and course management systems. Some of these projects have noted the need for going beyond database searching and evaluation.[4] The intent of this chapter is to develop a rationale for teaching students the system of knowledge production, recording, distribution, and use as it applies to the library research process. Based on statistical and critical evidence of student abilities, a conceptual analysis of what might be termed neo-bibliography will show its benefits in addressing the metaliteracy needs of the Age of Information and educational choice.[5]

The need of library users for help in finding their way through the records of knowledge is, of course, not new. In 1876, Samuel S. Green advocated "personal relations between librarians and readers:" "If you gain the respect and confidence of readers, and they find you easy to get at and pleasant to talk with, great opportunities are afforded of stimulating the love of study and of directing investigators to the best sources of information."[6] Without such respect and direction from librarians, many students flounder. A 2013 qualitative study by Project Information Literacy describes how so many students continue to have difficulties in the library.[7] Despite years of education, "students needed additional assistance with the research process."[8]

In 2000, to address the continuing deficit in bibliographic knowledge, the Association of College and Research Libraries (ACRL) established a set of *Information Literacy Competency Standards for Higher Education*. Fourteen years later, the first revisers of the document acknowledged that the current standards are showing their age, because they don't …adequately address student understanding of the knowledge creation process as a collaborative endeavor [or] emphasize the need for metacognitive and dispositional dimensions of learning throughout ALL steps of conducting research."[9]

Information scientist Michael Keresztesi defines bibliography as "metaknowledge."[10] The value of this understanding in the research process is what Ray Land et al. describe as a "threshold conception: …the interaction of all these elements in a process of ever-increasing complexity."[11] In the 2014 revision, the ACRL committee included threshold concepts, "*core understandings* about the evolving information system" and a "greater need for sense-making and metacognition."[12] To the objection that there is no more time or budget for adding extra lessons, new courses, or additional graduation requirements, the American Library Association (ALA) Code of Ethics directs librarians to "provide the highest level of service." For library epistemologist John Budd, "the goal is knowledge (for its own sake *and for application in practice*)" but also as radical educator Neil Postman reminds us, "to improve social life …to contribute to human understanding and decency."[13]

Entering a new world of discourse in college, it should not be surprising to find that students have no concept of subjects as disciplines or what a professor means by the terms *scholarly literature, literary criticism,* or *plagiarism.* Nor do they always "understand why their professors consider plagiarism such an important topic."[14]

> While the student is learning to write a paper within certain confines for one course, he may be enrolled in other courses that require self-reflection or other personal writing, or collaborative writing with other students, for which he must internalize an entirely different set of criteria about what constitutes original thought and moral behavior. Such mixed messages must certainly lead to confusion.[15]

Issues of agency and confidence also affect student writing:

> A university education can be a humbling experience for students. They are exposed to ideas that shake the foundations that have always held their worldview erect. In addition, they are faced with a highly educated faculty who (arguably) know more than they themselves are ever likely to learn in their particular subject area. As if that is not daunting enough, now they must grapple with the mysterious and ever-changing notion of intellectual property as they learn within each subject area. Not only is each student's body of knowledge questioned, but also his autonomy.[16]

Blaming students (or faculty or universities or "the Internet" itself) is counterproductive, even mean-spirited. Some of their difficulty lies with the rapid pace of change, when media interfaces seem to change faster than one can master them. Other difficulties include cultural, economic, and political issues. Nontraditional students also must balance the needs of their children, parents, and jobs. ACRL describes the variety of undergraduate students, many of whom share the following characteristics or needs:

1. They are beginning to acquire the research skills needed to exploit the university library's potential.
2. They need a user-friendly environment, where assistance is offered and questions are encouraged.
3. They need to be introduced to the academic nature of the services and resources available in university libraries.[17]

At certain times of the semester, some of these students sometimes pause at the reference desk, hesitate, and then whisper, "I need to find a book." Usually it is not a particular book they want, however, but a source citation for a class assignment. Within the context of library research, a source is information used for one's own work of expanding knowledge but originally discovered or created by someone else: "second-hand knowledge," to use Patrick Wilson's phrase.[18] In her teaching of "information structure," Elizabeth Frick insists that "students must acquire two basic skills in order to progress independently: (1) discrimination or judgment and (2) an understanding of bibliographic structure."[19]

As a critical study, bibliography (Greek for "book-writing") now includes not only the analytical description of information records regardless of format but also their historical, cultural, and material conditions of production. Given the varieties of print and electronic media (books, journals, discs, film, websites, archives), the definition of a textual source has remained relatively stable: In whatever medium (or multimedia) of transmission, a record of information is created, formulated, or discovered by one or more persons and distributed by speech, writing, or publishing. According to Keresztesi, "Bibliography as an intellectual pursuit must concern itself with the total process of how an information apparatus evolves through its interaction with the discipline or field it serves, and how this process creates the end products, the inventory artifacts, together with the printed and electronic information instruments."[20] Though style and format vary across disciplines, teaching the principles of bibliographical description and organization as a system is a user-enabling solution to student confusion, frustration, and plagiarism based on ignorance.[21]

Rebecca Moore Howard and Laura J. Davies argue for this solution: "Students don't need threats: Students need pedagogy."[22]

How and why research sources are documented is a function of their creation, material production, and use in context. Perhaps because formatting is more formulaic, learning to document sources is more frustrating than to evaluate them. "X writing commentary on Y began in the ancient world and has flourished in every culture that possessed a formal, written canon," as English historian Anthony Grafton indicates.[23] Aristotle referenced his predecessors to acknowledge them respectfully as well as to show the breadth of his own knowledge.[24] Formal documentation, which Grafton defines as "precise references to the section of an authoritative text from which a given quotation in a later work comes," developed later. From such notes, researchers discover new sources in the books and articles they read. "Footnotes are, after all, the traditional medium whereby scholars communicate with each other."[25] Source citations "seek to show that the work they support claims authority and solidity from the historical conditions of its creation ... To do so they locate the production of the work in question in time and space."[26]

This should hold true in student work as well, whether on math tests ("show your work") or in research writing. In the pre-digital past, unintentional documentation errors were usually a combination of laziness, haste, and faulty learning of the rules. Linguistic anthropologist Susan D. Blum, who studied students on residential college campuses, concludes that their plagiarism behavior arises from a combination of morality and pragmatics.[27] Add to this the 21st-century media explosion, and writers now have more reasons to be unsure about the nature of authorship and the procedures to avoid plagiarism.[28] Whereas the covers and title pages of books and journals usually indicate their provenance, online sources are often more opaque yet easier to manipulate. Word-processing programs make quotations easy to copy and paste without attribution; citation software requires users to input correct information. Trinity University's Benjamin R. Harris acknowledges the limited usefulness of citation software as he indicates their chief pedagogical flaw:

> These resources are indeed valuable. They save time and reduce errors in citation format. However, any philosophy behind giving attribution is completely lost with the deployment of these tools. In their efforts to make citation tasks more efficient and error-free, programs such

as InCite and RefWorks remove some of the intellectual
work of including sources.[29]

Even within databases, "citation generators produce a wide range of
variations when trying to reference the same document in a specific style."[30]
Like spell-checkers, citation programs are most effective when users have
learned bibliographical concepts and formats rather than copying and pasting
by rote. "The assumption that the information of all kinds found on the web—
individuals' correspondence, databases, and electronic primary works—is free
for the taking is probably one of the greatest impediments to the teaching of
correct attribution."[31]

Not even professional writers are free from this fallacy. Former *Wired*
magazine editor Chris Anderson was accused of and later apologized for
plagiarizing *Wikipedia*.[32] The ALA added to its Code of Ethics a clause to
"advocate balance between the interests of information users and rights holders."[33]
Defenders of plagiarists from Martin Luther King Jr. to US Senator Rand Paul
have argued that context is more important for citation than rules learned in
school.[34] This view reinforces the mistaken opposition of public knowledge
conventions and "school rules" for academic integrity. Careless writers and
inexperienced researchers need a sense that they work within a community of
users with language traditions, whose forms often make reading, writing, and
ethical research much easier. Teaching in the Google era must attempt to correct
the view that information is there for the copying and pasting, rather like food
that comes not from plants or animals, factories or cooks, but from a store.[35]
(Though in stores, no one is allowed to take food without paying.)

Such teaching might in the future also reduce the multiplication of
disciplinary standards of documentation format. Consider the following
example:

yntuZ$#&Mlastl!Brw214

With a little time and ingenuity, one could figure out what this group of
symbols means.[36] Had it been written in standard orthography, however, one
quick reading would suffice. Similarly, if scholarly publishing were to adopt a
single format for documenting research sources, the resulting efficiency would
free time for less standardized work. The writer's task would be simpler if all
disciplines used the same format. Unfortunately, more than one standard format

for bibliography now exists: APA, MLA, and Chicago styles are frequently used in undergraduate writing. Sixty years ago a short ACRL monograph surveyed the field:

> Four types of bibliographical style manuals, or brief style sheets, or handbooks of research have been issued for students and authors…. It is impractical to study all the style manuals, style sheets, and directions used in scholarly documentation… It is important to realize that professional associations, scholarly research journals, publishing houses, government agencies, and many individuals are concerned with the problems of documentation.[37]

Since then, bibliographical documentation has grown more complicated and various, though it cannot keep up with the proliferation of textual media, despite the desire of cataloguers and disciplinary arbiters to make it uniform. Even the American National Standards Institute failed to impose its 2005 Z39.29 protocol for bibliographic references, despite a committee representing scholarly publishers, universities, and library groups.[38] As a result, citation styles are multiplying—along with unnecessary confusion—despite the prevalence of three standard formats.[39] The Modern Language Association enlarged its handbook six times after the original "Style Sheet" was published in 1951,[40] while the APA Publication Manual is in its sixth edition since "its inception as a brief journal article in 1929."[41] The Chicago Manual of Style has seen 16 versions since 1891, when the University of Chicago Press used a "single sheet of typographic style fundamentals drawn up by the first proofreader."[42] Publishing media are being developed faster than bibliographical description, whose forms then need to be adapted by their users.

Regardless of format, the current academic model of documentation requires that any information from a source outside one's own brain or general common knowledge must be formally acknowledged. Information comes from external or outside sources, including interviewing another person, reading a book or article, or otherwise looking up information; not to acknowledge this is unethical, unhelpful to the readers, damaging to the writer's credibility, and sometimes illegal. The list of sources used in a research document serves readers in three important ways: It demonstrates authorial credibility; it credits earlier work in the subject; and it directs the readers to more information on the subject. Hence, an item in such a list normally includes four pieces, or "bites," of descriptive metadata: author, title, publisher, and date. Most formats now also indicate medium; others ask for electronic location information. Although some bites need additional bits ("publisher," for example, has become "source" in many database records), four bites of information are necessary and sufficient to identify and locate most graphic sources. This should be explained in the teaching of bibliography—even in a one-shot lesson.[43]

When printed books were the only graphic sources used for research, the four-bite structure worked almost perfectly. Then magazines, newspapers, and journals entered the source pool, and the original pattern was adapted to include them. With the invention of sound recordings and films, formats were stretched further. Then came microfilm, Internet databases, and other electronic media. Websites seem to be the most difficult to fit into a standard citation because authorship and publishing information can be difficult to locate on a webpage. However, with thoughtful adaptation of the basic four-bite description, almost anything can be documented: Twitter feeds, Yahoo ads, library pathfinders, election handbills, home movies, YouTube videos. And having studied the production of knowledge, students would know whether and how to use electronic ephemera as research sources. Biographer William Manchester observed that "the value of even the most perceptive eyewitnesses comes later, when their recollections can be matched against one another in tranquility. As long as events are still unfolding, the observations of each individual are as meaningless as a single jagged fragment in a thousand-piece jigsaw puzzle."[44]

Although it is the researcher's task to assemble the puzzle, there may be more than one solution, and all the source pieces need not be used. Though a study of composition rubrics would show differently, academic research is not a mechanical process expressible as an operation, say, $Q + T(\theta/i)$, where Q is the research problem, T is time, theta equals thought, and i is the number of information bits needed to think about the problem.[45] The venerable and authoritative *MLA Handbook for Writers of Research Papers* describes the research assignment as a tool for exploration and for communication.[46] Composition teachers assign research papers to develop students' critical thinking and writing skills as well as their ability to find and use information. Yet because of the many other skills needed by freshmen, instruction librarian Barbara Fister recommends eliminating it from the first-year curriculum.[47] Literature professor Kate Koppelman suggests slowing it down instead, to give college students time to begin to learn the fundamentals of their subjects.[48] Upper-level student researchers then can learn the literature, the values, and the methodology of their disciplines as well as in-depth knowledge of a particular topic.

The school research assignment can correct the mistaken views that everything is on the Internet, all sources are equal, and short sources are best ones. Assignments with long rubrics that specify the number and type of sources can reduce a useful and potentially interesting learning process to a scavenger hunt for objects with confusing numbers. The result, too often, is that students work superficially instead of learning. A scavenger hunt is an example of this, especially when the assignment directs students to take pictures with their phones rather than answering questions from the items they seek.[49] An annotated bibliography may also seem meaningless to secondary and early college students, but the assignment can be presented as an exploration and also a means of lifelong learning.[50]

Paulo Freire's criticism of the "banking concept of education" in *Pedagogy of the Oppressed* led to movements such as critical information studies and critical pedagogy, which urge a shift from instruction and "information retrieval" to education for lifelong learning.[51] David F. Noble defines education by contrast with job training as "the utter integration of knowledge and the self."[52] Over time, the primary purpose of libraries has shifted from collection to reference to this type of educational instruction.[53] An essay in the open journal *In the Library with the Lead Pipe* sums up the current situation: "Educators, including librarians, have responded to the challenges of 21st-century learners by identifying skills, competencies, fluencies, and literacies to be taught, but these are also in flux, with the concepts and methods often contested. Learning and literacy are core values in librarianship."[54] In a study of the structure of this change, Keresztesi observed, "Today, with the advent of the 'information age,'… the library's function is being transformed from that of a public warehouse of cultural goods to one of a social dynamic institution of communication and knowledge dissemination."[55]

Library theorist Budd argues "in favor of our profession thinking seriously about what constitutes knowledge in LIS,"[56] while Australian philosopher Colin Lankshear describes "profound changes in our conceptions and experiences of time, space, relatedness, and what it is to know things."[57] In Aristotle's well-known words, "All men by nature desire to know," or "to have knowledge" (in a more accurate translation).[58] The acquisition and use of knowledge is a subject not only for education and for libraries but also for action and evidence and truth. The business corporation Forbes, for example, maintains a "Thoughts on Knowledge" section in its online "Thoughts on the Business of Life."[59] Philosopher Keith Hossack suggests that "knowledge is a relation between a mind and a fact."[60] Friedrich Nietzsche asked, "What, then, is truth? A mobile army of metaphors, metonyms, and anthropomorphisms—in short, a sum of human relations which have been enhanced, transposed, and embellished poetically and rhetorically, and which after long use seem firm, canonical, and obligatory to a people."[61]

Drs. Daniel J. Rader and Emil deGoma declare that "in reality the 'truth' is not based on any single study but on an overall body ('totality') of evidence."[62] Information scientist Reijo Savoleinen asserts that "knowledge is an inherent part of action."[63] Acknowledging collaborative pedagogies and online/electronic learning, Alvin I. Goldman founded *Social Epistemology*, a journal of what he called "epistemics:" "the study of the social dimensions or determinants of knowledge, or the ways in which social factors promote or perturb the quest for knowledge."[64] In 2014, the ACRL affirmed that "authority is constructed and contextual" and that students should understand not only the circumstances of knowledge creation and production but also their own participation and purposes in learning or researching.[65]

Reinforcing the need for learning, Fister voices the lament that students are taught to find sources but not to read them.[66] English professor Mark Bauerlein criticized schools' overreliance on electronic media as insufficient preparation for college work. He argues against the displacement of complex texts in high schools by "blogs, wikis, Facebook pages, multimedia assemblages and the like, [which] do little to address the primary reason that so many students end up not ready for college-level reading…. That cause is, precisely, the inability to grasp complex texts."[67]

To address these concerns, professors Nicholas Delbanco and Alan Cheuse created "the first of its kind" college literature textbook for the Internet generation. *Literature: Craft and Voice* has a "fresh, inviting design and accompanying rich video program. Digital support is provided through CONNECT Literature, which will be totally integrated with the Blackboard CMS."[68] A critique of this "inviting design" by Laura Gruber Godfrey counters that instead of focusing attention on the literary text, the interspersion of stock images mimics "the everyday experience of reading the Internet."[69] Fear and loathing of new technology are recorded as early as Plato.[70] Marshall McLuhan's *The Gutenberg Galaxy* and Elizabeth Eisenstein's magisterial work, *The Printing Press as an Agent of Change: Communication and Cultural Transformation in*

Early-Modern Europe, analyzed the effects of the European printing press.[71] After Nietzsche began to use a typewriter in 1882, it was noticed that his prose style became "tighter, more telegraphic."[72] Though this wasn't necessarily a criticism, the philosopher acknowledged that "our writing equipment takes part in the forming of our thoughts."[73]

Stanford University professor Andrea Lunsford is pleased with students' fluency in new media and nonlinear organization. "Writing isn't just black marks on white paper. It's full of sound, images, color."[74] But those sensory effects arise first in the attentive reading of textual marks, and they are not present in all types of writing.[75] Godfrey quotes Nicholas Carr's description of multimedia texts to show the paradox: "The Net seizes our attention only to scatter it." She concludes that "the misfortune is that to insist on teaching only the words themselves, only an unadorned text, can sound like cultural elitism," whereas the inability to read an "unadorned text" precludes extended logical thinking.[76] A better way to solve the problem of shallow literacy is "to learn to work with computers in a way that maximizes their great ability to streamline analysis and data management, without turning the users into bleary-eyed idiots."[77] The "rise of the centaurs," a mythological combination of man and beast, is used by competitive chess players for the partnership of a human and a computer to accomplish a task using the strengths of each.[78]

"Every new tool shapes the way we think," writes Clive Thompson, but there are multiple ways of thinking.[79] Use the slower technologies of pencil and paper and print to browse journals, peruse books, study archives, analyze narratives, and evaluate analytical arguments. Leave the computers to answer queries, do brute-force pattern-matching, and store data. Work with computers to generate multimedia and expedite communication and research. A contextually appropriate embrace of slow thought and single focus, contrary though it is to the lightning-fast electronic world, would improve both the real and the virtual worlds. As a cataloger, Michael Gorman appreciated the difference between computers and older technologies, "between information (data, facts, images, quotes and brief texts than can be used out of context) and recorded knowledge (the cumulative exposition found in scholarly and literary texts and in popular nonfiction)."[80]

The systematic bibliographical instruction advocated here will enrich the teaching of research as well as its practice, justifying the curricular investment of resources by improved student engagement in writing and critical thinking as well as proficiency in information use. Instead of merely instructing users in interfaces and formats (whether electronic, print, or other), teach the information search process and its associated documentation systems as human work intellectually and socially productive. Researchers are investigative epistemologists: Who made these ideas? Where? When? How? Why? What are they named? How credible are these texts? Without bibliographical knowledge, writers can plagiarize, hunt robotically for sources, and let software assemble their papers. One such program claims to "help you better organize your education so you can focus on the important things—your dreams," as though education is not important or connected with one's dreams.[81]

"In conclusion, I wish to say that there are few pleasures comparable to that of associating continually with curious and vigorous young minds, and of aiding them in realizing their ideals."[82]

Notes

1.   Jesse H. Shera made this prediction more than forty years ago in "The Sociological Relationships of Information Science," *Journal of the American Society of Information Science* 22, no. 2 (1971): 76–80.

2.   Aristotle, "Psychology I," trans. J. L. Creed and A.E. Wardman, in *The Philosophy of Aristotle* (New York: New American Library, 1963), 235.

3.   Hans-Christoph Hobohm, "Can Digital Libraries Generate Knowledge?" *Historical Social Research* 37, no. 3 (2012): 218.

4.   Quite a literature is developing in the area of information instruction studies. An analytical annotated bibliography was assembled by Erin L. Ellis and Kara M. Whatley, "The Evolution of Critical Thinking Skills in Library Instruction, 1986–2006: A Selected and Annotated Bibliography and Review of Selected Programs," *College and Undergraduate Libraries* 15, no. 1-2 (2008): 5–20, doi: 10.1080/10691 310802176665. Two articles in particular that describe bibliographical study are (1) John G. Dove and John Shawler, "The Road to Mastery," *Library Journal* 137, no. 18 (2012): 10–12; and (2) Anne Marie Gruber, Mary Anne Knefel, and Paul Waelchli, "Modeling Scholarly Inquiry: One Article at a Time," *College and Undergraduate Libraries* 15, no. 1-2 (2008): 99–125, doi: 10.1080/10691310802177085.

5.   Patrick Wilson sensibly and philologically suggested that "insofar as they deal with texts, one might call them all bibliographers" (*Second-Hand Knowledge: An Inquiry into Cognitive Authority* [Westport, CT: Praeger, 1971], 171), so I will use the term to denote the wider and deeper information-literacy instruction for which this chapter is an argument.

6.   Samuel S. Green, "Personal Relations between Librarians and Readers," *American Library Journal* (November 1876): 78–79. An abridged version was published in Library Journal 118, no. 11 (1993): S4–S5.

7.   Alison J. Head, *Learning the Ropes: How Freshmen Conduct Course Research Once They Enter College*, http://projectinfolit.org/images/pdfs/pil_2013_freshmenstudy_fullreport.pdf. Some of the most prevalent difficulties reported by students were

> Conduct[ing] online searches for academic literature. Nearly three-fourths of the sample (74 percent) said they struggled with selecting keywords and formulating efficient

search queries. Over half (57 percent) felt stymied by the thicket of irrelevant results their online searches usually returned.

Learning to navigate their new and complex digital and print landscape plagued most of the freshmen in our sample (51 percent). And once they had their sources in hand, more than two-fifths of the freshmen (43 percent) said they had trouble making sense of, and tying together, all the information they had found (page 3).

A table comparing the research habits of high school and college students is on page 25.

8.   David Mazella, Laura Heidel, and Irene Ke, "Integrating Reading, Information Literacy, and Literary Studies Instruction in a Three-Way Collaboration," *Learning Assistance Review* 16, no. 2 (2011): 42.

9.   "The Future of the Standards," *Framework for Information Literacy for Higher Education.* September 2013. http://acrl.ala.org/ilstandards/?page_id=19.

10.   Michael Keresztesi, "The Science of Bibliography: Theoretical Implications for Bibliographic Instruction," in *Theories of Bibliographic Education: Designs for Teaching,* ed. Cerise Oberman and Katina Strauch (New York: Bowker, 1982), 24.

11.   Ray Land et al., "Threshold Concepts and Troublesome Knowledge (3): Implications for Course Design and Evaluation," in *Improving Student Learning Diversity and Inclusivity* (Oxford: Oxford Centre for Staff and Learning Development, 2005), 53–64, http://www.ee.ucl.ac.uk/~m-flanaga/ISL04-pp53-64-Land-et-al.pdf. Land and Jan Meyer's previous work is the basis for "threshold concepts." A threshold "conception" is more fundamental than a threshold concept.

12.   Association of College and Research Libraries, *Framework for Information Literacy for Higher Education,* accessed August 20, 2014, http://acrl.ala.org/ilstandards/wp-content/uploads/2014/02/Framework-for-IL-for-HE-Draft-1-Part-1.pdf, pages 4, 2. See also Deanna Kuhn, "Education for Thinking Project," accessed August 15, 2014, http://www.educationforthinking.org/, esp. parts 2–4.

13.   John Budd, *Knowledge and Knowing in Library and Information Science* (Lanham, MD: Scarecrow Press, 2001), 291–92; Neil Postman, "Social Science as Theology," *ETC: A Review of General Semantics* 41, no. 1 (Spring 1984): 22–32.

14.   Lori G. Power, "University Students' Perceptions of Plagiarism," *The Journal of Higher Education 80, no. 6 (2009): 658.*

15.   Ibid.

16.   Power, "University Students' Perceptions of Plagiarism," 651–52.

17.   *"Guidelines for University Library Services to Undergraduate Students,"* Association of College and Research Libraries, accessed August 20, 2014, http://www.ala.org/acrl/standards/ulsundergraduate.

18.   Wilson describes source knowledge as from others in contrast to first-hand experience in *Second-Hand Knowledge.* Although elsewhere in this collection, it is argued that a "source" is actually another person and not a document at all; library research as discussed in this chapter involves textual records as sources. See also Stephen K. Stoan's contrast between scholarly "research" and "library searching" (using tertiary sources and other reference tools), which he sneeringly says is only done by reference librarians, in "Research and Library Skills: An Analysis and Interpretation," *College and Research Libraries* 45, no. 2 (1984): 99–109.

19.   Elizabeth Frick, "Teaching Information Structure: Turning Dependent Researchers into Self-Teachers," in *Theories of Bibliographic Education: Designs for Teaching,* ed. Cerise Oberman and Katina Strauch (New York: Bowker, 1982), 197.

20.   Keresztesi, "The Science of Bibliography," 6–7.

21. And not only for students. Soo Young Rieh's qualitative study of faculty and graduate students validated his grounded-theory method based on the subjects' awareness of their own search and evaluation behaviors in "Judgment of Information Quality and Cognitive Authority in the Web," *Journal of the American Society for Information Science and Technology* 53, no. 2 (2002): 145–61, http://rieh.people.si.umich.edu/~rieh/papers/rieh_jasist2002.pdf.

22. Rebecca Moore Howard and Laura J. Davies, "Plagiarism in the Internet Age," *Educational Leadership* 66, no. 6 (2009): 64–67.

23. Anthony Grafton, *The Footnote* (Cambridge, MA: Harvard University Press, 1977), 26–27.

24. Henry Small, "Referencing Through History: How the Analysis of Landmark Scholarly Texts Can Inform Citation Theory," *Research Evaluation* 19, no. 3 (2010): 186–87, doi: 10.3152/095820210X503438.

25. Stephen K. Stoan, "Research and Library Skills: An Analysis and Interpretation," *College and Research Libraries* 45, no. 2 (1984): 99–109.

26. Ibid., 103.

27. Susan D. Blum, *My Word! Plagiarism and College Culture* (Ithaca, NY: Cornell University Press, 2009).

28. The problem has become so common that National Public Radio's Neal Conan featured it on his program *Talk of the Nation:* "Cut and Paste Plagiarism," February 14, 2006, radio broadcast, 36:35, http://www.npr.org/templates/story/story.php?storyId=5205929. For one high-profile example, see Jim Rutenberg and Ashley Parker, "Though Defiant, Senator Accused of Plagiarism Admits Errors," *New York Times*, November 5, 2013, http://www.nytimes.com/2013/11/06/us/politics/after-plagiarism-charges-paul-announces-office-restructuring.html?pagewanted=1and_r=1andnl=todays headlinesand emc=edit_th_20131106.

29. Benjamin R. Harris, "Credit Where Credit Is Due: Considering Ethics, 'Ethos,' and Process in Library Instruction on Attribution," *Education Libraries* 28, no. 1 (2005): 6, http://files.eric.ed.gov/fulltext/EJ849007.pdf.

30. Greg R. Notess, "Sighting Cites and Citing Sites," *Online Searcher* 37, no. 3 (2013): 62.

31. Necia Parker-Gibson, "From the Womb to the Web: Library Assignments and the New Generation," *Reference Librarian* 44, no. 91-92 (2005): 83–102.

32. Siva Vaidhyanathan, "Anderson's Wiki-versy," *Publishers Weekly,* June 29, 2009, http://www.publishersweekly.com/pw/by-topic/columns-and-blogs/soapbox/article/1861-anderson-s-wiki-versy.html.

33. "Code of Ethics of the American Library Association," American Library Association, http://www.ala.org/advocacy/sites/ala.org.advocacy/files/content/proethics/codeofethics/Code%20of%20Ethics%20of%20the%20American%20Library%20Association.pdf, section IV.

34. See, for example, Chris M. Anson, "Fraudulent Practices: Academic Misrepresentations of Plagiarism in the Name of Good Pedagogy,"*Composition Studies* 39, no. 2 (Fall 2011): 29–43, http://www.compositionstudies.uwinnipeg.ca/archives/392.html.

35. Kim McMurtry, "E-Cheating: Combating a 21st Century Challenge," *T.H.E. Journal* 29, no. 4 (2001). See also Rieh, "Judgment of Information Quality and Cognitive Authority."

36. "Why don't you use [expletive deleted] MLA style?" (Brown 2014).

37. Mary R. Kinney, *Bibliographical Style Manuals: A Guide to Their Use in Documentation and Research* (Chicago: Association of College and Reference Libraries, 1953), 1 and 18, http://babel.hathitrust.org/cgi/pt?id=mdp.39015036759424;view=1up;seq=1.

38. National Information Standards Organization. ANSI/NISO Z39.29, Bibliographic References. http://www.niso.org/apps/group_public/download.php/12969/Z39_29_2005_R2010.pdf.

39.   Karcher, Sebastian. "Why You Should Be Excited There Are 6000+ CSL Styles." The Zoteroist (blog). http://zoteromusings.wordpress.com/2013/04/30/why-you-should-be-excited-there-are-6000-csl-styles/.

40.   Rosemary G. Feal, "Foreword," in *MLA Handbook for Writers of Research Papers, 7th ed.* (New York: The Modern Language Association of America, 2009), xiv.

41.   *Publication Manual of the American Psychological Association, 6th ed.* (Washington, DC: American Psychological Association, 2010), xiii.

42.   *Chicago Manual of Style, 13th ed.* (Chicago: University of Chicago Press, 1982), vii.

43.   In my own classes, I use these five bibliographical bites as a structure, which includes database searching and critical thinking about topics and sources.

44.   William Manchester, *The Death of a President: November 20–November 25, 1963* (New York: Harper and Row, 1967), 262.

45.   With a grant from LSU Eunice, I will conduct this study in 2014–15. For now, see Mark A. Stellmack et al., "An Assessment of Reliability and Validity of a Rubric for Grading APA-Style Introductions," *Teaching of Psychology* 36, no. 2 (2009): 102–07; Maja Wilson, "Why I Won't Be Using Rubrics to Respond to Students' Writing," *English Journal* 96, no. 4 (2007): 62–66, http://www.jstor.org/stable/10.2307/30047167?origin=crossref; Heidi Goodrich Andrade, "The Role of Instructional Rubrics and Self-Assessment in Learning To Write: A Smorgasbord of Findings" (paper, American Educational Research Association, Montreal, Canada, April 21, 1999), http://files.eric.ed.gov/fulltext/ED431029.pdf.

Andrade, Heidi Goodrich. "The Role of Instructional Rubrics and Self-Assessment in Learning To Write: A Smorgasbord of Findings." (April 21, 1999): *ERIC*, Andrade, Heidi Goodrich. "The Role of Instructional Rubrics and Self-Assessment in Learning To Write: A Smorgasbord of Findings." (April 21, 1999): *ERIC*, Andrade, Heidi Goodrich. "The Role of Instructional Rubrics and Self-Assessment in Learning To Write: A Smorgasbord of Findings." (April 21, 1999): *ERIC*, Andrade, Heidi Goodrich. "The Role of Instructional Rubrics and Self-Assessment in Learning To Write: A Smorgasbord of Findings." (April 21, 1999): *ERIC*,

46.   *MLA Handbook*, 3–5.

47.   Barbara Fister, "Decode Academy" (presentation, LOEX Conference, Nashville, TN, May 3, 2013), 7, http://homepages.gac.edu/~fister/loex13.pdf.

48.   "Literary Eavesdropping and the Socially Graceful Critic," in *Teaching Literary Research: Challenges in a Changing Environment,* ed. Kathleen A. Johnson and Steven R. Harris (Chicago: Association of College and Research Libraries, 2009), 41–60, esp. 42–46. This entire collection is a thoughtful investigation of the relationship of literature professors and librarians, in a way that informs the theory and suggestions of the present work.

49.   Ellie Collier, "Stepping on Toes: The Delicate Art of Talking to Faculty about Questionable Assignments," *In the Library with the Lead Pipe* (March 18, 2009): http://www.inthelibrarywiththeleadpipe.org/2009/stepping-on-toes-the-delicate-art-of-talking-to-faculty-about-questionable-assignments/.

50.   Eugene A. Engledinger, "Bibliographic Instruction and Critical Thinking: The Contribution of the Annotated Bibliography," *RQ* 28, no. 2 (1988): 195–202.

51.   Paulo Freire, *Pedagogy of the Oppressed,* trans. Myra Bergman Ramos (NY: Continuum, 1970), chap. 2; Siva Vaidhyanathan, "Afterword: Critical Information Studies: A Bibliographic Manifesto," *Cultural Studies* 20, no. 2-3 (2006): 292–315, doi: 10.1080/09502380500521091; for two different perspectives, see (1) Lauren Smith, "Critical Information Literacy Instruction for the Development of Political Agency," *Journal of Information Literacy* 7, no. 2 (2013): 15–32, doi: 10.11645/7.2.1809; and (2) Troy Swanson, "A Critical Information Literacy Model: Library Leadership within the Curriculum," *Community College Journal of Research and Practice* 35, no. 11

(2011): 877–94.

52.   David F. Noble, "Technology and the Commodification of Higher Education," *Monthly Review* 53, no. 10 (2002): http://monthlyreview.org/2002/03/01/technology-and-the-commodification-of-higher-education/. Noble identifies the problem in achieving this shift in a time of political reluctance to fund higher education:

> Quality education is labor-intensive; it depends upon a low teacher-student ratio, and significant interaction between the two parties—the one utterly unambiguous result of a century of educational research.

53.   Matthew Battles, *Library: An Unquiet History* (New York: W.W. Norton, 2003). See also John Mark Tucker, "User Education in Academic Libraries: A Century in Retrospect," *Library Trends* 29, no. 1 (1980): 9–27, https://www.ideals.illinois.edu/bitstream/handle/2142/7115/librarytrendsv29i1c_opt.pdf?sequence=1, and Lisa O'Connor, "Information Literacy as Professional Legitimation: A Critical Analysis," *Journal of Education for Library and Information Science* 50, no. 2 (2009): 79–89.

54.   Eveline Houtman, "New Literacies, Learning, and Libraries: How Can Frameworks From Other Fields Help Us Think about the Issues?" *In the Library with the Lead Pipe* (November 6, 2013): http://www.inthelibrarywiththeleadpipe.org/2013/new-literacies-learning-and-libraries-how-can-frameworks-from-other-fields-help-us-think-about-the-issues/.

55.   Keresztesi, "The Science of Bibliography," 2.

56.   Budd, *Knowledge and Knowing in Library and Information Science*, 203.

57.   Colin Lankshear, "The Challenge of Digital Epistemologies," *Education, Communication and Information* 3, no. 2 (2003): 167–86.

58.   Aristotle, "Metaphysics I," trans. J.L. Creed and A.E. Wardman, in *The Philosophy of Aristotle* (New York: New American Library, 1963), 40.

59.   On April 4, 2014, the quotations were by writers from Franklin P. Adams to Ludwig Wittgenstein. www.forbes.com/quotes.

60.   Keith Hossack, *The Metaphysics of Knowledge* (Oxford: Oxford University Press, 2007).

61.   Frederich Nietzche, "On Truth and Lie in an Extra-Moral Sense," accessed April 5, 2014, http://oregonstate.edu/instruct/phl201/modules/Philosophers/Nietzsche/Truth_and_Lie_in_an_Extra-Moral_Sense.htm.

62.   Daniel J. Rader and Emil deGoma, "The Latest Study Isn't the Final Word," Room for Debate: When Medical Experts Disagree, *New York Times*, November 17, 2013, http://www.nytimes.com/roomfordebate/2013/11/17/when-medical-experts-disagree/the-latest-medical-study-isnt-the-final-word.

63.   Reijo Savoleinen, "Epistemic Work and Knowing in Practice as Conceptualizations of Information Use," *Information Research: An International Electronic Journal* 14, no. 1 (2009): http://www.informationr.net/ir/14-1/paper392.html.

64.   *The Cambridge Dictionary of Philosophy*, s.v. "social epistemology."

65.   On April 4, 2014, ACRL released the second part of the draft of *Framework for Information Literacy for Higher Education:* http://acrl.ala.org/ilstandards/wpcontent/uploads/2014/04/Framework-for-IL-for-HE-Draft-1-Part-2.pdf.

66.   Fister, "Decode Academy," 7.

67.   Mark Bauerlein, "Too Dumb for Complex Texts," *Educational Leadership* 68, no. 5 (2011): 28. A more accurate title would have been "Not Too Dumb for Complex Texts" or at least "Too Dumb for Complex Texts?"

68.   Nicholas Delbanco and Alan Cheuse, *Literature: Craft and Voice, 2nd ed.* (New York: McGraw-Hill, 2013).

69.   Laura Gruber Godfrey, "Text and Image: The Internet Generation Reads 'The Short Happy Life of Francis Macomber,'" *Hemingway Review* 32, no. 1 (2012): 39–56.

70.   See Socrates' lament in the *Phaedrus,* discussed by Clive Thompson in Smarter than You Think: How Technology Is Changing Our Minds for the Better (New York: Penguin, 2013), 68–69.

71.   Marshall McLuhan, *The Gutenberg Galaxy* (Toronto, Ontario: Toronto University Press, 1962); Elizabeth L. Eisenstein, *The Printing Press as an Agent of Change: Communication and Cultural Transformation in Early-Modern Europe* (New York: Cambridge University Press, 1979).

72.   Nicholas Carr, *The Shallows: What the Internet Is Doing to Our Brains* (New York: W.W. Norton, 2010).

73.   Ibid., 19.

74.   Andrea Lunsford quoted in Josh Karp, "Does Digital Media Make Us Bad Writers?" Spotlight on Digital Media and Learning, http://spot light.macfound.org/featured-stories/entry/does-digital-media-make-us-bad-writers. Lunsford's work is also discussed in Thompson, *Smarter than You Think*, 66–68.

75.   Of the many reader-centered theorists, Stanley Fish has probably the widest reputation: *Is There a Text in This Class?* (Cambridge, MA: Harvard University Press, 1980).

76.   Godfrey, "Text and Image," 54.

77.   Brian Brenner, review of *The Dumbest Generation by Mark Bauerlein, Leadership and Management in Engineering* 9, no. 2 (2009): 91, doi: 10.1061/(ASCE)1532-6748(2009)9:2(90).

78.   Thompson, *Smarter than You Think,* 17.

79.   Ibid., 7.

80.   Michael Gorman, "Google and God's Mind," *Los Angeles Times,* December 17, 2004, http://articles.latimes.com/2004/dec/17/opinion/oe-nugorman17.

81.   Cite Lighter: 21st Century Critical Thinking Platform, www.citelighter.com.

82.   Green, "Personal Relations between Librarians and Readers," http://polaris.gseis.ucla.edu/jrichardson/DIS220/personal.htm.

CHAPTER 8

Towards an Assumption Responsive Information Literacy Curriculum:

Lessons from Student Qualitative Data

Rob Morrison and Deana Greenfield

In our experience, information literacy is grounded in the assumption that students arrive at higher education lacking the requisite skills, knowledge, and experience to find, use, and evaluate information. The term *information overload* can create the perception and assumption that students are information illiterate while equally charged terms, such as *digital natives, millennials, generation X,* and *generation Y,* unconsciously influence our perceptions of who students are and what they know.[1] Librarians face changing student populations, rapidly evolving digital technologies, and a constantly changing information landscape. When we began teaching credit courses on digital information literacy, we sought to confront our assumptions about students and their learning. By integrating multiple responsive teaching tools, we were able to create a two-way exchange of information that informed us of student assumptions; allowed us to respond to their questions, concerns, and opinions; and ultimately disrupted many of the categories into which students are unfairly lumped.

Constructivism and Critical Reflection

The constructivist approach to learning values student experiences where students actively participate in their learning.[2] Constructivism is an active process of engaging and interrogating knowledge. Students learn how to build on prior experience, construct meaning, and make sense of their experiences in direct contrast to the banking approach of filling the student with knowledge.[3] In our teaching, students are active participants in their learning rather than empty vessels to be filled. We also believe that "learning is the construction of meaning from experience."[4] Traditional information literacy instruction is rooted in behaviorism where learning is observable and objective.[5] Grades and learning outcomes are examples of how behaviorism manifests in current educational practice. Behaviorism values demonstrable skills; what students can do and prove reinforces the banking approach to education. Students' experiences, emotions, cultures, and environment are often secondary or completely ignored in a strictly sequential process model. Our teaching philosophy goes beyond viewing information as an observable fact that is neutral and requires mastering; we emphasize helping students develop a consciousness about information and its social development in the world.[6] The problem, as we see it, is that librarians who adhere to a simple process model risk valorizing specific skills that can detract from viewing information as socially constructed, interconnected, and complex, demanding critical reflection and thinking.

Critical reflection and critical thinking are integral parts of student engagement and integrating a constructivist and critical approach to teaching. We crafted a definition of critical reflection using adult educator Stephen D. Brookfield's terminology and philosophy where being "critical" means actively investigating and revealing dominant beliefs, power structures, and practice. In this process, assumptions are uncovered by being checked and "hunted" in order to develop different perspectives.[7] Librarians and students who do not integrate this form of critical reflection into their practice risk falling back on ideologies and structures that dictate how the world operates instead of critically thinking and questioning. We practice "critical information literacy," which integrates traditional information literacy skills with a critical eye towards social and cultural boundaries. We challenge students to dig deeper into the social construction of information and engage with the larger and more complex contexts. Examining knowledge construction involves looking at the "why" behind beliefs we take for granted and acknowledging that information is not neutral or value free. One example is that for students to effectively evaluate all information, we must take them beyond the traditional "academic information literacy" of learning and idolization of scholarly sources.[8]

Educators can make assumptions about student learning, experiences, and knowledge because it is easy, but this outlook can also impede student learning as a process of inquiry.[9] In our experience, teaching information literacy is more effective in context and comprises more than just a series of tasks.[10] Librarians can prepare lesson plans without *always* knowing student competencies and knowledge. To address this issue, we resolved to uncover student assumptions in a face-to-face credit course on digital information literacy.

Library Credit Courses at National Louis University

National Louis University (NLU) was founded in Chicago in 1886 to train kindergarten teachers. Today, around 8,500 students are enrolled online and at campuses in Illinois, Wisconsin, Florida, and Poland and at field sites, usually businesses or other schools. NLU has three distinct colleges: the National College of Education (NCE), the founding college, and two newer ones, College of Arts and Sciences and the College of Management and Business that are now combining into a single college. NLU has mainly served nontraditional working adults and has focused on recruitment of minority and underserved populations as part of our social justice mission. Many courses are accelerated (three weeks to a full semester) with some undergraduate programs completed in a year and doctoral programs in three years. Library instruction has been challenging for a distributed campus model and accelerated programs where in-class sessions are generally short and follow-ups conducted by phone or e-mail. Librarians are faculty at NLU and for years taught an undergraduate credit course on using library resources as adjuncts for the College of Arts and Sciences. In 2008, recognizing that NLU students needed to learn digital skills, library faculty proposed and created a course called Digital Information Literacy.

LIBR 200: Digital Information Literacy is a two-quarter hour credit course that was initially offered as a three-week fully online general education elective.[11] This course introduced students to a critical consideration of information in digital formats. In 2009, ten sections were taught, four as part of an accelerated undergraduate business management program. Enrollment in these courses was small and did not exceed ten students in a single class. This was our first experience developing and teaching an extremely short credit class where time constraints made even skill building a challenge. Our experience with teaching digital information literacy online was helpful, but in 2010 we were asked to create a blended but mainly face-to-face version for a pilot program that spurred us to test assumptions and reflect on our pedagogy and educational practice.

In the fall of 2010, NLU started a daytime college program for traditional-aged students, a departure from its historical service to adult learners with evening and weekend classes. The daytime program was an attempt to recruit younger students from diverse populations for weekday classes in Chicago at our downtown campus. Undergraduate programs involved were elementary education, business management, and human services. LIBR 200 was taught as a face-to-face class in 2010, initially meeting twice a week over four weeks. The following year, we extended the class over ten weeks, meeting once a week for one and a half hours. After the first year, readings, discussion boards, and assignments were all placed online in a learning management system: WebCT, BlackBoard, and, today, Desire2Learn. In 2010 and 2011, four sections of LIBR 200 were taught in the fall with two sections in Fall 2012. One section was taught in Spring 2011 and Winter 2012. In addition, nine sections of LIBR 200 were taught entirely online as a five-week undergraduate elective course from Fall 2012 to Summer 2013.

Librarian Assumptions

The daytime program was an opportunity for librarians to participate more deeply in the student learning experience. The mixed population of returning adults and traditional-aged students was the catalyst for our wanting to learn more about students' prior search experience and their use of technology in order to quickly identify baseline information-seeking skills. Recognizing that critical thinking requires students to grapple with complex issues of authority, knowledge production, and privileged academic sources, we sought to further understand students' preexisting assumptions and experiences that impacted their information-seeking process. We view information literacy education as more than developing search skills and as more effective in context rather than a series of tasks.[12] Our desire to update the online class was another catalyst for reexamining our curriculum and practice.

The face-to-face class was an opportunity for us to work in person with students over an extended time frame. We had prior experience teaching students who had little experience with technology (computers, word processing programs), and in the fully online courses, students had to have some level of experience or comfort learning with technology. This new in-person/blended version was taught in a computer lab, and one of the first things we wanted to know for certain was if students could work online at home or only at the campus computer labs. Concern about students' experience with technology and Internet access was one of the catalysts for our decision to obtain hard data and avoid making assumptions. Other assumptions we did *not* want to make included students' search experience (knowledge of effective searching on the Internet and subscription databases); students' ability to evaluate information; students' familiarity with citing and academic honesty concepts; and students' critical thinking about searching for information. We had experience working with academically underprepared students and expected (assumed) that most students would not be proficient with searching, citing, and evaluating information. This course presented us with an opportunity to interrogate our assumptions and integrate active learning assignments in response.

Qualitative Data Collection Tools

Data was collected from 12 face-to-face classes taught from Fall 2010 to Fall 2012 that enrolled 163 students. We did not collect demographic information from students (age, ethnic identity, employment, income, etc.). The majority of students were Latino and African American and in their first year of college classes; some had taken community college courses. This information was confirmed by student advisors, who worked closely with all faculty to monitor student progress.

We used a variety of tools in the class to uncover assumptions and to help us "hunt" for them in the student learning process. The following tools collected qualitative data that provided depth and context to our assumptions and to student learning: pre-class survey, critical incident questionnaire, and end-of-course evaluations.

Pre-Class Survey Results

The first step in understanding student assumptions was implementing a survey to determine their access to and current use of technology. We considered the survey a pretest as it was administered early during the first day of class. Initially titled "Technology Survey," this instrument served as a form for students' self-reported use of technology, where they initially searched for information, and how they evaluated sources for credibility. The responses informed us on the students' experiences and assumptions and provided initial data on their search habits, favored resources, and evaluation criteria. This pre-class survey was most useful in determining how many students had access to the Internet outside of the classroom and prior experience searching online for information.

In response to the first question, "Where is the first place that you go to look for information?," the majority of responses were "Google," "Internet," or "library." This feedback confirmed one of our assumptions: Students' first stop for information is the Internet. We discovered through class discussions that some students had used a public library in their community for group study and reading purposes. We did see some thoughtful responses to this question related to the topic being the determining factor: "It depends on what type of topic I'm trying to find information on" and "the topic determines where I look" reflect a deeper level of critical thinking.

We asked several technology questions such as "Do you have a computer at home with Internet access?" and "Do you own a cell phone, iPhone, or other mobile device?" The percentage of students who did not own a computer at home with Internet access was around ten percent. This data confirmed our assumption that not every student would be able to work on assignments outside of class time. Using this information, we allotted more in-class time to assignments over the years and noted that many of the online discussion boards and quizzes were completed by students the day of class during school hours. Most students reported owning some type of portable device, usually a cell phone. As sometimes the cell phone was their only access to the Internet off-campus, we made sure that our course shells and activities were mobile friendly. After several years of asking this question about cell phones, we expanded the language to "What type of digital tools do you have or have used?" in an effort to be inclusive of apps and other programs students may have encountered. Examples of responses included websites, apps, iPhone, iPad, digital cameras, Flickr, Google Drive, etc. Overall, students self-reported a high level of comfort with technology, especially in regards to social media websites and messaging applications (Facebook reigned supreme).

Our assumption that students entered the classroom unfamiliar with the concepts of citation and information evaluation was proven false. On the question of "How do you acknowledge someone else's ideas or exact words?," we found the majority of responses were "citing," "quoting," "paraphrasing," "in a bibliography," "footnote," and "by giving them credit." However, performance on later class assignments showed that students were not knowledgeable of the specifics of academic citation styles such as APA or MLA. In response to the question, "What information do you consider as reliable and credible?," most students provided examples of various academics sources: books, journals, websites, evidence, encyclopedias, textbooks, specific websites, "from professionals," "have credentials," "from experts." Other students offered more general statements on the nature of credible information such as that which is "supported by statistics" and "theories that have proof." Several students acknowledged the difficulty of determining credibility: "The kind of information that I consider reliable and credible is the information that is written by professionals but then again it's always hard knowing because there is so much information that may or may not be true on google." In addition, the anonymity of the survey allowed for honesty as some students answered "I don't know" and "I am not sure," which led to further in-class discussion.

The question "What types of websites do you use for school assignments/projects?" revealed many students had been exposed to academic sources and directed to use them:

- "I choose carefully from the sites given to me. I stay away from blogs, and .coms and prefer .edu's, and .govs."
- "The Internet sites that have a .edu or .org ending also newspaper articles from reputable places. In addition, scholarly articles from college databases."

The comments about scholarly sources being credible and using material from professionals and experts revealed many students had some classroom experience with these concepts and used criteria to evaluate sources. We also saw the typical anti-*Wikipedia* ideology in comments: "not wikipedia" and "wiki is evil." Our takeaway from the survey is that many students were exposed to or had experience searching, citing, and evaluating information; their expertise, skills, and actual knowledge, though, would be demonstrated through classroom assignments and discussions. Our assumption that students were used to searching the Internet but did not differentiate between websites and databases was confirmed in search assignments. This data also revealed that students had prior search experience and exposure to some types of academic sources (books, encyclopedias, not scholarly journals) and "exhibit information literacy competencies in their own way."[13] We knew that we could not jump to advanced lesson plans on searching and evaluating sources based on this self-reported qualitative data, but it did challenge our assumptions that every student came to this course with no experience.

Critical Incident Questionnaire

The critical incident questionnaire (CIQ) is a tool designed by Brookfield to anonymously identify issues, concerns, and problems from students.[14] CIQs are comprised of five open-ended questions that ask learners about the most engaging and distancing moments, the most affirming and confusing actions, and the most surprising moments in the classroom.

Anonymous in nature, CIQs can help uncover unspoken thoughts and reveal assumptions by both students and instructors. In our course we used the CIQ to "take the temperature" of the class around the third or fourth week. The CIQs provided a rich source of information that informed our assumptions about student learning and revealed the emotional highs and lows of student learning. In addition, the CIQ questions encouraged reflective learning as students noted their own emotional responses to course content and discussions.

We asked five questions on our CIQ:

1. At what moment in class did you feel most engaged with what was happening?
2. At what moment were you most distanced from what was happening?

3. What action that anyone (teacher or student) took did you find most affirming or helpful?
4. What action that anyone took did you find most puzzling or confusing?
5. What about this class surprised you the most? (This could be about your own reactions to what went on, something that someone did, or anything else that occurs).

The first question, "At what moment in class did you feel most engaged with what was happening?," illuminated student learning styles. Numerous comments supported the value of group discussions and activities; we received more positive than negative comments:

- "Discussions: The time when we got to discuss our opinions. It lets me know our teachers care about how we feel and what we think."
- "When we do activities as a class."
- "During the in class debate"
- "When we all get into groups and take the time to put what we have learn [*sic*] from the lecture"
- "Also, I enjoy the discussions that we had because it is a great way to learn from others."

Seemingly contradictory comments, such as "I feel more engaged when we have discussions" and "I get more distracted after a discussion," both showed evidence of engagement with content. These comments comprised a majority of responses, confirming our assumptions on the value of active engagement and discussions. The third question, "What action that anyone (teacher or student) took did you find most affirming or helpful?," provided positive feedback on active learning assignments: "visual aids," "videos," and "group discussions and projects." A few students reported a preference for individual work: "I felt most engaged when we are pretty much on our own and we are working on our projects." This comment confirmed that some students may want to work individually, not in groups. We had a variety of assignments where students worked both in groups and individually (their final project was a solo venture); the CIQ confirmed that students had different learning styles and preferences.

Comments on what was most surprising included negative comments about other students' behaviors ("it's annoying how many people still, continuously come to class late") and positive comments on the value of group discussions ("how everyone had the chance to say what they thought about a topic and we didn't have to hear the teacher lecture the whole time"). These comments helped verify the impact of specific behaviors and dynamics observed in class by librarians. Also confirmed were our assumptions that students were building on searching, citing, and evaluating information skills in the class, based on the initial survey data:

- "There are a lot of things out there that I never knew about."
- "How there were certain databases that provide different information from search engines."
- "I thought it was going to be a class on how to use the Internet, but it has actually been helpful. For example, I had never heard of Google books."
- "Overall I have been surprised by all the new information that I have to learn. It has helped me a lot and this class has been informative."
- "It surprises me that even with everyone in the class depending on the technology for everything, their responses were of 'waiting' to do research the old-fashioned manual way."

Students demonstrated through these comments that our assumptions concerning the need and value of this class were substantiated.

End-of-Course Course Evaluations

We conducted our own end-of-course evaluations on the final day to obtain feedback as official university evaluations were almost never completed by students. Data from two key questions, "How could this course be improved?" and "What did you learn in this course? What was new?," confirmed the value of creating active lesson plans, using guiding questions to frame content, and challenging students to dig deeper were effective tools. We also received useful feedback on how to construct meaningful activities.

We received multiple comments from students who wanted to spend more in-class time on assignments: "more practice," "more activities," "I think it can improve by getting more group involvement," "it can have more social activities that help the student participate and share their thoughts," "more involvement, less lecture," "could improve on more activities where students talk more and are forced to participate," "be nice if you made more group activities that way people can get to know each other a little more," and "I think that we could have worked in groups more and made it a little bit more fun." In the first year, lectures were a group activity followed by in-class discussion; in subsequent years, lectures were moved to online homework, leaving more time for discussion and other activities in class. The "flipped" classroom model operates under an assumption that students will actually review videos, lectures, and other materials prior to class; in our experience, many students did not, so group activities often ended up incorporating lectures for context and support.

The comments on common knowledge helped verify classroom interactions when students made oral comments that demonstrated critical thinking and learning when discussing knowledge that is shared by all. Our lesson plan on plagiarism, "Why We Cite," critically explored the reasons and benefits of citing to expand upon learning citing skills. Comments such as these demonstrated critical thinking that was not superficial:

- "I learned that common knowledge is a bit vague because it mainly depends on who you are and where you come from."
- "I learned how to analyze a source in a new way that proved to be useful and efficient. Before taking this course I had no real way of knowing if a source was actually credible, or just looked credible."
- "I really like how the teacher made us think critically and how he would challenge the students on their responses."

One student did not know the fictitious story of George Washington and the cherry tree during an exercise on identifying common knowledge, providing a powerful teaching moment for the class that not all knowledge is shared or conventional in nature.

Curriculum Revisions

The data collected helped us to revise assignments that focused on the student experience, provide reflective evaluation, and exercise critical thinking that emphasized connections to process-oriented lessons. We integrated a constructivist approach to teaching by having students "engage concepts… through a process of inquiry, reflection and application."[15] Through reflection journals and classroom discussions, students were encouraged to explore their initial assumptions and examine the process of knowledge construction while still acquiring skills necessary to locate information.

The major revisions to LIBR 200 (face-to-face and online) were

- lectures were moved to homework;
- an increase in class time to write evaluations and practice citing;

- the number of reflection journal entries were reduced to two in 2012 and then incorporated into the final project in online classes starting in 2013;
- writing specialists were integrated into curriculum development and teaching (helped with writing annotations in 2011 and 2012); and
- an increase in discussion time, group activities, videos, and graphical materials (added after 2010).

We focused on evaluating information and allocating more in-class time to this activity where students applied critical thinking strategies as a means to developing information literacy skills.[16] One reason for this change was many students had inadequate reading and writing skills; this became more evident as the term progressed and convinced us that integrating writing specialists into the course was essential. Our assumption that an information literacy class could be taught without this essential piece and that students were developing writing competencies in other classes was proved incorrect.

Many students had difficulties writing and communicating in English. We invited writing specialists into the class to help with students and learned that this issue required considerably more time and attention. In 2011, the University Library was combined with all tutoring services into a unit called Library and Learning Support; in the future LIBR 200 will be revised by a team of librarians and learning support specialists to more effectively address student writing and citing needs.

LIBR 200 was revised every year; some revisions were minor (updated tutorials, new articles) and others were more substantive. Reflection journals were a part of every learning module in 2010 in the face-to-face classes. In 2011 and 2012, we reduced the number of modules from five to three: the impact of technology, academic integrity, and evaluating information. This change was for several reasons: We wanted students to spend more time on assignments; we thought the CIQs provided an additional reflection tool; and we increased points for the final project.

In 2013, we piloted moving the reflection journal to the final project in the online classes. We assumed students would reflect critically on each assignment; this did not happen, particularly in the online classes. We believe this change will also facilitate assessment of student learning. One student in our 2013 online class provided a reflection that demonstrates our objective to foster critical thinking and focuses on the purpose of citing:

> Citing and academic honesty is not merely a requirement, it is a demonstration of ethics and scholarly professionalism. When works are cited it is not a sign of personal weakness in a subject, it is evidence of solid research. It shows how scholars build on other works to better express their views and validate their ideas. Not only is citing about academic honesty and enforcing policies, it protects the work of original authors, and greatly aids in the educational process by inspiring study and academic growth.

We also incorporated more hands-on activities in response to student comments and framed learning modules with guiding questions. Asking "why" helps students examine their assumptions and focuses on critically analyzing information as part of the evaluation process.[17] Posing questions is a strategy that facilitates moving away from assumptions.[18] Lectures were moved to homework with a follow-up class discussion and additional hands-on activities to respond to comments from the CIQs and course evaluations. More class time was devoted to writing annotations and evaluations when students struggled the most with these activities. When students reported that group discussions, videos, and other visual media were engaging, we increased their role and use in the class.

The data also verified our strategy of not assuming students could demonstrate what they reported on the pre-class survey. The best example is being familiar with citing. Many students did not know APA style (we expected this), and many reported citing as a means to provide attribution on the surveys. The number of assignments turned in with incomplete citations was another factor; many students submitted partial APA citations for their final project. The comments on CIQs, course evaluations, and in-class on common knowledge supported our assumption that academic honesty policies and citing had to be critically presented and explored in class. By discussing and examining the definition of common knowledge, we were able to open the door to exploring knowledge construction and privilege (who defines knowledge?).

Conclusion

Our assumption responsive curriculum is one potential model to bridge the gap between the "how" and "why" of information literacy instruction in any classroom setting. Librarians used guided lesson plans to provide a structure and framework for students, many who arrived with little preparation for college-level coursework and were balancing jobs, family, and school. The qualitative data we received informed our assumptions, lesson plans, and engagement strategies; this experience was transformative in the sense that we understood our students' habits and thoughts better and were able to verify or expand active learning lessons. Many students did demonstrate critical thinking skills that went beyond viewing information as simple containers and clearly learned new perspectives on search tools and strategies as evident in the course evaluations.

We learned more about how students think, feel, and experience the research process. Assumptions are easy to make and not difficult to uncover; we all make them, and the tools discussed in this chapter are effective for making them visible. We learned that an assumption responsive curriculum is part of an overall strategy to facilitate student learning. Developing this type of curriculum requires multiple strategies. First, detailed interaction and assessment with students. The CIQs greatly facilitated learning students' thoughts and feelings in addition to providing useful feedback. Second, assumption checking must be ongoing and embedded in practice and teaching; librarians must consistently reflect on their practice and lesson plans. All NLU librarians and adjuncts teaching credit courses are required to write a teaching reflection for every course to share issues, problems, successes, strategies, and assumptions with colleagues. Third, critical reflection and thinking are integral to the process and must be practiced by librarians and students. In the words of Brookfield, "A critically reflective stance towards our practice is healthily ironic, a necessary hedge against an overconfident belief that we have captured the one universal truth about good practice."[19] Exploring student assumptions also helped us to check our own assumptions about individual students search habits and experience. We learned how to more effectively provide a highly responsive curriculum and class environment where students practiced critical reflection and demonstrated critical thinking.

Notes

1.   Association of College and Research Libraries, *Information Literacy Competency Standards for Higher Education*, accessed September 5, 2013, http://www.ala.org/acrl/sites/ala.org.acrl/files/content/standards/standards.pdf; Rosemary Green, "Information Illiteracy: Examining Our Assumptions," *Journal of Academic Librarianship* 36 (2010): 313–19.

2.   Nancy Pickering Thomas, Sherry R. Crow, and Lori L. Franklin, *Information Literacy and Information Skills Instruction: Applying Research to Practice in the 21st Century School Library* (Santa Barbara, CA: Libraries Unlimited, 2011), 78.

3.   Stephen D. Brookfield, *Becoming a Critically Reflective Teacher* (San Francisco: Jossey-Bass, 1995); Sharan B. Merriam, Rosemary S. Caffarella, and Lisa M. Baumgartner, eds., *Learning in Adulthood* (San Francisco: Jossey-Bass, 2007); Penny Bealle, "Using Constructivism to Engage Students in an Online Credit IL Course," in *Best Practices for Credit-Bearing Information Literacy Courses,* ed. Christopher V. Hollister (Chicago: American Library Association, 2010); Ibid., 242–55; Kenneth R. Howe and Jason Berv, "Constructing Constructivism, Epistemological, and Pedagogical," in *Constructivism in Education: Opinions and Second Opinions on Controversial Issues, ed. D.C. Phillips* (Chicago: University of Chicago Press, 2000), 19–40; Paulo Freire, Pedagogy of the Oppressed, trans. Myra Bergman Ramos (New York: Continuum, 2003).

4.   Sharan B. Merriam and Lara L. Bierama, *Adult Learning: Linking Theory and Practice* (San Francisco: Jossey-Bass, 2014), 36.

5.   Ibid.

6.   Freire, *Pedagogy of the Oppressed.*

7.   Stephen D. Brookfield, *Teaching for Critical Thinking* (San Francisco: Jossey-Bass, 2012), 11.

8.   James Elmborg, "Critical Information Literacy: Implications for Instructional Practice," *Journal of Academic Librarianship,* 32 (2006): 192–99.

9.   Carolyn B. Gamtso and Susanne F. Paterson, "Guiding Students from Consuming Information to Creating Knowledge," *Communications in Information Literacy* 5 (2011): 118.

10.   Thomas, Crow, and Franklin, *Information Literacy and Information Skills Instruction.*

11.   Details on the development of credit courses in digital information literacy are chronicled in this paper: Marisa Walstrum, Larissa Garcia, and Rob Morrison, "From Embedded to Integrated: Digital Information Literacy and New Teaching Models for Academic Librarians" (paper, Association of College and Research Libraries National Conference, Philadelphia, Pennsylvania, April 1, 2011), http://www.ala.org/acrl/sites/ala.org.acrl/files/content/conferences/confsandpreconfs/national/2011/papers/from_embedded.pdf.

12.   Thomas, Crow, and Franklin, *Information Literacy and Information Skills Instruction.*

13.   Green, "Information Illiteracy: Examining Our Assumptions," 316.

14.   Stephen D. Brookfield, "Critical Incident Questionnaire," accessed July 15, 2013, http://www.stephenbrookfield.com/Dr._Stephen_D._Brookfield/Critical_Incident_Questionnaire.html.

15.   Bealle, "Using Constructivism," 242.

16.   Ibid., 243.

17.   Gamtso and Paterson, "Guiding Students," 117–26.

18.   Bealle, "Using Constructivism," 246.

19.   Stephen D. Brookfield, "The Concept of Critically Reflective Practice," in *Handbook of Adult and Continuing Education,* ed. Arthur L. Wilson and Elisabeth R. Hayes (San Francisco: Jossey-Bass, 2000), 46.

CHAPTER 9

Expertise and Authority in an Age of Crowdsourcing

William B. Badke

It scarcely needs to be asserted that students in higher education struggle with evaluating the multitude of resources they have available to them for research. The rise of *Wikipedia* and the ubiquity of Google have challenged traditional notions of academic expertise. Why do we need experts when we have a crowdsourced encyclopedia like *Wikipedia* that, according to a 2005 *Nature* article, is almost as accurate as Britannica?[1] This is the era of the wisdom of crowds and of a diminished appreciation of expertise. What is more is that Google and *Wikipedia* are the preferred initial research resources for many students in higher education, leading to a much wider concept of "useable information" than existed in the more restrictive academic environments of the past.[2]

This contributes to a rather limited notion of what is required to be an "expert." If you as a professor claim to your class, "I know more than you do," does that make you an expert? If so, then students can counter by arguing that our current access to information makes mere knowing an unnecessary attribute. Knowledge is a cheap commodity today. What we don't know, we can look up. Who needs a knowledge expert?

Even if we were to find that expertise and its resulting declaration of authority are still necessary in our world, the current information environment makes it exceedingly difficult to determine what resources are worthy of respect. Imagine a keen student who comes across the following article in a Google Scholar search: "Cultural-Institutional Persistence under Autarchy, International Trade, and Factor Mobility" (http://www.santafe.edu/media/workingpapers/13-01-003.pdf). The paper looks like a scholarly work (citations and bibliography), and the authors have high credentials, but there is no journal title in the PDF. Is this a pre-peer-review posting of something that will later go through the regular publishing process, ending up in an established journal? Or has it simply been published to the web without any vetting? The answer is "neither." It has been posted by the Santa Fe Institute as a "working paper." That is, while having been written by competent people and perhaps reviewed to some extent by the institute, it has been posted as a work in progress, with actual peer review possibly in its future.

Changing understandings of expertise and authority, tied with the long-standing challenge that evaluation is difficult for any student who lacks subject knowledge and is unfamiliar with the conventions of the discipline, make evaluation of resources a difficult prospect. In order to understand the nature of the problem and its potential solutions, we must first trace recent developments in our growing uncertainty about the nature of expertise and authority.

The Era of Crowdsourcing
Where We Were

Harry M. Collins and Robert Evans have described the evolution of thinking about expertise in the sciences as comprising three waves.[3] Wave One of the 1950s and 1960s saw scholars being accepted as authoritative simply by virtue of their education and expertise. Collins and Evans argue, "Because the sciences were thought of as esoteric as well as authoritative, it was inconceivable that decision-making in matters that involved science and technology could travel in any other direction than from the top down."[4]

Wave Two arose out of a growing recognition that Wave One was circular: Information is authoritative because it is produced by authorities, who in turn are authorities because their qualifications make their pronouncements authoritative. For Wave Two, there must be some alternative way of measuring authority beyond saying, "I am an authority because I am an authority."[5] Thus there was greater interest in public participation and evaluation, along with the recognition that the work of experts has a political aspect to it that may influence authoritative statements. In fact, the boundary between expert and nonexpert was perforated to such an extent that it became difficult to determine what statement was actually authoritative and what was not. This led to Wave Three, a corrective to Wave Two, in which expertise is questioned and challenged but still recognized if it passes the test.

Wave Two, as described in Collins and Evans's study is of particular significance in that it fits with developments in the 1960s and beyond that tended to level all knowledge, challenging the very concepts of expertise and authority.

The New Consciousness

There has been a steady movement in the past few decades away from the traditional concepts of expertise and authority, both in academia and in popular culture, driven by parallel movements in the theory and democratization of knowledge.

In knowledge theory, the pervasive label for the spirit of our age is likely "postmodernism," which emphasizes the subjectivity of authors and readers, along with an increasing uncertainty about the authority or even validity of authoritative pronouncements.

Closely linked to postmodern thinking is the increasing recognition that knowledge dissemination is intensely political rather than objective and disinterested. Consider, for example, the works of Paolo Freire and Brian Martin.[6] Freire wrote of a pervasive "banking concept of education," in which the expert instructor bestows knowledge upon the "ignorant" student. Seeing this as a method for oppression, Freire proposed a process of "problem-posing education" in which professor and students learn together. Tellingly, he argued: "In this process, arguments based on 'authority' are no longer valid; in order to function, authority must be *on the side of* freedom, not *against* it. Here, no one teaches another, nor is anyone self-taught. Men teach each other, mediated by the world, by the cognizable objects which in banking education are 'owned' by the teacher."[7]

Freire's strong critique of knowledge oppression has been highly influential in helping to move instruction from "sage on the stage" to "guide on the side." But it has also rendered suspect the idea that anyone should claim to be a knowledge authority. Authority, to Freire, results in oppression.

Martin took a slightly different tack, arguing that academia, in essence, forms a guild intended to accentuate the difference between the expert and everyone else. Even the use of terminology can become a means to elevate authority illegitimately: "The specialised language and concepts of the discipline are convenient for those in the know. They also are convenient for ensuring that outsiders can't quickly see through to the essence of the issues."[8] The academic guild for Martin is intensely political. Once experts have all-encompassing control over knowledge, it is in their best interests to make sure that nonexperts are excluded. The result is that mediocre research, which has the approval of the academy, passes peer review, while potentially better material that is new or radical does not see the light of day. Martin's critique casts doubt on the notion that information is authoritative just because it is academic or peer reviewed. To enlist the perspective of Collins and Evans, academia, for Martin, perpetuates First-Wave thinking: Something is authoritative because the academic guild says it is authoritative.

Philip Schlesinger more recently has argued that academics are driven by interests that go far beyond disinterested use of expertise as they try to make authoritative statements uninfluenced by outside forces. Rather than being guided by their own academic culture, they are compelled by market forces:

> As opposed to the first model of an internalized culture that supplies the public sphere with spontaneously generated intellectual work, this is a *necessity-driven, demand-led model.* Ideal-typically, you produce research and engage in knowledge exchange in line with what is requested in order to justify your existence. Public intellectuality, therefore, is wanted but only on certain, quite instrumental, terms.[9]

The politicization of expertise and authority to meet utilitarian goals is, for Martin, Schlesinger, and many other scholars, a path to perverting the purposes of genuine scholarship, thus casting the whole notion of academic authority into disarray.[10]

Yet much of the current challenge in the field of authority comes less from the theorists than from the practical realities of the World Wide Web, which has led to the democratization of knowledge. Though it has been scarcely more 20 years since the web was created, it has transformed our understanding of what constitutes valid and significant information. From a restrictive but far more certain environment of peer review and other gatekeeping processes that limit publication, we now have anyone able to publish their ideas to the world. With the ubiquitous Google having become the tool of choice for student research, we are left with a challenge of epic proportions: How can we determine what has authority, or even what can be believed?

There is now an alternative to the authoritative scholar: Information produced by the crowd. The classic example is *Wikipedia*, which, rather than developing through contributions of recognized scholars, has been written by the people, the "great unwashed," or so the mythology goes. The theory behind crowdsourcing has actually been with us for quite some time. In 1907, Francis Galton published an article in *Nature* in which he demonstrated that 800 people, averaged out, could actually judge the weight of an ox to within one percent of its actual weight.[11] This concept has been described as "the wisdom of the crowd" and posits that, given enough people working on a single problem, a result can be produced that is comparable in value to the finding of an expert. In recent years, it has been popularized by the enthusiastic writings of journalist James Surowiecki.[12]

While it is commonly asserted that *Wikipedia* developed in just such a fashion, this is not entirely true. Sabine Niederer and José van Dijck point out that much of the mechanism that keeps *Wikipedia* from degenerating into chaos is controlled by editors and software: "The technicity of *Wikipedia* content … lies in the totality of tools and software robots used for creating, editing and linking entries, combating vandalism, banning users, scraping and feeding content, and cleaning articles. It is the complex collaboration not of crowds, but of human and nonhuman agents combined that defines the quality standards of *Wikipedia* content."[13]

The late Aaron Schwartz found, through discussion with the originator of *Wikipedia* and his own research, that while *Wikipedia* "outsiders" provide most of the initial content, a cadre of insiders do most of the edits.[14] Aniket Kittur and Robert E. Kraut have demonstrated that explicit coordination of editors in the development of *Wikipedia* articles is crucial to their success.[15] In essence, the power of *Wikipedia* is not in the supposed wisdom of the crowd but in a carefully designed and extensive system of quality control.

Google, similarly, constitutes a wisdom of the crowd in that Google's algorithms are based strongly on the links other sites make to a target site. Websites that have more external links made to them tend to rise to the top of search results, on the premise that heavy use by others indicates that such a site is inherently better than one that is ignored. External links form a crowd opinion about a website, thus giving it higher standing.[16]

James Goldman's dissertation on "collective intelligence" found that, while crowdsourced knowledge creation holds promise, it has yet to overcome the challenge that experienced users of the World Wide Web do not attribute the same credibility to creations of the collective that they do to sources that they view as having "cognitive authority."[17] Thus, while alternative approaches to the expertise-authority issue exist in our time, there is less trust in their validity than there is with more traditionally produced information. This leads to confusion. If we are not sure we can trust our "authorities," but we dare not rely too much on the crowd, how do we determine what information we can reliably use?

Now that authority structures are under challenge and the new options available to access information have varying levels of authority (in the traditional academic sense of the word), a new consciousness has risen. The result is, as Adam Frank has so ably described it, that we have entered an "age of denial" in which the pronouncements of authorities, particularly scientific authorities, are simply dismissed as one person's view that can easily be rejected by those who choose not to believe it.[18]

The Loss of Guideposts

With the role of authority figures in academia under challenge and the increasing growth in digital information that has not been peer reviewed or otherwise controlled by any traditional models of gatekeeping, today's student lives in a decidedly ambiguous and confusing academic environment.

MaryBeth Meszaros, in fact, has labeled this problem a "crisis:" "The word crisis may at first seem hyperbolic, but when one considers what is at stake—the ability of a citizenry to render reflective judgments, to weigh knowledge claims, to generate evaluations based on something more substantive than mere taste and feeling—the designation is apt.[19]

This growing uncertainty about the authority of academic assertions has been a phenomenon for several decades. Peter J. Pels and Lorraine Nencel, writing in 1991, referred to their fellow anthropologists as all being "uncertain about our projects" and all doubting "the representation of local knowledge in local texts."[20]

Not everyone shares this sort of pessimism. Mark E. Warren argues that authority is challenged only when it appears to be "unjustifiable." Thus we do not have a crisis, but an increasing pluralism in authority structures.[21] Warren's approach, unfortunately, is of little comfort to students who lack the subject knowledge and evaluation criteria to discern even what is justifiable and what is not.

The growth of digital culture through the Internet has exacerbated the problem. The University of California's commission on the future of the Berkeley Library stated the challenge cogently:

> Paradoxically, the massive and largely unregulated expansion of scholarly materials and information on the Internet has made it more difficult for scholars to locate authenticated materials and related services and to discover new resources. Expensive investments are underutilized as are cheaper and equally useable alternatives. For students, the challenge of finding appropriate materials in both print and e-forms and of distinguishing between reliable and non-reliable sources has become evermore difficult.[22]

What is it about the mere existence of a digital culture that makes it problematic for assessing authority of resources? Ray Land refers to the changeable nature of electronic texts that can be edited or altered at will, along with the constant increase in commentary on existing texts. Digital texts are thus "characterised by their volatility, multivocality, and radical contestability [which] become implicated in the 21st-century university's difficulty in maintaining and asserting its traditional authority."[23]

A recent paper from the International Federation of Library Associations describes a challenge to the very notion of the authorship and ownership of information: "New digital content is being created at an unprecedented pace, and is crowdsourced, computer-generated, and remixed as well as created by individuals. It can be easily shared and distributed, with impacts on markers of authorship, exercising of control and notions of 'ownership.'"[24] If we cannot determine authorship, our evaluation of authority very much depends only on our assessment of the final product. For students not familiar with the subject matter of the discipline under study, such evaluation is bound to be fraught with uncertainty and will likely not be done well.

While students show appreciation for the freedom of expression and interpretation afforded by the current emphasis on subjectivity and the openness of the Internet, there is also frustration with the lack of certainty that such freedom brings. If there are no absolute authorities or absolute answers, how can there be closure in any debate? Consider this comment from a student: "I just get so frustrated. Of course there are no definitive answers, so it seems to me we aren't supposed to argue anything—just merely accept that there are many different sides and nothing can be resolved. I get tired of saying, 'This seems most likely to mean this, because of these examples… but, of course, it could also mean that, because anything is possible.'"[25] In such an environment, a fruitful analysis of the validity, reliability, and importance of any resource used in research seems virtually unattainable.

Student Perceptions of Expertise and Authority
The Authority of the Professor

There has been a shift in student recognition of the authority of professors over the past number of decades, comparable with the growing confusion about expertise and authority in general. While students still tend to rely on the expertise of their professors, the authority they recognize may well be more "administrative" than "cognitive," to borrow the terminology of Patrick Wilson.[26] That is, they respect the authority of the professor because of the professor's position rather than, necessarily, because of any supposed superiority of knowledge or expertise.

Even though the expertise and authority of professors is more likely to be challenged today than it would have been in 1950, there is one sense in which professorial authority as administrative can enable students to choose resources that embody higher levels of expertise and authority.[27] Simply put, the professor determines both the requirements and grade for assigned research projects. Finding out "what the professor wants" is a clear priority for most students who want good grades, but it is noteworthy that, despite this "administrative" power of the professor to prescribe elements of research quality, students remain confused about the resources they are to use.[28] One would think that clear instructions from the professor as to what resources are acceptable (and where those resources could be found) would raise the level of authority in student bibliographies. But the inclusion of nonacademic or popular sources still abounds in student "academic" writing.[29] Somehow, professorial requirements are either not being stated clearly or are being misunderstood or ignored.

The Authority of Academic Literature

The high level of student confusion about the definitions of terms like "academic" and "scholarly" as well as a lack of understanding of why author credentials are important are phenomena encountered by academic librarians on a daily basis.[30] Even when students are able to cobble together bibliographies that meet their instructors' expectations, they are often not able to grasp why it matters that their resources should have a certain level of scholarship.[31] It is as if they believe they have been sent out to play an academic game whose rules are set by the professor for reasons unknown.

This is hardly surprising, given the disparity between professorial understanding of valid resources for research and the actual information world of the average student. A large number of research studies which show that students use Google and nonacademic Internet resources predominantly.[32] Many students satisfice with websites that provide "good enough" information. Even *Wikipedia* articles, after all, have endnotes and bibliographies. Discerning what more is needed to make information "scholarly" is baffling, even to students who are further along in their studies.

The Contradictory Authority of Student Experience

The Citation Project found that 77 percent of all student citations relate only to the first three pages of a source, regardless of its length.[33] This means that students are not engaging with their resources to any great extent. Neil Hogan and Connie Varnhagen discovered that, even when students do demonstrate understanding of criteria for critical evaluation of sources, they are not using those criteria to evaluate their sources in actual practice.[34]

Overall, many students fail to see the importance of evaluating resources.[35] There is a widespread preference for convenience of access over a more challenging search for more authoritative works.[36] In general, evaluation, when it is anything like a priority, is reserved for situations in which the research assignment demands such evaluation.[37] For the most part, students seem very trusting of most information they receive and view the demand of professors to evaluate sources as an unnecessary requirement.

The Nature of Expertise and Its Resulting Authority
The Nature of Expertise and Authority

It is a truism that the authority embodied in any piece of information relies to a large extent upon the expertise of its author. Expertise comes through knowledge development and experience. In essence, expertise involves the ability to demonstrate a mastery of subject matter and to operationalize that subject matter in order to demonstrate a superior grasp of problems and solutions in a particular field. As such, it must both be developed over time and recognized by colleagues as well as by those who receive the pronouncements of "experts."[38] The resulting acknowledgment by the recipients of the expertise that it is valid and has power to lead to sound decisions constitutes the authority in the expertise.

Academic Challenges to Authority: Postmodernism and a New Information Environment

Let's take a moment to assess the background to the current challenges preventing ready evaluation of expertise and authority.

Expertise, by its very nature, separates the expert from the nonexpert. Such separation has led to many criticisms of the role of experts and, indeed, the means by which we may determine what is authoritative. Martin has put the problem this way:

> Once a group of experts has established itself as having exclusive control over a body of knowledge, it is to their advantage to exclude nonexperts. This occurs in many ways. A long and expensive training is commonly demanded before a newcomer can be accepted as an expert…. Most experts are full-time professionals. Those

who might like to make an occasional contribution are
not made welcome. Finally, many experts are arrogant,
displaying contempt or hostility to amateur interlopers.[39]

Postmodernism, as embodied in the writings of Jean Francois Lyotard and
Jacques Derrida, challenges all claims to authority, arguing that knowledge is
mediated by the subjectivity of the receiver and thus can bear no claim to truth.[40]
Postmodernism, indeed, has become pervasive in modern society despite clear
signs that it is waning in some philosophical circles.[41] Peter Broks summarizes
the influence of postmodernism as follows: "Indeed, there are no authorities. No
final court of appeal to which we refer (or defer)."[42] The world of nature under
postmodernism does not, for the scientist, reveal what we once thought it did:
"What it tells us is no longer a single, unmediated, transcendent truth, but a
historically contingent collection of stories in an anthology of little narratives. Its
epistemological authority is shattered into a thousand pieces, a thousand local
knowledges."[43] This, essentially, dissolves the boundaries between expert and
layperson, making everyone an expert.

We see the results in the growing challenges to scientific and other
authorities as well as in the common belief of our students that all information is
essentially of the same nature, with none having more authority or believability
than any other.[44] While we may applaud a new order that is breaking down the
wall between the expert and the novice, thus allowing greater public involvement
in the knowledge economy, it represents a significant challenge to students who
must sift through a mass of information and discern which resources are more
reliable than the rest. If there is no such thing as the authority of information,
then we lack the means to discern what information is most worthy of our
consideration. In contrast, academia asserts the principle, at its very foundation,
that academic knowledge has an inherent authority.

Finding Equilibrium in Expertise and Authority

Collins and Evans have summarized the problem as follows: "Our question is:
'If it is no longer clear that scientists and technologists have special access to the
truth, why should their advice be specially valued?' This, we think, is the pressing intellectual problem of the age."[45] In response, several scholars have found
useful ways to navigate the postmodern landscape while at the same time not
abandoning expertise and its resulting authority.

John Hardwig argues that, in our current context of specialization, knowledge is built through teamwork based on the trust of scholars toward one another. He writes, "For the alternative to trust is, often, ignorance. An untrusting, suspicious attitude would impede the growth of knowledge… Trust in one's epistemic colleagues is not, then, a necessary evil."[46] Therefore, as long as there is good reason to trust the statements of those who provide rational reasons for what they say, nonexperts should be able to rely upon those statements.

More recently Hardwig has argued that even experts must rely upon other experts from other fields in order to have the evidence to support what they are saying, so that, in the face of subject areas in which any of us lack expertise, we must trust others to speak to us reliably. To this end, he suggests an ethics of expertise for those appealing to experts. Specifically, his instruction is to seek the best-qualified expert but not to demand that this expert share your values or goals; recognize that what you are seeking may not be known or may be a matter of considerable disagreement among experts; understand that expert opinion is not infallible; and know that experts may be tempted to say what you want to hear, so that you need to correct for that tendency.[47]

Steve Fuller, responding to Hardwig's earlier work, has argued that simple trust in experts is fraught with the common problem that the goals of the expert and those of the novice are often different or even contradictory. To follow Hardwig's approach is to give in to an "authoritarian theory of knowledge" in which there is no logical reason to challenge the authority of an expert. For Fuller expertise only goes so far, and the receiver of expertise must then decide what to do with it, something the expert is not qualified to determine for anyone.[48]

In an attempt to reconcile these two views, Robert Pierson has argued that it is not rational to assume that a layperson can evaluate the claims of an expert: "The layperson lacks the training and competence of the expert. And, in lacking these qualities, she will likely be unable to understand the expert's reasons, or, even if she does understand them, she may not be able to appreciate why they are good reasons."[49] Thus, the layperson is not the peer of the expert. As Pierson puts it, "Hardwig grants sole epistemic authority to experts, while Fuller, to the contrary, grants it to laypeople."[50] The best course for Pierson, however, lies between these extremes. While we may have to defer to the expertise of those who are authorities in their fields, it is only rational for a layperson to challenge an expert's findings when those findings impinge upon the layperson's future course of action. Thus the expert may be seen as right, but the layperson is not thus required to follow the plan that expertise lays out. Warren, in agreement, argues that authority in a democratic system must always be tempered by ongoing opportunity for critical challenge of that authority, even though not every authoritative utterance will necessarily be challenged.[51]

It is precisely in the potential abuse of expertise or authority that most scholars of this issue register their cautions. Daryl Koehn warns that the very concept of expertise may become the enemy to true authority. Expertise actively seeks a goal, and that goal may well be self-serving. True authority rests in the profession of the scholar, a profession that is guided by objective principles.[52] Thus, to the degree that any assertion comes from an expert whose motives may be in a conflict of interest with the objective goals of the profession or discipline, that assertion is open to challenge.

We might, in fact, wonder whether the academy as an authority vehicle is not just another version of the wisdom of the crowd, but on steroids. There are significant differences, however. The crowd is not governed by rules of evidence or even by a particular loyalty to the discipline under discussion. The academy carries with it a rich history, clear methodology, and deep expertise (the product of many hours working within the discipline, along with many debates among its members before judgments are finalized). We may challenge the whole academy as wrongheaded, out of date, and so on, but the very purpose of the academy, as elitist as it may seem, is to ensure that it has the mechanisms for quality control well in place.

A further warning comes from the work of Jojanneke Van der Toorn, Tom R. Tyler, and John T. Jost whose study revealed that those who feel most dependent upon an authority will be the most likely to defer to that authority and even to the prescriptive counsel of the authority.[53] Thus students, when they are dependent on the use of peer-reviewed literature for their ultimate grade, may be more inclined to accept that literature as true and valid simply because of their level of dependence on it.

We are left with a challenging mix of views about expertise and authority. Postmodernism, the World Wide Web, and the mythology of the wisdom of the crowd have ensured that uncritical acceptance of authority (if that ever existed) can no longer be sustained. Indeed, for many of our students, knowledge is flat, with none of it having more inherent authority than any other. This, of course, is an illusion, because none of us know enough not to need the guidance of those who know more than us. For academia, the exercise of cognitive authority is foundational. Our students need to acknowledge that reality but must also understand both how to discern it and when to challenge it. This is a difficult prospect for the average student who lacks deep subject knowledge and thus possesses neither the criteria nor the skills to evaluate it effectively.[54]

Restoring Appreciation of Expertise and Authority in Our Students: The Options
The Professorial "Big Stick"

One fairly certain way to raise the level of authority of resources used by students is to encourage faculty to specify more clearly what "scholarly literature" actually means. Many students see the world of academic writing as a mystery: What makes a work scholarly? How do I find the scholarly? How will I know it when I find it? Professors should be taking a strong role in opening up the worlds of scholarship within their disciplines so that students can begin to grasp what makes a certain work important and another peripheral.

Librarians, as well, can facilitate this professorial agenda by guiding students to the types of resources that are more likely to win a professor's approval. Here, showing students how to determine level of scholarship in books is one approach. With regard to journals, those libraries who still provide access to individual academic databases (as opposed to discovery tools) can guide students in selecting academic or peer-reviewed articles from their result lists, often with the single click of a link to a scholarly subset of the citations in their result list. While not perfect, a database link to scholarly resources is better than no link.[55]

We might assume that simply setting the parameters narrowly would compel students to raise the authority level of their resources, but such an assumption is naïve. Raising the level of authority is no substitute for giving students the ability to evaluate resources well. A scholarly article may be deeply flawed in its arguments, yet a blanket professorial statement that peer reviewed is good and non-reviewed is bad can give the impression that students must believe what they find in scholarly literature. Clearly that is not always the case.[56] In addition, there are solid resources available that are not part of the peer-review system but may have been produced with all the rigor of peer-reviewed scholarship.

Let Them Figure It Out

Alternatively, we could leave the decisions about the authority of resources to our students in the hope that, over time, they will begin to discern what information is most reliable. Miriam J. Metzger argues that students do better at the task of evaluation of resources when their motivation is high.[57] If professors base grades on a requirement to use high-quality resources, the motivation of students is increased, and they should make more effort on their own to find better information.

In essence, this approach is the status quo in academia, with professors often providing minimal standards and minimal criteria in the hope that students will find high-quality resources on their own.[58] The main problem here is that students, lacking deep content knowledge, are unlikely to choose well even if they know the best criteria to use and are well motivated. Sadly, for the majority of students, neither knowledge of criteria nor motivation to spend time evaluating is a prominent factor in their research.

The Checklist Approach

There are numerous checklists available that provide point-by-point guidance for evaluating information.[59] Particularly among novice students, checklists allow a step-by-step approach to thinking through the main evaluation criteria. Yet checklists are not without their critics, particularly Marc Meola, who argues in favor of "chucking the checklist."[60] Among his many criticisms, the following is salient:

> Another problem with the application of the checklist model in practice is that it can serve to promote a mechanical and algorithmic way of evaluation that is at odds with the higher-level judgment and intuition that we presumably seek to cultivate as part of critical thinking. The checklist format can give the impression that the checklist is a kind of machine that spits out correct website evaluations when given the right input.[61]

In Meola's view, the checklist results in students surrendering evaluation to a mechanical process and thus deprives them of the opportunity to further their own critical faculties.

It is possible to argue that checklists are not totally useless. They can be employed as general guides to the sorts of criteria students should look for in evaluating any piece of information. However, it is unlikely that many students, except the most motivated, pay much attention to checklists. As Meszaros writes, "The *A* word that matters most to the undergraduate researcher is accessibility, not authoritativeness. Thus, a mechanical method applied to information evaluation—the checklist approach—often does little to address and challenge undergraduate epistemological beliefs because it is based on premises that undergraduates frequently discredit."[62]

The Alternatives

Several non-checklist approaches have been suggested. Meola puts forward a three-step process: promoting peer-reviewed resources, comparing sources, and finding corroboration for statements that are made.[63] Metzger suggests using a variety of approaches, from checklists to more basic intuitive evaluations, depending on how important it is that the information be evaluated.[64]

Steve Borelli and Corey Johnson make a strong case for professors introducing students directly to the literature of their field, explaining the nature of scholarly work as opposed to popular and teaching students what to look for within scholarly articles in order to derive the most benefit from them. Faculty should, as well, address the motivations of students in order to align these with a choice of resources that better fit the requirements of the discipline.[65] Wilson, in this regard, comments:

> Evaluation of a piece of the literature is clearly better when the particular work is seen in relation to the other works in the field; attempts at evaluation of a work in isolation are generally pointless. Seeing a work as part of a structured field is seeing it in an appropriate context for informed evaluation. Seeing a structured body of literature as a whole is also a prerequisite for informed evaluation of the whole literature.[66]

Sara Robertson Seely, Sara Winstead Fry, and Margie Ruppel found through empirical research that formative assessment by librarians of the evaluation work done by preservice teachers resulted in enhanced evaluation skills. Simply providing feedback on previous evaluation work may well be a strong path to improving students' appreciation of the criteria and judgments needed in evaluating information.[67]

A Way Forward

It might appear that insisting on peer-reviewed resources, along with teaching how to use a checklist, should be sufficient to ensure that students are discovering expertise and using resources that are authoritative. But we live in an age in which everyone is an expert (or no one is), an age dominated by search engines that lack the ability to grade information as to its level of authority. Thus, for good or ill, our students are often left without the skills to make good evaluations and, indeed, without an understanding of why they should need to do so.

The previous age is not going to return. Thus we must work with our current reality. The following are several suggested steps to improving student ability to discern expertise and authority:

1. Faculty need to be made aware that lack of information ability and a disinclination to find material of higher authority is a significant challenge to student education. The solution is not merely to insist on peer-reviewed resources but to teach students how the academic information in the discipline actually functions. Students need to read closely and interact with actual literature in the field to begin getting a feel for what constitutes a valid resource and what does not. To put it colloquially, they need to begin knowing it when they see it.

2. Librarians must stress to students the special nature of academic information. As an experiment, a colleague and I team-taught library orientation sessions to three sections of 150 students each. We established the following scenario: A student is required to find five peer-reviewed journal articles, from the previous five years, on climate change in the Arctic. My colleague did a search on Google and eventually found one article from *Nature* that fit the bill. Despite a great deal of effort, that was all he was able locate. I then used Academic Search Premier, enlisting its many search features. Within a few minutes, I had narrowed the topic dramatically with faceting (down to the plight of polar bears due to the climate change-related loss of Arctic ice) and located more than five highly relevant peer-reviewed articles from the past five years. The students were impressed. The lesson to take away was that authoritative academic literature is different from the run-of-the mill Google fare. Finding it takes special tools, and appreciating it requires recognition that it operates at a different level from the average website.

3. Students, almost counterintuitively, need to understand that we live in an age in which slavishly accepting information that is deemed authoritative because it is academic is as wrong as assuming that all information is flat and of the same kind, thus needing no special evaluation. Whether they use checklists or other methods such as those suggested above, they must become critical users of information in their own right. As their content knowledge grows and their understanding of the ethos of information in their disciplines becomes more finely tuned, their skills will develop.

4. We must recognize that no intelligent evaluation of the authority of sources happens without deliberate input from professors and librarians. We live in an increasingly complex and convoluted information environment. Including that environment in our instruction, that is, developing students who understand and can work well with the kinds of information available to them, is just as important as teaching content. Education about information as a system must come into its own as something integral to higher education as a whole.

The complexities of the concepts of expertise and authority in our information age demand more intentional solutions. Educators must teach those complexities and provide students with the ability to navigate the information environment with discernment. Anything less is a failure to educate.

Notes

1. Jim Giles, "Internet Encyclopaedias Go Head to Head," *Nature* 438, no. 7070 (2005): 900–01.
2. Lynn Silipigni Connaway, "'I Always Stick with the First Thing That Comes Up on Google:' Motivating Student Engagement with the Digital Information Service Environment," *Libraries in the Digital Age (LIDA) Proceedings* 12 (2012): http://ozk.unizd.hr/proceedings/index.php/lida/article/view/93/67; Meg Raven, "Bridging the Gap: Understanding the Differing Research Expectations of First-Year Students and Professor," *Evidence Based Library and Information Practice* 7, no. 3 (2012): 4–31.
3. Harry M. Collins and Robert Evans, "The Third Wave of Science Studies: Studies of Expertise and Experience," *Social Studies of Science* 32, no. 2 (2002): 239; compare Harry M. Collins and Robert Evans, *Rethinking Expertise* (Chicago: University of Chicago Press, 2008).
4. Collins and Evans, "The Third Wave of Science Studies," 239.
5. Collins and Evans, "The Third Wave of Science Studies," 241.
6. Paulo Freire, *Pedagogy of the Oppressed,* trans. Myra Bergman Ramos (New York: Seabury Press, 1970); Brian Martin, "The Politics of Research," in *Information Liberation: Challenging the Corruptions of Information Power* (London: Freedom Press, 1998), 123–42, http://

www.uow.edu.au/~bmartin/pubs/98il/il07.html.

7.   Freire, *Pedagogy of the Oppressed*, 67.

8.   Martin, "The Politics of Research," 130.

9.   Philip Schlesinger, "Expertise, the Academy and the Governance of Cultural Policy," *Media, Culture and Society* 35, no. 1 (2013): 34.

10.   For example, Stephen Turner, "What Is the Problem with Experts?," *Social Studies of Science* 31, no. 1 (2001): 123–49; Peter J. Pels and Lorraine Nencel, "Introduction: Critique and the Deconstruction of Anthropological Authority," in *Constructing Knowledge: Authority and Critique in Social Science*, ed. Peter J. Pels and Lorraine Nencel (London: Sage Publications, 1991), 1–21.

11.   Francis Galton, "Vox Populi," *Nature* 75 (1907): 450–51.

12.   James Surowiecki, *The Wisdom of Crowds: Why the Many Are Smarter than the Few and How Collective Wisdom Shapes Business, Economies, Societies, and Nations* (New York: Doubleday, 2004).

13.   Sabine Niederer and José van Dijck, "Wisdom of the Crowd or Technicity of Content? *Wikipedia* as a Sociotechnical System," *New Media and Society* 12, no. 8 (2010): 1376–77.

14.   Aaron Schwartz, "Who Writes *Wikipedia*?," last modified September 4, 2006, accessed August 20, 2014, http://www.aaronsw.com/weblog/whowriteswikipedia.

15.   Aniket Kittur and Robert E. Kraut, "Harnessing the Wisdom of Crowds in *Wikipedia*: Quality through Coordination" (paper, Research Showcase @ Carnegie Mellon University, 2008), http://repository.cmu.edu/cgi/viewcontent.cgi?article=1098&context=hcii.

16   Sergey Brin and Lawrence Page, "The Anatomy of a Large-Scale Hypertextual Web Search Engine," *Computer Networks and ISDN Systems 30, no. 1 (1998): 107–17.*

17.   James L. Goldman, "The Cognitive Authority of Collective Intelligence" (PhD diss., Drexel University, 2010), https://idea.library.drexel.edu/bitstream/handle/1860/3254/Goldman_James.pdf?sequence=1. The term "cognitive authority" originated with Patrick Wilson, "Bibliographic Instruction and Cognitive Authority," *Library Trends* 39, no. 3 (1991): 259–70.

18.   Adam Frank, "Welcome to the Age of Denial," *New York Times*, August 21, 2013, http://www.nytimes.com/2013/08/22/opinion/welcome-to-the-age-of-denial.html?_r=0.

19.   MaryBeth Meszaros, "Who's in Charge Here? Authority, Authoritativenes, and the Undergraduate Researcher," *Communications in Information Literacy* 4, no. 1 (2010): 5–11, http://www.comminfolit.org/index.php?journal=cil&page=article&op=view&path%5B%5D=Vol4-2010PER1&path%5B%5D=110.

20.   Pels and Nencel, "Introduction: Critique and the Deconstruction of Anthropological Authority," 15.l></related-urls></urls></record></Cite></EndNote>

21.   Mark E. Warren, "Deliberative Democracy and Authority," *American Political Science Review* 90, no. 1 (1996): 59.

22.   Commission on the Future of the UC Berkeley Library, *Report of the Commission on the Future of the UC Berkeley Libra*ry, accessed November 1, 2013, http://evcp.berkeley.edu/sites/default/files/FINAL_CFUCBL_report_10.16.13.pdf, 5.

23.   Ray Land, "Speed and the Unsettling of Knowledge in the Digital University," in *Digital Difference: Perspectives on Online Learning*, ed. Ray Land and Siân Bayne (Boston: Springer, 2011), 63.

24.   International Federation of Library Associations and Institutions, *Riding the Waves or Caught in the Tide? Navigating the Evolving Information Environment*, accessed November 1, 2013, http://trends.ifla.org/files/trends/assets/insights-from-the-ifla-trend-report_v3.pdf.

25.   Susan Ostrov Weisser, "'Believing in Yourself' as Classroom Culture," *Academe* 91, no. 1 (2005): 28.

26.   Rosemary Chang, Gregor Kennedy, and Tom Petrovic, "Web 2.0 and User-Created

Content: Students Negotiating Shifts in Academic Authority," in *Hello! Where Are You in the Landscape of Educational Technology?*, ed. Roger Atkinson and Clare McBeath (Burwood, Victoria, Australia: Deakin University, 2008), 165–68, http://ascilite.org.au/conferences/melbourne08/procs/chang.pdf; Wilson, "Bibliographic Instruction and Cognitive Authority;" compare Meszaros, "Who's in Charge Here?."

27. Weisser, "'Believing in Yourself' as Classroom Culture."

28. Alison J. Head and Michael B. Eisenberg, *Finding Context: What Today's College Students Say About Conducting Research in the Information Age*, accessed August 15, 2014, http://project-infolit.org/images/pdfs/pil_progressreport_2_2009.pdf.

29. A study of 174 research papers from 16 universities found that fewer than half the citations were from books, journals or government documents; the remainder were websites and news sources: Sandra Jamieson and Rebecca M. Howard, "The Citation Project: Preventing Plagiarism, Teaching Writing; Initial Data from the Citation Project Study of Student Use of Sources in Researched Papers from Sixteen US Colleges and Universities," last modified August 2011, accessed November 1, 2013, http://site.citationproject.net/wp-content/uploads/2011/08/Sources-Cited-in-the-Paper.pdf.

30. Meszaros, "Who's in Charge Here?," 6–7.

31. There is some evidence that students with clear guidelines can find the scholarly resources they require: Stephanie Rosenblatt, "They Can Find It but They Don't Know What to Do with It: Describing the Use of Scholarly Literature by Undergraduate Students," *Journal of Information Literacy* 4, no. 2 (2010): 50–61no. 2 (2010, http://ojs.lboro.ac.uk/ojs/index.php/JIL/article/view/LLC-V4-I2-2010-1.

32. The plagiarism resistance company Turnitin has done research on its extensive database of student papers that provides a clear statistical picture of the sources students use. Nonacademic resources predominate. The Citation Project found the same: Turnitin, "White Paper: What's Wrong with *Wikipedia*? Evaluating the Sources Used by Students" (Oakland, CA: Turnitin, 2013); Turnitin, "White Paper: The Sources in Student Writing" (Oakland, CA: Turnitin, 2013); Jamieson and Howard, "The Citation Project."

33. Ibid.

34. Neil Hogan and Connie Varnhagen, "Critical Appraisal of Information on the Web in Practice: Undergraduate Students' Knowledge, Reported Use, and Behaviour," *Canadian Journal of Learning and Technology* 38, no. 1 (2012): 174.

35. Arthur Taylor, "A Study of the Information Search Behaviour of the Millennial Generation," *Information Research* 17, no. 1 (2012): http://informationr.net/ir/17-1/paper508.

36. Kyung-Sun Kim and Sei-Ching Joanna Sin, "Selecting Quality Sources: Bridging the Gap between the Perception and Use of Information Sources," *Journal of Information Science* 37, no. 2 (2011): 179; Meszaros, "Who's in Charge Here?."

37. Melissa Gross and Don Latham, "Undergraduate Perceptions of Information Literacy: Defining, Attaining, and Self-Assessing Skills," *College and Research Libraries* 70, no. 4 (2009): 336–50.

38. For an incisive analysis of expertise, see E. Summerson Carr, "Enactments of Expertise," *Annual Review of Anthropology* 39 (2010): 17–32.

39. Martin, "The Politics of Research," 135.

40. Jean Francois Lyotard, *The Postmodern Condition: A Report on Knowledge* (Minneapolis, MN: University of Minnesota Press, 1984); Jacques Derrida, *Of Grammatology* (Boston: JHU Press, 1998).

41. Robert L. McLaughlin, "After the Revolution: US Postmodernism in the Twenty-First Century," *Narrative* 21, no. 3 (October 2013): 284–95.

42. Peter Broks, "The Authority of Science and the Postmodern Reformation," *Interdisciplinary Science Reviews* 28, no. 2 (2003): 81.

43. Ibid.

44. Frank, "Welcome to the Age of Denial;" Meszaros, "Who's in Charge Here?."

45. Collins and Evans, "The Third Wave of Science Studies," 236.

46. John Hardwig, "The Role of Trust in Knowledge," *The Journal of Philosophy* 88, no. 12 (1991): 707. Compare Tyler Burge's assertion, "A person is apriori entitled to accept a proposition that is presented as true and that is intelligible to him, unless there are stronger reasons for not doing so," in Tyler Burge, "Content Preservation," *The Philosophical Review* 102, no. 4 (1993): 469.

47. John Hardwig, "Toward an Ethics of Expertise," in *Professional Ethics and Social Responsibility*, ed. Daniel E. Wueste (Lanham, MD: Rowman and Littlefield, 1994), 83–101.

48. Steve Fuller, *Social Epistemology* (Bloomington, IN: Indiana University Press, 1988), chap. 12.

49. Robert Pierson, "The Epistemic Authority of Expertise," *PSA: Proceedings of the Biennial Meeting of the Philosophy of Science Association* 1 (1994): 401.

50. Ibid., 403.

51. Warren, "Deliberative Democracy and Authority."

52. Daryl Koehn, "Expertise and the Delegitimation of Professional Authority," *American Behavioral Scientist* 38, no. 7 (1995): 990–1002.

53. Jojanneke Van der Toorn, Tom R. Tyler, and John T. Jost, "More than Fair: Outcome Dependence, System Justification, and the Perceived Legitimacy of Authority Figures," *Journal of Experimental Social Psychology* 47, no. 1 (2011): 127–38.

54. See, particularly, Teun Lucassen and Jan Maarten Schraagen, "Factual Accuracy and Trust in Information: The Role of Expertise," *Journal of the American Society for Information Science and Technology* 62, no. 7 (2011): 1332–42; Teun Lucassen et al., "Topic Familiarity and Information Skills in Online Credibility Evaluation," *Journal of the American Society for Information Science and Technology* 64, no. 2 (2013): 254–64.

55. In this regard, see Troy A. Swanson, "A Radical Step: Implementing a Critical Information Literacy Model," *Portal: Libraries and the Academy* 4, no. 2 (2004): 259–73.

56. See Barbara Fister, "Decode Academy" (presentation, LOEX Conference, Nashville, TN, May 3, 2013), accessed November 1, 2013, http://homepages.gac.edu/~fister/loex13.pdf, 11.

57. Miriam J. Metzger, "Making Sense of Credibility on the Web: Models for Evaluating Online Information and Recommendations for Future Research," *Journal of the American Society for Information Science and Technology* 58, no. 13 (2007): 2078–91.

58. See the evidence from the Turnitin and Citation Project studies, note 30.

59. For a number of examples, see Western Michigan University: The Evaluation Center, "Evaluation Checklists," accessed November 1, 2013, http://www.wmich.edu/evalctr/checklists/evaluation-checklists/.

60. Marc Meola, "Chucking the Checklist: A Contextual Approach to Teaching Undergraduates Web-Site Evaluation," *Portal: Libraries and the Academy* 4, no. 3 (2004): 331–34.

61. Ibid., 338.

62. Meszaros, "Who's in Charge Here?," 8.

63. Meola, "Chucking the Checklist." For more on the role of corroboration see Alvin I. Goldman, "Experts: Which Ones Should You Trust?," *Philosophy and Phenomenological Research* 63, no. 1 (2001): 97.

64. Metzger, "Making Sense of Credibility on the Web."

65. Steve Borrelli and Corey Johnson, "Information Evaluation Instruction," *Communications in Information Literacy* 6, no. 2 (2012): 173–90, http://www.comminfolit.org/index. php?journal=cil&page=article&op=viewFile&path%5B%5D=v6i2p173&path%5B%5D=154.

66. Wilson, "Bibliographic Instruction and Cognitive Authority," 268.

67. Sara Robertson Seely, Sara Winstead Fry, and Margie Ruppel, "Information Literacy Follow-Through: Enhancing Preservice Teachers' Information Evaluation Skills through Formative Assessment," *Behavioral and Social Sciences Librarian* 30, no. 2 (2011): 72–84; compare William B. Badke, *Teaching Research Processes: The Faculty Role in the Development of Skilled Student Researchers* (Witney, UK: Chandos Publishing, 2012).

Bibliography

Badke, William B. *Teaching Research Processes: The Faculty Role in the Development of Skilled Student Researchers.* Witney, UK: Chandos Publishing, 2012.

Brin, Sergey, and Lawrence Page. "The Anatomy of a Large-scale Hypertextual Web Search Engine." *Computer Networks and ISDN Systems* 30, no. 1 (1998): 107–17.

Borrelli, Steve, and Corey Johnson. "Information Evaluation Instruction." *Communications in Information Literacy* 6, no. 2 (2012): 173–90. http://www.comminfolit.org/index.php?-journal=cil&page=article&op=viewFile&path%5B%5D=v6i2p173&path%5B%5D=154.

Broks, Peter. "The Authority of Science and the Postmodern Reformation." *Interdisciplinary Science Reviews* 28, no. 2 (2003): 76–82.

Burge, Tyler. "Content Preservation." *The Philosophical Review* 102, no. 4 (1993): 457–88.

Carr, E. Summerson. "Enactments of Expertise." *Annual Review* of Anthropology 39 (2010): 17–32.

Chang, Rosemary, Gregor Kennedy, and Tom Petrovic. "Web 2.0 and User-Created Content: Students Negotiating Shifts in Academic Authority." In *Hello! Where are you in the Landscape of Educational Technology?,* edited by Roger Atkinson and Clare McBeath, 165–68. Burwood, Victoria, Australia: Deakin University, 2008. http://ascilite.org.au/conferences/melbourne08/procs/chang.pdf.

Collins, Harry M., and Robert Evans. *Rethinking Expertise.* Chicago: University of Chicago Press, 2008.

———. "The Third Wave of Science Studies: Studies of Expertise and Experience." *Social Studies of Science* 32, no. 2 (2002): 235–96.

Commission on the Future of the UC Berkeley Library. *Report of the Commission on the Future of the UC Berkeley Library.* Accessed November 1, 2013. http://evcp.berkeley.edu/sites/default/files/FINAL_CFUCBL_report_10.16.13.pdf.

Connaway, Lynn Silipigni. "'I Always Stick with the First Thing that Comes Up on Google:' Motivating Student Engagement with the Digital Information Service Environment." *Libraries in the Digital Age (LIDA) Proceedings* 12 (2012).

Derrida, Jacques. *Of Grammatology.* Baltimore: JHU Press, 1998.

Fister, Barbara. "Decode Academy." Presentation at the Annual LOEX Conference, Nashville, TN, May 3, 2013. Accessed November 1, 2013. http://homepages.gac.edu/~fister/loex13.pdf.

Frank, Adam. "Welcome to the Age of Denial." *New York Times,* August 21, 2013. http://www.nytimes.com/2013/08/22/opinion/welcome-to-the-age-of-denial.html.

Freire, Paulo. *Pedagogy of the Oppressed.* Translated by Myra Bergman Ramos. New York:

Seabury Press, 1970.

Fuller, Steve. *Social Epistemology*. Bloomington, IN: Indiana University Press, 1988.

Galton, Francis. "Vox Populi." *Nature* 75 (1907): 450–51.

Giles, Jim. "Internet Encyclopaedias Go Head to Head." *Nature* 438, no. 7070 (2005): 900–01.

Goldman, Alvin I. "Experts: Which Ones Should You Trust?" *Philosophy and Phenomenological Research* 63, no. 1 (2001): 85–110.

Goldman, James L. "The Cognitive Authority of Collective Intelligence." PhD diss., Drexel University, 2010. https://idea.library.drexel.edu/bitstream/handle/1860/3254/Goldman_James.pdf?sequence=1.

Gross, Melissa, and Don Latham. "Undergraduate Perceptions of Information Literacy: Defining, Attaining, and Self-Assessing Skills." *College and Research Libraries* 70, no. 4 (2009): 336–50.

Hardwig, John. "The Role of Trust in Knowledge." *The Journal of Philosophy* 88, no. 12 (1991): 693–708.

———. "Toward an Ethics of Expertise." In *Professional Ethics and Social Responsibility*, edited by Daniel E. Wueste, 83–101. Lanham, MD: Rowman and Littlefield, 1994.

Head, Alison J., and Michael B. Eisenberg. *Finding Context: What Today's College Students Say About Conducting Research in the Information Age*. Accessed November 1, 2013. http://projectinfolit.org/pdfs/PIL_ProgressReport_2_2009.pdf.

Hogan, Neil, and Connie Varnhagen. "Critical Appraisal of Information on the Web in Practice: Undergraduate Students' Knowledge, Reported Use, and Behaviour." *Canadian Journal of Learning and Technology* 38, no. 1 (2012): 1–14.

International Federation of Library Associations and Institutions. *Riding the Waves or Caught in the Tide? Navigating the Evolving Information Environment*. Accessed November 1, 2013. http://trends.ifla.org/files/trends/assets/insights-from-the-ifla-trend-report_v3.pdf.

Jamieson, Sandra, and Rebecca M. Howard. "The Citation Project: Preventing Plagiarism, Teaching Writing: Initial Data from the Citation Project Study of Student Use of Sources in Researched Papers from Sixteen US Colleges and Universities." Last modified August 2011. Accessed November 1, 2013. http://site.citationproject.net/wp-content/uploads/2011/08/Sources-Cited-in-the-Paper.pdf.

Kim, Kyung-Sun, and Sei-Ching Joanna Sin. "Selecting Quality Sources: Bridging the Gap between the Perception and Use of Information Sources." *Journal of Information Science* 37, no. 2 (2011): 178–88.

Kittur, Aniket, and Robert E. Kraut. "Harnessing the Wisdom of Crowds in *Wikipedia*: Quality through Coordination." Paper presented at the Research Showcase @ Carnegie Mellon University, 2008. Accessed August 15, 2014. http://repository.cmu.edu/cgi/viewcontent.cgi?article=1098&context=hcii.

Koehn, Daryl. "Expertise and the Delegitimation of Professional Authority." *American Behavioral Scientist* 38, no. 7 (1995): 990–1002.

Land, Ray. "Speed and the Unsettling of Knowledge in the Digital University." In *Digital Difference: Perspectives on Online Learning*, edited by Ray Land and Siân Bayne, 61–70. Boston: Springer, 2011.

Lucassen, Teun, Rienco Muilwijk, Matthijs L. Noordzij, and Jan Maarten Schraagen. "Topic Familiarity and Information Skills in Online Credibility Evaluation." *Journal of the American Society for Information Science and Technology* 64, no. 2 (2013): 254–64.

Lucassen, Teun, and Jan Maarten Schraagen. "Factual Accuracy and Trust in Information: The Role of Expertise." *Journal of the American Society for Information Science and Technology* 62, no. 7 (2011): 1232–42.

Lyotard, Jean Francois. *The Postmodern Condition: A Report on Knowledge.* Minneapolis, MN: University of Minnesota Press, 1984.

Martin, Brian. "The Politics of Research." In *Information Liberation: Challenging the Corruptions of Information Power.* London: Freedom Press, 1998. Accessed November 1, 2013. http://www.uow.edu.au/~bmartin/pubs/98il/il07.html.

McLaughlin, Robert L. "After the Revolution: US Postmodernism in the Twenty-First Century." *Narrative* 21, no. 3 (October 2013): 284–95.

Meola, Marc. "Chucking the Checklist: A Contextual Approach to Teaching Undergraduates Web-Site Evaluation." *Portal: Libraries and the Academy* 4, no. 3 (2004): 331–44.

Meszaros, MaryBeth. "Who's in Charge Here? Authority, Authoritativenes, and the Undergraduate Researcher." *Communications in Information Literacy* 4, no. 1 (2010): 5–11. http://www.comminfolit.org/index.php?journal=cil&page=article&op=view&path%5B%5D=Vol4-2010PER1&path%5B%5D=110.

Metzger, Miriam J. "Making Sense of Credibility on the Web: Models for Evaluating Online Information and Recommendations for Future Research." *Journal of the American Society for Information Science and Technology* 58, no. 13 (2007): 2078–91.

Niederer, Sabine, and José van Dijck. "Wisdom of the Crowd or Technicity of Content? Wikipedia as a Sociotechnical System." *New Media and Society* 12, no. 8 (2010): 1368–87.

Pels, Peter J., and Lorraine Nencel. "Introduction: Critique and the Deconstruction of Anthropological Authority." In *Constructing Knowledge: Authority and Critique in Social Science,* edited by Peter J. Pels and Lorraine Nencel, 1–21. London: Sage Publications, 1991.

Pierson, Robert. "The Epistemic Authority of Expertise." *PSA: Proceedings of the Biennial Meeting of the Philosophy of Science Association* 1 (1994): 398–405.

Raven, Meg. "Bridging the Gap: Understanding the Differing Research Expectations of First-Year Students and Professor." *Evidence Based Library and Information Practice* 7, no. 3 (2012): 4–31.

Rosenblatt, Stephanie. "They Can Find It but They Don't Know What to Do with It: Describing the Use of Scholarly Literature by Undergraduate Students." *Journal of Information Literacy* 4, no. 2 (2010): 50–61. http://ojs.lboro.ac.uk/ojs/index.php/JIL/article/view/LLC-V4-I2-2010-1.

Schlesinger, Philip. "Expertise, the Academy and the Governance of Cultural Policy." *Media, Culture and Society* 35, no. 1 (2013): 27–35.

Schwartz, Aaron. "Who Writes Wikipedia?" Last modified September 4, 2006. Accessed August 20, 2014. http://www.aaronsw.com/weblog/whowriteswikipedia.

Seely, Sara Robertson, Sara Winstead Fry, and Margie Ruppel. "Information Literacy Follow-Through: Enhancing Preservice Teachers' Information Evaluation Skills through Formative Assessment." *Behavioral and Social Sciences Librarian* 30, no. 2 (2011): 72–84.

Surowiecki, James. *The Wisdom of Crowds: Why the Many Are Smarter than the Few and How Collective Wisdom Shapes Business, Economies, Societies, and Nations.* New York: Doubleday, 2004.

Swanson, Troy A. "A Radical Step: Implementing a Critical Information Literacy Model." *Portal: Libraries and the Academy* 4, no. 2 (2004): 259–73.

Taylor, Arthur. "A Study of the Information Search Behaviour of the Millennial Generation." *Information Research* 17, no. 1 (2012). Accessed November 1, 2013. http://informationr.net/ir/17-1/paper508.

Turner, Stephen. "What Is the Problem with Experts?." *Social Studies of Science* 31, no. 1 (2001): 123–49.

Turnitin. "White Paper: The Sources in Student Writing." Oakland, CA: Turnitin, 2013.

———. "White Paper: What's Wrong with Wikipedia? Evaluating the Sources Used by Students." Oakland, CA: Turnitin, 2013.

Van der Toorn, Jojanneke, Tom R. Tyler, and John T. Jost. "More than Fair: Outcome Dependence, System Justification, and the Perceived Legitimacy of Authority Figures." *Journal of Experimental Social Psychology* 47, no. 1 (2011): 127–38.

Warren, Mark E. "Deliberative Democracy and Authority." *American Political Science Review* 90, no. 1 (1996): 46–60.

Weisser, Susan Ostrov. "'Believing in Yourself' as Classroom Culture." *Academe* 91, no. 1 (2005): 27–31.

Western Michigan University: The Evaluation Center. "Evaluation Checklists." Accessed November 1, 2013. http://www.wmich.edu/evalctr/checklists/evaluation-checklists/.

Wilson, Patrick. "Bibliographic Instruction and Cognitive Authority." *Library Trends* 39, no. 3 (1991): 259–70.

CHAPTER 10

Knowledge Societies:
Learning for a Diverse World

Alison Hicks

This chapter will build on the author's conceptual exploration of critical information literacy (CIL) in the foreign languages to examine what such a program could look like in reality.[1] Inspired by the author's increasing dissatisfaction with information literacy (IL) models that are decontextualized from broader, multicultural information landscapes, this chapter will present an instructional approach that draws from the experience and assessment of a pilot Spanish IL program at the University of Colorado Boulder (UCB). However, while the chapter will focus specifically on the study of foreign languages, it will be of interest to educators who work with global populations. Changing demographics as well as the evolution of communication technologies means that the capacity to act within multicultural information societies is more important than ever before, and learning for a diverse world is a core goal on many US campuses.

The class was also driven by the author's recognition of the growing exclusion of cultural knowledge and worldview from our information landscapes. While IL has been credited with empowering people to "locate, evaluate, apply, and create information within cultural and social contexts," traditional IL standards such as the

2.1 The Nature of Expertise, Authority, and Credibility

Association of College and Research Libraries' (ACRL) *Information Literacy Competency Standards for Higher Education* often seem to promote a "single, fixed way of knowing and learning."[2] In addition, the representation of different voices or cultures on the web is often muted, from *Wikipedia* to specialized systems of scholarly communication. Accessing culturally situated knowledge in information systems that tend to support traditional, global flows of information or established interests is a challenge.[3] While new technologies are often seen as a way to bridge cultural divides—for example, by allowing people to access a diversity of views or opinions—it is clear that in other ways, the Internet actually reinforces existing social biases or divisions. This can be seen most clearly in the design of tools, for example, algorithms that are weighted towards their designers' biases or search engine personalization trends that narrow our information experiences. More subtlety, it can also be seen in terms of access to information as the shape and reach of our personal networks mediates our information experiences.[4] These realities complicate our information landscapes and affect our expectations about the world.

A critical approach to IL, however, moves beyond the narrow focus on dominant cultural information practices. A CIL framework questions the "structures, functions, habits, norms, and practices that guide global flows of information."[5] In this way, it can help meet campus and foreign language curricular goals by enabling an exploration of cultural representations of information. At the same time, CIL also aims to develop the learner's understanding of "who she is (identity) and what she can do (agency)."[6] This enables a reflection on differences between languages, cultures, and communities, core aspects of transcultural and foreign language learning. In this way, CIL can be defined as "engendering lifelong learning, empowering people, promoting social inclusion, redressing disadvantage, and advancing the well-being of all in a global context," an approach that is ideally suited to the challenges of multicultural information societies.[7]

The chapter will start with an overview of the foreign language information environment, including a brief review of relevant background literature that informs this work. It will then center on describing the CIL framework that was used to design a series of two core advanced Spanish writing classes. The author will subsequently analyze student reflective prompts to explore student learning within SP3010: Advanced Rhetoric and Composition, the second of the two classes. The chapter will end by looking at future objectives for this program as well as exploring how this design could be adapted for other global learning initiatives on campus.

Background

Several bodies of work inform this study, including foreign language education practices, CIL literature, and work in critical information or Internet studies. A brief overview of each of these areas will serve to situate this paper.

Foreign language educational goals form the driving impetus for this program.[8] The university or college campus is an increasingly diverse location. This can be attributed to changing demographics, including the increase in nontraditional and international students as well as numbers of students who have studied abroad.[9] It can also be linked to the growth of global communication technologies and the subsequent effect on the education system and workplace needs.[10] Either way, internationalization, which refers to the incorporation of "global perspectives into teaching, learning, and research," is seen as increasingly important throughout higher education.[11] These realities are also gradually starting to influence disciplinary student learning goals as can be seen through the changing priorities of the Modern Language Association (MLA). Traditionally, foreign language education was very hierarchically structured. Lower-division language courses fed into upper-division studies of canonical literature, and language learning was based around the goal of acquiring near-native linguistic competence. Needless to say, few learners ever reached this level, and the foreign languages were seen as increasingly irrelevant in a world where understanding different cultures was more important than ever before.[12] As a consequence, a 2007 report urged departments to reconsider the wider purpose of language study by situating learning goals within broader cultural, historical, and geographic frames. In this way, learning would be reconfigured around transcultural rather than just linguistic competence, focusing on the ability of learners to reflect on the world, their society, and themselves "through the lens of another language and culture."[13]

The redefined goals provide an interesting challenge for librarians because traditional IL practices often seem to fail to structure these disciplinary aims. The emphasis that established IL standards and research place on identifying commonalities in information practices, for example, makes it hard to design IL instruction that allows students to acknowledge and reflect on difference.[14] In addition, the typical focus on developing efficient information retrieval skills leaves little space for students to develop broader language awareness such as considering the sociopolitical nature of language use.[15] In this way, it is clear that a more extensive approach to IL is needed in order to design integrated disciplinary instruction. CIL is one such approach. Drawing from critical pedagogy and literacy studies, CIL is hard to define yet can be seen as an approach to IL that is grounded in the development of a student's critical consciousness or disposition in and with complex information landscapes. On the one hand, this means that CIL engages learners with the broader social and cultural contexts of information questioning, "how knowledge is defined, by whom and for whom, and how these processes contribute to the reproduction, mediation, or transformation of power relations."[16] On the other hand, it indicates that CIL supports a personal approach to learning, drawing from the learner's past experiences to develop their ability to "critically construct, shape and negotiate knowledge, practices, and identities."[17] This focus on scaffolding the learner's personal development within broader cultural narratives does not just demonstrate that CIL can support the educational goals of the foreign languages; it also means, more importantly, that CIL can become "a key part of a student's knowing process in the foreign languages," thereby creating an opportunity for thoughtful instructional practice.[18]

While CIL literature helps to frame the course, class content is informed by literature that explores the political, social, and cultural dimensions of information practices. This literature is not commonly addressed in IL, yet studies that explore the hidden subcontexts of common research tools can help librarians consider the resources that they are teaching in a more critical light. These questions are especially important in foreign language studies because, as Project Information Literacy notes, students tend to rely on the same set of tried and true resources.[19] However, as students seek to reflect on the world and understand themselves as a member of a society that is foreign to others, the perceived universality of English language tools that are typically used as research starting points can be troublesome. Although a full exploration of all these fields is beyond the scope of this paper, the author will highlight various studies of search engines, *Wikipedia,* and library systems that helped her question foreign language information landscapes, which, ultimately, drove her IL instruction design.

One of the most relevant areas of interest for the foreign languages is research into the search engine, the starting point for much academic and personal research. Search engines have rapidly become our window onto the world, yet this can be problematic in a foreign language context. Although search engines "house and surface the long tail information that goes beyond the mass taste of the public," the parameters that humans set for indexing or algorithmic ranking mean explicit editorial choices are made.[20] This can decrease access to minority language or cultural materials as search engines seek to maximize search success by catering to majority interests.[21] Liwen Vaughan and Yanjun Zhang found that US sites were more likely to be indexed on Google than sites from China, Taiwan, or Singapore.[22] At the same time, Google defends these ranking and indexing choices as "an objective reflection of reality."[23] This supposition causes issues in foreign language information environments because it fails to consider cultural context as the experiences of journalists from Sahara Reporters whose reports about police brutality in Nigeria were censored demonstrates.[24] It can also promote offensive racial or cultural stereotypes about women of color as Safiya Umoja Noble and Latanya Sweeney describe.[25] Access to culturally relevant materials is further complicated by current trends for search engine personalization or customization, which can limit access to results based on location, past search history, or what is deemed "newsworthy." In turn, this restricted presentation of information can influence "our expectations and information about the world" as the search engine becomes "a means to know what there is to know and how to know it."[26]

Wikipedia, a common research resource, is another problematic tool in foreign language research. Issues, however, go beyond the typical preoccupation with credibility and center around how contributors and the *Wikipedia* structure affect access to foreign language information and knowledge. On the surface, *Wikipedia* prides itself on its low barriers to access and create knowledge. However, research into country-specific versions of *Wikipedia* shows that contributors from countries with higher levels of development participate more frequently in *Wikipedia*. This causes problems as local or country specific knowledge remains "largely left out of one of the world's most important and visible sources of information."[27] In turn, these skewed contributor demographics (who are also predominantly male and young) affect what counts as knowledge as the deletion of the entry on Makmende, a Kenyan meme that was not considered important enough for the English *Wikipedia*, demonstrates.[28] Further issues that affect the representation of knowledge in *Wikipedia* can be seen in an examination of geotagged entries. Research has shown that in large swathes of Africa, local people write fewer than five percent of *Wikipedia* edits, meaning that some populations are almost exclusively represented by foreigners.[29] This overrepresentation of topics of Western concern may then skew datasets or search engines. Lastly, *Wikipedia* is a predominantly textual source that relies on Western concepts of sources and citations. In this way, its very structure can be hostile to representations of indigenous or oral culture as well as "nuanced understanding of local notability" and the use of local sources.[30]

Lastly, a critical examination of academic search tools shows that the library too can be problematic in foreign language research. The scarcity of foreign language scholarly resources in libraries is a known problem.[31] Many common databases have very narrow representations of foreign language materials and index few non-Anglophone journals.[32] However, this is further complicated by documented problems that non-Western or Anglophone scholars face when they try and publish in major English-language disciplinary journals, including prejudice about what counts as locally and globally relevant knowledge.[33] While the growth of open access materials in many countries is helping to mitigate issues, invisible exclusionary practices have a significant effect on the production, funding, and visibility of broad academic knowledge. Access to and representation of foreign language material may also be limited by the classification systems used in the library. As Hope Olson points out, language choice in "universal" classification systems invariably reflects the biases of the creator; in the case of the Dewey Decimal System, this is based on the presumptions of Western philosophies.[34] Through the "systemic effect of continuing to privilege colonizers over colonized," this impacts the placement of topics as well as terminology issues and omissions.[35] It also affects the representation of minority materials as well as making foreign language material inaccessible to various groups and cultures.

In sum, scholars are starting to examine global flows of information, both in terms of production of and access to information as well as the representation of different voices or cultures on the web. Through these studies it is clear to see that in Anglophone-dominated environments, foreign language information landscapes are highly complex. Nonetheless, a critical approach to IL can help reveal these issues, thereby helping learners develop deeper cultural and linguistic competence. The remainder of this chapter will explore what this might look like.

Course Planning

The paper will now move to examine the pilot foreign language IL program that was introduced at UCB. A brief outline of the series of two classes that form the program will situate the paper before the author focuses more extensively on SP3010, the second of the two classes.

Context

At UCB, Spanish majors are required to take two three-credit advanced Spanish writing classes, SP3000: Advanced Spanish Skills and SP3010: Advanced Rhetoric and Composition. SP3000, the first course, is a transitional class that focuses on writing skills as well as introducing students to courses that tend to be offered in the department such as Iberian and Latin American literature, cultural events, and topical issues. Within SP3000, students write a five to seven page research paper in Spanish that relies predominantly on Spanish sources. While topics vary, many students write about contemporary current affairs topics that draw from their personal or study abroad experience. As part of this course, the Spanish librarian conducts one 50-minute seminar for each class section. Designed to introduce students to Spanish research, learning outcomes center round being able to carry out research in a Spanish context. More specifically, this involves developing an understanding of everyday and academic research tools that are used by Spanish speakers as well as being able to work within these tools, for example, constructing an appropriate search strategy. Although students have considerable experience doing research in English by the 3000 level, assessment data demonstrates that students have rarely undertaken any research in Spanish before this class and that they are extremely nervous of the process.

SP3010 builds upon SP3000 to develop student writing through the lens of social justice. This includes the study of Iberian and Latin American culture, linguistics, sociopolitical and economic reality, and literature and criticism. Within this class, students are expected to produce five pieces of written work, of which the *reseñas y comentarios de recursos* (summary and commentary of sources) paper and the *exposición* (exposition) paper have to include at least three to four credible Spanish sources. Topics are varied but tend to focus around social problems in Spain and Latin America such as trash collectors, access to education, or natural resource exploitation. Due to the number of prerequisite modules that need to be taken before this class, the course is normally taken in a student's final year of study.

Goals

SP3010 is driven by several jointly developed librarian and instructor teaching goals, which entwine foreign language and CIL in powerful pedagogical practice. Drawing from the MLA recommendations that linguistic competence should be developed through the analysis of a variety of cultural narratives, this class positions IL as a way for students to develop deep cultural knowledge. In this way, the primary goal of SP3010 is to develop the student's linguistic and transcultural competence through a critical engagement with Spanish information environments. As the previous section explained, the complexity of foreign language information environments is often obscured by our reliance on common English language research tools. Accordingly, questions about the political economies of information or knowledge ownership and control, for example, can help students develop their knowledge of the foreign language societies they are studying, a core foreign language learning goal. This will also help them understand the background realities that underpin Spanish cultural narratives. At the same time, the research process can be used as a bridge point where students can compare and contrast English and Spanish information practices.[36] By juxtaposing student experiences in the native culture as well as the foreign one, neither culture is positioned as dominant or universal. Instead, the librarian is enacting a process targeted at understanding rather than exotifying foreignness. In turn, this can help learners consider the position and role of cultural knowledge in their own societies, core aspects of transcultural learning goals.

This goal of linguistic and transcultural competence is supported by the class focus on real world information scenarios instead of academic goals. High levels of globalization and immigration mean that Spanish is growing increasingly important for a wide range of traditional information-seeking positions in the US, including the communications, medical, and legal professions.[37] Yet while workplace IL is highly distinctive, IL within higher education tends to be developed around academic goals with the expectation that this will be transferable to the workplace.[38] In this way, and recognizing the importance of Spanish IL in the workplace, the class focuses on facilitating critical engagement with the information systems and practices that students may encounter in their future careers. This enables learners to develop the independent habits of a lifelong learner who is positioned to step out and act in a variety of information environments. In addition, by structuring the class around the open web or asking students to grapple with concepts of trust and credibility rather than relying on checklists, the librarian positions the student to engage more profoundly in the information environment. This enables the development of a more sensitive knowing of the language and culture, a core goal of the foreign languages.

The librarian and the instructor's focus on slowing down the research process also supports transcultural learning goals. Students often see research as a confusing and procedural exercise. As Barbara Fister points out, "By making it sound as if the point of the paper is to find and use sources, we're practically *begging* them to patchwrite."[39] In addition, the focus on expert formal scholarship practices means that academic investigation can be considered unapproachable.[40] However, by focusing on scaffolding intermediate steps in the research process, students are deliberately given time to reflect on their process and their understandings of the research experience in different cultural contexts. This is particularly important when students encounter scenarios and questions that they may not have considered before, for example, the role of social and political systems in knowledge production. In addition, this shift from "a final product to the experience of inquiry" also allows students to see research as a dynamic conversation that they can enter, thereby reinforcing the goal of helping them become more deliberate in their actions as well as more aware of what they are becoming.[41]

Structure

Librarian engagement in SP3010 is structured around a research seminar and the administration of three reflective surveys. The in-person, hands-on research seminar is designed to initiate a more critical understanding of Spanish information environments. Held just before the second writing assignment is due, the librarian draws from pre-class survey answers to briefly revise elements introduced at the SP3000 level. However, the majority of class time is spent on engaging students in deeper, more problematic questions, such as access to and use of information in Spanish contexts, rather than the mechanics of the research process.

The first half of the class focuses on using the open web to find Spanish resources. Individually or in groups, students find one resource related to their topic, recording their choice on an online form. As they find this information, students are asked to make a note of how they found the source, including successful search techniques, tools, and evaluation criteria. After 10–15 minutes, the class comes back together to build a list of successful tips and strategies on the whiteboard. Through the ensuing discussion, the librarian facilitates further reflection on these findings, including probing for information that students expected to find but didn't or how their search strategies differed in a Spanish context. The conversation then moves on to discuss how the class chose and evaluated this information. The librarian builds a similar list of criteria that can be used to evaluate information on the whiteboard. She further probes student answers, for example, focusing the discussion on search personalization or the *Wikipedia* editing process. The second half of the class repeats the same exercise using the library webpage. A new list of tools, techniques, and evaluation criteria are added to the whiteboard as the librarian facilitates further reflection around these findings. She also probes for differences that students have noticed between doing English and Spanish research on the library webpage before pushing students to reflect on differences between research on the open web and the library webpage. While the class discussion varies according to student responses, students are provided with a handout of guiding questions to help start the reflective process (see Appendix 10A).

In this way, the class is structured around helping students to explore Spanish information environments critically. Instead of being presented with a checklist of differences, however, the class draws from personal experiences. This approach has several benefits. By compiling lists of resources and techniques as a group, the class draws from each student's knowledge to create a much wider and deeper understanding of Spanish information landscapes. This active approach creates a practical list of takeaway approaches and strategies for future research needs. More importantly, however, it also acknowledges students' prior knowledge and participation, thereby making the research process more meaningful and creating more opportunities for critical analysis. Ensuing discussions about differences between Spanish and English research are equally participatory. By engaging students in reflection about differences between their native and the foreign language culture, the class pushes students to think more broadly about their own world and society rather than simply marveling at the exotic. This is also far more inclusive in a class that could consist of native English speakers as well as heritage and native Spanish speakers from around the world. And, while the short amount of time allows only basic observations to be made, the reflective surveys are designed to build on these concepts to push students to develop their thinking even further.

The three reflective surveys are designed to inform both teaching and learning needs (see Appendix 10B). While they are optional, surveys are seen as an integral part of the class, and students are given class time to reflect on their process beyond the one-shot seminar format. Design of the prompts draws heavily on the work that the author and three colleagues did at a UCB Assessment Institute as well as the work of Troy Swanson and Claire Kramsch.[42]

The first survey is delivered before the research seminar to assess student needs and prior knowledge. In this way, it helps students begin to articulate and reflect on their goals and process. The questions also help to remind students of some of the complications of doing research in Spanish, thereby preparing them for class. At the same time, prompts that look at student topics and knowledge of Spanish information realities aim to help the librarian understand learner needs and guide plans for the upcoming seminar.

The second survey is administered immediately after the research seminar. Like the first survey, prompts about the research process help students reflect on their learning by articulating new strategies or approaches that they have adopted after the seminar. Answers also help the librarian assess comprehension and application of concepts, thereby helping her to understand what parts of the seminar work or are meaningful to students. These responses also allow the librarian to decide if further clarification is needed. The last reflection is delivered at the end of semester. This allows students to consider their research process holistically and reflect on their experience over the whole semester. At the same time, questions that probe the transferability and application of this knowledge help the librarian gauge whether students have retained these concepts. Responses also allow the librarian to decide whether she needs to make changes to her teaching in future semesters.

Results and Discussion

This class has been offered in three different semesters, starting in Fall 2012. Overall, 71 Spanish students have taken this class (Fall 2012: 20; Spring 2013: 20; Fall 2013: 31). While demographics of each class were not collected, as an illustration, in Fall 2012, there were 323 declared Spanish majors at UCB, of whom 71 percent are female and 21 percent have a minority race or ethnic status. Due to the number of prerequisites needed for this class, most students take the course as a senior. Student reflective prompts are analyzed during the semester to provide necessary feedback and follow up for student needs. In Fall 2013, the librarian combined and coded data from all three semesters to conduct a thematic analysis and draw broad conclusions. She also obtained IRB approval to quote from the reflective prompts in order to assess student responses to this course.

Pre-Class Survey

In the pre-class survey, most students indicated that they were at a very early stage of research. Their topics were still fairly broad, and they had a fairly superficial understanding of the issues and the people who would be interested in their area of research. Nonetheless, for the most part, students displayed a mature understanding of the steps that they felt they would need to take to be successful in this assignment. As most students who take the class are graduating seniors, these answers are not unusual. The comfort that students showed regarding the research process, however, was not borne out by their understanding of Spanish information environments. Only a few students demonstrated the experience or knowledge that they would need to interpret difference or to be successful in different cultural contexts. For instance, while most students recalled at least one method to find Spanish results in Google (for example, using the advanced search to specify the region or language), an even larger proportion indicated that they also expected to find significant material on sites that had worked in the past for English language research papers such as EBSCO or JSTOR. In fact, some students expressed mild frustration at the thought of having to attend the workshop because they "already know how to navigate the library webpage." In this way, it is clear that while students enter the class feeling comfortable doing research, few demonstrate extensive experience of carrying out research in a Spanish context.

Post-Class Survey

The second survey was administered a week after the research seminar. However, at this stage, and in direct contrast to the pre-class survey, student answers are more likely to be characterized by frustration as unexpected hitches and problems mar their research progress. Students quickly discover that few academic publications investigate the Latin American social justice issues, such as trash collectors, that are the topics of their papers. In addition, even if this information exists, the library does not always provide easy access to it:

> Algunos de los retos incluyen: la falta de información sobre América Central y basura, También, los sitios de web como Ethnic Newswatch que nos recomienda no funciona. (Some of the challenges were: the lack of information about Central America and trash, also, websites like Ethnic Newswatch that you recommended don't work.)

Furthermore, students see that this lack of information is not just limited to the academic sphere. Typical Google searches, for example, fail to pull up the amount of information to which students are accustomed:

> Algunos de los retos de mi investigación son que mi tema es algo muy complicado—hay muchas causas y efectos—pero no hay mucha información académica en la internet para países específicas. (Some of the challenges of my research were that my topic is quite complicated— there are many causes and effects—but there is not much information in the Internet about specific countries.)

While students are obviously frustrated, these answers demonstrate that they are making important progress in their growth as a Spanish researcher. The failure of expected successful search strategies as well as encountering the surprisingly limited visibility of Spanish information means that students are starting to recognize common pitfalls. In turn, this will help them develop a far more meaningful understanding of Spanish information landscapes. Interestingly, of all these challenges, student responses demonstrate that they struggle the most with the relative lack of academic sources. Accustomed to relying on databases as an indicator of credibility, students worry about using non-scholarly sources in their paper as well as the challenges of evaluating and integrating nontypical sources into their papers such as government websites, NGO reports, or social media. The discomfort that students feel working with this type of information also validates the decision to base the class around real world information environments.

At the same time, frustration forces the students to think more deeply about these problems and develop strategies to combat difficulties. One major strategy includes becoming more aware of keyword choices, especially the need to think about regional vocabulary:

> Hay muchas diferencias entre países de america latina, así que cuando busco en español ahora sé que tengo que tomar en mente que la palabra que conozco tal vez no la usan en otro país y debería de buscar otro. (There are many differences between Latin American countries, so when I search in Spanish, I know that I have to take into

consideration that the word that I know may not be used
in another country and I need to look for another.)

Another major strategy that students employ is rethinking their evaluation
process, moving from trusting information because of its place of publication
towards looking more critically at the concepts within the work:

Tengo confianza en información que yo encontré en
otros fuentes. También, no estoy de acuerdo con un pe-
dazo de informacion si no puedo encontrarlo en otros
fuentes. (I trust information that I also find in other
sources. Also I don't agree with a bit of information if I
can't find it in other sources.)

At the same time, students acknowledge that their lack of cultural
experience adds to their difficulties in working out how to trust information:

Creo que todo esta bien, porque busque cada hecho en
varios fuentes para verificar. Como yo no estoy familiar con la Ciudad de México y no sé realmente que esta
pasando estaba muy nerviosa que la información sería
incorrecta. Algunas veces los periódicos daban información en conflicto, por eso era difícil saber la verdad.
(I think it's ok because I have looked for each fact in
several sources to verify. Because I am not familiar with
Mexico City and I don't know really what is happening,
I was nervous that the information would be incorrect.
Sometimes newspapers give conflicting information, so
it's hard to know the truth.)

In sum, these responses show that although students are challenged by
the requirements of this class, they also start to develop sophisticated strategies
to overcome these problems. This indicates that students are starting to
demonstrate a growing sense of their own agency within information landscapes,
for example, by evaluating information critically and independently. These habits
will be particularly useful in the workplace and throughout their personal and
professional lives. Answers also show that students are starting to develop a much

broader understanding of the Spanish information environment. However, this understanding goes beyond being able to name or navigate core tools in the field towards starting to reflect on differences between English, Spanish, and Latin American information realities, for example, concerning publication, access to information, and its availability in an Anglophone setting.

End-of-Semester Survey

By the end of semester, when the third survey was administered, responses show that students have developed a far more critical understanding of the Spanish information landscape. This can be seen in the increasingly sophisticated analysis that marks student reflections on the information environment and their research process. For instance, beyond recognizing differences in academic and popular publishing, students also reflected at length on web publishing and its role in giving voice to minorities:

> Mucha de la gente, los pobres o los que no tienen accesso a educacion o tecnologia, no puede publicar sobre un tema. Sus historias son importantes pero ellos no tienen voces. La gente que puede publicar sobre un tema es la gente que normalmente tienen dinero y tiempo para acesar algunos recursos. Las voces de los profesores, y la gente academica estan incluidos, mientras las voces de los pobres estan exluidos.(Many people, the poor or those who don't have access to information or technology, can't publish on a topic. Their stories are important, but they don't have a voice. The people who can publish on a topic are the people who normally have money and time to access some resources. The voices of the teachers and academic people are included, while the voices of poor people are excluded

At the same time, some students also recognize that access to technology is not enough and that information systems are sometimes stacked subtly against specific groups:

> La gente excluido son la gente que no sabe las reglas de la academia o no entiendan las reglas. (The excluded

people are the people who don't know the rules of the
academy or don't understand the rules.)

This increasingly sophisticated perspective is carried over into students'
ability to evaluate information as they learn to critique sources in increasingly
insightful ways.

- Es bien aceptar la informacion que ve en las noticias a un punto cier-
to, sin embargo, la gente debe que preguntar todo y ser critico. (It's
good to accept the information you see in the news up to a certain
point; however, people should question everything and be critical.)
- Buscas por los dos lados de todas historias.(You look for the two
sides of all the stories.)

The previous failure of the students' usual research process means that
students have had to engage more fully with information instead of merely
accepting sources because they were published in a librarian-approved source.
This ensures that they have to think more deeply about how they work with
information, which also provides them with valuable experience for IL practices
beyond the academic sphere.

The final question in the reflective survey aimed to encapsulate the
student's transcultural learning experiences by requiring students to move away
from their native culture and demonstrate their understanding of research from
an outsider's perspective.[43] Answers showed that, for the most part, students have
developed an ability to see the world through another person's eyes while also
remaining aware of their own identity, key aspects of transcultural competence.
Key differences that students highlighted included comments about the relative
visibility of English and Spanish information in knowledge and research systems:

Para mi, una investigación española requiere que uno
busca más en el internet que los otras fuentes de información. (For me, Spanish research requires one to look
more in the Internet than other sources of information.)

This can also be seen through the strategies that students recommend
using to be successful in information environments:

Les diria que debieran usar sinonimos cuando buscan
informacion. Por ejemplo, si les gustarian decir "casa"

en su busqueda, pueden tambien usar la palabra "hog-
ar." (I would tell that they should use synonyms when
they look for information. For example, if they like to
say "house" in their search, they can also use the word
"home.")

In this way, it is clear that by the end of the semester, students are far
more comfortable with the research process. Their insightful analysis of
information practices shows the students have developed a deeper knowing
of Spanish information environments. The students' ability to evaluate a wide
range of sources demonstrates growing confidence in their agency within these
environments. Lastly, student reflections on the differences between English
and Spanish information environments show their capacity to think about the
world in a different way, one of the primary goals of this class.

Program Review

This program was established as a pilot in order to start to examine what a critical approach to IL could look like in the context of foreign language education.
Accordingly, while student responses demonstrate that this approach had significant success, other aspects of the pilot did not accomplish their original aims.
This section will attempt to analyze the reasons for this as well as outlining plans
for the future.

Over the course of the semester, students developed a critical
understanding of Spanish information environments. Three important factors
can explain this success: the librarian-instructor partnership; the librarian-
program integration; and the librarian's push to think more broadly about
Spanish information landscapes. The librarian-instructor partnership is one of
the biggest reasons for the success of this course. Over a period of four years, the
librarian and the instructor have worked together to design for and develop two
language classes. This has led to the creation of a supportive relationship that
encourages experimentation and research into teaching practices. Each of us
pool expertise and experience developed from our own fields, which, combined
with an openness to change, prove to be highly complementary for redesigning
the class. More importantly, however, the success of the partnership can be
linked to the shared premise that IL is the responsibility of both the librarian

and the instructor. In this way, research components of the course are designed collaboratively, and the instructor reinforces IL at key points throughout the class. This understanding has also supported the evolution of course goals and learning outcomes, in particular, the wish to slow down the research process and to focus on research in the real world.

Another reason that the partnership has been successful can be linked to the librarian and the instructor's attempts to understand each other's environment better. This is exemplified by the librarian's sharing of relevant literature with the instructor, for example, the accessible Project Information Literacy reports. At the same time, the librarian has also developed her understanding of the foreign language disciplinary context. Her participation in language pedagogy and technology workshops as well as reading more broadly about foreign language education has enabled her to develop a deep understanding of what constitutes IL in the field. This knowledge has allowed her to take a holistic approach to IL that adapts instruction to the disciplinary context rather than merely focusing on tools and resources.

While the establishment of a supportive relationship such as this may not be unusual in IL literature, the worth of this partnership should not be understated in the foreign languages. The traditional rigid divide between language and content courses in foreign language departments means that most foreign language support has been focused on upper-division literary courses taught by tenure track faculty rather than instructor or graduate student taught lower-division language courses.[44] However, as the 2007 MLA report points out, neither the one-sided focus on literary studies nor the two-tiered system of education is beneficial for foreign language students.[45] As the library also moves from serving as a warehouse of traditional scholarship to a focus on lifelong learning and inquiry, it is important that IL is not confined to traditional "content-based" foreign language courses. Instead, this chapter highlights the value of building IL instruction throughout the curriculum as well as the importance of reaching out to language instructors to fulfill this goal.

The librarian-programmatic integration is a second reason for the success of this course. While this chapter has focused on the SP3010 course, it is clear that this class would not have been as successful if the librarian had not worked extensively with Spanish majors at the SP3000 level too. The one-shot seminar format has been widely criticized within the library literature, yet demands of time and the curriculum as well as scalability issues mean that it remains a common feature of academic instruction. While the librarian is hopeful that the close relationships that she has built up with the Spanish department may eventually result in the further redesign of Spanish research assignments and one-shot seminars, her in-person involvement in both SP3000 and SP3010 currently remains limited to one class session. Notwithstanding, she has worked with the Spanish department to maximize this contact time by mapping the curriculum and ensuring that she is integrated into the department's structure at the most appropriate points. This means that she can sequence and scaffold increasingly complex learning goals over the two courses while also ensuring that students can fulfill the mechanics of the assignment for each class. This approach also has the added benefit of forming a baseline for other advanced Spanish content classes.

Lastly, the success of this course can be linked to the librarian's ability to think beyond traditional IL literature and practices. The field of foreign language IL is relatively underdeveloped, perhaps due to the more typical focus on collection development. Literature that explores CIL went a long way to fill this gap. It is clear that CIL, with its focus on multiple ways of knowing, forms a useful approach for scaffolding foreign language learning goals of transcultural competence. However, beyond this literature, the author found that it was equally important to draw upon research in the field of critical Internet studies. While this type of research is rarely mentioned in LIS, it forms a vital part of investigation into the changing implications of information landscapes and knowledge societies in the digital, global age and proved to be highly influential on the librarian's thinking.

Although this class has been successful on a number of levels, the librarian encountered several challenges and problems that require future research or work. The reliance on the typical research assignment that forms the heart of the course is one such area that the librarian is working on changing. Often seen as a procedural exercise, the traditional research assignment does little to introduce students to the dynamic nature of inquiry in global knowledge societies. While librarians are starting to design alternative research assignments that focus on the research process as much as the product, their implementation requires a modification of course and support structures that may be intimidating for instructors.[46] In future, the librarian will continue to attempt to integrate more meaningful research assignments into these courses.

Within the class structure, the librarian plans to develop further components that look more closely at concepts of trust and source evaluation. Experience has showed her that students are often able to parrot lists of "approved" evaluative criteria yet are often unable to put this knowledge into practice. Future iterations of the class will concentrate more explicitly on these topics. The librarian also hopes to continue revising the course structure. Designing, teaching, and writing about this class was not a comfortable process for the librarian. Through writing this chapter, she has finally come to terms with the positive yet out-of-control feeling that characterized her experiences in these classes. At the same time she also realized that she was too ambitious in the initial scope of the class, trying to do too much all at once. CIL is exciting, but the passion that it often engenders means that it can also be overwhelming. In addition, the relative lack of literature about the integration of CIL into the classroom means that any instructional approach has to be developed haphazardly or by trial and error. In future, while the librarian's interest and belief in this approach remains undiminished, she will endeavor to narrow the scope of the class to expand its impact. In this way she hopes to use these experiences to keep building on these promising beginnings, thereby enacting her own lifelong learning process.

Conclusion

This chapter set out to explore what an IL program that focuses on preparing students for global knowledge societies could look like. Recognizing the unique realities of foreign language information landscapes as well as the need to integrate IL into the disciplinary context, the author explored how IL is constituted in Spanish knowledge societies. She then demonstrated how librarians, in conjunction with instructor and departmental goals, could draw from CIL literature to prepare students to act in rich multicultural information futures. Student responses over the semester demonstrated a growing awareness of how information works in Spanish contexts, moving from knowledge of specific sources to reflecting critically on broader differences between English and Spanish research.

While the chapter has focused on IL for foreign language students, it is clear that transcultural competence is a core goal of many institutions of higher or further education. As campus and workplace become more globalized, students must be able to function in multicultural societies. Accordingly, further research must be done to see whether the concepts outlined in this paper could be adapted to related IL programs such as those focused on international students, international affairs, or global studies. More research should also be done to investigate whether these concepts could be adapted for bilingual societies, for example, in Canada or Wales. It is also unclear what effect this course has on students' familiar or everyday information practices, whether in Spanish or in English. Future research could endeavor to carry out in depth follow-up interviews in subsequent semesters to try and engage with these broader questions. This program forms one librarian's attempt to design IL around core goals of diversity and multiculturalism, and it is to be expected that this topic will only grow more important in the future.

At the same time, it is clear that traditional IL, with its focus on one way of knowing, cannot help students meet these goals. Instead, an approach that is based on CIL can create a more appropriate and meaningful experience. Yet, CIL cannot merely be adopted as a set of alternative ACRL standards. Instead, librarians need to work to develop their own critical consciousness before they can effect transformative change. This involves recognizing biases, beliefs, and privileged positions in the classroom. It also involves moving beyond the functional view of IL and of librarianship to re-professionalize our positions from the "de-skilled technician" who can be replaced by Google to the transformative intellectual who strives for educational advancement and personal transformation.[47] More succinctly, our teaching can no longer center on database demonstrations; our research can no longer just focus on library tools. IL is a core capacity for the digital age, and librarians, as critical information professionals, are ideally suited to scaffold these needs.

Appendix 10A: Class Lesson Plan

In your group:

- Find a Spanish resource on the web and record it in this online form.
- As you work in your group, consider the following questions:
  — Search strategies
    - How did you find this resource? How did this differ from English searching?
    - What keywords did you choose?
    - When you were looking at the list of results, what type of resources did you find? What didn't you find?
    - Who can publish on a specific topic?
    - Who can't? And why?
    - What tips do you have for your classmates (e.g., a great webpage, search tip, etc.)?
  — Evaluation
    - Why did you choose that resource?
    - How did you evaluate the results?
- Find a Spanish resource on the library webpage and record it through this form.
- As you work in your group, consider the following questions:
  — Search strategies
    - How did you find this resource? How did this differ from English searching?
    - What keywords did you choose?
    - When you were looking at the list of results, what type of resources did you find? What didn't you find? How did this differ from the web search? Who can publish on a specific topic? Who can't? And why?
    - What tips do you have for your classmates (e.g., a great webpage, search tip, etc.)?
  Evaluation
    - Why did you choose that resource?
    - How did you evaluate the results? Did this differ from your web search?
- On the whiteboard, build up a list of search strategies for the class and a list of criteria to evaluate resources.

Appendix 10B: Reflective Surveys

Survey 1

- What do you already know about your research topic?
- What do you need to know about your topic?
- Where might you discover this information?
- If you wanted to find information about, for example, solid waste in Guatemala, where would you look?
- When you use Google, how would you look for information in Spanish?

Survey 2

- What changes did you make to your initial searches in order to improve results?
- What prompted you to make those changes?
- What are some of your research challenges? How have you dealt with them or what do you need help with?
- Thinking about the information sources you have found so far, what information do you trust? What causes you to disagree with a piece of information?

Survey 3

- Who can publish on a specific issue? Who cannot and why? Whose voice is included/excluded?
- What information is trusted by society? Do you agree?
- What takeaways from this project or process will you use in your future career or studies?
- You have been offered a position teaching English in Costa Rica. You have two sessions to teach students who are about to study abroad how to conduct research in the US. What points will you emphasize, knowing what you know about the differences between Spanish and English research?

Notes

1.   Alison Hicks, "Cultural Shifts: Putting Critical Information Literacy into Practice," *Communications in Information Literacy* 7, no. 1 (2013): 50–65.

2.   UNESCO, "The Alexandria Proclamation on Information Literacy and Lifelong Learning," accessed November 18, 2013, http://archive.ifla.org/III/wsis/BeaconInfSoc.html; Rob Morrison, "Culturally-Relevant Information Literacy: A Case Study" (EdD diss.,National Louis University, 2010), http://digitalcommons.nl.edu/cgi/viewcontent.cgi?article=1020&context=diss.

3.   Safiya Umoja Noble, "Missed Connections: What Search Engines Say about Women," *Bitch Magazine* 54 (2012): 36–41.

4.   Danah Boyd, *It's Complicated* (New Haven, CT: Yale University Press, 2014), 172.

5.   Siva Vaidhyanathan, "Afterword: Critical Information Studies; A Bibliographic Manifesto," *Cultural Studies* 20, no. 2-3 (2006): 303.

6.   Douglas Thomas and John Seely Brown, *A New Culture of Learning: Cultivating the Imagination for a World of Constant Change* (Lexington, KY: CreateSpace, 2011), 56.

7.   Heidi Jacobs, "Information Literacy and Reflective Pedagogical Praxis," *Journal of Academic Librarianship* 34, no. 3 (2008): 257.

8.   The author will refer to "foreign languages" throughout this paper in accordance with common US higher education terminology, despite her personal preference for other terms.

9.   American Council on Education, *Mapping Internationalization on US Campuses: 2012 Edition*, accessed November 18, 2013, http://www.acenet.edu/news-room/Documents/Mapping-Internationalizationon-US-Campuses-2012-full.pdf.

10.   Hilary Hughes and Christine Bruce, "Cultural Diversity and Educational Inclusivity: International Students' Use of Online Information," *International Journal of Learning* 12, no. 9 (2006): 33.

11.   American Council on Education, *Mapping Internationalization*, 3.

12.   Modern Language Association, *Foreign Languages and Higher Education: New Structures for a Changed World*, accessed August 15, 2014, http://www.mla.org/pdf/forlang_news_pdf.pdf.

13.   Ibid., 4.

14.   Bonnie Cheuk, "Exploring Information Literacy in the Workplace: A Process Approach," in *Information Literacy around the World: Advances in Programs and Research*, ed. Christine Bruce, Philip C. Candy, and Helmut Klaus (Wagga Wagga, New South Wales, Australia: Centre for Information Studies, 2000), 184.

15.   B. Kumaravadivelu, *Beyond Methods: Macrostrategies for Language Teaching* (New Haven: Yale University Press, 2003), 164.

16.   Christine Pawley, "Information Literacy: A Contradictory Coupling," *Library Quarterly* 73, no. 4, (2003): 445.

17.   Troy Swanson, "Applying a Critical Pedagogical Perspective to Information Literacy Standards," *Community and Junior College Libraries* 12, no. 4 (2004): 67; Alan Luke and Cushla Kapitzke, "Literacies and Libraries: Archives and Cybraries," *Pedagogy, Culture and Society* 7, no. 3 (1999): 486.

18.   Hicks, "Cultural Shifts," 59.

19.   Alison Head and Mike Eisenberg, *Lessons Learned: How College Students Seek Information in the Digital Age*, accessed August 15, 2014, http://projectinfolit.org/images/pdfs/pil_fall2009_finalv_yr1_12_2009v2.pdf.

20.   Laura Granka, "The Politics of Search: A Decade Retrospective," *The Information Society*

26, no. 5 (2010): 370; Eric Goldman, "Search Engine Bias and the Demise of Search Engine Utopianism," *Yale Journal of Law and Technology 2005–2006* (2006): 112.

21.   Ibid., 116.

22.   Liwen Vaughan and Yanjun Zhang, "Equal Representation by Search Engines? A Comparison of Websites across Countries and Domains," *Journal of Computer-Mediated Communication* 12, no. 3 (2007): 888–909.

23.   Evgeny Morozov, *To Save Everything, Click Here: The Folly of Technological Solutionism* (New York: Public Affairs, 2013), 144.

24.   Ibid., 141.

25.   Noble, "Missed Connections;" Latanya Sweeney, "Discrimination in Online Ad Delivery," *Queue* 11, no. 3 (2013): 1–19.

26.   Siva Vaidhyanathan, *The Googlization of Everything: (And Why We Should Worry)* (Berkeley, CA: University of California Press, 2011), 80; Tarleton Gillespie, "The Relevance of Algorithms," in *Media Technologies*, ed. Tarleton Gillespie, Pablo J. Boczkowski, and Kirsten A. Foot (Cambridge, MA: MIT Press, 2014).

27.   Mark Graham, "Geographies of Information in Africa: *Wikipedia* and User-Generated Content," *R-Link*, January-March 2013, 40–41.

28.   Ethan Zuckerman, "Makmende's So Huge, He Can't Fit in *Wikipedia*," *My Heart's in Accra* (blog), March 24, 2010, http://www.ethanzuckerman.com/blog/2010/03/24/makmendes-so-huge-he-cant-fit-in-wikipedia/.

29.   Mark Graham, "What Percentage of Edits to English-Language *Wikipedia* Articles Are from Local People?" *ZeroGeography* (blog), March 25, 2013, http://www.zerogeography.net/2013/03/what-percentage-of-edits-to-english.html.

30   Heather Ford, "Isolated vs Overlapping Narratives: The Story of an AFD," *Ethnography Matters,* March 13, 2013, http://ethnographymatters.net/2013/03/13/isolated-vs-overlapping-narratives-the-story-of-the-operation-linda-nchi-wikipedia-article/.

31.   Alison Hicks, "Research in the Foreign Languages," in *Research within the Disciplines: Foundations for Reference and Library Instruction*, 2nd ed., ed. Peggy Keeran and Michael Levine Clark (Lanham, MD: Rowman and Littlefield, 2014), 301–22.

32.   José Octavio Alonso Gamboa and Jane Russell, "Latin American Scholarly Journal Databases: A Look Back to the Way Forward," *Aslib Proceedings* 64, no.1 (2012): 32–45.

33.   Theresa Lillis and Mary Jane Curry, *Academic Writing in a Global Context: The Politics and Practices of Publishing in English* (New York: Routledge, 2010).

34.   Hope Olson, "Sameness and Difference Classification," *LRTS* 45, no. 3 (1999): 117.

35.   Ibid., 120.

36.   Claire Kramsch, *Context and Culture in Language Teaching* (Oxford: Oxford University Press, 1993).

37.   "Career Resources," University of Colorado Boulder: Anderson Language and Technology Center (ALTEC), accessed November 18, 2013, http://altec.colorado.edu/employment-resources.shtml.

38.   Annemaree Lloyd, "Informing Practice: Information Experiences of Ambulance Officers in Training and On-Road Practice," *Journal of Documentation* 65, no. 3 (2009): 398; Alison Head et al., "What Information Competencies Matter in Today's Workplace?" *Library and Information Research* 37, no. 114 (2013): 74–104.

39.   Barbara Fister, "Sources of Confusion," *Library Babel Fish* (blog), *Inside Higher Ed*, August 17, 2011, http://www.insidehighered.com/blogs/library_babel_fish/sources_of_confusion.

40.   Gloria Leckie, "Desperately Seeking Citations: Uncovering Faculty Assumptions

about the Undergraduate Research Process," *Journal of Academic Librarianship* 22, no. 3 (1996): 201–08.

41.   Caroline Sinkinson and Alison Hicks, "Unraveling the Research Process: Social Bookmarking and Collaborative Learning," in *The Plugged-in Professor: Tips and Techniques for Teaching with Social Media*, ed. Sharmila P. Ferris and Hilary Wilder (Oxford: Chandos, 2013), 49–60; James Elmborg, "Literacies, Narratives, and Adult Learning in Libraries," *New Directions for Adult and Continuing Education* 127 (2010): 71.

42.   Megan Bresnahan et al., "Assessment Institute Report," University of Colorado Boulder: Faculty Teaching Excellence Program, accessed November 18, 2013, http://www.colorado.edu/ftep/events/assessment_institute/reports/BresnahanGraberHicksSinkinson.htm; Troy Swanson, "Information Is Personal: Critical Information Literacy and Personal Epistemology," in *Critical Library Instruction: Theories and Methods*, ed. Emily Drabinski, Alana Kumbier, and Maria Accardi (Duluth, MN: Library Juice Press, 2010), 265–78; Kramsch, *Context and Culture in Language Teaching*.

43.   Ibid., 231.

44.   For example, see Peter Kraus, "Information Literacy for German Language and Literature at the Graduate Level: New Approaches and Models," *Library Philosophy and Practice* (2008): http://www.webpages.uidaho.edu/~mbolin/kraus2.htm; Heidi Madden and Anne Marie Rasmussen, "Hiding in Plain Sight: Print Literary Histories in the Digital Age," *CRL News* 74, no. 3 (2013): 140–43.

45.   Modern Language Association, *Foreign Languages and Higher Education*.

46.   Sinkinson and Hicks, "Unraveling the Research Process."

47.   Mark Alfino and Linda Pierce, "The Social Nature of Information," *Library Trends* 49, no. 3 (2001): 475; Kumaravadivelu, *Beyond Methods*, 13.

CHAPTER 11

Student Author(ity):
Engaging Students in Scholarship

Brian W. Young and Daniel Von Holten

Introduction

Library instruction at the University of Mississippi located in Oxford for first-year composition courses is generally scheduled in conjunction with a research paper assignment and limited to one class session with emphasis on teaching students how to use the discovery service, catalog, or databases to find resources. Instructing students how to navigate these resources, though, leaves little class time to devote to information literacy skills such as evaluating source credibility, authority, and validity. For these assignments, instructors generally require students to locate, read, and comprehend a certain number of peer-reviewed sources to ensure students incorporate quality research into their writing. This presents a twofold problem. The requirement reinforces a binary view of scholarship and authorship that excludes student writers, presenting "real" writers as those granted authority by journal editors and peer reviewers. Another challenge is that peer-reviewed sources, particularly in sciences or engineering, are not easily understood by first-year students, which encourages students to approach research in a way that runs counter to the intent of research assignments—use patchwriting techniques rather than critically engage and integrate scholarly sources.

As a potential solution to this problem, we used a semester-long approach integrating multiple, co-taught sessions that focused on both resource navigation and broader research concepts. Students worked throughout the semester on a single research assignment that the instructor divided into steps (field notes, annotated bibliography, literature review, and final report). In addition to developing research and information literacy skills, the assignment's goal was both to develop and increase students' awareness of their own authority. To accomplish this goal, we introduced an electronic repository to the research assignment that would house student-created work and be accessible by later institutional generations. The repository would then be an entry point to introduce students to the concepts of source authority and validity by discussing prior peer research as authoritative and valid sources. In doing so, we hope that current students will then perceive themselves as capable of creating authoritative and valid research. To support this goal, we needed to change our approach to focus more on validity than authority when evaluating information while also helping students recognize the authority and validity of their own work.

Pilot Assignment

In addition to general first-year composition courses (FYC), the Center for Writing and Rhetoric at the University of Mississippi offers a specialized curriculum for freshman engineering students that meet the same objectives as the traditional FYC courses while focusing more on engineering writing genres and student collaboration. More importantly, students work on their research project for the entire semester rather than the more traditional three to four weeks, which allows students to develop their project in a staged process that more closely imitates academic research. The longer assignment addresses a common concern of research assignments in composition classes by providing the instructor and librarian time to give more guidance on the research and writing process.

Including a fieldwork component was important for this specific set of students because it appeals to engineering students' disposition for process-oriented approaches and hands-on analysis. It also provides students the opportunity to study in-depth something that impacts them or that they use on a daily basis, thereby potentially creating a more personal investment in the project. Moreover, limiting students to local systems in Oxford reduced the potential for plagiarism, but more importantly, it provided topics that have little to no published research material—academic or otherwise. Developing the research assignment in a way that required the students to develop knowledge on something to which there is no "go-to text" compels them to engage with their sources more fully, which helps establish their authority on their topic.

For the assignment, students, initially individually and later as groups of three to four students, were asked to analyze a dynamic local system such as the bus transit system or traffic at an intersection or roundabout. Individual observations took the form of a brief exploratory study requiring one week (four one-hour observations) and, optionally, secondary research. Afterwards, each student reported on the feasibility of the system for long-term study and whether it was usable for the larger group assignment. Requiring students to upload their brief studies to an electronic repository allowed students from all four first-year composition for engineering (FYCe) sections to review each studied system and decide, with their group members, which system to investigate further for the larger project.

The remaining parts of the final project were scaffolded as a series of assignments, which, in aggregate, would produce the bulk of the research paper. The first assignment asked students to design a fieldwork study by reviewing research on similar systems. To prepare students for secondary research, we co-taught an instruction session where emphasis was placed on locating appropriate sources to support their own study design. Rather than using an instructor-led method, such as lecture, we provided space and tools, such as whiteboards, to facilitate brainstorming and rotated around each group to discuss their methods and provide one-on-one instruction on locating sources to help guide their study design. In one instance, the librarian overheard students jokingly discuss performing a system analysis of a bar and then dismiss it as not academic, which the librarian quickly refuted by showing the students how to access relevant academic studies on bars, including variables they could include in their own study should they choose to pursue the topic. We later co-taught additional sessions in conjunction with other major components (e.g., research contextualization and annotated bibliography). As students completed each section of their project, they uploaded the documents (field notes, annotated bibliography, project abstract, etc.) to the electronic repository.

The repository took the form of a wiki intended to be used as a collaborative space and an archive of student research. Ideally, subsequent generations (i.e., future engineering students who later take the same course and work on the same assignment) would be able to use the archive as a starting place for their research and possibly improve or update prior research, thus mirroring the iterative research process that is common in academic disciplines. The particular platform (PB Works) we used did not work as well as we had hoped for collaborative writing because restrictions in the platform prevented multiple users from generating content simultaneously.[1] It did, however, serve well as a shared repository accessible to students in multiple sections of the same course and, as a proof of concept, demonstrated the potential in having students access other students' work.

In retrospect, asking students to reflect on their research experience would have been helpful to determine the efficacy of this assignment to achieve our stated goals. However, the composition instructor believed that the reliance on and integration of scholarly resources was improved in comparison to prior iterations of the course. Examples include the aforementioned group ultimately using two studies to form the basis of their own research design to study a local bar; groups using technical jargon found through journal articles (e.g., dead mileage in one study of the Oxford bus system); and groups using articles to support their own observations (articles relating to queuing time and impact on customer satisfaction). In one of the more successful projects, each member (n=4) of a group rode a different bus route between the hours of 11:00 a.m. and 4:00 p.m. They noted that during their study, there seemed to be noticeable difference between what they termed the "popular" and "unpopular" bus routes. Based on these observations, one of their conclusions was that the use of large buses, especially for unpopular routes, results in gas inefficiency, and the city of Oxford should consider purchasing smaller buses to use for these routes. While their findings would require much more exhaustive research to confirm, which they noted in the suggestions for further research section of their final report, it is a worthwhile observation and indicative of the critical thinking we hoped would occur using the pilot assignment.

Source Validity and Authority

Commonly, FYC instructors at the University of Mississippi require the use of peer-reviewed articles. In support of this, library instruction sessions focus not only on how to use the discovery service or individual databases but also on how to use facets to refine their searches to include only journals with peer-reviewed articles. The pilot assignment, though, did not have any explicit requirements related to source authority. Rather than focus on authority and require students to use only peer-reviewed articles, we co-taught an instruction session focused on guiding students to determine who would publish similar studies to their own topics, why they would publish them, and where and how those studies may be published. Student groups then further developed concepts for their studies and, with our help, located sources to inform their designs. Sources used ranged from government transportation reports to similar analyses on various groups' topics (bars, roundabouts, bus routes).

When discussing methods for locating peer-reviewed articles, it can be easy to describe it in the context of the right, or best, way to research, which would invalidate other approaches, including our students' prior experience working with information. Rolf Norgaard has cautioned librarians and instructors to be mindful of our approach to teaching information literacy because suggestions and guides to research can easily be perceived as mandates, or in his words, "oughts."[2] The change in our approach to discussing sources was subtle, yet important. If we had focused on source authority through a prescriptive approach (i.e., articles in peer-reviewed journals and available through a peer-reviewed facet are "right"), we would have reinforced a binary concept of authority that precludes students from being authoritative writers. We chose, then, to frame our discussions on research and source use within the lenses of evidence-based practice and critical information literacy (and, by extension, critical pedagogy). Through these lenses, we sought to improve students' understanding of research and self-awareness of their authority.

Nancy Adams compared Association of College and Research Libraries' information literacy standards to evidence-based practice (EBP) and discussed the implications for library instruction. In evidence-based practice, source credibility and authority (i.e., who and where) as traditionally viewed by librarians are generally considered weak evidence. Instead, evidence-based practice places more emphasis on validity, which focuses on whether the source is "[free] from bias and error" (internal validity) and is "[applicable] to the question at hand" (external validity).[3] We, like Adams, recognize that most sources in the context of EBP would generally be considered authoritative (i.e., they are peer reviewed) and, therefore, it is expected that internal and external validity would be emphasized. Moreover, freshman researchers would have difficulty reading and determining the internal validity of a typical engineering journal article, so we focused the discussion of sources on external validity. Through lecture and one-on-one conversations with individual groups, we ensured our students were able to locate comparable studies applicable to their research. Further, by requiring students to develop a fieldwork study with the guidance of external literature, we could expect students to consult authoritative sources because they are, largely, the only place students could locate similar research. However, by framing the primary discussion of sources on validity and not authority, we hoped to create a concept of authorship and authority in which students could situate themselves—something we did not feel was as possible when focusing on authority in a binary, prescriptive manner.

Critical information literacy also supports changes to the traditional research process, especially when those changes empower students by encouraging them to view information literacy instruction and the research process as more than information transfer.[4] Critical information literacy, derived from critical pedagogy, encourages instructors (librarians and teachers) to recognize students' preexisting knowledge and experience. Troy A. Swanson (2004) recognized that college students interact with information sources in their daily lives, and this knowledge can influence their research and reception to information literacy instruction. Using students' experiences as starting points, Swanson led several library sessions that guided students from their beginning knowledge of information to a more academic understanding of information sources and their applicability in various contexts.[5] Similarly, we recognized that students are already accustomed to searching for answers to specific questions, so by framing the discussion of sources on external validity, students were asked to use their everyday information-seeking process (e.g., searching Google for answers to a specific question) to locate sources.

Barbara Fister has argued that students are unable to fully engage with scholarly material often due to time constraints that can prohibit instructors from discussing the proper way to read and evaluate journal articles.[6] Reframing the conversation on source material and modifying expectations of how students approach that material may change how we, as librarians and instructors, perceive students' use of sources. While we have no data at this time to support our observations, our students seemed to use sources as we envisioned—as guides to design their research study and to contextualize their findings.[7] This introduction to reading and integrating scholarly material is especially appropriate when we view students as novice scholars learning their craft and accept that they should not be expected to use sources in the same manner as more experienced researchers.

Once we shift our perception of students to that of novice researchers, and then view their research skills not as right or wrong but as developing, it becomes easier to accept that the expert-researcher model does not work for students who are generally unable to engage in intermediate to advanced research tasks (e.g., following citation trails or recognizing and reading important scholars).[8] Research projects are challenging for students at least in part because of their developing research skills and their need to establish their authority on their topic.[9] For this reason, it is beneficial to not require peer-reviewed resources, which generally leads to librarians demonstrating peer-reviewed facets in discovery services and/or databases, thereby enforcing the view of authority as dichotomous. Singular focus on peer-reviewed sources, by default, excludes students and encourages the perception that students should not be perceived as scholars. Instead, focusing attention on source credibility and validity accomplishes the same purpose (i.e., students reading and incorporating quality sources), but it does not restrict students to a specific type of material and, more importantly, does not prioritize a genre (peer-reviewed research) that, for the most part, excludes them.[10]

Being cognizant of how we teach students to perform library research can only do so much in regards to how students perceive their own authority. Limiting students to local systems and requiring fieldwork, though, helps establish our students' credibility and authority because not only are they active participants of their system (library space, traffic intersections, bus transit, etc.), they can design their study based on traditionally authoritative texts (scholarly material) and locally authoritative texts (previous generational student work found in the local repository). Moreover, by streamlining the initial research steps, especially topic selection, and by centralizing the project to local systems, it is more likely that our students will overcome possible library anxiety and be more effective in locating secondary sources, further establishing their authority on the topic.

Designing the assignment to position students as authors embraces the notion that students can be, and are, capable of writing authoritatively as scholars. Laurie Grobman has stated that students can gain authorship and authority through undergraduate research and publication.[11] She also calls for undergraduate research to be viewed as part of a "continuum of scholarly authority" and states that student scholars should be "*author*ized," thus removing the binary concept of student writer vs. author.[12] By encouraging students to take the mantle of authority for themselves, they become better acquainted with the purpose of research in the academy.

Electronic Repository

From a practical standpoint, the repository would eventually, as more classes add documents, provide an abundant number of sample annotated bibliographies, data collection instruments, and system analyses for future students to review. Homework assignments can be developed that require students to use the repository such as critiquing a past group's methods or choosing and summarizing a past report that they found to be interesting and discussing its effectiveness. In this way, the repository becomes much more than a collection of examples; it becomes a pedagogical tool—one used to shape student's understanding of the research process by critiquing and summarizing previous research.

For the pilot semester, the repository allowed students to interact with documents created by students outside of their class (i.e., in a different section). More important to students' understanding of their authority is that the repository will act as an archive of studies on local systems and, as a repository of citable student work, will act as a logical starting place to discuss the "academic conversation" and how students can participate. In future semesters, students will be able to refer to the repository for both examples of how to complete their project and for sources to critique when designing their study and writing their final report. The latter is important as we seek to widen the audience of student work to more than just instructors and current classmates and position students as authors and scholars.

Previous discussion in this chapter outlined how we approached bibliographic instruction in a way that we thought would allow students to perceive themselves and their prior experiences as inclusive in the scholarly process. The repository as a place to "publish" student work is a tangible artifact that represents our students' place, albeit at the lower end, in the authority continuum. Approaching the idea of scholarly communication in this way actively demonstrates the Burkean parlor conversation that occurs by providing students the authority and opportunity to actively participate and interjecting them directly into the conversation.[13]

Students researching more traditional topics may have difficulty understanding the ongoing discussion in the scholarly literature when they only read a small number of journal articles. By focusing on a local topic and having students populate the repository, it would be possible for future students to read all material published on the topic (i.e., all previously uploaded student work related to their topic) and then supplement those documents with contextualizing pieces from the broader literature. Abstract concepts about information production and scholarly literature, such as the idea that knowledge and authority is constructed and dependent on the writings and interpretations of a series of researchers, becomes more "real" when students (over the course of several iterations of the class) have been the creating the literature.

Imitating the process and directly inserting students into a scholarly conversation should improve their understanding of the research process and improve their understanding of authority by positioning them as authorities as viewed by Grobman and others. As the repository becomes more populated with studies about each system, future generations of students will have first-hand experience synthesizing multiple studies on a precise topic, reviewing secondary literature to support their conclusions from the synthesis, and then writing their own research analysis. This addresses some of the practices recommended by Joyce Kinkead and Grobman as students are taking part in a more authentic research experience that involves authentic inquiry.[14] The inquiry involves students engaging with authoritative work but not just solely peer-reviewed works.

As a pilot, no previous documents inhabited the repository, but in future iterations of the class, students would consult (i.e., review, critique, cite, etc.) the documents in the repository as they would documents found in a discovery service or database. The repository, then, serves the dual purpose of being an archive and a controlled environment or database, where freshman can conduct research. It is in this phase of their academic careers that we want them to continue developing critical thinking skills and begin to read and integrate outside thoughts into their own. In this beginning phase of learning how to locate and write their own research, a "go-to database" related specifically to their assignment can be used to scaffold the introduction to broader resources such as a library discovery service or database listing. The difference between the instructor handing out sample final projects and students looking in the repository is the emulation of the research process. Skimming abstracts and looking through a collection of papers in the repository is similar, albeit much scaled down, to the process expert researchers use, for example, when skimming through a particular subject heading in a database. In both cases, the novice and the expert are scanning for potential sources to inform and further their own research.

Conclusion

Compositionists and librarians have discussed the need for scaffolded approaches to the research assignment.[15] Karen Keiser Lee, who has studied the history of the research paper in relation to undergraduate writing courses, notes faculty criticisms, chiefly that such assignments "oversimplify the research process or confine it to a single, often laborious task."[16] Studies on undergraduate student perceptions of research paper assignments show that students often fail to understand the instructor's intended purpose: The research assignment is a recursive process that involves revising a viewpoint as research is integrated into the work. Many students instead focus on strategies that allow them to quickly present information they find or present a topic after cursory research.[17] Often, this results in students "patchwriting"—locating and integrating quotes into their paper without having fully read or understood the cited articles. Based on results from the Citation Project, a multi-institutional study that investigates how students use sources, students tend to paraphrase or directly quote from small sections, often from the abstract or first few pages of journal articles.[18] This, of course, is not the desired result of requiring students to use academic journal articles. With the pilot assignment, especially the fieldwork component (both the design and observation), we hoped to engage our students in the assignment. More importantly, though, we hoped for our students to engage in scholarship by discussing sources in a purposeful manner and presenting the repository to students as an archive, one that would be consulted by future students.

Framing conversations about sources primarily on validity and introducing an online repository were the two key components of our pilot approach. Scaffolding the research project over many weeks, instead of just a few, afforded students the opportunity to engage with their project in a manner that more closely imitates "traditional" research, which, in turn, afforded us the opportunity to discuss more broadly the information cycle, specifically the academic conversation and requirements and methods for participation.

Outside of anecdotal comments (e.g., "it is cool to think that someone may reference my work next year"), we cannot definitively claim that this approach had any impact on student perceptions. We believe, though, that this approach, or one similar, has potential for overcoming identified threshold concepts of information literacy instruction.[19] Published student work in the repository provides not only a logical starting point for discussing iterative research but also "format as a process."[20] Instructors or librarians, in the future, could juxtapose the creation process of students' work in the repository with that of researchers' work in a journal article. Introducing this juxtaposition in the context of Grobman's continuum of authority could be the basis of a classroom discussion about how novice researchers, such as themselves, do not undergo as rigorous of a vetting process, and so, for example, their methods must be critiqued and considered more closely if used as models for designing a system analysis study.

The repository, then, becomes more than just a storage device; it is an archive of novice authors and scholars whose research emphasis is on dynamic systems local to Oxford. This establishes a community—one where students, as knowledgeable peers, establish norms and decide which texts are valued.[21] Much as Grobman's basic writers felt more comfortable with citing sources from their own discourse community (the web), we expect future engineering students will feel more comfortable, that is, more authorized, to actively engage with sources accessed through the repository and therefore be more likely to enter the discourse community tangibly represented by the repository.

We want students to view themselves as authors, not *student writers*. This requires changing their perceptions as well as our own as to what constitutes an author and an authoritative and/or valid text. Librarians and composition instructors, like us, must be aware of the underlying implications of prioritizing peer-reviewed texts. Introducing students to and informing them about the information cycle in the academy (e.g., peer review) is important, but just as important is developing students as critical thinkers and creating a place for them in the academy, which includes engaging them in scholarship and encouraging them to perceive themselves as authors—writers with authority. To accomplish the latter in our classroom, we chose to discuss sources in the context of validity and in the context of an authority continuum, rather than as a binary concept. Moreover, archiving student work in a repository with the intent for future students to cite that work is a step towards creating a local community of scholars and helping students recognize their positions as authors, not just passive participants in the academy.

Notes

1. PBworks: http://pbworks.com/.

2. Rolf Norgaard, "Writing Information Literacy: Contributions to a Concept," *Reference and User Services Quarterly* 43, no. 2 (2003): 126.

3. Nancy Adams, "A Comparison of Evidence-Based Practice and the ACRL Information Literacy Standards: Implications for Information Literacy Practice," *College and Research Libraries* (forthcoming).

4. James Elmborg, "Critical Information Literacy: Implications for Instructional Practice," *The Journal of Academic Librarianship* 32, no. 32 (2006): 193.

5. Troy A. Swanson, "A Radical Step: Implementing a Critical Information Literacy Model," *Portal: Libraries and the Academy* 4, no. 2 (2004): 265–68.

6. Barbara Fister, "Decode Academy" (presentation, LOEX Conference, Nashville, TN, May 3, 2013), http://homepages.gac.edu/~fister/loex13.pdf.

7. Examples include students using a Polish article on bars to determine which variables to study and gas emission data for car and buses to support conclusions of a study on the bus transit system.

8. Gloria J. Leskie, "Desperately Seeking Citations: Uncovering Faculty Assumptions about the Undergraduate Process," *The Journal of Academic Librarianship* 22, no. 3 (1996): 201–08.

9. Ibid., 203.

10. While undergraduate research journals do exist, composition instructors and librarians are generally not speaking of these journals when discussing peer-reviewed publications.

11. Laurie Grobman, "The Student Scholar: (Re)Negotiating Authorship and Authority," *College Composition and Communication* 61, no. 1 (2009): 176–77.

12. Ibid., 177–79.

13. Kenneth Burke, *The Philosophy of Literary Form: Studies in Symbolic Action* (New York: Vintage Books, 1957).

14. Joyce Kinkead and Laurie Grobman, "Expanding Opportunities for Undergraduate Research in English Studies," *Profession* 1 (2011): 227.

15. Karen Keiser Lee, "The Research Paper Project in the Undergraduate Writing Course," in *The New Digital Scholar: Exploring and Enriching the Research and Writing Practices of NEXT-GEN STUDENTS*, ed. Randall McClure and James Purdy (Medford, NJ: American Society for Information Science and Technology, 2013), 41–63; Richard Larson, "The 'Research Paper' in the Writing Course: A Non-Form of Writing," *College English* 44, no. 8 (1982): 811–16; Fister, "Decode Academy;" Leskie, "Desperately Seeking Citations," 201–08.

16. Lee, "The Research Paper Project in the Undergraduate Writing Course," 45.

17. Ibid., 48–51

18. The Citation Project: http://site.citationproject.net.

19. Amy R. Hofer, Lori Townsend, and Korey Brunetti, "Troublesome Concepts and Information Literacy: Investigating Threshold Concepts for IL Instruction," *Portal: Libraries and the Academy* 12, no. 4 (2012): 387–405.

20. Hofer, Townsend, and Brunetti define *format as process* as "what makes a book a book and a newspaper article a newspaper article has nothing to do with how one accesses it (print/digital), but with the process that went into creating it. Understanding this principle helps students… evaluate it according to the process underlying its creation."

21. Elmborg, "Critical Information Literacy," 195.

Bibliography

Adams, Nancy. "A Comparison of Evidence-Based Practice and the ACRL Information Literacy Standards: Implications for Information Literacy Practice." *College and Research Libraries* (forthcoming).

Burke, Kenneth. *The Philosophy of Literary Form: Studies in Symbolic Action*. New York: Vintage Books, 1957.

Elmborg, James. "Critical Information Literacy: Implications for Instructional Practice." *The Journal of Academic Librarianship* 32, no. 2 (2006): 192–99.

Fister, Barbara. "Decode Academy." Presentation presented at the LOEX Conference, Nashville, TN, May 3, 2013.

Grobman, Laurie. "The Student Scholar: (Re)Negotiating Authorship and Authority." *College Composition and Communication* 61, no. 1 (2009): 175–96.

Hofer, Amy R., Townsend, Lori, and Brunetti, Korey. "Troublesome Concepts and Information Literacy: Investigating Threshold Concepts for IL Instruction." *Portal: Libraries and the Academy* 12, no. 4 (2012): 387–405.

Kinkead, Joyce, and Laurie Grobman. "Expanding Opportunities for Undergraduate Research in English Studies." *Profession* 1 (2011): 218–30.

Larson, Richard L. "The 'Research Paper' in the Writing Course: A Non-Form of Writing." *College English* 44, no. 8 (1982): 811–16.

Lee, Karen Kaiser. "The Research Paper Project in the Undergraduate Writing Course." In *The New Digital Scholar: Exploring and Enriching the Research and Writing Practices of NEXT-GEN STUDENTS*, edited by Randall McClure and James P. Purdy, 41–63. Medford, NJ: American Society for Information Science and Technology, 2013.

Leckie, Gloria J. "Desperately Seeking Citations: Uncovering Faculty Assumptions about the Undergraduate Process." *The Journal of Academic Librarianship* 22, no. 3 (1996): 201–08.

Norgaard, Rolf. "Writing Information Literacy: Contributions to a Concept." *Reference and User Services Quarterly* 43, no. 2 (2003): 124–30.

Swanson, Troy A. "A Radical Step: Implementing a Critical Information Literacy Model." *Portal: Libraries and the Academy* 4, no. 2 (2004): 259–73.

CHAPTER 12

From Counting Sources to Sources That Count:

Reframing Authority and Accountability in First-Year Composition

Nicole Walls and Amy Pajewski

Midway through our third semester of collaboration, a student arrived to class worried about the upcoming firsthand research deadline. He had reached someone from the US Copyright Office and had requested an interview, but the potential source could not agree without first checking with the office's ethics department. The interview would be no problem if it were for a class paper, the contact had explained, but because the researched essay would be published online, the contact needed permission to disclose. In the end, the student never got the interview, and ultimately, we don't really care. We assume, of course, that the interview would have been of great value, primarily for its potential to move the student further into the role of accountable, authoritative researcher; however, students in the introductory course must manage their time and energy carefully. They must maintain momentum and cannot afford to abandon all other obligations to chase a lead. Moreover, despite its premature end, the student's communications with the contact were not void of value; for the student, the experience reinforced the lesson that writing *matters*—that the information and perspectives he manifests through research and invention are active, consequential forces. For us, we were reminded that assignment specifications and product requirements are related but not the same: Rather than establishing definitive end goals, assignment specifications motivate inquiry and method, which develop in conjunction and in largely unpredictable ways.

For three semesters we collaborated to revise English 1302: Academic Research and Writing toward a more challenging and rewarding experience for students. A core option at West Texas A&M University, English 1302 is designed as a first-year composition (FYC) course in which instructors introduce academic research methods and materials and guide students in developing a written researched argument. From our perspective, the instructor and librarian are two resources among many who contribute to an expansive support system as students navigate a new spectrum of research writing activities and negotiate new values and identities. Our contributions to this system overlap in many areas, but our roles differ to account for our respective disciplinary and institutional responsibilities. The librarian's instructional role, in broad terms, is to demonstrate and frame the capabilities for secondary research based on criteria explicitly articulated according to the Association of College and Research Libraries' standards and outcomes.[1] Similarly, writing programs and instructors across Texas public institutions are responsible for upholding national standards and working from corresponding objectives. Outcomes for both information literacy and core writing are largely communicated and internalized as "techniques rather than content," establishing as our primary concern what students should learn to *do* and inviting us to define academic foundations in terms of skills and practices as a result.[2]

For FYC, this dynamic sustains a reliance on process paradigms, which combine both the theoretical rationale and the underlying practices for a process-based pedagogical approach. Though problematized in composition theory and scholarship for their capacity to reduce research writing into a linear series of discrete steps, process paradigms reflect and shape FYC pedagogy more or less explicitly across many institutions. As A. Abby Knoblauch argues, "Though few instructors would purport to conceptualize or teach writing as 'a lock-step sequence of prewriting, writing, and rewriting,' most instructors still incorporate revision practices and expectations as fundamental writing activities, making the division between process and post-process [a] rather tenuous one."[3] In useful ways, process paradigms are highly accommodating; they provide an inventory of generic practices (e.g., searching, collecting, prewriting, drafting, peer review, and revision) around which courses can be designed and implemented by instructors with divergent personalities and levels of experience. They accommodate personalization and experimentation as well since generic practices can take many possible forms and are not contingent on any particular topical focus. Within any given program or department, applications of process pedagogy can vary substantially.

Despite ample, valuable room for practical variation, a process-based theoretical framework could not accommodate our collaborative goals, which inevitably changed over time to account for areas of weakness or struggle. In "New Directions in Writing Theory," John R. Hayes notes the potential of activity theory "to help make sense of the complex social and environmental factors that influence writing," considering that it "is designed to describe actions that a person or a group of people undertakes by relating the actions to the environments in which they take place."[4] For us, the activity system has been particularly useful in allowing us to reconceptualize introductory research writing as more complex than an inventory of discrete practices, arranged into a linear process that divides and designates responsibilities. As represented in Figure 12.1, an activity system includes seven interrelated components: subjects, division of labor, tools, object/motive, outcome, rules/norms, and community.[5] These components can account for an array of elements; a number of those common to FYC research writing are categorized in Table 12.1.

Figure 12.1. Diagram of generic activity system

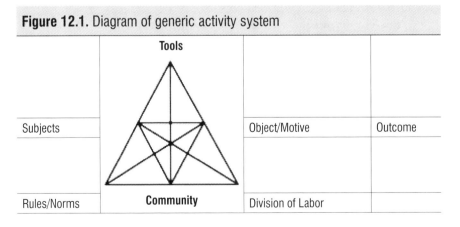

| Subjects | Tools | Object/Motive | Outcome |
| Rules/Norms | Community | Division of Labor | |

Table 12.1. Generic components and context-specific examples of elements

Subjects:	Teachers, students, librarians, tutors, etc.
Division of Labor:	Roles of subjects
Tools:	Classroom, pen and paper, computer, databases, thesaurus, etc.
Object/Motive:	To challenge, teach, learn, improve, pass, etc.
Outcome:	Understanding, grade, contribution
Rules/Norms:	Arguability, MLA format, deadlines, etc.
Community:	Social relations within classroom, university, US, etc.

All frameworks invite a limited range of possible interpretations and applications, of course, and the activity system is no exception; however, we value this framework as much for what it does not do as for what it does. As a descriptive framework, it does not prescribe relationships among elements, either within or across categories; it does not, in other words, establish a hierarchy, pair specific motives with specific outcomes, or assign roles to subjects. Rather, it invites us to consider influences we might otherwise overlook and to imagine new dynamics as we acknowledge multiple participants in multiple alternating roles—expert, novice, reader, writer, reviewer, etc.—working to develop and navigate the best possible system for pursuing meaning and sustainable knowledge appropriate for FYC research writing courses as "liminal spaces that mark a boundary between the inside and the outside of the academy."[6] However systematized, liminal spaces are intrinsically active, and our resource value derives in large part from our ability to render introductory research writing viable to students as a dynamic system of variables to be negotiated collaboratively and in context.

This chapter accounts for some of the key instructional and reflective endeavors that have brought us to see introductory research writing in these terms, changing what we consider meaningful collaboration between writing instructor and instructional librarian in this particular academic context and perhaps beyond. We maintain that the librarian must be more deliberately embedded in the course if he or she is to integrate his or her knowledge in ways that students will retain and trust; however, we have had to reconfigure our additive approaches to co-instruction. If we want to improve our collective value to students, we must work to understand where and why our investments do and do not align and collaborate according to negotiated priorities to which we commit as both co-instructors and co-learners. Otherwise, we risk mistaking *more* for *better*, expanding a system that accommodates our divergent principles and practices but not the potential contributions and transformations of our students.

Instructional Authority and the Division of Labor

It is appropriately commonplace for instructors to worry over their authority. They may feel it lacking, for example, or inconsistent and, at the very least, a work of perpetual progress. Initially, then, the extent to which students can privilege the instructors' direct guidance over that of other resources can seem a contradiction of sorts. From the moment their career begins, the instructors work to establish and refine their authority, and then when a situation arises where they want to relinquish some of that authority for sound pedagogical reasons, they find they can't shake it. More accurately, however, this scenario draws attention to default authority that FYC students ascribe to the instructor as a supervisory and evaluative figure, abstracted from years of compulsory schooling. Even in spite of an instructor's direct advice to consult others, many of our FYC students rely on the instructor as exclusively as possible. This tendency is restrictive to both students and instructors and, from our perspective, persists well beyond where it should.

Initially, Nicole and Amy communicated under standard pretenses to work out the details of Amy's instructional session for Nicole's English 1302 students; however, our discussions took a more critical turn, and we began to reconsider the librarian's conventional role in the research writing course. Practically speaking, the expectation that a librarian transfer sufficient, sustainable skills and knowledge in a single session of 50–75 minutes is unreasonable. Epistemologically, this model devalues information literacy and library research and does little to disrupt the instructor's default authority, which often reduces research to an assignment's most quantifiable requirements—a number of pages to produce, for example, and a number of sources to find. As Barbara Fister explains, "While faculty in the disciplines are masters of the content in their fields, they don't have the perspective librarians do on the complexity of the political and economic ecosystems that circulate those ideas."[7] Indeed, writing instructors cannot replicate librarians' understanding of information literacy or capacity to navigate and organize library resources. The use of LibGuides, for example, reflects efforts on the part of libraries to accommodate the shift to Web 2.0 technologies with guides more "social" in appearance and ethos, suitable for the socially networked web. Presumably, providing students and other library users synthesized library information relevant to a course or project is more reasonable and effective than expecting users to search a comprehensive A–Z list of databases.

Amy developed a research guide that gathered resources—databases, journals, websites, etc.—relevant to the project's theme of reputation in context, and to enhance her presence in the course, she linked the guide to the class's learning management system site, through which students could both access the guide and contact Amy to request help or an appointment. We incorporated a second instructional session in the library as well, designating additional time for Amy to help students navigate the guide and locate any resulting sources, whether electronic or material. It is difficult to determine how students perceive these guides, of course, or how they use them independently. Many librarians maintain that guides are appealing to both creators and researchers: Librarians can easily create content and can quickly make edits as links go dead or research needs change, while students can easily surf via links and tabs and can contact the subject librarian with a simple click on the librarian's "profile box." Based on our students' final products and communication activity throughout the term, however, few seemed to rely on the guide as these arguments would suggest or as we intended. If they did consult the guide outside of class and conferences, they did so quietly as though in accessing the guide they had exhausted Amy as a resource.

We assume that the utility of research guides is shaped by the larger research context and that some activity systems render them more valuable than others, even if they do not change students' preferred search methods. As Barbara Valentine's 2006 study concluded, undergraduate students prefer to run searches "quick and dirty."[8] In 2008, Vanessa Earp found that search engines provided the preferred approach among graduate students as well.[9] In the following section, we discuss in further detail how students worked with sources and how the nature of this work changed after the first semester. Changes to students' use of the guide, specifically, are unclear and ultimately less important to us than the extent to which students interacted differently with Amy and with sources. LibGuides respond to certain changes and challenges in technology that increase and direct online activity, making some ways of using the Internet feel easy and natural and others more difficult. LibGuides mean to align intuitive ways of navigating the web with academic research, and for researchers who understand the purposes and principles of this research, guides may constitute a solution. But for FYC students, a problem does not yet exist as they are not really seeking new, easier ways to conduct their academic research. The real challenge of introductory research writing comes with helping students engage in academic research activities, methodologically new and epistemologically strange, in order to develop an understanding of why academic research happens in the first place.

By the start of our third semester, we had come to question our working division of instructional space as it delineates participation and authority by extension. We had tried to move students into Amy's domains, where she is the primary expert, but these spaces were additional, not integral, and so was her authority. For Fall 2013, we adopted the theme of intellectual property, an area of shared interest and knowledge, and Amy worked more often with students in the regular classroom as primary instructor. Though these additional interactions did not result in additional consultations outside of class, Amy's advice made explicit appearances in concept or application quizzes, and differences between these final projects and those from earlier terms attest to her influence on the range of sources and information students were able and willing to consult. More time in the classroom with Amy meant more opportunities for Amy to clarify and reiterate distinctions between academic and public sources, for example, and methods of source identification and evaluation. It meant opportunities for Amy to move beyond modeling research and to facilitate inquiry and application in the context of students' individual projects.

Authority, Accountability, and the Rules of (Re)source Engagement

In 2012, Dan Berrett reported in *The Chronicle of Higher Education* findings from the ongoing Citation Project, "a multi-institution research project responding to educators' concerns about plagiarism and the teaching of writing."[10] Berrett's article, "Freshman Composition Is Not Teaching Key Skills in Analysis, Researchers Argue," focuses specifically on what principle investigators Rebecca Moore Howard and Sandra Jamieson shared about "how students find, evaluate, and use the sources they cite."[11] Howard and Jamieson presented initial findings at the 2011 Conference on College Composition and Communication, reporting that "students rarely look past the first three pages of the sources they cite and often stitch together a patchwork of text, with little evidence that they absorb their sources' content along the way."[12] The following year, after further work with data, Howard and Jamieson were able to share the "good news" that "70 percent of the students in the study chose government documents, journals, books, or news sources to cite, which [Jamieson] said are the kinds of materials that librarians and teachers of composition encourage students to seek out."[13]

Unfortunately, the positive implications were offset by a "closer look at how students are using these sources," which suggests a superficial or otherwise problematic engagement with source content.[14] Berrett does not include such evidence in his summation, however, and instead continues with the following:

> Ms. Jamieson offered an example of a student who wrote a research paper on eating disorders. The student cited ten works, including the *Proceedings of the National Academy of Sciences* and two books. One of those books, however, was *Skinny Bitch*, a best-selling diet book written by a former agent for a modeling agency along with a former model who earned a master's degree in holistic nutrition. "This was a student who was really trying, but just fell flat when dealing with the sources," Ms. Jamieson said.[15]

Though some of the project's findings resonate with our experience, the report draws important attention to the variability of interpretation. Whether the student referenced above "fell flat when dealing with the sources," for example, seems highly arguable. For one, the inclusion of a single weak source among several credible sources does not seem the kind of mistake that would render a paper a total loss in the introductory context; and for another, the inclusion of a source on a list of works cited does not indicate how that source is used in the paper any more than "a paper on eating disorders" indicates the argument's purpose. Presumably, investigators examined the writer's use of the source and found that the writer gave it undue authority; however, the example as presented in Berrett's report implies that the ability to evaluate credible sources and the ability to analyze their content are one and the same. These capacities are related, of course, but they are not the same: A student can meet sufficient number of established criteria to select credible sources but fail to understand them thoroughly, engage them critically, and/or represent them fairly. Moreover, established criteria often exclude sources that are valuable for reasons other than accuracy of information. Unless the sole purpose of a research paper on eating disorders is to collect and report information, *Skinny Bitch* and other popular texts that participate in shaping cultural ideals may prove quite valuable, depending on the student's argument and angle.

At the end of our first semester, the collective of student work presented a disheartening number of problems that reflect a disregard for citation style conventions and/or academic-authorial integrity. One student followed her list of works cited with "I have 8 sources," an accurate statement with regard to the list but not to the argument. The argument includes a total of four citations—one for each of her firsthand sources—and a few decontextualized and unattributed quotes scattered throughout. Another student appears to have grown tired of providing full bibliographic information, listing the final four entries as follows:

>Mellissa Stormont—Beyond Behavior
>John R. Wooden—They Call Me Coach
>The Lombard Rules
>Tony Dungy—Quiet Strength

Neither Stormont nor "The Lombard Rules" are referenced in the student's argument, and Wooden and Dungy are poorly contextualized. The reference to Dungy is particularly problematic as the discussion suggests a biography rather than a memoir:

>Tony Dungy was a coach for the Indianapolis Colts and one of the most historical coaches in the National Football League. He is a perfect example of my thesis statement. There is a book called Quiet Strength written about Tony Dungy. In the book it shows the way he had gotten his players to win the Super Bowl. The book states that Tony was a quiet man that established his authority by respecting his players.

More carefully contextualized in the argument are the writer's two firsthand interviews; however, neither appears in the list of works cited.

We understand how Moore and Jamieson would conclude that the standard assignment—the search for appropriate sources toward a heavily weighted research paper—ought to be eliminated and replaced with smaller assignments that accommodate slower, guided analysis of fewer sources that are provided by the instructor. However, we have real reservations about how the Citation Project's findings might be interpreted in ways that further reduce FYC research writing to the sum (or the worst) of a product's sources. Rather than accepting our first batch of products as indicative of student ability, we believe it was more productive to consider their problems a reflection of a dysfunctional activity system, open to change.

As originally conceived, our assignment required a level of abstract thinking and synthesis beyond what FYC students have typically experienced, and it did so deliberately. Students were to select a professional or public context and to develop through primary and secondary research an understanding of how reputation functions in that context as a complex system of players and practices. The hypothesis was that, insofar as the prerequisite to synthesis is analysis, a more advanced synthesis requirement might compel students to focus more carefully on the content of their sources, which would likely require they more eagerly pursue help from resources—the writing center, a dictionary, us, etc.—as they located, interpreted, and analyzed unfamiliar kinds of texts. Across two instructional sessions, Amy introduced students to the course LibGuide, accessed Academic Search Complete, and modeled searches, proving that a rich and relevant body of knowledge is, in fact, out there—beyond Google, beyond Bing. Yet many students could find "nothing." They resisted the idea that sources need not bring the context and reputation together explicitly—that they could consider them respectively in research and connect them in synthesis—and they limited their searches accordingly. Rather than increasing students' willingness to consult and evaluate new sources in new ways, the assignment discouraged research altogether.

In the end, many abandoned the mission in order to fulfill seemingly more concrete obligations, such as the required primary research, and ultimately, the required number of words on a page and number of sources in a list. These obligations became the new mission, which became manageable as a checklist of discrete elements. The argument, the in-text citations, and the list of works cited were thus accounted for as discrete practices, only abstractly related. Moreover, the majority of arguments relied on personal interviews with individuals who were chosen for their familiarity and/or accessibility—instructors, family members, neighbors, for example—who could finally provide a direct answer to the research question.

That the assignment felt an impossible challenge did not mean that we would dismiss it altogether, but we would make a number of revisions based on our discussions regarding interactions with students and project outcomes. The following semester, Nicole introduced Google Scholar and modeled a "quick and dirty" method for conducting preliminary research, running searches that brought concepts associated with reputation together with contexts—searches with phrases like "innovation in the field of biology" and questions like "How does gossip affect athletes?" Students were then instructed to conduct preliminary searches in order to determine the context through which they would explore reputation—before their first class in the library with Amy. Also, we divided secondhand and firsthand research so that they did not overlap, provided new guidance and guidelines for each, and aligned our vocabulary with the textbook, distinguishing between "firsthand" research and evidence from "secondhand" and using these terms rather than "primary" and "secondary." Not only had our moving back and forth between the two sets of terms meant inconsistencies across the text, assignments, lectures, and discussion, but considering students' conspicuous overreliance on personal interviews, we suspected the term "primary" had taken on unintended meanings.

Collectively, second-semester practices and projects reflected students' willingness to pursue a new range of sources and to see assignment elements as parts of a whole. Most students struggled with scholarly materials throughout the search and as they wrote, but they did so in ways that indicated they were actively grappling the relative values of personal experience, opinion, testimonial, academic credentials, qualitative and quantitative data, methodological disclosure, etc. Ultimately, final products integrated a balanced enough variety of sources and enough attention to attribution and citation that we could analyze projects for more subtle tendencies.

Scholarly vs. public (or popular) will always guide research writing instruction for students new to scholarly materials; however, we saw a person vs. text variable that amounted to students' putting more trust into sources with visible bodies and/or audible voices. These sources were given names and space in projects, while text sources—scholarly or otherwise—were introduced by title and had little to say. A student, whose research focused on the reputation of rock musicians, for example, integrates information from academic journals, including *Regional Studies* and *Journal of Law and Economics*; public sources, such as the *Wall Street Journal* and salary.com; and three personal interviews. She is careful to credit information to her sources, which she introduces primarily in signal phrases and secondarily in parenthetical citations that include more information than required. Still, her representation of interviewees is distinctive in how she introduces them by role and refers to them by first name. Also, she concludes her contribution with a statement from an interviewee, who has explained to her that "his favorite part of being a musician isn't the money" but rather the experiences from close collaboration among band members to inspiring responses from audiences. She uses her source's final words as her own not because they relate in some summative way to reputation, but because they resonate with her as a person, and as a person, she can assume they will resonate with her audience as well.

A student, whose paper considers the nature and value of reputation in professional athletics, refers to interviewees by first name and engages their ideas with distinctive care. This student, like the student who discussed rock musicians, introduces secondhand sources with concise signal phrases, if at all—some are referenced only in parenthetical citations, while firsthand sources are introduced by their full name and their relation to the topic as in "Jim Jones, a Junior Varsity Soccer coach at Panhandle High School says, 'I want....'" Following such quotes, the student interprets the statement and connects it to the larger argument: "You can see that Jim, as a coach puts a very high standard on how he expects his athletes to have positive publicity, a good reputation." At one point, the student evaluates a statement as "very true." However, she does not expect this truth to be self-evident but rather supports the claim of its truth with further interpretation that once again connects the idea to her own.

Also across the papers are places where information is attributed to a text: The title of an article, rather than the author(s), "writes," "reports," or "states." Of course, personal interviews do not afford the option to signal information by title, but personal introductions and use of first names contrasts significantly with the use of titles to signal secondhand, namely scholarly, information. Perhaps the contrast reflects parallel rhetorical moves to establish credibility: The use of titles highlights the scholarliness of the source and the intrinsic credibility of the information, while the personal introductions establish interviewees as credible for their relationship to the issue. Ultimately, these various distinctions draw attention to how direct lessons on source evaluation account only partially for our students' interactions with sources; our instructional discourse is always shaping how students will understand and value others' ideas and information.

Wendy Holliday and Jim Rogers argue, for example, that if we talk about "finding sources," we emphasize containers; if we talk about "learning about" an issue, it puts the focus on the ideas that spill out of containers for students to consider.[16] Expanding on this insight, we propose that the term "idea" signifies thought, drawing attention to the human mind(s) that developed and shared that idea. The term "source," by contrast, refers interchangeably, if not ambiguously, to a text and its producer(s), whose interests and labor are more easily obscured so that a text becomes more an object to be handled than a communication to be understood, evaluated, and dialogically engaged.

Conclusion: Student Participation and Collaborative Authority

To what extent do students see their future products as objects, thereby obscuring their own interests and the real requirements of labor? If students have a difficult time seeing the person behind any given source text, how can they see their own text as a meaningful reflection of their person? Some do as evidenced by their efforts and growing investment over the course of the project; however, the identity these efforts and investments reflect is that of a student who wants to perform well, not a person who wants to contribute, who wants to be heard. Joyce Walker and James Purdy believe that "the construction of a powerful, directed research identity is necessary for students to engage in learning about and making knowledge in both academic and nonacademic environments." They see students as researchers before they enter the university and worry that "our instructions, methods, and tools ignore, disregard, or even suppress the knowledge on which their existing identities are based."[17] Instructors, librarians included, reinforce the student identity by way of instructing. With each directive, correction, restriction, and evaluation, the instructor reaffirms the distinction between teacher and student, and as the librarian navigates databases, determine key words, and runs successful searches, students are reminded that they are not researchers.

These practices are among our instructional obligations, communicating the directives and expectations that engage students in activities that are integral to academic research writing. These activities are not comprehensive, however, until students engage with regard for the principles that substantiate and motivate them. Considering our shared investment in students' accessing new library materials in new ways, the use of Google Scholar may appear a desperate move that responds to previous outcomes, rather than larger, ideological objectives. Similarly, the decision to divide secondhand research, firsthand research, and writing may imply a reductively contrived approach that ignores "how academic research actually happens."[18] More accurately, however, these decisions are the products of two forces: (1) the fact that a real challenge common to the FYC context is getting students to start working with their sources in writing, and sometimes this challenge requires focusing less on how a practice happens elsewhere and more on making certain a practice happens at all; and (2) the fact that cross-disciplinary collaboration broadened the range of possible decisions that we could make and that we could make for viable pedagogical reasons.

Jennifer E. Nutefall Ryder and Phyllis Mentzell report that librarians and FYC faculty differ in how we conceptualize research for students and how our approaches to research pedagogy differ as a result:

> From the librarians' perspective, starting narrowly prepares students for the research process because it provides direction and rhetorical purpose…. In contrast, faculty describe the initial stages of research in more fluid terms and seem comfortable when students invest an extended period of time and effort arriving at a workable research focus. For them, the starting point is not a narrow question but rather a large and admittedly unwieldy one that must be honed down through research as the student becomes familiar with the materials and the discourse of the issue.[19]

These divergent perspectives map well enough onto our early approaches that the dynamic between class instruction and library instruction was less complementary than contradictory, primarily because librarian instruction is designed to assist students in narrowing their focus and in generating search terms that are operable in the database searches.[20] Meanwhile, compositionists Walker and Purdy, concerned about the potential stifling of students' existing research identities (as discussed above), argue that "positioning the library as the required starting place for academic work is both impractical and inaccurate: Students are already looking to more easily accessible online resources first," as confirmed by a study they conducted in 2007.[21] The use of Google Scholar, then, accommodates a synthesis of criteria: Students rely on an accessible variation of a familiar tool to conduct preliminary research that allows them to decide on a topic and research question. Their decision is based not only on personal interest or curiosity but also on the encouraging certainty that relevant and useable information on the topic does exist, in at least one place. The introductory library session extends their work into new and better places and provides advice on search terms that takes on real meaning as they learn through immediate application. This represents the ideal relationship between instruction and outcomes, of course, and it accounts only for the first week of at least a month-long endeavor that is inevitably, deliberately challenging.

When it comes to research instruction, the disciplinary histories of library science and composition studies reveal parallel efforts to understand and work from what is familiar to students. Sometimes, these efforts direct our focus toward objectives and outcomes with such (well-intentioned) resolve that they obscure the complexities of difference and our own limitations. If we acknowledge social networking as an activity system, or range of systems, for example, we cannot expect that appropriating some of its tools within a different community for different objectives will make the work of academic research feel like Facebooking. Similarly, using students' nonacademic Googling practices as evidence that they are already researchers will not make shopping for shoes feel like searching for sources or vice versa. The motives and objectives for these activities are not part of the same system—at least for our students, not yet. For Nicole, Google and Google Scholar are integral to academic research and instruction. For Amy, Facebook is integral to many activities of academic life— professional networking, idea and resource sharing, etc. Disciplinary experience ensures that we both know better than to expect our students to perceive, value, and experience academic activities as we do; however, Ryder and Mentzell's study reminds us that our "own research projects and processes [may] provide a backdrop against which [we] unconsciously construct [our] ideal of a 'good' research process."[22] Fortunately, disciplinary experience also obliges us to confront such possibilities.

Working within our respective fields, we are more likely to inflate the significance of the decisions we make on behalf of our FYC students, to evaluate students according to our discipline-shaped intentions, and to use these evaluations as bases for more decisions. Working together in the FYC context, compositionists and librarians can check one another's assumptions about what exists and what is ideal and can allow one another to see variables in instruction that might otherwise go unconsidered in pedagogical revision. Our intentions for further collaboration include increased interactions between students and librarian, with the librarian as instructor of regularly scheduled classes, which students see as both obligation and opportunity. Once we realized that students genuinely valued their time with Amy in the classroom, we realized that this approach more successfully displaced the default authority of the instructor than invitations to visit the library outside of class. Moreover, what we present as extra opportunities, students may see as extra obligations—perhaps not unlike the opportunities we are given to serve on new committees, all of which will "make an important difference." We will also continue and increase the librarian's role in the classroom to extend beyond the search and into the writing, which does not signify the end of critical engagement with information but rather the evaluation and interpretation of information as new activities, with new purposes and new conventions.

We will be more attentive and responsive to disciplinary differences that can go overlooked in light of complementary knowledge and shared pedagogical goals. We will continue, for example, to examine the terms we use—how they function within and across our fields, and how their instructional use may invite interpretations that neither field intends. This kind of analysis allows us not only to better serve our students in any given moment, but to negotiate pedagogies that better address our institutional and larger academic responsibilities. In this pedagogical context, we are not teaching students how to research and write from discipline-specific perspectives; rather, we are introducing students to ways of thinking and practicing that embody the value of academic work, and that contribute to students' lives outside of the university as they make "nonacademic" decisions as educated people.

Notes

1.   Association of College and Research Libraries, *Information Literacy Competency Standards for Higher Education*, accessed August 18, 2014, http://www.ala.org/acrl/sites/ala.org.acrl/files/content/standards/standards.pdf.

2.   Grace Veach, "At the Intersection: Librarianship, Writing Studies, and Sources as Topoi," *Journal of Literacy and Technology 13, no. 1 (2012): 106.*

3.   A. Abby Knoblauch, "First-Year Composition in US Higher Education," in *Teaching Academic Writing*, ed. Patricia Friedrich and Paul Kei Matsuda (New York: Continuum, 2008), 15–16.

4.   John R. Hayes, "New Directions in Writing Theory" in *Handbook of Writing Research,* ed. Steve Graham and Charles A. MacArthur (New York: The Guilford Press, 2006), 28, 37.

5.   Ibid.

6.   Joyce R. Walker and James P. Purdy, "Liminal Spaces and Research Identity: The Construction of Introductory Composition Students as Researchers," *Pedagogy* 13, no. 1 (2013): 10–11.

7.   Barbara Fister, "Practicing Freedom in the Digital Library: Reinventing Libraries," *Library Journal*, August 26, 2013, http://lj.libraryjournal.com/2013/08/future-of-libraries/practicing-freedom-in-the-digital-library-reinventing-libraries/.

8.   Barbara Valentine, "Undergraduate Research Behaviour: Using Focus Groups to Generate Theory," *Journal of Academic Librarianship* 19, no. 5 (1993): 304.

9.   Vanessa J. Earp, "Information Source Preferences of Education Graduate Students," *Behavioral and Social Sciences Librarian* 27 (2008): 73–91.

10.   "What is the Citation Project?" *The Citation Project: Preventing Plagiarism, Teaching Writing*, http://site.citationproject.net/.

11.   Dan Berrett, "Freshman Composition Is Not Teaching Key Skills in Analysis, Researchers Argue," *Chronicle of Higher Education* 58, no. 30 (2012): A29, http://chronicle.com/article/Freshman-Composition-Is-Not/131278/ (accessed September 29, 2013)

12.   Ibid.

13.   Ibid.

14.   Ibid.

15.   Ibid.

16.   Wendy Holliday and Jim Rogers, "Talking about Information Literacy: The Mediating Role of Discourse in a College Writing Classroom," *Portal: Libraries and the Academy 13, no. 3 (2013): 260–61.*

17.   Purdy and Walker, "Liminal Spaces and Research Identity," 10.

18.   Ibid., 23.

19.   Jennifer E. Nutefall Ryder and Phyllis Mentzell, "The Timing of the Research Question: First-Year Writing Faculty and Instruction Librarians' Differing Perspectives," *Portal: Libraries and the Academy* 10, no. 4 (2010): 444.

20.   Ryder and Mentzell, "The Timing of the Research Question," 444.

21.   Purdy and Walker, "Liminal Spaces and Research Identity," 18.

22.   Ryder and Mentzell, "The Timing of the Research Question," 446.

Making It Work: Teaching Students about Information

2.2 Point of View, Belief, and Source Bias

CHAPTER 13

Through a Mirror Darkly:

A Postmodern Approach to Teaching Expertise, Authority, and Bias

Stephen A. Sanders

Why, in a book of this nature, include a chapter on postmodern philosophy? Why grapple with a school of philosophy that is (in)famously obscure and demanding? I believe practitioners in our field can gain a great deal from these philosophical "gadflies." As noted by Gilles Deleuze, philosophy is best viewed as "an elaborately developed question, and nothing else; by itself and in itself, it is not the resolution to a problem, but the elaboration, *to the very end*, of the necessary implications of a formulated question."[1] In our case, I would pose the following question: "As we think about our present pedagogy, what are the typically unquestioned assumptions informing what we do?" And, as a corollary to that: "How might our approach be different if we looked at these assumptions through postmodern eyes?"

In this chapter, I want to compare postmodern philosophy to a long room with a series of windows that look out on a scenic vista. While every window "frames" the same landscape, we quickly notice that the glass's shape, quality, and coloration causes a variation in the way the background appears. This fact reminds us that a window not only conducts light but also (sometimes obviously and sometimes subtly) changes it. We find our eyes shifting focus back and forth between the view and the glass through which we are observing. Finally we come to one window that "feels" right because of its familiarity. The way the window encloses the scene is what we are "used" to. Then a question comes to mind: Could our long acquaintance with this particular window "blind" us to the fact that it too not only transmits but also distorts the view beyond? At the moment we take that thought seriously, we've become postmodernists.

The window that seems so familiar, with such a comfortable outlook, could be called "modernism." In the first section of this chapter, I'll trace how this view became the *de facto* standard. In subsequent sections, I'll show how postmodernists put some "cracks" in the glass of modernism and thereby called into question some of our most deeply held library and information science (LIS) assumptions. In the conclusion, I'll look at how the questions raised by postmodern philosophers might influence our approach as we move "beyond what button to press."

The Modern "Outlook"

Where have we gotten our collective sense that the "modern" window is right?

The modern era is usually dated to the time of Francis Bacon (1571–1626). He inherited an intellectual world in which people looked "up" toward the authority of God or "back" to the ancients for the most reliable information. In contrast, emerging modern thinkers viewed the past as a "dark" age and hierarchical authority as a barrier to perception. They assumed that progress would now inevitably occur as the imprisoning ideas of ancient times were jettisoned and replaced with verifiable truth.[2] For this new breed of thinker, factual knowledge could be found by looking out at the world for data (a view that would come to be known as empiricism), and/or within for clear and certain ideas (a view that would come to be known as rationalism). Thus knowledge ran along a horizontal line that formed a continuum from the mind to the world.

The excitement generated by this new approach was palpable and giddy. The concept of time—which had been circular to the ancients and providentially destined for eschatological blessings according to the church—was now viewed as progressive, not due to divine imposition, but rather human progress. The ability to "make all things new," previously reserved for God, was now within the reach of humanity.[3] The religious rejection of the body as the seat of sinful desire was now replaced by respect for mental processes as the place of salvational human creativity.[4]

Perhaps no figure better illustrates modernism's adherence to empiricism than Bacon. He turned "natural philosophy" (what we now call "science") away from the theoretical, which was syllogistically determined, and toward the practical, which was inductively determined.[5] A syllogism is a statement that reasons from a broad concept to a narrower application. (Example: Plato is a person. All persons are mortal; therefore Plato is mortal.) Inductive reasoning, which Bacon championed, is moving from a series of observations to a generalization. (Example: Every insect observed in an extensive study has six legs; therefore insects have six legs.)

This empiricism continues to be a defining characteristic of modernism. For example logical positivism, developed by a group of philosophers called the "Vienna Circle" and published as a manifesto in 1929, taught that sensory perceptions lead to the *only* certain form of knowledge.[6] Any language we use that cannot be verified through observation is at best an opinion and at worst nonsense.

If the empirical (externally based) side of modernism is illustrated in the works of Bacon, then the rationalist (inward) perspective is demonstrated by the French philosopher René Descartes. Perhaps it was his experience as a "gentleman" soldier in the Thirty Years War between Catholics and Protestants that convinced him that there must be a better basis for establishing certainty than religious fervor. While he was "wintering" in Neuberg, Germany, he had a series of dreams that led to a new method of determining truth.[7]

Descartes's earliest works were in mathematics, a field that seemed to reveal certainty. Could he find a way to establish this same certainty for our beliefs about ourselves, the material world, and God? Since according to rationalism the mind not only interacts with the world but can also be a source of knowledge, Descartes made a journey within to look for truth. And just as mathematics breaks down the complex into its simplest parts, he utilized "radical doubt" to tear every belief to its foundation. In doing so, he was looking for *a priori* knowledge, that which we know *prior to* experience.

What is the result? C.G. Prado summarizes it thusly:

> Descartes sets out to ground human knowledge on ab-
> solute certainty. He does so for its own sake, but also

to insure that there never again would be occasion for errors to prompt challenges to and revisions of established knowledge. To ground knowledge on certainty, he begins by doubting everything he can doubt, seeking even a single truth that he cannot doubt because of its evidency: its clarity and distinctness. Once he has one indubitable truth, he can rebuild his beliefs by comparing their constituents to that one truth. In his view, the same procedure will allow us to develop human knowledge to its fullest extent.[8]

That "single truth" is found in the fact that he, as a doubting person, cannot question his own existence. ("I think, therefore I am.") From this base Descartes rebuilds his belief in the mind, the body, the external world, and even God.

Rationalism continues to be a defining characteristic throughout the modern period. The German philosopher Immanuel Kant (1724–1804) also believed that the mind is an active creator of what it knows. His method, called transcendental idealism, expounds the idea that *both* the external world *and* our minds *combine* to produce what we call "reality."[9] To illustrate, think about the activity we call "seeing." Upon reflection, we realize it is a combination of light, which originates in the *external* world, and the eye, which is *internal* to us. For "seeing" to occur, each must be present in a synthesizing unity. Analogously, for the mind to function it requires empirical content, but that content is structured, processed, and packaged by our mental (rational) capacities.

The ramifications of modernism are far-reaching, and only a few of them can be mentioned here. A belief in the innate capacities of humanity contributed to the rise of the institutions of democracy, the nation-state, and the free market. Religion was now relegated to the private sphere, where it could help reform private morals or contribute to therapeutic health. One modernist redefined religion as that which an individual does with his or her own solitariness.[10] The "God hypothesis" was unnecessary given science's (seeming) ability to eradicate famine, exposure, ignorance, and disease.[11]

So what is the problem with all this? The modernism window seems clear, comfortable, and familiar. What happened to cause the glass to seemingly warp and crack?

LIS as Ideology

According to Gary P. Radford, LIS is committed to our own form of positivist thought. We've developed libraries around the idea that we can, in a rationalist manner, give order to chaos by means of a "place where each item within it has a fixed place and stands in an a priori relationship with every other item." Our classification system "imposes a rigid structure of expectations that come to define the library experience for both librarian and library user."[12] John Budd calls our unquestioning loyalty to modernism a form of scientism, which is "the belief that knowledge growth in all disciplines depends on the application of the methods of natural science." In absolutist fashion, "scientism purports to provide, not only *a* means of conduct, but *the* means of conduct."[13] There's a word for the kind of thinking they're describing—ideology.

Ideology can be defined as a connected group of ideas that leads to an outlook or worldview on life. In any given culture, contradictory ideologies can be held by diverse groups, differing according to social class and relative power. To adherents, a particular ideology appears obvious and commonsensical and is usually unexpressed and assumed as "natural" or "right."[14] I would compare ideology to the atmosphere that we breathe. We really don't notice it unless it changes by becoming, for example, acrid or thinner. Then and only then does the air we breathe rise into consciousness.

For the purposes of this essay, the most important aspect of an ideology is the function of legitimating the power of a dominant social group. According to Terry Eagleton, a domineering class will use ideology to promote itself by using at least six strategies:

> A dominant power may legitimate itself by *promoting* beliefs and values congenial to it; *naturalizing* and *universalizing* such beliefs so as to render them self-evident and apparently inevitable; *denigrating* ideas which might challenge it; *excluding* rival forms of thought, perhaps by some unspoken but systematic logic; and *obscuring* social reality in ways convenient to itself… In any actual ideological formation, all six of these strategies are likely to interact in complex ways.[15]

Ideology not only blinds the ascendant class, but it also causes them to see a higher power at work in that which is historically contingent. For example, male domination has been attributed to the "nature of things," and various diseases such as AIDS have been interpreted as punishment for sin.[16]

Going back to the long room with various windows, as we walk along contemplating the various views, we are suddenly accosted by an ideologue, who quickly escorts us to one particular window. "*Only* this one is correct," he assures us. "All the others are designed to mislead you, so stick with this window."

How should this affect LIS, and bibliographic instruction in particular? I think it is more a matter of attitude than anything else. Postmodern thinkers remind us that we need to be more circumspect and judicious in our pronouncements. In other words, we need to admit that everyone is looking through ideologically tainted windows. There is no such thing as pure objectivity, an Archimedean point that is above and beyond perspective. The interests of class, societal position, and institutional power inevitably "color" our "outlook."

I teach a one-hour for-credit information literacy course that is required in about half the majors at my university. It contains all the usual "suspects" such as a section on critical thinking and bias. I now teach both concepts as a continuum rather than a dichotomy. I tell my students, "Of course, there's no such thing as a purely unbiased source. As researchers, the most we can do is 'move the needle' toward the goal of objectivity."

One effective illustration I've used is Alfred Hitchcock's movie *The Birds*. In one harrowing scene the town is under avian attack with several dire events happening all at once—a gas fire, an attack on a phone booth, and darting victims, just to mention a few. At this precise moment, Hitchcock pulls above the action and, quite literally, shows a bird's eye view of the bedlam below. I tell my students that we, all of us, are *in* the action, not *above* it.

LIS and Metanarratives

The most famous definition of postmodernism is offered by is Jean-François Lyotard (1924–1998). This French philosopher was both deeply influenced and then profoundly disillusioned by ideological Marxism, which in his interpretation turned out to be just another form of cultural imperialism. In *The Postmodern Condition*, he defines postmodernism as "incredulity toward metanarratives."[17] This means that all totalizing theories that are used to legitimate the interests of any group are met with deep skepticism. Instead, Lyotard want to make room for "little narratives" (*petit récit*) that are locally determined. He advocates simply allowing these various explanations to messily bump into each other, resisting the temptation to homogenize them by establishing a new norm of understanding.[18]

To discern "little narratives" while operating under the aegis of a controlling narrative, we must learn to look obliquely. A nonnormative truth, in the words of Lyotard, "never appears where it is expected." It is an "aberration" when compared to accepted knowledge. Little narratives can only become visible when we have "renounced the madness of unity, the madness of supplying a first cause in a unitary discourse, the fantasy of the origin."[19]

Members of our profession are becoming more sensitive to the need to "other" truths that go beyond our historic metanarratives. For example, archivist Joseph Deodato notes that from "the postmodernist perspective, every discourse, every text, every document, every artifact, is just one representation of reality; one narrative among many, and inevitably, one constructed by the most powerful elements in society."[20] We thus find ourselves living in the paradoxical tension of needing standards yet simultaneously recognizing the need to open space to "little narratives" by, for example, increasing access points and expanding descriptors.

I am still thinking this one through, but one change I have made in my class and my reference work is to rethink the use of jargon. Specialized language sets up an aura that causes the uninformed student to view the librarian as an autonomous "expert," a decidedly modern concept. This is also a hierarchical "one-up and one-down" relationship that is inconsistent with a postmodernist approach.[21] Thus a classification system is an "address," stacks are "bookshelves," and circulation is "the place you check stuff out." The approach to teaching should be more collaborative, with assignments that have multiple answers and approaches. While it has become a tiresome cliché, the teacher as "guide on the side" rather than "sage on the stage" is a refreshingly postmodern perspective.

Another implication concerns our proprietary databases. Are they patterned on the (modernist) assumption that information can be packaged in a "one-size-fits-all," unifying structure? What then happens to local knowledge? Is it important to know that crawfish in Louisiana are often called "mudbugs"? I think all of us should do our part to preserve and celebrate "truths" that are situated in particular times and places. "Used for" is not a synonym for "inferior."

Returning to our room of windows metaphor, as we look through glass that is sponsored by a powerful and wealthy patron, we notice in the corner of our eye a temporary wall that has been erected. "What's behind that barrier?"

we ask. Our host replies, "Oh, those are the works of some 'others' and are so deeply flawed; we try to keep them out of view. We're even considering having them destroyed, so don't let those windows concern you." I would counter that as librarians, we need to be *very* concerned to protect access to nonmainstream perspectives.

LIS and Genealogy

Among the more trenchant criticism postmodernists direct toward modernism is the challenge to its theory of knowledge, or epistemology. The modernist metanarrative is normative because it is thought to be both objective and value free. As in a geocentric universe, human self-understanding revolves around this central point in a grid of assumptions often called "genealogies." The name most associated with this type of criticism of modernity is the French philosopher Michel Foucault (1926–1984).

How can we learn to see our own genealogical metanarratives? According to Foucault, the best way is to look at history because human self-understandings change over time. This, in turn, allows us to readily see patterns of differences between ourselves and the people of the past. To use an earlier illustration, the "atmospherics" are different, and this fact renders it visible to those with a different "mix" of assumptions and patterns of life. However, this method of investigation will only work if we remember two things. First, we must be careful to not import our understandings into the past— as for example when a contemporary reader of the Bible sees individualistic capitalism or 21st-century American sexual controversies reflected in its pages. To avoid this tendency, Foucault summarizes past genealogies with lots of data and a minimum of interpretation. Second, we must avoid the idea of inevitable progress toward today's superior pinnacle of understanding—after all that is *our* ideology!

The cumulative effect of reading Foucault's genealogies is astounding. It slowly dawns on the reader that the societies under consideration saw self-evident "truth" in understandings that we today would find appalling and shocking. Take for example the subject of insanity, which Foucault extensively researches. In the Middle Ages the "sinful" and "spiritually dangerous" insane were banished from society by such means as a "ship of fools." During the Renaissance, madness was considered a gift rather than a disease. The insane "were considered to be under the influence of 'folly'—a wise or even revelatory, mode of thought."[22] With the coming of the Enlightenment and industrialization, they were detained in prisons and hospitals, where their primary crime was "laziness." This incarceration conveniently became a large pool of cheap labor for business and factory owners. With the ascendency of scientific reason, madness was viewed as a shameful phenomenon in which the insane person must be tamed like an unevolved frenzied animal. In Victorian times, the asylum took a parental approach and sought by means of discipline, rules, and punishments—such as isolation and dipping in cold water—to treat madness. This punishment was meted out by the patriarchic "head" of the family, namely the (male) doctor, who held almost limitless authority over the patients as well as nurses and assistants. It was thought that the insane were responsible for their condition and, like aberrant children, could be treated with negative and positive reinforcement so that they might gain the ability to rule themselves. With the advent of the medicalization of insanity, the exact opposite is assumed, and insanity is treated as an illness for which the individual is not responsible. We currently seek cures by the use of pharmaceuticals and a treatment regimen.[23]

Adherents to all the above genealogies based their ideas on "self-evident" truth. They sought and found multiple justifications for each perspective and tended to view with disdain the "barbarism" of their past. Ostensibly based on detached rationalism or unadorned objectivity, each approach was largely a reflection of the *culture* in which it originated. We can see this because we live in a different milieu with a different set of assumptions. In an insight that goes back to the German philosopher Martin Heidegger (1889–1976), we tend to "prove" our results by presupposing them. This is because our language and form of life are the unavoidable lenses through which we see the data.[24] In sum, our metanarratives make certain "facts" stand out as obvious and render inconvenient counterexamples otiose.

LIS, at least in modern times, has been deeply influenced by the seeming precision and exactness of science. For example, our subject headings imply that most areas of knowledge can fit into a hierarchical (biological) grid with clearly demarcated subjects. I think this blurs the fact that subjects are often context dependent, which implies a more horizontal than vertical relationship. Perhaps medieval alchemists were correct "that the universe is intrinsically and intricately interconnected."[25] If this is so, then the goal of distinct subject headings becomes problematic.

How can we awaken students to the role of society in learning? In my classes, I seek to find shocking or counterintuitive ways to challenge the cultural assumptions of the day. Here are just a few examples:

- Has the ability to multitask made us more efficient, or does it merely give us the ability to do more things badly?
- Does the capacity to do well on a standardized test indicate that a person is more knowledgeable, or is simply good at taking standardized tests?
- Are you more or less safe having a gun in the house?
- Are we truly "rugged individuals," or do we depend on each other far more than is realized?

In every instance above, studies can be found that challenge conventional wisdom. Again the idea is to shock students out of the assumption that if our culture widely believes something, it *must* be true.

As we walk along the room full of windows, we gaze out and notice that some prominent features from the landscape are completely missing, while other elements are highlighted. We shake our heads at the realization that glass can act as a powerful filter.

LIS and Collective Thinking

As already noted above, postmodernists enable us to appreciate the group's considerable role in learning. This means that knowledge is more intersubjective and less individualistic and autonomous than we assume. For example, Descartes was convinced that he arrived at his rationalistic understandings in splendid solipsistic isolation, but it is remarkable how culturally bound many of his conclusions were. According to one educator deeply influenced by postmodernism, the world "we see is not the world as it is, but the world as we have learned to see it, oriented in large part by an inherited language with its already established obsessions and webs of associations."[26] Put succinctly, reality is a social construction.

This insight is important for how we approach the teaching of bias. We tend to teach this subject in an individualistic way that assumes that the solitary individual can and should change his or her privately held thinking patterns. I now see that approach itself as a form of cultural bias.

Heidegger, who has deeply influenced postmodern thinking, saw this as early as 1927 when he wrote his most famous work, *Being and Time* (*Zein und*

Seit). The human person, whom he calls (usually untranslated) *Dasein*, can be authentic or inauthentic, depending on his or her relationship to others, here called the "they-self."

> The self of everyday Dasein is the *they-self*, which we distinguish from the *authentic self*, that is, the self which has explicitly grasped itself. As the they-self, Dasein is *dispersed* in the they and must first find itself… "I" "am" not in the sense of my own self, but I am the others in the mode of the they.[27]

In this powerful and original insight, Heidegger is saying that the dominance of norms dictates that humans automatically tend to conform. We thus "level" down and adapt the customs, manners, and viewpoints of those who matter to and/or surround us.[28]

The difference between authenticity and inauthenticity is a matter of awareness. We either realize that class, education, geography, and social networks shape us, or we do not. Bias isn't in *my* head; it's in *our* heads. Heidegger writes:

> We enjoy ourselves and have fun the way *they* enjoy themselves. We read, see, and judge literature and art the way *they* see and judge. But we also withdraw from the "great mass" the way *they* withdraw, we find "shocking" what *they* find shocking. The they, which is nothing definite and which all are, though not as a sum, prescribes the kind of being of everydayness.[29]

As a result of this profound insight, I now teach bias with "the they" in mind. In a lighthearted way, I'll show an "outrageous" fashion trend from the past and ask, "How did this come to be thought of as normal, as acceptable, as stylish?" Then I'll look at my students, who dress remarkably alike, and ask, "How did 'gym clothes' get out of the gym and into the classroom?" (The nice thing about this illustration is that it can be updated and reapplied as fashions change!) On a much more serious note, I've shown propaganda clips directed toward or against particular groups and asked students to reflect on the subtle and not so subtle "we versus them" messages contained therein. Somewhere in-between the silly and serious, I'll use language to illustrate this principle. For example, why might one group call a particular levy an "estate tax," while another group might refer to that same practice as a "death tax"? (Because I'm a bit of a ham, I intone the former with a British-accent affectation and the latter with a sinister cackle.)

In our windows gallery, for perhaps the first time, we notice that people always gravitate as groups toward particular windows. A glimpse around the room reveals that window makers from different cultures and geographic locations use different geometric patterns for their windows. While we definitely prefer the familiar rectangular model, we notice that the shapes of some of the other ones allow quite different views. For example, the long and tall skinny one opens our vision to a mountain that was "outside the frame" of our preferred window. Could we learn to value the opportunity to view vistas outside our group's normal "frame" of reference? (Of course, to do so is quite a "stretch"!)

LIS and Power

As librarians, we like to say, "Knowledge is power." Postmodernists, however, would challenge us by noting it's more reflective of reality to say, "Power is knowledge." Consider the fact that the parameters of knowledge are by and large defined and set by the controlling metanarratives of the powerful of any particular culture. By way of illustration, think about the history of warfare, which is usually written by the victors. For example, most of our accounts of the Punic Wars (264–146 BCE) between ancient Rome and Carthage are written by the Romans. What would we see differently if Hannibal had won rather than Scipio Africanus? Hannibal's city was eventually razed to the ground, while Rome went on to establish an ever-expanding empire. The records of Rome were largely preserved, while most of those of Carthage quite literally went up in smoke.

Power is a process that becomes visible in several different ways. Some are quite physical, as in the power of the gaze, which Foucault calls "panoptic modality of power."[30] Other means are more covert as when patterns of discourse put us in our "place." Examples include devaluing terms such as criminal, deviant, sinner, "the little woman," the uneducated.[31] All these means of expression and many more limit both who we are and what we can become. In this and many other ways, power takes human malleability and "shapes" us in accordance with the mores of dominant groups.

Those of us in LIS need to see that we too are part of a "power grid" that refracts everything we do and say. Only partially tongue in cheek, we as librarians are part of the Higher Education Industrial Complex. More specifically, we are also a part of what I would term the Proprietary Database Industrial Complex. Do we really think that this fact does *not* influence our attitudes toward such entities as (free) search engines?

Our power is reflected in the way we use language because, as the postmodernists never tire or reminding us, discourse is always enmeshed with systems of power. Potent words such as "authoritative," "scholarly," and "peer-reviewed" are designed to put other sources of knowledge "in their place." Step back and think, for a moment, what it must sound like to speak of "controlled vocabulary." Does this imply that our patrons were "out of control" before?[32]

Returning to our hall of windows, we now notice who has the power to get "center stage." Has someone blocked off a particular "outlook" so as to render it "invisible"? Did someone use his or her access to deface or spray paint a particular window (perspective)?

LIS and Deconstrution

By now our hall of windows' visitors are confused and dazed. "Is there any way we can recover those aspects of the landscape that *all* these windows filter or distort?" While postmodernists would bristle at the term "technique," there is a way to recover some of what has been lost—specifically "deconstruction." This is a term that is associated with the French philosopher Jacques Derrida (1930–2004).

Deconstruction can be thought of as a means of resisting all universalistic metanarratives.[33] In an interview Derrida states that deconstruction is

> what disrupts the totality… The privilege granted to uni-
> ty, to totality, to organic ensembles, to community as a
> homogenized whole—this is a danger for responsibility,
> for decisions, for ethics, for politics. That is why I insist-
> ed on what prevents unity from closing upon itself, from
> being closed up… And this prevents totalitarianism, na-
> tionalism, egocentrism, and so on.[34]

Thus, for example, if a totalitarian regime wrote a political treatise, we would want to pay special attention to what they *do not* say. The voice of the oppressed is in the margins, the periphery, the blind spots, and the lacunae that the powerful ignore. Deconstruction can break the human tendency wherein unexamined assumptions "prove" preconceived conclusions. It brings to the "foreground" elements that go unnoticed in the "background."

In addition to the concept of deconstruction, Derrida is also (in)famous for saying "There is nothing outside of the text." By this comment he is pointing to the fact that no one, himself included, can step outside human (textual) time and space and assume a God-like perspective.[35] In other words, we are finite, historical, and temporal beings.[36] Honesty demands that we admit that we are stuck looking out of windows.

Deconstruction teaches me to reflect the local discourses that are incommensurate with many of our mainstream (one-size-fits-all) databases. (Remember "mudbugs"?) Noting such interesting variations from the norm helps nourish many of the "little narratives" that sustain us as populations and cultures.[37]

Conclusion

The title of this book implies that our field is coming out of a long period of breathtakingly rapid change. Only now can we step back and rethink the theory that informs our day-to-day pedagogy. I submit that postmodern thought can make a valuable contribution at this precise moment as we develop an educational philosophy that matches the contours of the 21st century.

As we move forward, we need an LIS pedagogy that reflects a wrestling with the challenges of postmodern thinking. In particular, we should remember that

- Our hierarchical and vertical organization of knowledge often obscures the horizontal interconnectedness of information.
- Our rugged individualistic "metanarrative" masks the fact that we are deeply and perhaps decidedly influenced by the groups to which we belong or aspire to belong. This means that teaching bias is less about expounding principles for the individual and more about challenging the power of "the they."
- We ourselves are part of a power system that, along with other power constellations, often utilizes ideology and language to protect our "turf."

- In my opinion the greatest gift postmodernism wishes to bestow upon us is awareness. If we can remember that we all see the same landscape, but view it through a variety of mediating "windows" that—sometimes subtly and sometimes overtly—filter what we see, then these philosophical "gadflies" will have done their job.

Notes

1. Gilles Deleuze, *Empiricism and Subjectivity: An Essay on Hume's Theory of Human Nature*, trans. Constantin V. Boundas (New York: Columbia University Press, 1991), 106 (emphasis in original). I became aware of Deleuze's definition of philosophy in Todd May, *The Philosophy of Foucault* (Montreal, Quebec: McGill-Queen's University Press, 2006), 2.

2. William J. Bouwsma, *The Waning of the Renaissance, 1550–1640.* (New Haven, CT: Yale University Press, 2000), 45.

3. Berman Marshall, "Why Modernism Still Matters," in *Modernity and Identity,* ed. Scott Lash and Jonathan Friedman (Oxford: Blackwell Publisher, 1992), 33.

4. Bouwsma, *The Waning,* 27.

5. Stephen Gaukroger, *Francis Bacon and the Transformation of Early-Modern Philosophy* (Cambridge: Cambridge University Press, 2001), 33.

6. Birger Hførland, "Empiricism, Rationalism and Positivism in Library and Information Science," in *Library and Information Science and the Philosophy of Science, ed. Birger Hførland* (Bradford, UK: Emerald Publishing Group, 2005), 137.

7. Michael Moriarty, introduction to *Meditations on First Philosophy with Selections from the Objections and Replies,* by Rene Descartes, trans. Michael Moriarty (Oxford: Oxford University Press, 2008), x.

8. C.G. Prado, *Starting with Descartes* (London: Continuum International Publishing Group, 2009), 50.

9. Marcus Weigelt, introduction to *Critique of Pure Reason,* by Immanuel Kant, trans. and ed. Marcus Weigelt (London: Penguin Classics, 2007), xxxi.

10. Alfred North Whitehead, *Religion in the Making: Lowell Lectures, 1926* (New York: Fordham University Press, 1996), 16–17.

11. "God hypothesis" is a phrase made famous by Richard Dawkins in *The God Delusion* (Boston: Houghton Mifflin Company, 2006).

12. Gary P. Radford, "Flaubert, Foucault, and the Bibliotheque Fantastique: Toward a Postmodern Epistemology for Library Science," *Library Trends* 46, no. 4 (Spring 1998): 617–18.

13. John Budd, *Knowledge and Knowing in Library and Information Science: A Philosophical Framework* (Lanham, Maryland: The Scarecrow Press, 2001), 15 (emphasis in original).

14. David J. Clines, *Interested Parties: The Ideology of Writers and Readers of the Hebrew Bible* (Sheffield, UK: Sheffield Phoenix Press, 2009), 10–11.

15. Terry Eagleton, *Ideology: An Introduction (London: Verso, 1991),* 5–6 (emphasis in original).

16. Slavoj Zizek, "The Spectre of Ideology" in *Mapping Ideology,* ed. Slavoj Zizek (London: Verso, 1994), 4.

17. Jean-Francois Lyotard, *The Postmodern Condition: A Report on Knowledge, vol. 10, Theory and History of Literature,* trans. Geoff Bennington and Brian Massumi (Minneapolis, MN: Uni-

versity of Minnesota Press, 1984), xxiv.

18. Ibid., 60–61.

19. Jean Francois Lyotard, "Taking the Side of the Figural," in *The Lyotard Reader and Guide,* ed. Keith Crome and James Williams (New York: Columbia University Press, 2006), 41–42.

20. Joseph Deodato, "Becoming Responsible Mediators: The Application of Postmodern Perspectives to Archival Arrangement and Description," *Progressive Librarian* 27 (Summer 2006): 54.

21. Mark Stover, "The Reference Librarian as Non-Expert: A Postmodern Approach to Expertise," *Reference Librarian* 42, no. 87-88 (2004): 276–77.

22. Alec McHoul and Wendy Grace, *Foucault Primer: Discourse, Power, and the Subject* (New York: Routledge Press, 2002), 15.

23. Lois McNay, *Foucault: A Critical Introduction* (New York: Continuum, 1994), 19–24.

24. Herman Philipse, *Heidegger's Philosophy of Being: A Critical Interpretation* (Princeton, NJ: Princeton University Press, 1998), 65.

25. Brent Davis, *Inventions of Teaching: A Genealogy* (Mahwah, NJ: Lawrence Erlbaum Associates, 2004), 44.

26. Ibid.,100.

27. Martin Heidegger, *Being and Time,* trans. Joan Stambaugh, rev. Dennis J. Schmidt (Albany, NY: State University of New York Press, 2010), 125.

28. Hubert L. Dreyfus, *Being-in-the-World: A Commentary on Heidegger's Being and Time, Division 1* (Cambridge, MA: MIT Press, 1991), 158–61.

29. Heidegger, *Being and Time,* 123.

30. Foucault, *The Foucault Reader,* 211.

31. McHoul and Grace, *Foucault Primer,* 23–24.

32. None of this is new, of course. As a baby boomer beginning college in the '70s, I can remember the first time I approached an academic library. The large, open spaces had a numinous quality about them. The librarian (the apotheosis of learning) was approached with a sense of reverence and entreated in hushed, confessional tones. Some libraries contained icons or statues of such figures as John Dewey and other sources of enlightenment (salvation). In short, the architecture was designed to impress on the trembling freshman the fact that he or she had entered a temple of learning.

33. David Couzens Hoy, *Critical Resistance: From Poststructuralism to Post-Critique* (Cambridge, MA: MIT Press, 2004), 175.

34. Jacques Derrida and John D. Caputo, *Deconstruction in a Nutshell: A Conversation with Jacques Derrida* (New York: Fordham University Press, 1997), 13–14.

35. Mark Dooley and Liam Kavanagh, *The Philosophy of Derrida* (Montreal, Quebec: McGill-Queen's University Press, 2007), 55.

36. David Tracy, *The Analogical Imagination: Christian Theology and the Culture of Pluralism* (New York: Crossroad Publishing, 1988), 102.

37. Nicholas Burbules, "Postmodernism and Education," in *The Oxford Handbook of Philosophy of Education,* ed. Harvey Siegel (Oxford: Oxford University Press, 2009), 526.

CHAPTER 14

Librarians and Students:
Making the Connections

Julie Obst and Joe Eshleman

2.2 Point of View, Belief, and Source Bias

"What's my motivation?" asks the method actor before plunging into an emotionally wrought performance. Perhaps the same thing can be said about the mindset of students beginning to wrestle with research papers on subjects that they may not find personally engaging. Students who are required to locate three "good" sources to support their ideas may struggle to be motivated and even question the point of research assignments. Librarians can facilitate this understanding by fostering connections with students and learning more about how they approach the research environment. This can enable librarians to develop instruction sessions and assignments that expand beyond "how to" and focus on this question of "why." In reaching the "why" questions, students can reflect on their own research process and better recognize their own motivation and incentive. Librarians who implement these types of reflective strategies and who connect with students "can also ease one of the most common frustrations of teaching librarians—not being able to interact with learners long enough to form a real connection with them."[1]

This chapter explores ways in which different types of students approach the information landscape and how this can impact the tactics and pedagogy of the instruction librarian. More importantly, assignment strategies are presented that connect students to librarians and also push students to think about how they interact with information. A close connection between librarians and students can provide a foundation that can help both. Librarians can expand their understanding of how individual students approach research; students can benefit by gaining a better grasp of the role of the librarian and how librarians can help them.

Knowledge of the potential chasms in the library instruction environment can promote empathy and build stronger bonds between librarian and student. How does the librarian reach out to the student and build a connection so that moving away from "where to click" advances to "who is clicking" and "why are they clicking"? Also considered in tandem with strengthening librarian and student bonds is how to respond as broader conceptions of information literacy emerge in reaction to an ever-changing information environment. Although proposed changes being made to the *Information Literacy Competency Standards for Higher Education* by the Association of College and Research Libraries (ACRL) are still in process at the time of this writing, in the current phase there is a shift from a set of "how-to standards" to a "why-based framework." It may be easier for the librarian to show "how to," but it may be much more important to answer "why" when it comes to students' motivation and approach to research. Although changing habits and commonly held beliefs require a great deal of effort from the student and the librarian, the potential transformation benefits both. Librarians can accomplish this student conversion by making concerted efforts to meet specific students on their plane of research understanding. Then they can use that knowledge to connect to students in a personal way. Finally, librarians can impress upon students the creative and transformative nature of research. This allows a student to feel a close connection to the work they create. Close connections help alleviate misunderstandings and diminish "why" questions.

Getting to Know Students

When students lament "Why do I need to do research?," what exactly is a student asking? Beyond the initial thought that they are protesting more work, perhaps there are additional concerns for students such as lack of confidence in their research skills or not understanding the need to support their ideas with sound evidence. The value of research can be expounded upon in a library instruction session, but students' self-questioning about their ability to do research still needs to be addressed. It is in the librarian's interest to make attempts to assess the research skills that students have so that there will be a teaching and learning parallel.

Making a rigorous effort to meet students on their plane of research understanding may be a bit easier than it seems. Just as any instructor must understand that different students have different learning styles, the librarian must realize that a full array of research styles will also be met in the library instruction classroom. Shouldn't the instruction librarian focus more time and energy communicating with individual students? Ask them how they feel about doing research? At first glance, getting to know students and working through a short hour-long transitory session appear to be incompatible. Yet what if some time was given towards connecting to the various types of students that are on campus? This effort could help when designing assignments and pedagogy that may be beneficial to those skillsets and needs. What strategies that can be employed by instruction librarians to get a clearer picture of student capabilities and demographics? As an example, as part of a personal librarian initiative on one of our campuses, the instruction librarian reached out through the learning management system (LMS—in this case, Blackboard) two weeks beforehand to students who would be attending a session and asked them to respond to some questions about their previous experiences (or lack of) with library instruction. This short foray into preparing for the differing types of student research experiences can aid with preparation and help to create both empathy and understanding.

There are a number of research skill sets, experiences, and dispositions in play, and library sessions and assignments need to take this into consideration. As in all classifications, it can be difficult to discern how to divide and define a whole group into smaller demarcations. Jessica Lange, Robin Canuel, and Megan Fitzgibbons are speaking directly about adult learners and continuing education students here, yet their assessment seems apt:

> The authors have found that for meaningful learning to take place it is essential to acknowledge this diversity and avoid making assumptions about students' background knowledge and skills. Some students, for example, have never used an open-stacks library and therefore need very explicit instructions on how to physically borrow a book. Others have not used a computer before coming

to the university. Yet others have completed advanced degrees and are quite experienced in research in other languages and settings. If the librarian targets the class at just one point of skill level along this continuum, the majority of students will not have their needs fulfilled.[2]

Further interrogation of the library literature supports the idea that librarians should acknowledge the diversity of their student populations and recognize the need to connect with different students in different ways. In 2000, Trudi E. Jacobson and Helene C. Williams edited *Teaching the New Library to Today's Users: Reaching International, Minority, Senior Citizens, Gay/Lesbian, First-Generation, At-Risk, Graduate and Returning Students, and Distance Learners.* The authors sought input from numerous librarians in order to gain perspective on multicultural and diverse students and then presented assorted approaches and strategies when teaching in the library. In the introduction, the editors point out that the underlying theme of the book (which is composed of individually authored chapters) is to treat students as singular entities, even if they are part of a group, and be aware of their differences.[3] As an excellent introduction into considering the extensive assortment of students that instruction librarians come in contact with, each chapter of *Teaching the Library to Today's Users* takes a look at separate types of viewpoints and gives valuable ways to address them. For example, Kwasi Sarkodie-Mensah offers a table that maps cultural groups to their predominate learning styles; in the international student focused chapter, Sara McDowell gives a self-assessing checklist that leads to insight that can help lesbian, gay, bisexual, and transgendered college students; and David A. Tyckosen suggests six ways to assist the first-generation student: schedule sessions during evening and weekend hours, design library assignments that do not discriminate, provide a family friendly environment, offer personalized service, establish a peer-mentoring program, and make an effort to become part of your campus's first-year experience. Tyckosen's focus on first-year and first-generation students makes for the best example here because it often the case that these primarily undergraduate students would be those most likely to struggle with doing research and have the most questions and frustration.

A more recent perspective can be found in the Ethnographic Research in Illinois Academic Libraries (ERIAL) Project. This project, a 21-month research study conducted from 2008 to 2010, investigated how different students conduct research and use library resources and services at five Illinois universities. A number of student populations were studied in the project, and first-generation students were of particular interest to several of the participating institutions. The book, *College Libraries and Student Culture: What We Now Know,* based on the findings of this study, examined how these students approached research. The ethnographic approach of the study was qualitative, which we appreciate because multiple viewpoints are considered and relationships are a key element. Challenges for the first-generation student included "limited technology and information literacy skills and a lack of familiarity with the research process."[4] Unfortunately, these students are not turning to librarians for assistance. The researchers concluded that the first-generation students at their institution "primarily turned to their instructors and their TA's for all kinds of help, including areas in which librarians could be most helpful."[5]

The growing interest in retention within higher education has led to more work that highlights at-risk students or those who may be candidates for leaving school. Often a formalized first-year experience program, sometimes with a library instruction element, is used as a salve to help with retention efforts. A chief reason for students leaving school is the feeling that they are alone on campus and have difficulty approaching others. Dona McDermott concentrates on library anxiety as a main impediment for students; she traces Long Island University's efforts to identify and work with students who might have difficulty understanding the library's (and the librarian's) role in their academic lives. She concludes that "one of the factors for achieving academic success in college is the recognition of the need to seek help; library instruction can encourage even reluctant students to feel comfortable doing this."[6]

Peter Collier and David Morgan see first-generation students as needing more time allotment and more detailed assignment definition than other students; differences occur between first-generation and traditional college students' understandings of faculty expectations."[7] As instruction librarians who have worked closely with faculty to create assignments, the authors can attest to numerous revisions that work towards highly detailed assignments to improve student understanding. These experiences reinforce the position that certain students find aspects of research difficult and clarification of terms sometimes need to be "spelled out." Oftentimes, library jargon can be a culprit as well as assumptions made about the research skill competences of students. However, adding more detailed explanations to an assignment can make it seem more complicated or difficult, creating a bit of a conundrum. A suggestion here would be to work with students when developing assignments to avoid excessive trial and error.

Stacey Brinkman, Katie Gibson, and Jenny Presnell find that first-generation students may experience more confusion about how services operate on campus and potentially feel as though they are outsiders. They suggest four tactics that directly target these students: be aware of library jargon to minimize anxiety, work towards creating a diverse staff, establish and foster relationships with other campus departments to connect to students' everyday lives, and seek to be mentors and/or become involved in student life and academic affairs programming.[8] Tiffany Wang also suggests the mentorship approach for first-generation students.[9] Gaining a better understanding of what the first-generation or first-year student may be experiencing when approaching research gives the instruction librarian the ability to step back and start from square one and then synchronize their teaching with the student's starting point.

Getting to know students may not always be at the forefront of a librarian's mind, yet the rewards for this type of outreach can benefit both. One consideration for the librarian when reaching out to students is the importance of emotion in both the students' worldview and in their information-seeking process. Studies show that emotional as well as cognitive dynamics affect research strategies. Carol Kuhlthau's landmark demarcation of the student's emotional stages: going from uncertainty, confusion, and frustration to optimism, confidence, and satisfaction form the basis of the information search process as seen through the user's perspective.[10]

Others support the value of the emotional component. Miriam L. Matteson, Omer Farooq, and David B. Mease explore how emotions affect information literacy competency and conclude that "understanding how emotional intelligence aids in prioritizing thinking and enables students to manage emotions in all aspects of their academic information-seeking behavior can help librarians decipher the points at which students might need intervention during information literacy instruction sessions."[11]

The litany of terms such as "not understanding," "misunderstanding," "intervention," and "unfamiliarity" portend that the instruction librarian should take caution to proceed slowly and stay with students. One concurrent theme in this literature is that there are additional challenges simply within the collegiate environment that many students bring with them to the library and these also must be considered. Instruction librarians can teach to diverse groupings of students within a semester, sometimes even within a day. The more that can be done to "line-up" teaching materials, activities, and outcomes with students' capabilities, the more familiar and understandable information literacy concepts will be. A deeper understanding of the variety of students and building connections to them can make for a more level situation.

Meeting the Students

How then does the librarian meet the student at the level that makes for the best progression? One of Susie Andretti's three concluding strategies in *Ways of Experiencing Information Literacy: Making the Case for a Relational Approach* is "start with the learner-information relationship and develop a customized information literacy profile for each learner."[12] Although it may seems as if this would require an inordinate amount of work, Andretti goes on to explain that "in practice, this means profiling the learners to establish from the outset what they 'don't know' in order to stimulate their motivation, and what they 'do know' to foster their confidence."[13] Alison Head recommends that "both professors and librarians may want to expand, if at all feasible, the hands-on services and support that are already provided to students… students valued one-on-one coaching sessions with these research 'experts.'"[14]

Research consultations between librarians and students often go undocumented and can seem to exist between the demarcations of instruction and reference. Yet it is here where a great deal of progress is made because there is an opening for the librarian to gain a better awareness of the research problems students might be experiencing. Additionally, students can take the time to ask questions that they may not in an instruction session. Offering these types of meetings to students should be a goal of the librarian who desires to create connections.

Steven Bell has commented that developing a meaningful library experience requires librarians to expand the role of gate-keepers to one of gate-openers: "Our future may depend on our ability to differentiate what libraries offer and what library workers contribute to communities. The library profession should consider an alternate vision for our future: the library worker as gate-opener. In that role we shift from a focus on creating access to resources to creating meaningful relationships with community members—both those who use and those who don't use our libraries."[15]

In a related vein, the question "Why don't students ask librarians for help?" is often raised and has been addressed by such factors as library anxiety and students not understanding librarian roles.[16] Susan Miller and Nancy Murillo tick off a number of other reasons from the library literature: Students do not want to be bothersome; they believe librarians would not necessarily want to help them; or they may feel foolish for not knowing how to do library research.[17] Miller and Murillo conclude that "students will seek help from those with whom they have established relationships… With institutional support, librarians can foster these kinds of relationships via peer-mentor programs, graded library assignments that emerge from faculty-librarian collaborations, and increased librarian outreach efforts to meet students in-person and online."[18]

In Project Information Literacy's report *Learning the Ropes: How Freshmen Conduct Course Research Once They Enter College*, one large insight and solution became clear: "Many freshmen appeared to be unfamiliar with how academic libraries—and the vast array of digital resources they provide—can best meet their needs. Included are recommendations for how campus-wide stakeholders—librarians, faculty, and administrators—can work together when instructing freshmen to be better researchers."[19] In essence, the report suggests four recommendations for helping incoming students: building bridges between high school and college libraries, creating an integrated approach to teaching information competencies, emphasizing the role of faculty and the value of apprenticing in the research process, and resetting expectations of the Google generation. As a final recommendation, the researchers conclude,

> One starting point could be to initiate a campus dialogue to increase awareness about the information practices of today's freshmen, including both the strengths and weaknesses they bring to the college. What challenges do freshmen themselves mention about completing course work that calls for finding, using, and retaining information? What do freshmen say helps them most when learning how to navigate the complex information landscape of their new campus?[20]

Working towards meeting students and creating relationships that foster an atmosphere in which students and librarians might thrive together is a goal worth pursuing. Imagine addressing students by first names as they enter the library and how that could diminish certain preconceived notions students may have regarding libraries and librarians. Of course, the size of the library and the responsibilities of the librarian are factors that influence this capability.

Despite that, there might be a lessening of mumbled "students these days" if librarians knew more about students. Once students become more three dimensional to librarians (and vice versa), an empathetic understanding and collaborative mindset might take hold. Possibly, the student sees the librarian as a steady and reliable source, an anchor on campus, or just another person to converse with minus any barriers. The librarian sees the student as a distinctive face in the library instruction classroom crowd and a researcher with his or her own set of challenges and achievements. Another benefit to reaching out to students in the library instruction is the building of authenticity that supports a sense of connection. Char Booth feels that to convey a sense of self is a large motivating factor for teaching and "authenticity is the capacity to communicate yourself—your personality and sense of identity—during instruction, an overarching concept that covers many qualities of instructional effectiveness."[21]

With this in mind, an assignment that would push students to think about information use and create an opportunity to form a relationship with a librarian (or at the minimum, get to know a librarian by name) would seem to be of assistance. Appendix 14A shows an example of an assignment created by one of the authors, which was given in a communications class in conjunction with library instruction. Concepts such as evaluation of information and using the information responsibly are presented and discussed in the session before handing out the work. This assignment requests that a student take some time to find a source, give some reasons for why it is reliable, and think about how the information fits properly into their demonstration speech. An additional element here is that the students are required to e-mail this information to the instruction librarian, who provides each student with feedback about the source, the evaluation, the citation structure, and how the information is being used. Also, as a way to show an example, the librarian sends back their response with an additional source that can help the student with the research for their speech. In this particular case, the assignment is not graded.

This exercise goes beyond a student's desire to quickly fulfill a research requirement and creates a communication opportunity for both student and librarian. Although there has not yet been any qualitative assessment of this assignment and concrete evidence does not currently exist for whether a consistent bond is forged, informally there have been conversations with students about how this type of exercise clarifies the importance of the research element of their speech and there is a broader sense of purpose and connection is established between student and librarian. An initial connection is forged, and students have spent some time amplifying their understanding of information use.

Establishing a connection is just the beginning, and more work may be required to keep the relationship moving forward. One way to further develop the relationship is to contact students after an initial meeting. A personal librarian program or an embedded librarian can send e-mails to students throughout a term. Linking to a class through the LMS provides current updates to assignments so that just-in-time correspondence can take place. This type of relationship can also be reinforced by taking a prolonged and discerning look at the diverse types of students librarians encounter every day. Thinking about the different types of students is a start to a deeper connection because understanding someone on a personal level can create stronger bonds. In our case, the realization surfaced that a great deal of students are unfamiliar with many aspects of the library and the role of librarians as well as how to accomplish college-level research. Familiarity with students lessens these issues.

Students Connecting with Research

As mentioned earlier in this chapter, struggling with a research paper can often be associated with the undergraduate student experience. In addition to some of the hurdles already mentioned such as unfamiliarity with research and hesitation to ask for help, other difficulties arise when students do not connect to the material or understand the reasons for doing research. Jody Passanisi and Shara Peters posit that "students can be overwhelmed by tasks that require time consuming research and they unsuccessfully scan pages of text as opposed to reading these pages of text for comprehension, therefore, they cannot tell whether or not the source they are looking at is applicable to their research question."[22] This is where the hard work of research comes in, and it should be something that librarians need to be honest about with students. Mixed messages can be sent when a "how-to" instruction session is presented as an easier way to find information and cite sources. The point here is to help show students how knowledge creation does not come easy, yet when it does, it can be quite rewarding. Margit Misangyi Watts quotes a student who expresses it this way: "Clearly knowledge is having an in-depth understanding of something that you can make useful in your own life. Merely storing information for keepsake is useless. Knowledge that proves to be useful has meaning; it actually benefits us to have obtained useful knowledge."[23] Once students understand that research is rewarding in this way, they are better able to articulate why research is necessary.

A great deal of conversation in the literature revolves around students becoming more aware of the creative nature of research and how that can lead to a greater ownership of their work. Barbara Fister has frequently explored the design of the research paper in her blog *Library Babel Fish* and writes about connecting to the process in a similar fashion, "When students realize that research is creative, that they can come up with ideas nobody has had before, that they have agency in the world of ideas, it's a huge revelation."[24] One substantial change for the instruction librarian would be presenting research as a way to enter a conversation and avoiding using terms like "finding sources" in an instruction session in favor of "learning about" so that there is a distinction between merely accessing information and creating something more than a short-lived work.

The steps outlined in the introduction have been followed. First, an effort by the librarian has been made to gain a more robust understanding of different student experiences and capabilities. Then some more work is done to develop relationships that help both librarian and student. How then to get students to understand why they are doing research and have a more vested interest in the creative and pragmatic aspects of the research paper? Librarians, in partnership with faculty could break the research paper into smaller components and emphasize the importance of each. Annotated bibliographies and literature reviews can accomplish these goals, especially when the objectives behind these exercises are highlighted. One overlooked element of the research paper that can offer introspection is the importance of topic choice. Students often wait until the final hour to pick a topic and seem to have a tendency to view this decision as an unimportant one. Yet this decisive moment may show whether the student is committed to the project at hand and how much ownership they will take when researching.

Appendix 14B provides an example of the type of assignment that may allay some of the research paper concerns that a student may have. A first step in realizing a more robust library instruction session is getting an individual to reflect upon or analyze his or her own motivation. This metacognitive approach is valuable because it can prompt the student to move away from rote information satisficing and can pave the way to a deeper understanding of the motivations behind the process. For example, pacing students through the steps that they take when choosing a topic and having them reflect upon why they are choosing it can lend more ownership to an aspect of a research paper that was formerly "glossed over."

This assignment was delivered by one of the authors in conjunction with English composition library instruction and was graded by the librarian. The feedback that has come from both the instructor and the students has been positive and generally involves comments that highlight the importance of spending more time thinking about topic choice and taking more initiative and ownership of the topic. Because the librarian was able to provide feedback, there were numerous cases where a student would suggest more than one topic and ask for advice from the librarian about which one to choose. This type of assignment can help students who struggle with choosing a topic before searching and complains when they cannot find anything about their last-minute choice.

A strong, impactful idea is sometimes referred to as a threshold concept, which at the time of this writing, is being considered as a supporting tenet for revising the 2001 ACRL's *Information Literacy Competency Standards for Higher Education.* The theories behind threshold concepts were developed by Ray Land and Jan Meyer and can be described as core concepts within a discipline that are central to a mastery of a subject. While the threshold concepts are yet to be fully defined within information literacy, the idea that a threshold concept is transformative, troublesome, and irreversible can help us to understand some of the ways it will be explored in this field.[25] The assignment described above aligns with the *Framework for Information Literacy for Higher Education* threshold concept example of "scholarship as conversation," that is, how students can gain an understanding of the ways in which the conversational and creative nature of research differs from merely finding and accessing information.

How can a student be able to converse in a scholarly way if the topic was chosen for them or they had no personal motivation to explore their choice? Showing a commitment to a topic (the main goal of this assignment) fulfills both an opportunity to become part of a conversation and a beginning consideration of the information landscape. Students also benefit by beginning to understand their own research habits and becoming more than passive observers of library instruction.

The aforementioned framework attempts to prompt all information users (not just students) to think more about the how the information ecosystem is constructed. One might say that there is more of an inclusive nature regarding the new framework because it attempts to move away from rigid standards and become a more expansive way to get students, librarians, and all information users to think about the whys of information use rather than stating they are information literate when a thoroughly checked list of standards is met. Another goal of implementing the framework is moving the responsibility for advocating for information literacy away from the sole province of the library. Advancing student understanding of information literacy involves many different strategies and many more promoters than the library and librarians. As a way to converse with other stakeholders on campus, the framework will allow for more discussion about how to advance students to the "next level," transforming them from consumers of information to active and committed creators.

Although a goal is to move information literacy initiatives beyond the realm of the library, perhaps students could also begin to understand librarians. At the core of this chapter is the threshold concept "librarians are resources." The transformative nature of this concept has yet to dawn on many students, particularly first-year students. Often, some of the more basic or ingrained ideas such as the understanding the goals of research and recognizing the helpfulness of librarians, go passing before our eyes because we think everyone already knows or values what we value. These basics are glossed over in an effort to get to concepts that appear more important at the time. But what could be more important than taking some time to sit down with a student and help to answer the question "Why do I need to do research?"

Appendix 14A: Demonstration Speech: Resource Assignment

Finding good, solid research sources about your topic is an important way to provide information to your audience. As part of your research, you will need three sources to support the information you present in your demonstration speech. You will need to e-mail one of the resources (or a link to it) plus the following information to the librarian who taught your class, Joe Eshleman (joe.eshleman@jwu.edu). You will receive confirmation and feedback on your source and citation, and you will be sent another source for your speech.

What is your speech topic?

Source Information

List your source using MLA format. The research goal for your source is finding information that is factual and interesting. Remember that just finding a website about your topic is not a source. For example, finding a website about how to make chocolate cheesecake or one with a recipe is not in and of itself a source (unless it does provide some interesting historical or statistical fact or perhaps a quote for your speech).

What are two reasons that your information qualifies as a reliable source?

What interesting fact (biographical, statistical, or historical information; quote; etc.) are you using from this source in your speech?

Appendix 14B: Thinking about Writing the Research Paper: Picking a Topic

Asking and Answering the Question, "What Can I Do to Make My Research Paper Experience Better?"

Step back for a moment and reflect on the reasons that you write a research paper and how you can improve your experience. In some of your other classes, for example, why you are practicing a particular skill in the kitchen, studying a trend in a certain hospitality industry, or learning how to write a particular business letter may be obvious. Take some time to think seriously about the ideas explored here and answer the questions honestly. Write complete sentences in paragraph form to answer each question.

The Importance of the Topic

When you are choosing a topic for a research paper, pick something that motivates you and creates passion about wanting to explore that idea. The topic is very important because what you choose motivates you to find information on it.

What specific topics would you choose to create an assignment that would produce enthusiasm and motivation?

Why would that choice of topic or topics get you interested in finding information about it?

Finding Information about Your Topic

Now that you have a topic that interests you and you are eager to find information about it, what do you want to find out about it?

Where could you find this information?

Notes

1.   Char Booth, *Reflective Teaching, Effective Learning: Instructional Literacy for Library Educators* (Chicago: American Library Association, 2011), 19.

2.   Jessica Lange, Robin Canuel, and Megan Fitzgibbons, "Tailoring Information Literacy Instruction and Library Services for Continuing Education," *Journal of Information Literacy* 5, no. 2 (2011): 70.

3.   Trudi Jacobson and Helene C. Williams, *Teaching the New Library to Today's Users: Reaching International, Minority, Senior Citizens, Gay/Lesbian, First-Generation, At-Risk, Graduate and Returning Students, and Distance Learners* (New York: Neal-Schuman, 2000), 11.

4.   Firouzeh Logan and Elizabeth Pickard, "First-Generation College Students: A Sketch of Their Research Process," in *College Libraries and Student Culture: What We Now Know*, ed. Lynda M. Duke and Andrew D. Asher (Chicago: American Library Association, 2012), 111.

5.   Ibid., 124.

6.   Dona McDermott, "Library Instruction for High-Risk Freshmen: Evaluating an Enrichment Program," *Reference Services Review* 33, no. 4 (2005): 433.

7.   Peter Collier and David Morgan, "'Is that Paper Really Due Today?:' Differences in First-Generation and Traditional College Students' Understandings of Faculty Expectations," *Higher Education* 55, no. 4 (2008): 425–46.

8.   Stacey Brinkman, Katie Gibson, and Jenny Presnell, "When the Helicopters Are Silent: The Information Seeking Strategies of First-Generation College Students," in *Imagine, Innovate, Inspire: Proceedings of the Association of College and Research Libraries 2013 Conference*, ed. Dawn M. Mueller, Indianapolis, IN, April 10–13, 2013, http://www.ala.org/acrl/sites/ala.org.acrl/files/content/conferences/confsandpreconfs/2013/papers/BrinkmanGibsonPresnell_When.pdf, 649.

9.   Tiffany R. Wang, "Understanding the Memorable Messages First-Generation College Students Receive from On-Campus Mentors," *Communication Education* 61, no. 4 (2012): 335–57.

10.   Carol C. Kuhlthau, "Inside the Search Process: Information Seeking from the User's Perspective," *Journal of the American Society for Information Science* 42 (1991): 366–67.

11.   Miriam Matteson, Omer Farooq, and David B. Mease, "Feeling Our Way: Emotional Intelligence and Information Literacy Competency," in *Imagine, Innovate, Inspire: Proceedings of the Association of College and Research Libraries 2013 Conference*, ed. Dawn M. Mueller, Indianapolis, IN, April 10–13, 2013, http://www.ala.org/acrl/sites/ala.org.acrl/files/content/conferences/confsandpreconfs/2013/papers/MattesonFarooqMease_Feeling.pdf.

12.   Susie Andretta, *Ways of Experiencing Information Literacy: Making the Case for a Relational Approach* (Oxford: Chandos Information Professional Series, 2012), 187.

13.   Ibid.

14.   Alison J. Head, "Information Literacy from the Trenches: How Do Humanities and Social Science Majors Conduct Academic Research?," *College and Research Libraries* 69, no. 5 (2008): 427–46, http://crl.acrl.org/content/69/5/427.full.pdf+html.

15.   Steven J. Bell, "From Gatekeepers to Gate-Openers," *American Libraries* 40, no. 8–9 (2009): 51.

16.   Barbara Fister, "Fear of Reference," *Chronicle of Higher Education*, June 14, 2002, http://chronicle.com/article/Fear-of-Reference/2928; Kirsty Thomson, "University Students Are Unaware of the Role of Academic Librarians," *Evidence Based Library and Information Practice* 7, no. 2 (2012): 68.

17.   Susan Miller and Nancy Murillo, "Why Don't Students Ask Librarians for Help? Under-

graduate Help-Seeking Behavior in Three Academic Libraries," in *College Libraries and Student Culture: What We Now Know*, ed. Lynda M. Duke and Andrew D. Asher (Chicago: American Library Association, 2012), 51.

18. Ibid., 69.

19. Ibid.

20. Ibid.

21. Booth, Reflective Teaching, 9.

22. Jody Passanisi and Shara Peters, "What's So Hard about Research?" Guest Blog (blog), *Scientific American*, June 19, 2013, http://blogs.scientificamerican.com/guest-blog/2013/06/19/whats-so-hard-about-research/.

23. Margit Misangyi Watts, "The Place of the Library versus the Library as Place," in *Challenging and Supporting the First-Year Student: A Handbook for Improving the First Year of College*, ed. M. Lee Upcraft, John N. Gardner, and Betsy O. Barefoot (San Francisco: Jossey-Bass, 2005), 355.

24. Barbara Fister, "From Things to Conversations," *Library Babel Fish* (blog), Inside Higher Ed, November 26, 2013, https://www.insidehighered.com/blogs/library-babel-fish/things-conversations.

25. "Threshold Concepts: Undergraduate Teaching, Postgraduate Training and Professional Development; A Short Introduction and Bibliography," UCL Department of Electronic and Electrical Engineering, last accessed August 18, 2014, http://www.ee.ucl.ac.uk/~mflanaga/thresholds.html#topofpage.

CHAPTER 15

Fragmented Stories:

Uncovering News Bias through Information Literacy Instruction[1]

Willie Miller

The press has significant power in society. According to Len Masterman, "The media tells us what is important and what is trivial by what they take note of and what they ignore, by what is amplified and what is muted or omitted."[2] Citizens look to news and media organizations to provide an accounting of the significant occurrences of the day. In the current age of the 24-hour news cycle, in which we have access to broadcast and written reporting at all times, the classic duties of news programs have given way to more fragmented and populist coverage.[3] Further, widely used wire services, such as Reuters and the Associated Press, have increasingly become embroiled in controversies regarding potentially biased stories, which are reprinted for readers all over the world.[4] As a result, it behooves the citizen to exercise critical information literacy (IL) skills in the daily consumption of news. Many undergraduate students are not equipped to parse through rhetoric to identify questionable reporting or agenda pushing. Because news media are pervasive institutions concretely entwined with everyday life, requiring critical analysis for responsible engagement, the news makes for an excellent frame in which to teach IL.

Often, IL skills are taught in the context of the classroom and in relation to a paper or a project, which can obscure their real world, everyday application. In her keynote presentation at the 2013 LOEX Conference, Barbara Fister makes the "outrageous claim" that librarians should stop teaching first-year students how to find information and focus on teaching students how to engage in the scholarly conversations.[5] Though, I would not go as far as to encourage librarians to eliminate information-seeking lessons from first-year curricula, I do believe information seeking is often one of the more simple research tasks in which one engages at this level, and librarians might redirect focus away from database demonstrations. As Google maintains its dominance in online search and proprietary databases become increasingly easier for the average person to navigate, the ease of information seeking provides the librarian educator to use the precious few moments he or she may have in-class with students toward the development of other competencies. Librarians could better serve the IL competency in low-level undergraduate courses by creating learning opportunities and lessons designed to guide students in critiquing information and its producers.

To cultivate IL skill in students enrolled in first-year seminar (FYS) courses in the School of Journalism and the School of Informatics and Computing at Indiana University-Purdue University Indianapolis (IUPUI), I created a lesson on evaluating news stories, in which students are given three articles that report on one event. At this time, I have used this approach in eight courses: four in Fall 2012 and four in Fall 2013. The FYS courses in which I used this lesson have no research component; however, the curricula do include a session on IL. This chapter will discuss news media, fragmentation, and the value in using news stories to demonstrate evaluation skills.

The Power of the Press

Inasmuch as the public is dependent upon the press to deliver information we might not otherwise know about the world, members of the press have an obligation to report on issues objectively and without bias. Theodore Peterson outlines, in his seminal chapter "The Social Responsibility Theory of the Press," six tasks of mass communication. Foremost among them is the task of "servicing

the political system by providing information, discussion, and debate on public affairs."[6] Peterson further challenges the press to not only report a fact, but
also the *truth* about that fact. Without the full context surrounding a fact, the
media suggests to its audience that it has not properly evaluated the credibility
of its sources, nor has it supplied the essential perspective needed to completely
understand a situation.[7] Thus, in the absence of this objectivity, it becomes the
responsibility of the audience to evaluate the media.

   Journalist and social commentator Walter Lippmann theorizes that mass
media reports create our mental pictures of the world around us.[8] In essence,
we internalize the images and perspectives we consume through media, and
those messages inform the ways in which we view society. Later, in one of the
most cited articles in the field, researchers Maxwell E. McCombs and Donald
L. Shaw found high, positive correlations between the news coverage of the
1968 election and the significance of political issues in the minds of voters in
Chapel Hill, North Carolina.[9] By showing a correlation between issues covered
in major news stories and the public's perception of the importance of the
issues, this study and many subsequent studies effectively proved Lippmann's
theory. McCombs and Shaw go on to conclude, though "mass media may not be
successful in telling us what to think … they are stunningly successful in telling
us what to think about."[10]

Fragmentation

The American public has had a long and, at times, tumultuous relationship with
the press. While promising to inform, the press sporadically misguides the public, sometimes by accident, other times by design. The newspaper leaders of the
19th century built the philosophical foundation on which modern journalism
has its home. On this, Lippmann (1922) provides keen insight:

> In the early years of the 19th century, papers used the
> news as a political weapon; it was distorted, biased, and
> suppressed to meet the needs of the moment. Later in the
> century newspapers began to confine their opinions to the
> editorial pages; they strove to record the news objectively,
> without personal intrusion and comment, and to present
> not just one side but all sides. True, there were econom-

ic reasons for the development of objective reporting, apart from a growing sense of professionalism. But there was a philosophical foundation as well. For by separating news and comment, by presenting more than one side, the press was expediting the self-righting process; it was making it easier for the rational reader to discover truth.[11]

The pursuit of objectivity became the hallmark of good journalism. The model journalist takes pride in presenting information in such a way that the average citizen can come to his or her own opinions without direct guidance. The fixation on objectivity is a laudable goal for the press to reach; however, the pursuit of objectivity can also result in monotony and conformity across mass media. Repetition in coverage and content, homogeneity, exhausts audiences.

As recently as 20 years ago, the press had a tendency to report on topics in a similar fashion. Timothy Crouse lambasted the inclination toward "pack journalism," in which most stories were essentially the same with infinitesimal variations.[12] A study of the press coverage of the 1992 US presidential election found a widespread similarity in the tone between newspaper and television broadcast stories.[13] However, homogeneity has arguably decreased in recent years as the prevalence of Internet journalism opened more possibility for news stories framed toward certain ideological perspectives to take hold of mass communication.[14]

Technological advances of the past 30 years allow for an increased volume of information available for news consumers.[15] Reports can be researched, written, and disseminated at increased speeds. Moreover, citizen journalists contribute increasing amount of new content into the media environment.[16] An upsurge in both media producers and products allow more choices for consumers, which leads to segmentation of the audience. A benefit of this era is a greater ability to target messages to specific audiences and more interaction between consumers and producers of media.[17]

Even in this new media age, vestiges of the old systems are in place. Most of the news content the average person sees comes from one in a handful of media conglomerates.[18] Walt Disney, News Corp. (now split into 21st Century Fox and News Corporation), Time Warner, CBS, and Viacom were the highest grossing conglomerates of 2013.[19] In addition, many news organizations rely on wire stories from the Associated Press or Reuters to reduce costs.[20] With this amount of consolidation and aggregation, the frustration of homogeneity still floods mass media, particularly newspapers and televised broadcasts. However, the proliferation of online news, particularly when mediated through social media or "micro media," provides niche content producers a large number of platforms for targeted exposure for specific audiences.[21]

With a simple click of the mouse, change of the channel, or file download, consumers can choose a news media outlet most aligned with their ideological preferences.[22] This is fragmentation in news. It provides more choice and possible exposure to wider perspectives in the news at the cost of a radical increase in the amount of biased or unbalanced reports propagating in mass media. This is a problem across all news media, but particularly visible in broadcast journalism on 24-hour news networks. Commentators and journalists are paid to view the events of the day with their own personal lenses. Many viewers cannot or do not care to differentiate between those editorial programs and programs that are hard-line, objective news. This results in a misguided citizenry. For example, on the May 30, 2013 edition of Fox News's *Fox and Friends* broadcast, contributor John Stossel wrongly asserted that no Americans died of hunger during the Great Depression.[23] Though he later issued a correction on his blog, the millions of viewers of the original broadcast who did not check Stossel's blog were misled by prevarication into believing that one of most difficult periods in American history was, in "fact," not that bad.

The current media environment resulting from technological advancement is, in many ways, opposed to Peterson's social responsibility theory. In this new fragmented reality, consumers' personal preferences play a larger role in media gatekeeping and control because individuals patronize media outlets that are most aligned with their personal beliefs. Instead of the homogeneous news world of the past, in which most stories and reports essentially were the same, the fragmented news era boasts a heterogeneous news environment wherein accounts of one issue, topic, or event can differ significantly depending on the source.[24] In such a time, Peterson would agree that it is essential for information consumers to be proficient with IL skills in order to cut through slanted accounts to the truth in reporting. In my experience as a librarian, I have heard students assert, "I don't trust any of the news. It's all lies." However, the teaching opportunity inherent in this frustration is for sharpened information evaluation skills. The belief that all reporters are biased liars is as equally naïve as the contrasting belief that reporters never lie or make mistakes: The problem is that truth is mixed in with fiction.[25] As news media are pervasive institutions concretely entwined with everyday life and require critical analysis for responsible engagement, the news makes for a prodigious frame in which to teach IL.

Institutional Context

IL is woven into the undergraduate curriculum at IUPUI through the university's six principles for undergraduate learning (PUL). The first principle on core communication and quantitative skill—defined as a student's ability to express and interpret information, perform quantitative analysis, and use information resources and technology—is noted as a foundational skill needed for student success. The PUL related to critical thinking is defined as the "ability of students to engage in a process of disciplined thinking that informs beliefs and actions." Further explanation reveals "a student who demonstrates critical thinking applies the process of disciplined thinking by remaining open-minded, reconsidering previous beliefs and actions, and adjusting his or her thinking, beliefs, and actions based on new information."[26] With outcomes including the ability to comprehend, interpret, and analyze ideas and facts and the ability to effectively use information resources and technology, this foundational skill is easily aligned with IL competency.

In addition to the well-known Association of College and Research Libraries' (ACRL) *Information Literacy Competency Standards for Higher Education*, which define IL as the ability to "recognize when information is needed and have the ability to locate, evaluate, and use effectively the needed information," the Accrediting Council on Education in Journalism and Mass Communication (ACEJMC) affirms that students should be able to critically evaluate, not only their work, but the work of others for "accuracy and fairness, clarity, appropriate style, and grammatical correctness."[27] In light of the similarities between these standards, some librarians have collaborated with journalism or mass communication professors to integrate IL instruction through a department's curriculum.[28]

IUPUI librarians are a part of the FYS instructional team; consequently, considerable time and attention is given to IL instruction in FYS courses. In addition, it is through FYS courses that most students are introduced to library resources and subject librarians. The problem with the course curriculum is often the lack of a research assignment. Because of this, students can seem unengaged in the IL instructional session. Without an explicit need to develop IL competency, like a research paper, students seem to view IL assignments as busy work and IL instruction as inapplicable. My goal was to create an IL session in which FYS students developed IL competency and experienced authentic learning. As an avid news consumer and as the subject librarian for the School of Journalism and the School of Informatics and Computing, I am familiar with fragmentation in news media. Much like McCombs and Shaw I decided to capitalize on one of the most regularly controversial seasons in the country—the US presidential election—to use news fragmentation as the lesson and motivation in refining IL skills to journalism and informatics students in FYS.[29] This endeavor led to several positive and highly effective lessons on navigating news and information.

Information Literacy through News Analysis: Lecture

I started employing this lesson during the Fall 2012 semester in two FYS courses in journalism and two FYS courses in informatics. Since it was an election year and most of my first-year students were preparing to vote for the first time, I took advantage of the news coverage of the presidential campaign to demonstrate the importance of information evaluation. While my students were very interested in analyzing election coverage, I feared future repetitions of the lesson would suffer under from a lack of election enthusiasm. However, I soon learned most political US stories, in which there are two prominent partial leanings (left/liberal and right/conservative), work well for the exercise. Since the election, I have successfully used local and national news stories on the government and officials to achieve learning outcomes.

As previously stated, the IL session addresses information evaluation, standard three of the ACRL IL standards, which is coincidentally similar to the ACJEMC standard on evaluating work for accuracy and fairness as well as to IUPUI's PUL on core communication and quantitative skills and critical thinking. With these standards in mind, I set the following student learning outcomes for the session: (1) describe bias in news media, (2) discuss methods of decoding bias in the news, and (3) illustrate examples of bias in the news.

Starting with a short lecture on IL and facts, opinion, and bias in reporting, I set up a discussion on decoding bias in news media. Also within the lecture, I reflect on the difference between news articles and opinion or editorial pieces by borrowing from "Think Like a Journalist," a news literacy guide written by the director of the Greenlee School of Journalism and Communication at Iowa State University of Science and Technology, Michael Bugeja (tables 15.1 and 15.2).[30] This is information that journalism students will cover more than once, but many others, including my informatics and computing students, will possibly never learn.

Table 15.1. News vs. opinion[31]

News	Opinion
Informs	Persuades
Based on multiple viewpoints	Based on singular viewpoints
Facts speak for themselves	Presents informed arguments
Objective and impersonal	Subjective and personal

Table 15.2. News and opinion formats[32]

News Formats	Opinion Formats
News Report: disseminating facts the public needs to know	Opinion: a stance about an issue, newsmaker or event
News Analysis: interpreting issues and events objectively and impersonally	Editorial: the voice of an entire publication such as a newspaper or television station
Special Report: focusing in-depth on an issue, newsmaker or event	Interview: questions and answers featuring a newsmaker or source
Breaking News: covering news events as they happen	Speech: spoken remarks by a newsmaker or source
Investigative Reporting: disclosing data, documents, and testimony	Comment: statement or blog post about issues, newsmakers and events
Poll: surveying the public about issues, newsmakers and events	

Further, the lesson uses Wm. David Sloan and Jenn Burleson Mackay's definition of journalistic bias as evidence of

- partiality;
- one-sidedness;
- unbalanced selection or presentation;
- tendency or inclination that prevents a fair of balanced approach;
- temperamental or emotional leaning to one side;
- favoritism that distorts reality;
- personalized, unreasoned judgment; and
- predisposition or preference.[33]

I give illustrations to provide context for the criteria, particularly the more ambiguous phrases. For example, I clarify "unbalanced selection or presentation" with the example of using more quotes from one side or political party. I also quantify "temperamental or emotional leaning to one side" by encouraging students to consider emotionally expressive language used in reporting. I encourage students to become critical readers and consumers of news by staying alert to the ways in which an author may intentionally or unintentionally express bias.

Information Literacy through News Analysis: Activity

To apply this knowledge through active learning in one instruction session, I give each student three articles on the most recent political controversy from one of several popular news media organizations. I typically use pieces from *New York Times*, National Public Radio (NPR), Fox News, Reuters, Associated Press, and *USA Today*, though I have also used transcripts from televised news reports available through LexisNexis. I intentionally choose one article with a politically left-leaning slant, one article with a right-leaning slant, and one article I determine to be fair, objective, and/or centrist. Within a 75-minute session, students have five to seven minutes for a close reading of each of the three articles. If, after consultation with the course instructor, I believe time is a concern, I highlight specific portions of each article in student copies. Like most librarians, who are generally invited guests into an existing classroom, I do not always have the benefit of the full class time of 70 minutes. However, I found this lesson to be easy to scale up or down. In these cases, the highlighted portions are emphasized as a representative example of questionable or fair reporting in the piece.

After the close reading, students engage in a class discussion on whether the article displayed examples of questionable reporting and whether the article was slanted in one party's or politician's favor. To offset potentially high emotional investment in the topic, I require students to take a formalist approach to criticism. Formalism is a school of literary criticism that postulates the scholar should address the literature rather than the milieu that surrounds it.[34] It requires the critic to develop his or her opinions on a piece of writing based exclusively on the words on the page. I instruct students to use quotes from the article to illustrate examples of questionable or fair reporting. I discourage students from arriving at a conclusion based on emotions or inclinations rather than textual examples. One common prejudice is against Fox News. If students know an article is from Fox News, they often jump to the conclusion that the article has a conservative slant. After first noticing this trend in Fall 2012, I concealed the name of the publisher in the four courses in which I used the activity in Fall 2013.

In addition, I modify the activity to fit the constraints of time and class size while maintaining the learning outcomes. For example, instead of each student reading each article, I split the class into groups of three to five members. Together, the groups closely read one of the given articles for five to seven minutes. Once groups finished reading, they are given about five minutes to discuss the article with each other to decide whether the article had examples of questionable reporting. After this time, each group reports to the class how it determined whether the article has evidence of bias.

Further, one can decide to incorporate computers for additional active-learning activities or homework. In Fall 2013, I taught this lesson in a computer classroom with a small class of eight informatics students. Though I allotted 45 minutes for the students to read and discuss three articles about the rollout of healthcare.gov, we completed the lesson in 30 minutes. To fill the time and explore a few new learning outcomes, I had students use library resources to find articles about the topic and quickly analyze them aloud for the class.

When I prepared this session for the two journalism FYS courses in 2012, it took place before the final presidential debate, and I was able to assign homework. Accordingly, the IL homework was to watch the next debate and find an example of questionable reporting of the final debate, preferably using one of the library's news databases: LexisNexis Academic, EBSCO Newspaper Source, or ProQuest Newsstand. Students were then asked to write a one-page paper illustrating the ways in which the article or report was biased, with textual examples, and to provide an APA citation for the article and any references.

During the discussion, students drew attention to the pre-highlighted portions of the articles, citing them in descriptions of the article's point of view. Once each article was discussed, class concluded with a final discussion on the importance of evaluating news even when it comes from a popular or well-regarded source. In addition, we conceptualized and discussed bias on a scale from fair to extremely prejudiced. We sometimes found that a generally impartial and equalized account had a few instances of unbalanced writing. The idea of a gauge allowed the discussion to reveal that questionable news is not totally black and white with regards to bias.

Results

Class discussions evaluating evidence of bias in the articles are usually fruitful—students engage in thoughtful debates with fellow students, arguing or seeking clarification on their views. I serve more as an informational and rhetorical coach, challenging students to find textual clues for their claims, rather than act as an omniscient judge. Through these formative discussions, students verbally and collectively navigate the complex process of information evaluation. For example, FoxNews.com published an article titled "Obama, Romney Battle over Economic Policies in First Presidential Debate" from which I highlighted the following troubling section: "Republicans seized on a comment by Biden in North Carolina Tuesday in which he said the middle class has been 'buried' over the last four years. Romney and running mate Paul Ryan pointed to the admission as proof of what they've been arguing all along."[35] In an article seemingly covering the result of the first presidential debate, the quote is discussion of a speech Vice President Joe Biden made days before. Discussion of this gaffe, which is not central to the debate the article alleges to cover, is a display of preferential treatment of the Romney-Ryan campaign. Students were able to identify this article's unbalanced presentation of the two presidential campaigns.

In some cases, I had to explain instances of dubious reporting, which students did not initially understand. A NPR article stated, "Romney looked straight at his opponent, often wearing a confident Mona Lisa grin."[36] I clarified for the unknowing students that this description could be taken as an insult by insinuating that Mitt Romney was smug at the debate. In addition, students have disagreed with my analysis of an article as biased or unbiased, and these moments have been thrilling. It is my hope that the class environment invites this kind of debate. It is never my goal to imply my own omniscience; I only want students to be able to use the tools of criticism I provide to developed well-reasoned opinions. As long as students can provide significant textual evidence, any opinion is valid. Students do not have to agree with me to achieve the learning outcomes in this lesson.

In the journalism classes, in which students were assigned homework, the papers on bias in reporting the presidential elections were among the finest work produced in the course, according to the instructional team. Through their analysis of articles on the debates, in most cases, students clearly displayed the ability to express and interpret knowledge, analyze facts, and evaluate the work of others for accuracy and fairness. For example, one student writes in response to a conservative leaning piece on the 2012 vice presidential debate:

The author fails to give the article balance on remarks, responses, and attitudes. Guffaws, snickers, interrupter, aggressive, chuckles, smirks, hammered, gaffes, feisty, are just some of the words used to describe Biden's behavior and attitude at the debate. Ryan got remarks such as, "maintaining a steady and comparatively reserved demeanor throughout." You are the judge here, but I call this article biased.

Another student found a *New York Times* article with evidence of temperamental or emotional leaning to one side:

Quotes describing Paul Ryan's statements used words such as said, declared, or pointed out. Biden's began or followed with words like sharply retorted, argued, and asked bluntly. The debate's analysis offered opinion of how the debate resonated with Republicans, describing Biden as annoyed and likened him to Al Gore rolling his eyes in his debate against President Bush.

Teaching faculty in the FYS courses are very pleased with this IL session. The professor leading the instructional team in the journalism FYS courses expressly requested I continue to present IL in this way in future years as the instruction was directly in line with ACEJMC standards.

Students in informatics and computing are not assigned homework. The assessment for the lesson in those courses are formative, often only through the class discussion. However, like in the example of the small class of eight, learning outcomes could be enhanced and easily evaluated by asking students to find additional articles online and to analyze an article spontaneously in class. I found students in these courses took to the concepts and activity well. Discussions with journalism students are often more lively; yet informatics and computing students find ease in discussing gray areas in reporting with the concept of the bias scale.

After successfully executing this lesson a few times, I shared my materials online with colleagues. One colleague who employed the activity found it a refreshing approach to teaching IL. Another found success with the lesson, though she cautioned that many first-year students are not politically engaged enough to read liberal or conservative bias in a news story without an explanation of the political landscape. In using this activity since the presidential election, I have found the need to give background information on a topic (e.g., the 2013 US government shutdown) before giving out the articles. This process has made me more sympathetic to journalists as I put in effort to not reveal my own political leanings in this process.

Conclusion

Framing IL instruction in the news allows the librarian to make real-world connections to information evaluation, inquiry, and use. For courses with no research paper or research assignment, I found this activity to rouse students toward authentic engagement with the instruction. This approach to instruction is not a new one; anecdotally, many teachers employ similar method to engage learners in information evaluation. However, with appropriate consideration, this activity should be added to the common toolbox of IL activities for its ability to engage students in a real world examination of complex rhetorical arguments. Many undergraduate students are not equipped or have not yet been challenged to parse through the rhetoric to identify media bias.

Moreover, this lesson plan could be used in a variety of settings and audiences. School librarians or teachers in K–12 environments could adopt this plan. The formalist approach and analysis relate to the Common Core English Language Arts Standards for Reading: Informational Text for grades 6–12. Public libraries and educational institutions with approaches for andragogy could engage adult learners in the activity to sharpen IL skills. And, of course, community college, college, and university librarians could employ this lesson, as I have, for the benefit of undergraduate students. Without concentration on database instruction, this lesson deepens the value of librarians as facilitators to IL competency.

The presidential debates provided an exemplary series of political events to cover; yet, it was simple to find another hot topic in the news. The government and politicians provide an abundance of options for this exercise—not only as a result of consistent controversy but also because of the two-party system of American politics. This allows for an approximate unequivocal division in rhetorical scale. However, other industries or interest areas could be considered. International affairs or sports news would easily work as there is often a significant amount of coverage provided by number of platforms.

The only requirement for this IL session to work is evidence of fragmentation in the news. The bittersweet reality is that even casual news consumption reveals substantially different accounts of issues and events as reported in the news. Teaching a student, especially a first-year undergraduate student, to examine media and to evaluate their strengths and failings is worth the time. It can prove its benefits immediately in the lives of students, and the skills will be valuable forever.

Notes

1.   A shorter version of this paper will appear in *LOEX Conference Proceedings* 2013.

2.   Len Masterman, *Teaching the Media* (London: Comedia Publishing Group, 1985), 5.

3.   Bruce A. Williams and Michael X. Delli Carpini, "Monica and Bill All the Time and Everywhere: The Collapse of Gatekeeping and Agenda Setting in the New Media Environment," *The American Behavioral Scientist* 47, no. 9 (2004): 1208–30.

4.   Jonathan Bailey, "Wrap Up: AP Controversy, Cowherd and More," *Plagiarism Today*, last modified March 29, 2006, accessed March 8, 2014, http://www.plagiarismtoday.com/2006/03/29/wrap-up-ap-controversy-cowherd-more/; Craig Silverman, "There Were 31 Incidents of Plagiarism/Fabrication in 2012," Poynter, last modified December 24, 2012, accessed March 8, 2014, http://www.poynter.org/latest-news/regret-the-error/197275/there-were-31-incidents-of-plagiarismfabrication-in-2012/.

5.   Barbara Fister, "Decode Academy" (presentation, LOEX Conference, Nashville, TN, May 3, 2013), http://homepages.gac.edu/~fister/loex13.pdf.

6.   Theodore Peterson, "The Social Responsibility Theory," in *Four Theories of the Press*, ed. Fred S. Siebert, Theodore Peterson, and Whilbur Schramm (Urbana, Il: University of Illinois Press, 1956), 74.

7.   Ibid., 88.

8.   Walter Lippmann, *Public Opinion* (New York: Macmillan, 1922).

9.   Maxwell E. McCombs and Donald L. Shaw, "The Agenda-Setting Function of Mass Media," *The Public Opinion Quarterly* 36, no. 2 (1972): 176–87.

10.   Donald L. Shaw and Maxwell E. McCombs, *The Emergence of American Political Issues: The Agenda-Setting Function of the Press* (St. Paul, MN: West Publishing, 1977), 5.

11.   Lippmann, Public Opinion, 88.

12.   Timothy Crouse, *The Boys on the Bus* (New York: Random House, 1973).

13.   Marion R. Just et al., eds. *Crosstalk: Citizens, Candidates, and the Media in a Presidential Campaign* (Chicago: University of Chicago Press, 1996).

14.   Jonathan S. Morris, "Slanted Objectivity? Perceived Media Bias, Cable News Exposure, and Political Attitudes," *Social Science Quarterly* 88, no. 3 (2007): 710; Diana Owen, "Media Consolidation, Fragmentation, and Selective Exposure in the USA," in *The Sage Handbook of Political Communication*, ed. Holli A. Semetko and Margaret Scammell (Thousand Oaks, CA: Sage, 2012), 401.

15.   Morris, "Slanted Objectivity?," 710.

16.   Owen, "Media Consolidation," 402.

17.   Jeffrey B. Abramson, Gary R. Orren, and F. Christopher Arterton, *Electronic Common-*

wealth: The Impact of New Media Technologies on Democratic Politics (New York: Basic Books, 1990).

18.   Ben H. Bagdikian, *The Media Monopoly* (Boston: Beacon Press, 1997).

19.   "Fortune 500 2013: Full List—Fortune," *Fortune,* accessed March 15, 2014, http://fortune.com/fortune500/2013/wal-mart-stores-inc-1/?iid=F500_sp_full.

20.   Owen, "Media Consolidation," 402.

21.   Ibid., 403.

22.   Morris, "Slanted Objectivity?," 710.

23.   John Stossel, "Fox's Stossel Dismisses Aid to Needy with Claim That No One Starved during the Great Depression," Media Matters for America video, 2:45, May 30, 2013, http://mediamatters.org/video/2013/05/30/foxs-stossel-dismisses-aid-to-needy-with-claim/194265.

24.   Darrell M. West, *The Rise and Fall of the Media Establishment* (Boston: Bedford/St. Martin's, 2001), 93–95.

25.   Alexandra Kitty, *Don't Believe It!: How Lies Become News* (New York: Disinformation, 2005), 18.

26.   "Principles of Undergraduate Learning," Indiana University-Purdue University Indianapolis, last modified 2007, accessed December 3, 2013, http://academicaffairs.iupui.edu/PlansInitiatives/Plans/Principles-of-Undergraduate-Learning.

27.   Association of College and Research Libraries, *Information Literacy Competency Standards for Higher Education,* accessed December 3, 2013, http://www.ala.org/acrl/sites/ala.org.acrl/files/content/standards/standards.pdf; "ACEJMC Principles of Accreditation," *Accrediting Council on Education in Journalism Mass Communications,* last modified August 2009, accessed December 3, 2013, http://www2.ku.edu/~acejmc/PROGRAM/PRINCIPLES.SHTML.

28.   Elizabeth J. Natalle and Kathryn M. Crowe, "Information Literacy and Communication Research: A Case Study on Interdisciplinary Assessment," *Communication Education* 62, no. 1 (2013): 97–104; Claudia Ruediger and Donald Jung, "When It All Comes Together: Integrating Information Literacy and Discipline-Based Accreditation Standards," *College and Undergraduate Libraries* 14, no. 1 (2007): 79–87.

29.   McCombs and Shaw, "The Agenda-Setting Function of Mass Media."

30.   Michael Bugeja, "Think Like a Journalist," *CBS,* last modified 2009, accessed November 14, 2013, http://newstrust.net/guides.

31.   Ibid.

32.   Ibid.

33.   Wm. David Sloan and Jenn Burleson Mackay, *Media Bias: Finding It, Fixing It* (Jefferson, NC: McFarland, 2007), 6.

34.   René Wellek and Austin Warren, *Theory of Literature* (San Diego, CA: Harcourt Brace Jovanovich, 1977), 130.

35.   "Obama, Romney Battle over Economic Policies in First Presidential Debate," Fox News, last modified October 4, 2012, http://www.foxnews.com/politics/2012/10/04/obama-romney-battle-over-economic-policies-in-first-presidential-debate/print.

36.   Alan Greenblatt, "Five Takeaways from the First Presidential Debate," NPR, last modified October 4, 2012, accessed August 20, 2014, http://www.npr.org/2012/10/04/162265100/five-takeaways-from-the-first-presidential-debate.

Making It Work: Teaching Students about Information

2.3 Interpreting the World

CHAPTER 16

Logical Fallacies and Sleight of Mind:

Rhetorical Analysis as a Tool for Teaching Critical Thinking

Jessica Critten, Anne C. Barnhart, and Craig Schroer

The primary *raison d'être* of media, whether online, television, cable, radio, print, etc., is the attraction and maintenance of an audience through some sort of persuasive offering (e.g., "fair and balanced," "the latest in breaking news," "funny or die," etc.). Consequently, the media ecosystem is structured to pander to the target demographic audience by using rhetoric that beckons for attention while also flattering and aligning the viewer's perception in a way favorable to the economic and political interests subsidizing the content. This manipulation takes many forms, depending upon the target demographic and the entertainment and information context, and can range from seamlessly subtle to artlessly overt. Teaching a framework for conceptualizing, understanding, and recognizing rhetorical misdirection and logical fallacies—whether language-based, aural, visual, or, in the case of most media, a combination of modalities—is fundamental to information literacy, media literacy, and the everyday practice of critical thinking. The skilled, reflexive, day-to-day exercise of critical faculties is a measure of educational success equal to and supportive of the mastery of any specific subject area.

To further this educational goal, librarians at the University of West Georgia (UWG) created an exercise to help students develop these vital critical thinking skills by examining verbal and visual rhetorical devices and logical fallacies as used in popular media (in particular, an episode of the television show *Penn & Teller: Bullshit!*). Being able to identify rhetorical sleight of hand allows students to feel more empowered as consumers of information, and this empowerment increases their confidence and willingness to engage with the material. Examining rhetorical tricks in popular media provides a wealth of tangible examples for teaching the abstractions necessary to critical thinking and does so in a manner that emphasizes "real-world" value and the extension of these skills outside of the classroom.

This chapter will discuss how the authors developed, adapted, and used this exercise to teach critical thinking in several instructional scenarios. It will address how students responded to this activity and its applicability and usefulness in workshops and one-shots (single-class settings) as well as part of a semester-long class. The exercise will also be discussed as a valuable formative assessment tool that measured how many rhetorical tricks students could identify in a one-shot as well as how many they could continue to identify in readings and in media discussed throughout a semester-long course. By providing a framework and vocabulary for describing recognizable but, for the most part, previously unnamed manipulative communication techniques, the authors were able to measure and document students' application of critical thinking skills.

Rhetoric and Multimodal Information Literacy

For the sake of clarity and brevity, an explanation of how the term "rhetoric" is used in this chapter is in order. Rhetoric as a word or part of a phrase has a multitude of meanings and uses. In Aristotle's *Rhetoric*, the word is used to encapsulate three modes of persuasion: *pathos* (appeal to emotion), *ethos* (appeal to authority or credibility), and *logos* (appeal to logic*)*.[1] A discussion of the word rhetoric is, in fact, the starting point for the *Penn & Teller: Bullshit!* exercise. For our purposes, rhetoric serves as linguistic shorthand when referring to slippery rhetorical devices, logical fallacies, or otherwise manipulative or distracting techniques employed in a manner so as to evoke an emotional response (pathos) to misdirect an audience's attention away from the logical underpinnings (logos) of the argument at hand.

The Association of College and Research Libraries' *Information Literacy Competency Standards for Higher Education* do not specifically address rhetoric; however, the value of identifying and understanding rhetorical devices are implied in standard three, performance indicator two. The outcomes from this indicator include "analyzes the structure and logic of supporting arguments or methods" and "recognizes prejudice, deception, or manipulation."[2] These standards are being updated, and the newer version will include more on metaliteracy and a focus on evaluating information in the "media-rich environment."[3] Librarians should be helping students develop these other literacy skills in the multimodal communication environment characteristic of social media.

When students and librarians focus only on evaluating the written text of resources, students may not learn how to evaluate the other kinds of information (visual and audio cues, infographics, etc). In an interview with Wade Mahon, Cheryl Ball notes, "In a writing class teachers think they're supposed to teach just writing, but with the communication patterns we are engaged in the world these days, it does students a disservice to only teach them how to write without tending to these other modes of communication."[4] When information literacy is restricted to textual evaluation, it is easy for consumers and producers of information to become distracted by the other modalities and not recognize or apply their critical reading skills when evaluating information presented in other formats. In his presidential address at the National Council for Teachers of English Annual Convention, Keith Gilyard said, "We need to double-down on promoting critical language awareness, on having students search and strive for intellectual substance rather than mere spectacle."[5] Teaching students to think about multimodal forms of communication empowers them to see through the distraction of the spectacle in order to focus on the strength of the actual arguments being presented (logos).

A Critical Framework

There are several educational philosophies gaining popularity in librarianship largely driven by instruction librarians' growing discomfort with "traditional" methods of teaching information literacy: a focus on search mechanics and an approach to establishing authority that lacks cultural context and nuance. The work of, among many others, Paulo Freire and bell hooks have helped shape the field of critical pedagogy, which asserts that education should provide a framework for questioning power structures that perpetuate social injustice and oppression.[6] As such, inherent to this education movement is praxis: The idea that learning and theory should inspire active and productive practice.

Cushla Kapitzke extends the work of critical pedagogy into the realm of librarianship in her discussion of critical information literacy, which reconstitutes information literacy as a "socially constructed discourse and discipline" that should provide "a space for the possibility of social transformation and disruption of the discourses and economies that produce and reproduce it."[7] Here, then, critical information literacy paints the process of becoming information literate as a fundamentally political and empowering act. Critical pedagogy positions the educator as a force of enfranchisement rather than an unchallenged authority. In this light, the role of the instruction librarian can be seen as providing those "spaces" and opportunities for students to engage content intellectually and, because of its "real-world" implications, emotionally. This engagement introduces an affective element that is beneficial to learning and encourages praxis, creating a positive feedback loop.

The exercise discussed in this chapter uses as a theoretical framework the philosophy of critical media literacy, which examines the intersection of critical theory, pedagogy, and information literacy specifically in the media apparatus. Douglas Kellner and Jeff Share write that critical media literacy "focuses on ideology critique and analyzing the politics of representation of crucial dimensions of gender, race, class, and sexuality … and expanding textual analysis to include issues of social context, control, resistance, and pleasure."[8] The exercise was consciously constructed to motivate students to examine implicit media messages presented within structures that are powerful because they are pleasurable; that is to say, the experience of having one's opinions and worldview reaffirmed in media narratives is comforting, and conversely, the idea that information and ideology are political and socially constructed is unnerving.[9] By giving students an accessible tool—the ability to recognize and name specific logical fallacies and slippery rhetoric—instructors can empower them to challenge oppressive or misleading media narratives, allowing students to begin the difficult process of thinking critically about how they interact with the world and how it influences what they choose to believe.

Background

In Summer 2012, the UWG started its inaugural College Transition program (later renamed "Ignite" for the 2013 program and all successive iterations.) This program was designed to allow first-year students entering the university at the lower end of the acceptance standards to take college classes and access supplemental programming to gain skills that would prepare them for the expectations of college work. All students in the program were enrolled in a university freshman orientation course (UWG 1101: First Year University Experience) that included an overview of the library. In addition to the standard library introduction, librarians were asked to lead separate workshops for the students as part of the freshman orientation course.[10]

As a general philosophy, UWG instruction librarians design one-shot lesson plans around a particular research project so students spend their time with library faculty more meaningfully.[11] However, the students enrolled in the program did not have a research project to work on at that point in the semester, so the librarians planning this workshop decided to focus on transferable, fundamental information literacy skills rather than a research tool or particular resource. These skills would also have the added effect of laying a foundation of knowledge that UWG librarians hoped to build upon as they used their ongoing curriculum mapping efforts to scaffold learning outcomes throughout the students' sophomore, junior, and senior years.

This session planning also coincided with an ongoing paradigm shift for many of the faculty in the instructional services department, who were beginning to shape their program around more critical approaches to instruction. Kellner and Share write, "When educators teach students critical media literacy, they often begin with media arts activities or simple decoding of media texts … with discussion of how audiences receive media messages."[12] One of the librarians brought to the group's attention a list of rhetorical tricks from the website Thou Shalt Not Commit Logical Fallacies.[13] This comprehensive list included, for example, common fallacies such as *ad hominem* and strawman attacks, which the librarians felt would be good for students to understand particularly in light of the media coverage leading up to the 2012 presidential election. After some deliberation it was decided to focus on a small set of common rhetorical devices as the framework for an interactive activity.

As a part of the project of teaching critical information literacy, Kaptizke writes that instruction should be moved "from the confines of the library to the arenas of language use and the social lives of youth."[14] The librarians decided to use an episode of the popular Showtime show *Penn & Teller: Bullshit!* as their central text for this exercise because of the bombastic way it utilized language; for example, it immediately captures interest with its provocative title. Librarians hoped that the show's graphic language would engage new college students unaccustomed to the use of profanity in educational settings. It was also an opportunity for the librarians designing the exercise to discuss with students that Penn and Teller were very conscious that the language they chose had power and impact. Penn Jillette explains in the show's pilot episode that they named the program *Bullshit!* both to get attention and to avoid legal problems. He observes, "If one calls people 'liars' and 'quacks,' one can be sued and lose a lot of one's money. But 'motherfuckers' and 'assholes' is pretty safe. If we said it was all scams, we could also be in trouble but 'bullshit,' oddly, is safe."[15]

College Transition Program Workshop

All students enrolled in this program attended this workshop as a program cohort together in the evening, after that day's classes were over. In the first iteration of this exercise, librarians had 90 minutes of class time. They began by dividing the approximately 50 students enrolled in the program into groups of seven or eight students as they entered the library's large flexible working space. Each group was given a two-sided dry erase easel on wheels and each student a piece of colored paper with either the number one or two on one side and a list of logical fallacies on the other. (See Appendix 16A for the lesson plan for the workshop.) Once students were settled, librarians showed a popular Old Spice commercial ("the man your man could smell like") to set up the discussion of rhetoric. The librarians then led a discussion of the ad, specifically asking students three questions: "What is the ad trying to persuade you of?," "What are they trying to sell you?," and "What tools or methods is this ad using to persuade you?."

Students were readily able to identify that commercials were trying to sell them something and that "something" was a tangible product. The librarians started the program thusly to establish that even in conspicuously manipulative media environments (commercials) there were different layers of manipulation, overt in the sense that the commercial was meant to sell them a product and less obvious in that the commercial was trying to "sell" or reinforce traditional ideals of masculinity. The hope was that as students began to notice that they were being influenced in ways they hadn't realized and that they could find value in identifying and challenging these methods of manipulation.

In the second portion of the exercise, students were then asked to have a discussion in their small groups to answer following questions" "Whom have you manipulated in the past?," "What were you trying to achieve?," and "What tools or methods have you used to persuade people?." Librarians circulated during this time to different groups to monitor the conversations and prompt students who were confused by the assignment or whose conversations were not moving forward. After they shared in their groups for a few minutes, students were asked to volunteer some of their answers with the larger group. These students recounted times that they had tried to convince a friend to help them with something or a professor to give them an extension on an assignment. This portion of the exercise was meant to evoke constructivist learning principles, which assert that content is more meaningful when students have the opportunity to build on prior knowledge and connect it meaningfully to something in their everyday lives.[16]

These discussions were designed to set a context for the next, and main, portion of the assignment. Students were asked to watch an approximately13-minute segment of a *Penn & Teller: Bullshit!* episode about genetically modified food entitled "Eat This."[17] The librarians chose this episode because they wanted a topic that, while controversial, was not likely to raise the passions of the student participants. First, students were asked to watch this clip all the way through and to pay attention to who was talking and reflect on the following questions: "When and how does Penn Jillette use profanity? Why?," "Where are the guests when they are being interviewed?," and "How does Jillette react to each speaker?."

After everyone watched the segment for the first time, students were given three minutes to review the list of logical fallacies they'd been given at the start of the program. The group then watched the segment again, this time pieced out in three-to-five minute clips. Students with a number one on their cards were asked to go on one side of the dry-erase easel and pay particular attention to the argument made by the hosts (who were for genetically modified foods) and the guests on the show who agreed with them. Students with the number two were asked to be mindful of the people arguing against genetically modified foods in the episode. All of the students, however, had to identify the logical fallacies they recognized in the show after each clip.

Students were also prompted to consider the settings in which the different voices are placed during each clip. Jillette's political agenda is quite prominent in how the show situates those representing the different sides; the interviewees who agree with Jillette's (and presumably, the show's) politics are presented in professional settings with flattering lighting. Those who are on the opposite side are often treated quite differently in front of the camera, positioned in apartments and otherwise nondescript rooms. Students were asked to explore these differences and the non-textual messages they were receiving.

The students were encouraged to speak with their small groups in between each section of the episode to compare what logical fallacies they found. Establishing groups as discussion spaces created an environment for constructivist learning as students collaborated to solve problems together. Students shared the fallacies they identified with the entire group once the episode was finished.

This final discussion was designed to give students more opportunity to draw conclusions and connections between the exercise, their college careers, and their everyday lives. For example, librarians asked students why the activity was designed the way it was: watching the episode all the way through once and then again in short clips with breaks to reflect on the language being used to craft arguments. The librarians wanted the students to learn to analyze how their professors introduce material to them. This was an effort to get the students to engage learning as a form of praxis by understanding the theoretical framework of how learning environments are designed. It also reflected the authors' critical pedagogy approach by encouraging the students to question the professor as absolute authority so that they can become critical consumers of their classroom experiences as well. Students were able to identify that the exercise gave them an opportunity to see how their perception of the arguments changed when they were aware (or at least more thoughtful) of the fact that they were being manipulated. However, they were not as readily able to pick up on the fact that they were consuming a text in this program in the way they might consider consuming a text for a class: reading or watching something all the way through at first to get a sense of it as a whole and then again in more depth. With some prompting, students were also able to discuss other media in which these sort of rhetorical tricks were in play, including commercials, social media, television pundit shows, presidential debates, and political radio shows.

This workshop had an unforeseen outcome: The day after the rhetoric program, one of the student workshop participants approached a librarian and asked where the *Penn & Teller: Bullshit!* DVDs were located. The student checked out several of these DVDs and was quite happy to learn that the library carried other popular films. A workshop on rhetoric and logical fallacies got a student interested in library resources!

Other Uses of Exercise Framework

Since it was created in Summer 2012, this exercise has been used and adapted by several different UWG librarians depending on the amount of time an instructor was able to devote to it and at what point in semester it would be used. The librarians who created the assignment always intended that the framework of using rhetorical devices should be a tool of critical evaluation and therefore flexible and transferable to any number of different kinds of information sources—news programs, advertisements, scholarly writing, interpersonal conversations, and so on. The choice of text for the workshop was fairly incidental; as the exercise continues to be used and adapted, *Penn & Teller: Bullshit!* will be replaced by a more timely resource when appropriate.

One-Shot

When adapting the workshop exercise for a standard 50- or 75-minute one-shot, the content had to be more focused. To get the students ready to discuss the issues, the librarian often started by showing a video clip of a commercial and asking students talk about what the commercial was implying. The librarian then referred to the handout the students received, which listed a selection of the more commonly used logical fallacies (including those fallacies used in the sample commercial) and asked the students to indicate which rhetorical device most accurately fit how they had just described the commercial. After discussing a few of the examples on the handout, the librarian showed a shorter clip from the *Penn & Teller: Bullshit!* episode used in the workshop ("Eat This"). At the time of writing, each episode was available on YouTube and broken into three segments, which made it easy to stream an eight-minute clip in class. As in the workshop, students were asked to pay attention to when and how Jillette used profanity and to note the rhetorical devices used. While the students watched the clip and tried to identify the devices, the librarian often wrote direct quotes from the segment on the board.

After watching the clip, the librarian asked the students to report what fallacies they heard and in what context. When there was a lull in the conversation, the librarian indicated one of the quotes on the board and asked the students which fallacy it represented. In different classes, librarians have experimented with both playing the shorter eight-minute segment used in one-shots all at once and pausing it after some of the fallacies. Depending on the personality of the class, both methods have worked for discussion. Pausing the clip after each example helped the students identify the fallacies but had the consequence of interrupting Penn and Teller's argument. Students struggled more to identify the fallacies when they watched the clip straight through; however, they could then discuss some affective learning outcomes if the conversation was directed to how they felt about the information and the way that it was presented.[18]

Credit-Bearing Course

One adaptation of the exercise was in an honors section of the library's semester-long information literacy class (LIBR 1101: Academic Research and the Library), which allowed the students to explore and apply the concepts in more depth and over the course of a semester. This LIBR 1101 section was focused specifically on critical media literacy (and informed greatly by cultural studies), and in the class, rhetoric was a "pillar of media literacy" along with hegemony, ideology, and representation. All of these concepts were introduced in a "flipped" classroom environment where students would encounter a new concept as homework and then process it in the classroom through discussion and other active learning exercises.

Students were asked to review the same abbreviated list of rhetorical tricks used in other versions of the assignment and identify and reflect on those tricks in 30 minutes of a news show of their choosing as a homework assignment on their personal class blogs. (See Appendix 16B for the homework and in-class assignments used.) In class, students were then asked to identify rhetorical devices from the same list in the episode of *Penn & Teller: Bullshit!*. The discussion that followed focused both on what students found in their homework and in the in-class version of the assignment. An obvious drawback of the initial version of the exercise was the short amount of time students had to review the list of rhetorical devices before identifying them in the episode of *Penn & Teller: Bullshit!* With introducing rhetorical devices as part of a homework assignment, students were much better equipped to identify those devices when they completed the exercise in class. As a result, the discussion was robust and almost completely student driven.

In the homework assignment, students had the opportunity to process the devices and the overarching concept of how language can be used to manipulate at their own pace and apply those concepts to a familiar text of their choosing. Having students interact with the concept in this way initially was designed to give them a space to be successful and, ideally, confident both with handling this potentially unfamiliar and challenging concept and the process of identifying rhetoric in a particular text.

This exercise was mostly assessed formatively; the course did not give traditional exams and instead used writing assignments parsed throughout the semester to determine student learning. Students had to write two longer essays at different points in the semester focused specifically on one of the course "pillars of media literacy" of their choosing, and almost all of the students chose rhetoric and the uses of manipulative language as one of their topics. Overall, students demonstrated a thoughtful understanding of the concept and, in addition to identifying rhetorical tricks, were also able to reflect on how rhetoric has both consciously and unconsciously shaped their ideologies. Students were also able to identify rhetoric in the media they confronted throughout the semester, noting in class discussions and on their personal blogs when specific rhetorical tricks were used in both the media they were analyzing and in the classroom.

Another librarian used this in an asynchronous online section of the credit-bearing information literacy course. In the online class, students were given links to Thou Shalt Not Commit Logical Fallacies and asked to watch a segment of the "Eat This" episode on YouTube. This time the students were asked to react to the episode and record the emotional response they had. In addition to identifying logical fallacies and manipulative video editing devices, they were asked to write down ten terms they did not recognize or names of people, events, or agencies that they would need to research in order to better understand the issues behind the video segment. Of the ten, students were asked to pick three and research them (while library databases were encouraged, *Wikipedia* was permitted as a source for this). Then the students were asked to re-watch the segment and respond again to the information presented now that they had some background knowledge. Some of the students were reflective about the affective learning outcomes. Some expressed irritation at the manipulative tactics used by Penn and Teller.

Unfortunately, however, a few other students did not think critically about what they were seeing or researching. One student hijacked a discussion board and merely repeated Jillette's arguments without evaluating the presentation or including the additional sources they were asked to consult. While non-reflective students also exist in face-to-face classes and this kind of discussion derailment is common, it is more difficult to manage in an asynchronous online environment because by the time the librarian instructor logged in and read the comments, other students began to post, doubting the conclusions they had reached in their independent work. In a face-to-face class, it would have been much easier to rein in the wayward student and redirect the conversation. Unfortunately, in online discussion boards there is no guarantee that any of the students actually reads the "corrective" posts an instructor makes. This is not dissimilar from the problem in a live classroom setting in which any number of students might not be paying attention or might not be understanding the discussion yet remain quiet.

While there were frustrations, the online experiment did produce satisfying results. After learning the logical fallacies, students agreed to not rely on them to make arguments in their discussion board posts. When students did use them, the instructor responded by citing which fallacy had been employed and encouraged the student to make his or her argument differently. At the end of the semester, students had to make a digital poster for an online poster session. They were also graded on how well they evaluated each other's posters. Several students pointed out the usage of logical fallacies or overtly manipulative pairings of images to text when evaluating the work of their classmates.

Conclusions and Further Applications

The success of the *Penn & Teller: Bullshit!* episode in a variety of settings has prompted a continual evaluation of how the exercise can best be structured to maximize its impact. One-shots continue to be a problem in that the limited amount of available time greatly constricts the ability to cover a select set of common logical fallacies while still leaving time for the actual exercise. In more expanded settings there is an opportunity to spend more time considering the nature of rhetorical tricks and logical fallacies and constructing examples. Ideal-ly, when this exercise is used as part of a multi-session set of information literacy classes there can be a build up wherein several different examples, class discus-sions, and exercises can be used to demonstrate and explore the use of logical fallacies and rhetoric. Active learning exercises have included handouts with, for example, ten brief arguments based on logical fallacies that match ten types of fallacies introduced in class. The authors also wanted to design an exercise to introduce the students to the concept of rhetorical devices and to provide them with the tools and confidence to identify them in popular media. As lower-di-vision students develop and build on their rhetorical awareness, it opens the possibility of applying the same skills to recognize the often more subtle uses of rhetoric and manipulation employed by scholars in academic texts.

Moving forward, the authors are continuing to develop this exercise and further examine its utility in future iterations of the semester-long LIBR 1101 course. For example, in the Spring 2014 honors section of LIBR 1101, instructors plan to position a continued analysis of rhetoric as an overall framework for the course. After doing the initial homework introduction and flipped-class discussion, students will choose one or two rhetorical devices to monitor in news, scholarly, and social media texts examined in the class throughout the semester. Students will then create an infographic using their chosen rhetorical trick, which will allow them to demonstrate that they have synthesized the concept and can not only identify it but also actively apply it. This course will also focus more intently on the reflective and metacognitive potential of the assignment, giving students opportunity to explore the praxis of how their newfound understanding of manipulative visual and verbal language can reshape their consumption and creation of information.

The reshaping of mental maps and examination of previously unexamined beliefs is an outcome that, ideally, should be a positive sign of maturation and acquisition of higher-level critical thinking skills. This intellectual growth, however, is not necessarily a comfortable or desirable space for students. In a presentation the authors gave on the exercise at the LOEX Conference in Nashville in May 2013, one of the attendees posed the problem, "What if students ask, 'How can you believe anything?'" This was a perceptive question and, in fact, accurately reflected the response of some students to the exercise. It is natural that an examination of the meaning and use of language leads to ontological questions, and for some people, whether it be fear, cynicism, or laziness, there may not be an interest in delving too deeply into such matters.

This "spiraling existential crisis," as one author responded, gives students an opportunity to begin to see the role that research plays in building a sound argument or establishing a valid point of view. Research becomes actualized as a tool that can be used to challenge existing "authoritative" structures. The potential of information literacy to empower students has informed the authors' overall philosophy of their work, which asserts that instruction librarians can and should emphasize larger cognitive skills rather than just mechanics. Specifically, the exercise discussed in this chapter was designed equip students with a conceptual framework and vocabulary that will empower them not just to consume but to also thoughtfully contribute to a larger global exchange of information and the shaping of cultural discourse.

Appendix 16A: College Transition Program Rhetoric Workshop Schedule

June 15, 2012

7:05–7:10: Get students situated—Give each student a colored piece of paper with a number on one side and our adjusted list of fallacies on the other.

7:10–7:20: Show large group of students AXE commercial.
> **What is the ad trying to persuade you of? (What are they trying to sell you?)**
> **What tools or methods is this ad using to persuade you?**

7:20–7:25: Introduce Penn and Teller activity.
> Explain: Why is it called BULLSHIT?

7:25–7:40: Watch whole section of episode all the way through. Before, ask students to
> **Pay attention to who is talking.**
> **Why does Penn Jillette use profanity when he does and how he does?**
> **Pay attention to the settings, or the context of the presenters: Where are they when they are being interviewed? How does Jillette react to each speaker?**

7:40–8:20: Watch chunks; introduce fallacies.
> Ask students with #1 to watch the chunks from Penn and Teller's (or their surrogates—the people who agree with them) position. What logical fallacies do they utilize to make their points?
> Ask students with #2 to watch the chunks from the opposition's side: What logical fallacies do they use to make their points?
> After each chunk, write your fallacies on your side of the board

8:20–8:30: Closing words:
> Why did we do it like this? (You are reading a text!)
> How was it different the second time you watched it?
> (If time, have you manipulated?)
> Where else have you seen these logical fallacies in play?

Appendix 16B: Homework and In-Class Assignments for LIBR1101-H

Spring 2013

Before completing this assignment, review the handout, "Common Rhetorical Devices," which lists a number of rhetorical tricks.

Rhetorical Tricks

1. Watch/listen to at least 30 minutes of a news program and identify at least two of these tricks. You can watch any program you like, but I've linked to some below that you might want to check out. (The pundit-y shows are generally—but certainly not always—more rich for this sort of thing than the nightly news.)

2. Post the tricks you identified and their context in the news program to your blog as well as a short write up of what you think a rhetorical trick is, based off of the examples you read on the handout. (Yes, you could just Google it, but where is the fun/learning in that?!)

I suggest watching your news program online, so you can pause if you need to. Or maybe you have a fancypants DVR you can use for that purpose—whatever works best.

Here are some news programs online you might check out:

- *The Rachel Maddow Show*
- *The War Room*
- *Hannity*
- *Talking Liberally*
- *Rush Limbaugh*

Common Rhetorical Devices (Does that Argument Make Sense?)

Ad Hominem
Attacking your opponent's character or personal traits instead of engaging with their argument.
After Sally presents an eloquent and compelling case for a more equitable taxation system, Sam asks the audience whether we should believe anything from a woman who isn't married, was once arrested, and smells a bit weird

Slippery Slope
Asserting that if we allow A to happen, then Z will consequently happen too, therefore A should not happen.
Colin Closet asserts that if we allow same-sex couples to marry, then the next thing we know we'll be allowing people to marry their parents, their cars, and even monkeys.

Appeal to Nature
Making the argument that because something is 'natural' it is therefore valid, justified, inevitable, or ideal.
The medicine man rolled into town on his bandwagon offering various natural remedies, such as very special plain water. He said that it was only natural that people should be wary of 'artificial' medicines such as antibiotics.

Appeal to Authority
Using the opinion or position of an authority figure, or institution of authority, in place of an actual argument.
Not able to defend his position that evolution 'isn't true' Bob says that he knows a scientist who also questions evolution (and presumably isn't a primate).

Appeals to Emotion
Manipulating an emotional response in place of a valid or compelling argument.
Luke didn't want to eat his sheep's brains with chopped liver and Brussels sprouts, but his father told him to think about the poor, starving children in a third world country who weren't fortunate enough to have any food at all.

False Cause
Presuming that a real or perceived relationship between things means that one is the cause of the other.
Pointing to a fancy chart, Roger shows how temperatures have been rising over the past few centuries, whilst at the same time the numbers of pirates have been decreasing, thus pirates cool the world and global warming is a hoax.

Anecdotal
Using personal experience or an isolated example instead of a valid argument, especially to dismiss statistics.
Jason said that that was all cool and everything, but his grandfather smoked, like 30 cigarettes a day and lived until 97—so don't believe everything you read about meta-analysis of sound studies showing proven causal relationships.

Composition/Division
Assuming that what's true about one part of something has to be applied to all, or other, parts of it.
Daniel was a precocious child and had a liking for logic. He reasoned that atoms are invisible, and that he was made of atoms and therefore invisible too. Unfortunately, despite his thinky skills, he lost the game of hide and go seek.

Black-or-white	Strawman
Where two alternative states are presented as the only possibilities, when in fact more possibilities exist.	Misrepresenting someone's argument to make it easier to attack.
Whilst rallying for his plan to fundamentally undermine citizens' rights, the Supreme Leader told the people they were either on his side, or on the side of the enemy.	*After Will said that we should put more money into health and education, Warren responded by saying that he was surprised that Will hates our country so much that he wants to leave it defenseless by cutting military spending.*

The Texas Sharpshooter	Genetic
Cherry-picking data clusters to suit an argument, or finding a pattern to fit a presumption.	Judging something good or bad on the basis of where it comes from, or from whom it comes.
The makers of Sugarette Candy Drinks point to research showing that of the five countries where Sugarette drinks sell the most units, three of them are in the top ten healthiest countries on Earth, therefore Sugarette drinks are healthy.	*Accused on the 6 o'clock news of corruption and taking bribes, the senator said that we should all be very wary of the things we hear in the media, because we all know how unreliable the media can be.*

Examples borrowed from Thou Shalt Not Commit Logical Fallacies (https://yourlogicalfallacyis.com).

NAME: _____

**As you watch this clip, try to answer the following questions:

Besides the fact that he doesn't want to get sued, why does Penn Jillette use profanity when he does and how he does?

Pay attention to the settings, or the context of the presenters: Where are they when they are being interviewed? How does Jillette react to each speaker?

Below, list the rhetorical tricks that you were able to identify from the clip. Try to also make note of what each trick is referring to. (*Example: Ad hominem* attack—they said the guy's mustache was ugly, so you can't take anything he said seriously.)

    1.

    2.

    3.

    4.

    5.

Notes

1.   Aristotle, *Rhetoric,* trans. W. Rhys Roberts, The Internet Classics Archive, http://classics.mit.edu/Aristotle/rhetoric.html.

2.   Association of College and Research Libraries, *Information Literacy Competency Standards for Higher Education,* accessed August 20, 2014, http://www.ala.org/acrl/sites/ala.org.acrl/files/content/standards/standards.pdf.

3.   The authors attended an online open forum on November 4, 2013 to discuss the formation of the new standards, hosted by a task force formed for this purpose. Recordings of this webinar can be found here: http://acrl.ala.org/ilstandards/?page_id=21.

4.   Wade Mahon, "Multimodal Composition and the Rhetoric of Teaching: A Conversation with Cheryl Ball," *Issues in Writing* 18, no. 2 (2010): 114.

5.   Keith Gilyard, "The 2012 NCTE Presidential Address: Literacy, Rhetoric, Education, Democracy," *Researching in the Teaching of English* 47, no. 3 (2013): 342.

6.   See Paulo Freire, *Pedagogy of the Oppressed,* trans. Myra Bergman Ramos (New York: Seabury Press, 1974); Bell Hooks, *Teaching to Transgress: Education as the Practice of Freedom* (New York: Routledge, 1994).

7.   Cushla Kapitzke, "Information Literacy: The Changing Library," *Journal of Adolescent and Adult Literacy* 44, no. 5 (2001): 453. For more information on critical information literacy, refer to James Elmborg, "Critical Information Literacy: Implications for Instructional Practice," *Journal of Academic Librarianship* 32, no. 2 (2006): 192–99; and Troy A. Swanson, "A Radical Step: Implementing a Critical Information Literacy Model," *Portal: Libraries and the Academy* 4, no. 2 (2004): 259–73.

8.   Douglas Kellner and Jeff Share, "Critical Media Literacy Is Not an Option," *Learning Inquiry* 1, no. 1 (2007): 62.

9.   Drew Westen studied what happens in the brain when political partisans are faced with information that confirms or refutes an opinion they have. When confronted with information that was in conflict with their partisan opinions, people lie to themselves to resolve the conflict. Upon lying to themselves, participants' brains released dopamine, a neurochemical associated with pleasure and reward. In other words, people do feel actual pleasure when their opinions are reinforced, even when that reinforcement is not supported by reality. For more information about Drew Westen's study, see the transcript of the October 12, 2012 *On the Media* broadcast in which he was interviewed, http://www.onthemedia.org/story/243320-your-brain-politics/transcript/ or his book *The Political Brain: The Role of Emotions in Deciding the Fate of the Nation* (New York: Public Affairs, 2007).

10.   Since they were already teaching two sections of the library's credit-bearing information literacy class (LIBR 1101) for the four-week program, librarians had to develop separate topics for the stand-alone workshop so as to not duplicate course content. Approximately one-third of students enrolled in the College Transition program were enrolled in LIBR 1101, so UWG librarians thought that this additional programming would be a good opportunity to build relationships with incoming students. At the time, rhetoric was not covered in the LIBR 1101 curriculum thus guaranteeing that students enrolled in the program would be building new, topical, and relevant skills.

11.   "One-shot" is librarian shorthand for a single stand-alone library instruction session typically offered in conjunction with a specific course or assignment.

12.   Kellner and Share, "Critical Media Literacy Is Not an Option," 63.

13.   Jesse Richardson, Andy Smith, and Sam Meaden, Thou Shalt Not Commit Logical Fallacies, accessed August 18, 2014, https://yourlogicalfallacyis.com/.

14.   Kaptizke, "Information Literacy: The Changing Library," 453.

15.   "Talking to the Dead," season 1, episode 1, *Penn & Teller: Bullshit!*, directed by Star Price, aired January 24, 2003 (New York: Showtime Entertainment, 2004), DVD.

16.   For an introduction to constructivism through the lens of information literacy, see Sarah E. Cooperstein and Elizabeth Kocevar-Weidinger, "Beyond Active Learning: A Constructivist Approach to Learning," *Reference Services Review* 32, no. 2 (2004): 141–48.

17.   "Eat This," season 1, episode 11, *Penn & Teller: Bullshit!*, directed by Star Price, aired April 4, 2003 (New York: Showtime Entertainment, 2004), DVD.

18.   *Framework for Information Literacy for Higher Education*, the new ACRL information literacy standards, draws from Tom Mackey and Trudi Jacobson's work on metaliteracy learning, which specifies four domains: behavioral, affective, cognitive, and metacognitive. See http:// metaliteracy.org/learning-objectives for more information.

CHAPTER 17

Scholarly Storytelling:
Using Stories as a Roadmap to Authentic and Creative Library Research

Rebecca Halpern and Lisa Lepore

The foundation of our first ever for-credit information literacy course for students in our undergraduate-completion program started with a hunch. Like so many teachers and librarians before us, we had a feeling that our students were engaging with their research assignments in the most superficial ways; indeed, our hunch was supported by the work of Project Information Literacy that assured us that the tendency for students to pull quotes from the first resource they find was not unique to Antioch University Los Angeles (AULA).[1] And, again like so many others before us, we as librarians struggled to guide our students to the most appropriate resources.

As librarians, our library sessions often felt flat. Covering the basics of generating keywords and tricks to using the databases left both the students and us feeling a little glazed and confused. Furthermore, after informally speaking with course instructors about ongoing problems students had in research assignments, we discovered that while students were mostly successful in locating scholarly works, they were significantly less successful in using those sources in purposeful or meaningful ways. We were left with concern about the disconnection of students to resources resulting in research papers lacking in spirit, coherence, and intelligence.

To test our hunch that students were shallowly engaged in research, we gathered as much data as we could. We spoke with handfuls of teaching instructors to ask them what they saw were the most common errors in student work, paid close attention to what students struggled with during reference appointments, and had dozens of conversations with both students and faculty on their frustrations in doing and teaching research. Additionally, we launched a citation analysis project to collect more quantitative data. Citation analysis has been an established method for assessing library information literacy instruction for at least the last decade and more recent studies helped inform the way in which we conducted our project.[2] Citation analysis is a relatively straightforward process by which instruction librarians identify several sections of one course, offer a particular intervention to one or more while leaving at least one section without the intervention as a control group, and then compare the bibliographies of the sections to assess particular learning outcomes. Common ways this method has been used are to determine what areas of information literacy instruction *aren't* effective, to serve as an introductory tool to strategize long-term information literacy curriculum, to evaluate the utility and quality of print and online library-specific resources, and to measure the comparative effectiveness of both one-on-one consultations and librarian-led workshops.[3] While most citation analyses focus on the quality and appropriateness of sources used, our goal was to go beyond this foundational step to discover how well students integrate and synthesize the information they find. We modeled our rubrics off a 2010 study that evaluated both the quality of sources and how well those sources were used.[4]

The results of our citation analysis indeed confirmed what our informal quantitative research had suggested: Overwhelmingly, our students were skillful in locating appropriate sources and struggled with integrating them. The curriculum at AULA encourages students to be active participants in their education and to challenge, investigate, and draw conclusions. The kind of spirit and enthusiasm typically found in student work was largely absent in research-heavy assignments. How could we get students to engage in the research process with as much curiosity as they exhibited in other assignments? In particular, we wanted to encourage the idea of authorial identity, or "the sense a writer has of themselves as an author and the textual identity they construct in their writing."[5]

When doing research, it is essential that we can see ourselves as writers, experts, colleagues, and contributors; without the understanding that research is an act of writing, research papers read more like book reports. Our students, like most others, displayed a disconnect between the research they found and the context by which they found it. After the citation analysis, we knew we needed to revise our information curriculum in a radical way.

Once we had a sense of where we were, it was time to consider where we needed to go. In particular, we wanted to revisit our goals: What do we want students to learn from library instruction? We spent the next several weeks exploring the idea of threshold concepts: Threshold concepts are those fundamental concepts of a discipline upon which all other concepts build.[6] While related to learning outcomes, instead of being a task-based assessment measure, threshold concepts are "gateways for student understanding that once traversed, transform the student's perspective."[7] Focusing on concepts instead of outcomes gave us the flexibility to design instructional content and delivery and allowed us to challenge some aspects of AULA's information literacy competency standards that don't reflect our student body or learning communities. Interestingly, while writing this chapter, the Association of College and Research Libraries began a radical revision to the standards as a response to these, and other, inadequacies. Teaching threshold concepts is one of the major revisions to the standards.

Eventually, we identified three primary threshold concepts that shaped our information literacy curriculum: (1) research serves as an ethos, (2) research is a mode of narrative, and (3) research is a conversation. Instilling a scholarly ethos served to answer the oft-asked question, "What does this have to do with me?" As the majority of students at AULA are in professional master's degree programs, they often have difficulty seeing how research-heavy assignments would help their professional goals. Framing our instruction sessions to help students develop an answer to this question means our students will be more engaged and our sessions will be more vibrant. By helping students to develop an authorial identity and understand how research solves problems, we hoped to reduce plagiarism and have students see themselves as agents (not visitors) to their own work (this is discussed in more detail later in this chapter). Along the same lines, we found it problematic that students do not consider research as a mode of narrative, a way to tell an important story as a means to solve problems. The social sciences and humanities have a rich tradition of recognizing storytelling as a powerful means to give marginalized groups a voice; likewise, philosophers like Søren Kierkegaard and Carl Jung understood that storytelling was central to meaning-making and cognition.[8] If we were to help students understand how research can be used as a powerful tool for problem solving, why wouldn't we frame it as a narrative process? Incorporating aspects of narrative and storytelling into research is a familiar way to explore the idea of authorial identity.

These being lofty concepts, we decided the best approach to test-drive the feasibility of this framework was in a for-credit quarter-long course. Of course we recognize that a for-credit long-format course is a rare privilege; however, having several weeks to grapple with pedagogy, learning activities, and course content meant we could have a much clearer direction for restructuring the entirety of the information literacy curriculum, including our digital learning objects and content of one-shot sessions. In other words, the long-format course gave us time to answer the question, "What are we really talking about here?" To frame the content of our course, we relied heavily on the concept of research as storytelling for several reasons. The rest of this chapter discusses the content and framework for our course and how we used what we learned to shape our information literacy curriculum as a whole.

Storytelling

Storytelling is a fundamental means of communicating, "central to human understanding" (ethos); through stories (mode of narrative), we learn about each other and ourselves (conversation).[9] Patrick J. Lewis writes, "We take in stories, our own and others, and tell them back to our self and to others in a recursive process that augments our understanding."[10] The relational aspect of storytelling offers a back and forth dynamic, a willingness to understand one another, and, often, assumes an audience. In their study on students' self-perception as writers, Gail Pittam et al. found that many students did not expect an audience for their papers; a lack of authorial identity meant they did not perceive their work suitable for real engagement.[11] This estrangement to their own work and to themselves as creators can result in dull, inauthentic, and rote papers. We find similar characteristics in much of the student library research we examine at our university. Selected resources seem a perfunctory choice, weakly integrated into students' papers. Does the same lack of authorial identity affect the quality of students' research, resulting in research that fulfills a requirement, but tepidly? It is worth looking at the quasi-standard directive students receive from their professors when writing research papers: "Find three peer-reviewed articles."

The assignment is not to "find the work of a specific researcher" or "assess an important journal in a discipline" or even to understand the influence of a work through citation evaluation. If the mandate to find peer-reviewed articles is an invitation to enter scholarship, it is an anemic one. It also impedes intellectual growth by forfeiting more robust ways of searching for material. Likely the directive points to a flailing effort on the part of faculty to get students to be engaged in their work, to follow and participate in conversations relevant to their fields of interest. But it also could suggest that there is a way that students are eavesdroppers and outsiders to academic conversations, causing the rootlessness of their scholarship. The Ethnographic Research in Illinois Academic Libraries (ERIAL) Project reported on students' "crude" research skills; students stumble when looking for resources, with unrefined ways of searching. But let's assume students *did* feel they had a story to tell, would that change not only their motivation to find applicable information but the ways and places in which they searched?[12] Our hypothesis is that if students self-identify as storytellers and invest in the importance of their narrative, they will forage for sources that are meaningful, credentialed in various ways. They will become more intrepid, resilient, and knowledgeable researchers. If being a storyteller means having both a story to tell and an audience to tell it to, a student's relationship to his or her work could be transformed, invigorating the process of research and writing and altering the quality of the work. Simply, in assigning a story-driven research paper, we wagered that students would want to tell a good story and that telling a good story must be predicated on solid research.

Storytelling is a personal, vernacular approach to scholarship. It is not a student imitating an academic voice but is the student's voice in the academy. Like "narrative expression," which "embodies multiple ways of knowing," storytelling corroborates the knowledge of the storyteller. Using one's voice assures the student's knowledge.[13] This is an important point and relates to the idea of an authorial identity. All undergraduate students at AULA read "Social Class and the Hidden Curriculum of Work," Jean Anyon's study of a socioeconomic cross section of fifth-grade students. In the study, the children are asked if they can "make knowledge."[14] The majority of students said no; only those in the executive elite school said yes, almost to a person. Inferring that the study captures the thinking of a majority of people, then the idea of being a knowledge maker (an author) is not a likely or comfortable identity. The student as storyteller provides a more natural and familiar venue for a student to communicate his or her ideas. The idea of a storytelling method for academic paper writing could counteract the existing perception of who can create, who can produce, and who can add to the body of knowledge.

Wanting to investigate this idea further, how storytelling could invite students into the academic conversation (including the possibility of knowledge production), we devised a core assignment that would allow for such explorations. Students were asked to write an historical biography research paper based on someone active in a social justice cause. Because stories are central to the crafts of history and biography, this seemed a natural fit to such a paper. Pushing the normal biographical paper, however, we permitted our students to write about a subject who was real or fictionalized. Although students had the choice to make their subject fictional, the biography would be steeped in research from real historical sources. Crafting a fictionalized character permits the student to be more creative, perhaps, but it also intentionally prompts important critical conversations about the veracity of history. Patrick H. Hutton contends, "What is called history is no more than the official memory a society chooses to honor."[15] A fictionalized character based on well-scrutinized research could be "more real" than a glossed-over figure of official memory. Students read a variety of works in the class in order to understand the ideas of "history as truth" and "manipulated histories." Donna Haraway argued that all knowledge is contextual, affected by situation and circumstance.[16] We wanted students to play with that idea. If history is a packaged deal supporting official memory, how does that inform an understanding of history? None of what Haraway calls the "ideology of direct, devouring, generative, and unrestricted vision" can exist in neatly packaged, non-contextualized stories of the world.[17] How does contending with a *restricted* vision inform an understanding of history, the role of stories, and the need to find alternative narratives? Where do students search for historical information about people on the other side of history, where those active in social justice causes are often found?

Our interest in adding a social justice element to the research paper was to compel students to search for information that might not be so easy to find, to search for histories that might be scarcely available, if available at all. This informs them as researchers and as purveyors of information. It is an excellent lesson about information access. Simply put, people active in social justice or civil rights causes often fall outside of official history, living in history's (if not society's) margins; a search for information about them would require alternative routes to nonobvious places. In addition to searching for history and stories *about* people who live in the margins, our students will be encouraged to look for stories *by* people who live in the margins. These stories are akin to *testimonios*, "expressions of resistance …defined as first-person narratives that bear witness to individual responses to systems of oppression."[18] Storytelling introduces a multitude of "narrative habits, patterns of seeing."[19] The storytelling by the "outgroups" becomes a way to sidestep the master narrative, allowing for alternative voices and acknowledging the fact that "social reality is constructed through stories and counter-stories."[20] So not only can stories and storytelling work for our students as a means of alternative communication in the academic setting, it also allows for a way to better understand the subjects about whom they write, finding them despite the winnowing of their narrative in the mainstream.[21]

If storytelling provides an alternative way for students to think of communicating ideas, it also provides an alternative way of understanding ideas. Richard Delgado explains, "Underneath everything is the sense, the fear really, that stories if well told can become part of the narrative base and so change the way we understand the world. That's truly subversive."[22] As students write these academic stories, by piecing together and enlivening information that lies in wait, they will contribute to the subversion, to the unmaking or remaking of fixed narratives and creating new possibilities of understanding. They will (however small) be challenging oppression *through* storytelling, in part by challenging social categories and beliefs.

The Teaching, or What We Did and Why

The class provided a framework for exploring research as a narrative, creative, exploratory enterprise. The assignments, lectures, and course activities were designed to help meet this goal. Inspired by critical pedagogy, we wanted to create an environment that allowed students as much freedom as possible to explore their existing relationships with research and scholarship and to invite students to think critically about their assumptions surrounding the creation and use of information. Through lectures, in-class activities, and carefully designed assignments, we utilized a critical pedagogy to encourage students to become more information literate.

Education scholars like Henry Giroux, Paulo Freire, bell hooks, and many others have developed critical pedagogy as an educational framework over several decades. Though this framework is relatively well rooted in teaching strategies, it has only just begun to be explored in library instruction.

Moving beyond basic bibliographic instruction, critical information literacy aims to develop a critical consciousness and understands library instruction as a dialogic process.[23] Instead of focusing on database how-to, critical library instruction exists as a mode of knowledge creation and challenges students to understand how library research is a means to develop their passions, academic curiosities, and positions in the sociopolitical world of information creation and distribution.[24] Rather than teaching our students where to click, we are involving students in solving real-world information-seeking problems in order to present information seeking as a fundamentally cooperative and political activity.

For librarians interested in examples of how a critical pedagogy can shape library instruction sessions, we highly recommend Maria Accardi, Emily Drabinski, and Alana Kumbier's *Critical Library Instruction* (*CLI*); we pulled much of our inspiration from those chapters. General strategies for creating a critical learning environment involve minimal lecturing, group discussions, student-led problem solving, classroom-flipping, and participative assessment.[25] Indeed, much of the challenge of teaching with a critical pedagogy is employing thoughtful learning activities to meet learning objectives. The learning activities we employed were conducive to the for-credit format but can easily be modified for use in standalone techniques in one-shot information literacy sessions.

In addition to *CLI* as a theoretical framework, we heavily borrowed from Pittam et al.'s work on authorial identity for our content, as described above.[26] In addition to their findings on the lackluster nature of student work when students fail to recognize themselves as authors, their study found that students who fail to see themselves as authors or participants in the research conversation, in addition to lacking spirit and cohesion, are at much higher risk of unintentional plagiarism. Because students do not necessarily recognize themselves as authors, they rely heavily on direct quotes and imperfect paraphrasing to construct arguments. Moreover, because students do not completely understand their role and responsibilities as authors, they struggle to meaningfully engage with and transform source material, which leads to inadvertent plagiarism. Indeed, in our own citation analysis project, we too found evidence that students who struggle to integrate themselves into their writing are more susceptible to the too-common phenomenon of "information dumping."

Pittam et al. recommends that in addition to teaching students the technicalities of proper citation, we should also include activities or discussions that help students understand their responsibilities as authors.[27] In other words, our job as research instructors is to demonstrate that excellent scholarship occurs when students see themselves not only as students but as creators and narrators as well. Thus, the main learning objectives for this course were to present research as a narrative process.

The course assignments were as follows:

- write a 10–12 page research paper, turned in incrementally starting in week two—
  - list of research ideas,
  - abstract,
  - outline,
  - annotated bibliography,
  - first draft,
  - second draft, and
  - final draft;
- maintain a blog; and
- give a final class presentation, using PowerPoint and touring the blog.

As discussed, the core project was an historical biography. Students either chose a real-life figure or invented a character based on a sociopolitical era; one student chose Julia Child and her relationship to feminism; one created a backstory for Christina, the subject in Andrew Wyeth's painting *Christina's World*; one wrote about her neighbor's miraculous immigration to California from Egypt and Armenia; and another contextualized her experience as an orphan in Europe. The rationale for allowing students to write about an enormous range of topics was three-fold. First, they will approach the subject of their research from a place of intrinsic curiosity. In fact, many students expressed gratitude for getting to tell a story they've always wanted to tell. Secondly, the nature of the assignment required students to explore the entirety of the information universe: primary documents and archives; newspapers; scholarly research; and their own imaginations, conversations, and experiences. Lastly, by requiring that the subject be sociopolitical, we expose students to how information creation, production, and distribution are ultimately deeply political acts with historical and social implications.

To write a convincing and accurate biography, students had to interweave research into their imaginations. We required students visit a physical archive to experience how primary and historic materials are organized, discovered, and used. Instead of providing instruction on locating archival materials, we had them speak with the director or head archivist of their archives. Historian Arlene Farge writes that the archive forces one "to engage with it. It captivates you, producing the sensation of having finally caught hold of the real, instead of looking through a 'narrative of' or 'discourse on' the real."[28] Archivists are not neutral "handmaidens" as they have been referred to in the past, but participants in existing power structures and relationships.[29] Randall C. Jimerson writes, "The archivist's role of interpretation, both in creating finding aids to guide users of records and in providing reference services, conveys stories of the human condition."[30] By speaking with an archivist, students got a sense of how the collection developed over time and how it is frequently used. Throughout the planning of this course, we talked a lot about the "spirit" of each assignment— what is it that we're hoping students will learn about the information universe? For instance, the small, handmade or community archive is an often-overlooked opportunity to access unpublished, essentially hidden information. Obscure, unfunded archives will have material not available anywhere else, perhaps deliberately rejected or overlooked by other archivists. Without these community archives, those stories (often the last tracings of a community) have no harbor. Jimerson argues that archivists should be cultivating outcast collections. He writes, "Archivists concerned about their role in society can provide a valuable foundation for social justice initiatives by fulfilling their professional responsibility to document all aspects of society, all segments of the populace."[31] Equipping our students with a hands-on relationship to an archive and an archivist as well as an understanding of the politics involved in creating and maintaining an archive became a crucial part of our instruction. Requiring an archives visit was somewhat contested, as one of us felt very strongly about it, while the other didn't see the use. Ultimately, we decided to include this element because primary and archival materials are oft forgotten in social sciences and embody the questions of access, digitization, appropriation, and attribution that are so critical to information literacy. Had this not been a long-format class, this element could be met by exploring local or topical digital archives.

Another element to the assignment was a standard annotated bibliography. In addition to being a very useful skill for students to learn as a way to organize and prepare for a large research project, this is where we really challenged students to view research as a sociopolitical conversation. Annotations had to include how the reference relates to the other references they'd found and identify how the reference demonstrates the sociopolitical nature of information. For instance, the student who wrote a fictional memoir of a young Chinese woman fleeing from the World War II-era Japanese invasion had to indicate if the source was generated during the conflict, the kind of bias it shows, and how it highlights or obfuscates certain elements of the conflict. These annotations first offered a way to summarize and organize research sources, but they also gave students the chance to realize that information is more than just good or bad but is in fact deeply entrenched in political, social, and cultural agendas.

Finally, the blogs allowed for a multimedia facet of a largely written research project. We wanted students to create content in an online medium. Students accessed WordPress, an easy-to-use platform.

Evaluating the Class

Writing the narrative-driven paper motivated our students. They were keenly interested in their subjects and in the research, reflected weekly in class discussions. Organically (that is, not scripted or planned for in the syllabus) students talked at the beginning of each class in detail about their research processes. Sharing tips, asking for assistance, and expressing interest in each other's projects was standard. The difficulty of finding an archive was a repeated discussion. *Talking* about researching became *a part of the research experience*. It was a dynamic cycle of information, an intersection of stories about the search for stories, through which students taught and learned from each other. It was also a confirmation of students' knowledge. The conversations were student initiated and led. As instructors, we participated in the conversations but were most often peripheral actors.

Turning in segments of the research paper throughout the quarter required regular contact with students, allowing for an ongoing critical examination of their research practices. E-mails and in-person discussions, in addition to any class time spent on research questions, was important in a few ways. It allowed us to know what, where, and how students were researching; have opportunities to dialog about their methods; and provide feedback and assurance to students. Students told us that these check-in sessions were very helpful. Undergraduate classes at AULA are usually small in number (they can range from three to 20 students); eight students enrolled in our course, and the small student size allowed for this kind of in-depth interaction. With more students, the level of engagement might need to be moderated but relatively significant amounts of interaction would still be recommended.

Charged with writing a historic-biography research paper about either a fictionalized or real subject, the students largely chose to write papers about real subjects. The two fictionalized papers focused on the woman in Andrew Wyeth's "Christina's World" and a Chinese immigrant fleeing oppression, both previously mentioned. The six nonfictional subjects were two women, Julia Child and Juliette Gordon Lowe, the founder of the Girl Scouts of America, both as feminist icons, and the remaining four nonfictional subjects were people the students knew: neighbors (Armenian political immigrants to the Soviet Union), two parents (a Jewish-American man with family ties to the Holocaust and a woman who survived abusive relationships through spiritual transformations), and a student writing about herself (an orphan). This possibility was not at all anticipated when designing the fictional/nonfictional aspect to the historical biography. The exploration of the fiction/nonfiction binary was intended to understand bias and selectivity in historiographies, examining who gets left out of official records and the consequential difficulty in finding information about them. It was also linked to the importance of stories as a way to enter and alter the historic record. Students taking the assignment as a means to investigate family lore presented a dilemma for us. How does a memoir become an academic research paper? Could it be anything but an exercise in journaling? Despite the paradigm of our entire class—the *invitation* to tell a story—the personalized quality of these papers made us initially struggle with their academic fit. It also made us question our fit as instructors, that in trying to get students to be creative researchers, we overreached; that our pedagogical inexperience allowed for papers that were more like memoirs. Perhaps this uncertainty tapped into a prevailing insecurity in the profession of librarian-as-professor or the role of library as faculty. But what allayed our doubts initially was the pure excitement these students had for their projects that they maintained throughout the quarter. By being storytellers, the act of research was not abstract or burdensome but integral to their work.

For the majority of our students (all adult students), making a blog was a new experience. They stated that they liked having a place to elaborate on and extend their written story. Knowing they could display images made them want to find images, motivating, even emboldening, their research. The documents displayed in the blogs included films clips; photographs; and images of drawings, maps, letters, badges, patches, clothing. Photographs of people and places were used more than any other medium. Students expressed a belief that the photographs validated their works, ensuring the truth or "realness" of their historical papers. Photographs were ubiquitous regardless of the paper's subject being fictional or nonfictional. For the students who wrote papers based on family members or themselves, the photographs of their subjects held an additional, even sentimental value, proof of the emotional lives of their subjects and their worth as topics of investigation.

Although encouraged to seek out whichever archives held material suitable for their needs as long as they were traditional and not online, our students gravitated to the smaller places. This makes sense as they were pursuing off-the-grid subjects. But the smaller archives come with challenges. They are usually not affiliated with institutions and are often community-based or in the charge of one person or a small handful of people. Often there are not catalogs, perhaps only summary notes; nor is the material always accessible; nor are the archives always open or with regular hours. "Cataloging standards and accessibility are often secondary to the compilation of material" for the smaller archives.[32] A couple of students were frustrated in their searches and had to settle for less significant material. The student who researched Armenians immigrating to the USSR found an archive with newspapers and communication on the topic but the proprietors (not archivists) had stopped allowing people to visit the collection. This provided an opportunity to discuss information as private (not public) resource and the scarcity of archival material available for people who fall outside of the mainstream. It also points to the amount of time research can take, particularly when searching a more obscure topic.

Conclusion

We offered the class "Scholarly Storytelling and Library Research: Creative Explorations" in an attempt to overcome the shortcomings with typical, library-based, one-off efforts to teach information literacy instruction in a college setting. In particular, we wanted to expand on the limited instructional opportunities and provide students the occasion to explore and evaluate information resources as a creative, intellectual act. We did this in part by motivating information literacy instruction concepts with a substantial research project. Sifting and winnowing scholarly sources would be an essential aspect of successfully conducting the research. By concentrating on the narrative aspect of their research, we hoped to engage students being aware of their own authorial identity, which would lead in turn to more authentic and deeply engaging papers. Finally, such properly motivated research would allow students to assess critical information literacy concepts such as assessing what is not available, what is missing, and how we provide access to which form of knowledge.

As we evaluated the class work—discussions, bibliographies, synthesis of sources into papers and blogs—and by student reflections and evaluations, we concluded that overall the students in the course became creative and enthusiastic researchers, even though there was still much to learn about finding quality resources. The students reported to us that the creative approach to academic research invigorated them. They were dedicated to their stories and to telling those stories well, intent on finding accurate resources and being explicit about the role that imagination and creativity played in the development of their project. The storytelling prompt was largely successful in freeing students from self-imposed constraints of "writing an academic paper," allowing for Haraway's "unrestricted vision."[33] In discussion post-course, students said that creating a narrative emboldened them. Initially tentative about their ability to yield a "legitimate" academic voice, they did recognize authenticity in their ability to tell a story (authorial voice); the research followed. Many found that the research fed the narrative, allowing for an unimpeded investigation of resources and material and a smooth back and forth between construction of a story and production of a paper. Students also felt the story form allowed for their differences to be integrated or accepted in a way unprecedented to their experiences, embodying the ideas of Delgado who sees stories as a matter of (and opportunity for) liberation. Overall, the bibliographies had wider, less-standard, and more diverse sources than we have seen in a typical research paper, from ephemera to obscure books to oral histories, although there were still some generic Internet news sources used. Most students ventured far in pursuing sources, wanting the correct, exact-fit document to ensure the integrity of their story; this was often a source of conversation in the class and a source of frustration when looking for an archive.

While we considered the quality of the storytelling in the papers to be a success, we were disconcerted that students did not access as much scholarship as we anticipated. Though not omitted, the peer-reviewed articles and books were underused and scholarly sources and perspectives were missing from some of the papers. Looking for primary sources in the archive was the dominant search, perhaps because finding archives initially proved elusive and took significant effort, leaving little time for more traditional library (in-house and online) research. But we also suspect that a richer understanding of the significance of scholarship was lacking in our students and would need to be addressed in the next iteration of the class. We also needed to pay more attention to the act of researching. We would revise the course syllabus in some basic ways. Merging some of the discussions, we'd free up room to discuss basic search skills. We would spend *more* time discussing the academic conversations and the importance of student engagement, both as active learners reading the works of others and through their own work as participants. The synthesis that some of the students provided of the literature in their research was still rather bare-bones, concentrating on synopsizing the literature that they did use, rather than truly assessing it in ways consistent with the ideals of critical information literacy. We would spend a class session going over the point-and-click of the database search and the evaluation of websites and establish from the where information is located and how it is organized. We would also evaluate and discuss schematically, in both a basic and thorough way, different kinds of information.

When we teach academic storytelling again, we will open the class with a question: "How do you research?" What we learn from our students and what they learn from us about our research habits will provide context and direction for our class as a body of researchers. Gretchen Kerr suggests that librarians, in an initial effort to assuage student trepidation about research, come forth with our own "feelings of discomfort" when researching something new and that "those feelings are just another part of the research process."[34] Such an admission on our part unsettles a little the hierarchy between teacher and student and, we would argue, promotes authenticity all around. Because this is a class about stories, it would have been a perfect opportunity to get stories like that going, talking about the ways we think of and deal with information—what our expectations and entitlements are in terms of access and how we seek it out. We plan to use *testimonios* and other forms of personal narrative in academic research to provide students with other examples of personally motivated research with similar narrative structures.

Our final assessment is that we accomplished much of what we set out to do but that the course must be viewed as a work in progress. Providing students with proper support (through persistent instruction) and motivation (through an engaging and persistent research project) is key in educating students in critical information literacy. Such activities are essential in transforming students from rather ineffective consumers of scholarship into effective students and even participants conducting authentic (and not merely imposed) research.

Finally, the long format course, with students motivated to conduct meaningful research and focused on engaging a wide range of information sources, is an opportunity to explore different approaches to research and to critical information literacy, an essential component of becoming not only a consumer but ultimately a producer of scholarship and knowledge. We understand that such skills, even when limited to only the abilities of critical information seeking and use, are developed over years of reading, analyzing, seeking, and responding and form the foundation of a scholarly mind. Aspiring to such goals, we feel our course can be useful, even a transformative exercise for those students initiating their careers as scholars, one brief but hopefully lasting invitation to students dedicated to contemplation and social change.

Notes

1.   Alison J. Head and Michael B. Eisenberg, *Lessons Learned: How College Students Seek Information in the Digital Age,* accessed August 18, 2014, http://projectinfolit.org/images/pdfs/pil_fall2009_finalv_yr1_12_2009v2.pdf.

2.   Karen Hovde, "Check the Citation: Library Instruction and Student Paper Bibliographies," *Research Strategies* 17, no. 1 (2000): 3–9, doi: 10.1016/S0734-3310(00)00019-7.

3.   Ibid; Beth A. Mohler, "Citation Analysis as an Assessment Tool," *Science and Technology Libraries* 25, no. 4 (2005): 57–64, doi: 10.1300/J122v25n04_05; Susan Hurst and Joseph Leonard, "Garbage in, Garbage out: The Effect of Library Instruction on the Quality of Students' Term Papers," *The Electronic Journal of Academic and Special Librarianship* 8, no. 1 (2007); Thomas A. Reinsfelder, "Citation Analysis as a Tool to Measure the Impact of Individual Research Consultations," *College and Research Libraries* 73, no. 3 (2012): 263–77; Stephanie Rosenblatt, "They Can Find It but They Don't Know What to Do with It: Describing the Use of Scholarly Literature by Undergraduate Students," *Journal of Information Literacy* 4, no. 2 (2010): 50–61, doi: 10.11645/4.2.1486.

4.   Ibid.

5.   Gail Pittam et al., "Student Beliefs and Attitudes," *Studies in Higher Education* 34, no. 2 (2009): 153.

6.   Lori Townsend, Korey Brunetti, and Amy R. Hofer, "Threshold Concepts and Information Literacy," *Portal: Libraries and the Academy* 11, no. 3 (2011): 853–69, doi: 10.1353/pla.2011.0030.

7.   Ibid., 855.

8.   Patrick J. Lewis, "Storytelling as Research/Research as Storytelling," *Qualitative Inquiry* 17, no. 6 (2011): 505, doi: 10.1177/1077800411409883; Adalberto Aguirre, "The Personal Narrative as Academic Storytelling: A Chicano's Search for Presence and Voice in Academia," *International Journal of Qualitative Studies in Education* 18, no. 2 (2005): 14–63.

9.   Lewis, "Storytelling as Research," 505–06.

10.   Ibid.

11.   Pittam et al., "Student Beliefs and Attitudes."

12.   Andrew D. Asher and Lynda Duke, "Information Literacy and First Year Students: Evaluating Knowledge, Needs, and Instruction" (presentation, National Resource Center Annual Conference on the First-Year Experience, Denver, CO, February 16, 2010), http://www.erial-project.org/wp-content/uploads/2010/03/FYE_Paper_Final.pdf.

13.   Petra Munro Hendry, "Narrative as Inquiry," *The Journal of Educational Research* 103 (2010): 72–80, doi: 10.1080/00220670903323354.

14.   Jean Anyon, "Social Class and the Hidden Curriculum of Work," *Journal of Education* 162, no. 1 (1980): 67–92.

15.   Patrick H. Hutton, *History as an Art of Memory* (Lebanon, NH: University Press of New England, 1993), 9.

16.   Donna Haraway, "Situated Knowledges: The Science Question in Feminism and the Privilege of Partial Perspective," *Feminist Studies* 14, no. 3 (1988): 575–99.

17.   Ibid., 582.

18.   Jeanne Pearlman, "Chronicles of Resistance: A Borderlands Testimonio" (PhD diss., University of Pittsburgh, 2010), iv, http://d-scholarship.pitt.edu/6740/1/PearlmanJeanne_Final_4-27-10.pdf.

19.   Richard Delgado, "Storytelling for Oppositionists and Others: A Plea for Narrative," *Michigan Law Review* 87, no. 8 (1989): 2411.

20.   Ibid., 2412, 2413.

21.   Aguirre, "The Personal Narrative as Academic Storytelling."

22.   Richard Delgado, *The Law Unbound: A Richard Delgado Reader* (Boulder, CO: Paradigm Publishers, 2007), 63.

23.   Kim Olson-Kopp and Bryan M. Kopp, "Depositories of Knowledge: Library Instruction and the Development of Critical Consciousness," in *Critical Library Instruction: Theories and Methods,* ed. Maria Accardi, Emily Drabinski, and Alana Kumbier (Duluth, MN: Library Juice Press, 2010), 55.

24.   Elisabeth Pankl and Jason Coleman, "'There's Nothing on My Topic!' Using the Theories of Oscar Wilde and Henry Giroux to Develop Critical Pedagogy for Library Instruction," in *Critical Library Instruction: Theories and Methods,* ed. Maria Accardi, Emily Drabinski, and Alana Kumbier (Duluth, MN: Library Juice Press, 2010), 3.

25.   Maria Accardi, Emily Drabinski, and Alana Kumbier, eds., *Critical Library Instruction: Theories and Methods* (Duluth, MN: Library Juice Press, 2010).

26.   Pittam et al., "Student Beliefs and Attitudes."

27.   Ibid., 153.

28.   Arlette Farge, *The Allure of the Archives* (New Haven, CT: Yale University Press, 2013), 7–8.

29.   Randall C. Jimerson, *Archives Power: Memory, Accountability, and Social Justice* (Chicago: Society of American Archivists, 2009), 280.

30.   Ibid.

31.   Ibid.

32.   Joshua Finnel and Jerome Marcantel, "Understanding Resistance: An Introduction to Anarchism," *College and Research Libraries News* 71, no. 3 (2010): 156–59.

33.   Haraway, "Situated Knowledges."

34.   Gretchen Keer, "Critical Pedagogy and Information Literacy in Community Colleges," in *Critical Library Instruction: Theories and Methods,* ed. Maria Accardi, Emily Drabinski, and Alana Kumbier (Duluth, MN: Library Juice Press, 2010), 157.

CHAPTER 18

Doing It Yourself:

Special Collections as a Springboard for Personal, Critical Approaches to Information

Lucy Mulroney and Patrick Williams

In academic libraries, we frequently encounter students whose research practices are informed exclusively by what is most familiar to them. Accustomed to writing essays using the resources that are easily available through the web and the library tools they know best, students often approach research with the assumption that they are looking for a solitary "right" answer and that the activity of research is disconnected from their own lived experiences. Moreover, their approaches demonstrate a lack of awareness of the impact their searching choices have on the sources they encounter. Such an approach results in gaps in students' understanding of the scope of available materials and methods, leaving them deprived of opportunities to develop effective skills for finding, evaluating, and using information in unfamiliar environments.

This chapter documents the collaboration between a curator of special collections, a subject specialist librarian, and a writing instructor to develop a different kind of instructional approach for undergraduate research and writing. We sought to use special collections as a springboard to create an environment in which students could investigate research questions that connect to their personal lives and interests; engage in various of modes of writing; conceive of the potential networks of production and circulation for their work; and identify the library as a locus for sustained, organic, social, and productive inquiry.

The opportunity for our collaboration came in the form of a new lower-division undergraduate pilot writing course entitled WRT 200: DIY Publishing. The instructor's aim for the course was to explore the do-it-yourself ethos through writing and publication in all of its forms, continuously asking two questions: "What is DIY?" and "What is publishing?" The instructor asked that the library be involved in the first unit of the course in order to provide students with a tangible, historical background in print communities to prepare them for digital work later in the semester. The subject specialist librarian and the curator of special collections designed a series of unique in-library sessions to meet this goal. At the culmination of the unit, each student self-published a "zine" on a topic of their choice, using the materials that they encountered in special collections as models for thinking about the modes available to them for writing styles, graphic layout, and format. Students then presented, read from, and distributed their zines in a public "Zine Fest," which was held in the library and open to the public.

Literature Review
Information Seeking and Traditional Research Assignments

Much of the research on the contemporary undergraduate research process deals with traditional research paper assignments, in which students are expected to write a paper that demonstrates deep knowledge of a current issue or topic, engages with the scholarly literature, and makes an argument. The challenges that this kind of assignment poses to library instruction is well documented in the literature. In 1996, Gloria Leckie noted that traditional research paper assignments "require a good understanding of the way that the scholarly literature works," something that instructors expect and students lack.[1] The core skill in constructing a good research paper is finding and critically examining primary and secondary sources. But as Lea Currie et al. observed, students can often discuss the criteria for evaluating credible sources but cannot necessarily apply them as their instructors expect.[2] Hannah Gascho Rempel, Stefanie Buck, and Anne-Marie Deitering have outlined similar problems with regard to students' ability to identify and choose scholarly sources, noting that the proliferation of disintermediated and federated search tools may not be helping students build an understanding about the links among information resources.[3]

While the scholarly literature points us to ways in which librarians can modify their instructional approaches to assist students in successfully completing traditional research assignments, another body of research also suggests alternative methodologies that might enable students to better understand the information landscape in personally meaningful and critical ways.

Divergent Interests, Epistemologies, and Attitudes

For most academic librarians, the claim that students in our information literacy and bibliographic instruction sessions come from a variety of backgrounds, interests, beliefs, and experiences—as well as the claim that these differences affect the way they approach the process of seeking information—are not shocking or controversial.[4] But it is equally important to remember that the same is true for librarians and instructors. The variety of interests, epistemologies, and attitudes that we all bring to the research process points to how important it is to cultivate a shared context in instructional situations.

It is also important to note that despite their enthusiasm and aptitude for electronic media, students often struggle to understand the differences among the formats and genres our electronic tools make available. Rempel, Buck, and Deitering caution that librarians and instructors must "recognize the role databases themselves play in shaping students' appreciation of source quality."[5] This is particularly problematic in that students often depend on the search interface itself to tell them what kind of source they have found.[6] At the same time, David Nicholas et al. caution against wrongly believing "that it is only students' information seeking that has been fundamentally shaped by huge digital choice, easy (24/7) access to scholarly material, disintermediation, and very powerful and influential search engines."[7] The research strategies of librarians and instructors have also been profoundly influenced by the digital. Thus, our ability to get students, librarians, and instructors on the same page, with common understandings of terms, expectations, and possibilities, may help us to guide students toward successful research outcomes and clearer and more accurate conceptions of how the information landscape is structured. It is our job to encourage the critical use of databases and help users understand the limitations, coverage, strengths, and weaknesses of the tools they employ. Archival finding aids can add crucial friction to this work, thanks to the ways in which they are situated in local collections, how they represent the interpretive and descriptive work of librarians, and how they challenge the implied completeness of the electronic tools students most frequently encounter.

Matching Tasks and Expectations through Collaboration

A deeper connection among librarians and instructors is frequently recommended in the literature as a means of strengthening the shared context in which undergraduate research takes place. Currie et al. suggests that "a closer collaboration between teaching faculty and librarians could result in greater student understanding of the academic research process and perhaps contribute to student success and retention."[8] Sonia Bodi recommends that librarians work with instructors to establish a set of guiding questions for an assignment that prompt students to be reflective and critical in their thinking about appropriate sources.[9] Susan Frey believes that librarians' unique awareness of student information-seeking behavior positions us to influence instruction in a manner that will lead students to "more realistic self-assessment of their research skills, and a deeper understanding of the complexity of the research process."[10] Additionally, Robert Detmering and Anne Marie Johnson see a role for librarians in advocating for students in pushing back on instructors "who may or may not understand the realities of the information landscape."[11]

Closer collaboration among librarians and instructors can increase the potential to align library instruction with course curriculum and to link course assignments to library collections. It can also make visible the connection among faculty and librarians as research partners, modeling the essential social elements of research to students. Van E. Hillard, writing of information in the literary research context, contends that librarians and instructors "can assist our students in assuming their social roles if we treat research not simply as contact with information, but as participation in the professional culture we call the library."[12] Jennifer Bonnet et al. in a recent article about an undergraduate apprentice researcher program, recommend that approaches to research instruction should emphasize the personal relationships and motivations upon which scholarly research is often built:

> Talking about research in terms of a scholarly network can help students understand the characteristics of scholarly literature: author credentials, bibliographies, and the contours of scholarly conversations. Librarians struggle to help students understand the context of scholarly discourse: Why is there such a thing as scholarly literature, and why is it important that students use it in their research? Students are often aware of terms like peer review, but when we ask them what it means, why scholarly communication matters in the academy, and why it is important to cite sources, the gaps become apparent.[13]

It is clear that students' understanding of the purpose of research can only come through students' reflection and engagement with the greater information landscape. Very often the keys to this knowledge lie implicit in the tools, systems, and structures around which libraries are organized.

Self-Efficacy and Information Seeking

For students to take ownership of the research process, they must feel empowered to do so. Many researchers view students' feelings of self-efficacy—the extent to which he or she expects to be successful in a task—as a powerful contributor to research performance. In *Social Learning Theory*, Albert Bandura presents self-efficacy as derived from performance accomplishments, vicarious experience, verbal persuasion, and emotional arousal.[14] These tenets of self-efficacy are often expressed in instructional sessions through activities involving hands-on practice, modeling, discussion, and active engagement. Updating the concept for the digital age, Matthew Eastin and Robert LaRose developed the construct of Internet self-efficacy to understand differences between novice users of the Internet and those who felt self-sufficient on the web.[15] In their study, the biggest factor affecting the user self-efficacy was prior experience, and they note that up to two years of experience may have been required before participants began to feel self-sufficient.

Bonnet et al. are critical that many of our traditional library instruction techniques, like "canned" searches, "do not always model the iterative process by which research is actually conducted; hence, students see neither the real frustrations and pitfalls of research, nor the real rewards." To combat this, they suggest models of student engagement establish "sophisticated, persistent, and hybridized modes of inquiry."[16] Adeyinka Tella's 2009 study found self-efficacy more strongly correlated with information seeking than with other variables (such as gender, enjoyment, and discipline) and offered the suggestion that students "also need to engage in vicarious experiences, such as observing their peers, that will further strengthen their information-seeking capability."[17] A preferred situation for engaging with students in the development of their information-seeking skills would accommodate critical engagement, reflective thinking, and the time and flexibility to make mistakes and learn from them.

We can draw from the literature that students struggle with traditional research assignments because they have not yet developed critical mastery in finding and evaluating sources, because these assignments have implicit expectations of standards of student preparedness that are inaccurate, and because the potential for collaboration among librarians and teaching faculty has not been maximized. What the research also exposes, however, is the need to identify opportunities to provide scaffolding for such assignments at earlier points in students' undergraduate careers. Librarians should seek out prospective instructional collaborations that strategically deliver—and better distribute over the course of the semester—the work that traditional "one-off" sessions must do. The collaboration described in this chapter reflects an attempt to do just this through the use of our university's special collections.

Utilizing Special Collections for Information Literacy Instruction

Traditionally, teaching students has not been at the heart of special collections. "Our first concern is—and has always been—supporting research and research-ers," writes Steven Escar Smith. "Acquiring, cataloging, and preserving material are indeed core activities and must remain so."[18] Thus the most common modes of instruction in special collections are the "show and tell" method and the be-dazzling, yet superficial, presentation of "university treasures." Smith contends that while we continue to pursue the core activity of collection development within special collections, "our commitment to teaching must also broaden and deepen."[19] Education and outreach not only bring people into our spaces, Smith suggests, but "they are also essential for justifying the expense" of building and maintaining special collections.[20]

In the six years since Smith's call for a deeper commitment to teaching was published, a number of studies and essays on instruction in special collections have appeared. One attribute shared by much of this literature is that instruction is often situated within the broader goal of "outreach" taken up by special collections departments. As a consequence, special collections instruction has been understood within the purview of other activities, such as exhibitions, tours, lectures, publications, and seminars, which function to publicize the collections and demonstrate their value and not to teach students *how* to use these collections in their own academic work. For example, the findings of the 2010 survey *Special Collections Engagement* found that "while the traditional methods of exhibits, events, and curricular instruction continue to be the emphasis of special collections' outreach programs, institutions are also embracing opportunities to be active physically beyond the borders of their campuses and virtually through blogs, social networking sites, and other Web 2.0 technologies."[21] Aligning instruction with publicity efforts such as social networking under the one heading of "outreach" may seem pragmatic, but there are unfortunate consequences to this way of framing special collections instruction. It suggests that instruction be understood and discussed as a supplemental and promotional activity rather than as an integral function and purpose of special collections.

In his article for *The Chronicle of Higher Education*, Scott Carson describes how a growing number of librarians "are trying to turn their library's rare holdings into promotional and marketing tools for their institutions, and for traditional research methods." Carson goes on to point out that "such collections may also help attract financial and political support, as libraries increasingly find themselves raising money to make up for budget shortfalls."[22] In this way, special collections instruction is tied up with efforts to demonstrate the value of the library within the shifting university landscape. For example, Matthew Reynolds's 2012 study, "Lay of the Land: The State of Bibliographic Instruction Efforts in ARL Special Collections Libraries," concludes that while bibliographic instruction in special collections is strong, "adequate staffing, properly sized and equipped instructional spaces, and effective communication with faculty are all areas in need of attention."[23]

In the past, questions about what is actually taught by special collections librarians and what are the methodologies they utilize have been relegated to the back burner if discussed at all. With the general increase in instruction within special collections, the profession's interest in instruction has recently started to change. For example, Anne Bahde has adopted innovative approaches for integrating special collections materials into campus instruction. Bahde contends, "Teaching faculty, administrative bodies, and even students are now beginning to understand what special collections librarians have always known: Working with authentic rare books, manuscripts, or archival documents produces a particularly stimulating educational environment, and physically handling original materials fuels lively discussion, generates uncommon ideas, and cultivates critical thinking."[24] Bianca Falbo suggests that "asking students to work with archival materials creates the opportunity for a more student-centered classroom."[25] Falbo explains, "Instead of telling students what I know about materials I have preselected, I focus on how and why they chose their particular documents and what makes these documents meaningful to them in the context of the particular course issue(s) we are investigating."[26] According to Magia G. Krauss, the primary sources held by special collections "offer contextual support for the concepts teachers describe, enhancing their meaning and grounding them in actual events and real people's lives. Using primary sources, students take multiple perspectives into consideration, making discernments about the authenticity and accuracy of the information presented to them."[27] In her most recent article, she explains that "the current generation of special collections librarians has had the privilege of 'growing up' in a transformative era for our profession, when access to materials has been raised to at least the same level of relevance in our eyes that preservation enjoyed in the past… we have been taught to get creative with the materials and to think imaginatively about research use beyond the obvious audiences. Who can use what for what purpose? When this question is inventively answered, our task then becomes to attract those people through the door of the department so we can get the 'stuff' into their hands."[28] Despite the complexity of interests and agendas that converge in special collections instruction, scholars seem to universally agree upon one point: Students benefit from direct engagement with special collections.[29]

The work of Bahde, Falbo, and Krauss all build upon Susan Allen's seminal 1999 study of the relationship between undergraduate education and special collections, which contended that "when students, alongside their teacher, gain access to original materials, then a conversation of mythical proportions becomes possible."[30] Allen continues, "Once object and student are brought together, they may be left somewhat on their own for the attraction to occur and the love affair to blossom."[31] While Allen contends that "a book or any other object in special collections is nothing until a human being interacts with it," she offers little substantive reflection on the modes of instruction that can take place within special collections. The role of the librarians is simply to be a "matchmaker." Allen explains that "most undergraduate students will still need to be wooed into special collections. However, once we have them there and the 'sacropower' of our wonderful collections begins to play on their 'minds and hearts,' then we matchmakers can sit back and relax. From that moment we can enjoy watching bibliophiles in the making."[32]

Here we reach a lacuna in the literature on special collections instruction. It is clear that instruction has a vital role in our ability to articulate the value and purpose of special collections to the mission of our home academic institutions and to the broader value of knowledge and critical thinking within our world. It is also clear that faculty and librarians share a belief in the educational value of having students directly engage with our collections. But how might special collections librarians engage with the current research on students' information-seeking practices and the development of self-efficacy in both traditional and digital search settings? Along these lines, Elizabeth Yakel has argued for the creation of a new paradigm for researcher education. Yakel writes, "Opening up discussion of what constitutes information literacy in archives is important for archivists and researchers in both the analog and digital realms… Identifying the knowledge and skills necessary for researchers to make effective use of the archives becomes more important as archival research—once done only in the reading room—can now be done, at least in part, in libraries, classrooms and at home."[33] Clearly it is not enough to "sit back and relax" once we we've successfully "wooed" the students into special collections.[34]

Our Case Study: Doing It Yourself

Based on the foci of our local special collections holdings, as well as shared interests and expertise, the subject specialist enlisted the curator of special collections to work with the instructor and his students. We saw this pilot course as an opportunity not only to put students in dialogue with the variety of DIY-inflected material available "hidden" in the library's special collections but also to invite them to interrogate the limits of the archive and the electronic tools we employ to represent it. Additionally, we were interested in having the students publicly showcase their work in the library and engage with a variety of library staff along the way, uncovering the different social and professional linkages among researchers and information professionals. We were also interested in introducing students to manuscript and rare book collections, exploring scarcity and serendipity in discovering personally meaningful items, and articulating the ways in which those materials were produced and distributed. And we wanted to accomplish this by working collaboratively with the instructor.

The Special Collections Research Center at Syracuse University is dedicated to preserving the history of radical movements in the United States and has significant collections documenting the artistic and literary expression of progressive ideologies and radical traditions in America. These include the papers of abolitionist Gerrit Smith, the records of the utopian Oneida Community, Communist Party General Secretary Earl Browder's papers, small press publications of the Black Arts Movement, and the records of the great publisher of the counterculture Grove Press. Thus our collections in radicalism and reform were easily linked to the concept of zines and DIY publishing in that zines are thought of as facilitating "a true culture of resistance ... a vernacular radicalism, an indigenous strain of utopian thought."[35]

At the culmination of the unit, each student created a zine on a topic of their choice, using the materials that they encountered in special collections as a springboard for considering their own work's writing style, audience, graphic layout, and format. Thus the project demanded that students engage in a deep personal and critical reflection on a chosen research subject and express that engagement through an alternative form of scholarly work: the publication of a zine—in multiple copies and with the intent to share. In the words of zine historian Stephen Duncombe,

> In an era marked by the rapid centralization of corporate media, zines are independent and localized, coming out of cities, suburbs and small towns across the USA, assembled on kitchen tables. They celebrate the everyperson in a world of celebrity, losers in a society that rewards the best and the brightest. Rejecting the corporate dream of an atomized population broken down into discrete and instrumental target markets, zine writers

form networks and forge communities around diverse identities and interests. Employed within the grim new economy of service, temporary, and "flexible" work, they redefine work, setting out their creative labor done on zines as a protest against the drudgery of working for another's profit. And defining themselves against a society predicated on consumption, zinesters privilege the ethic of DIY, do-it-yourself: Make your own culture and stop consuming that which is made for you.[36]

Taking the DIY ethos to heart, we tried to engage in a form of collaborative "creative labor" ourselves to facilitate a different kind of experience for everyone involved—the students, the instructor, the librarian, and the curator.

"Tactile Proof," the unit of the DIY publishing course in which we were involved, emphasized materiality and production techniques as a means of introducing students to the rich, generations-deep traditions of print culture that can be obscured by the web and electronic resources students most often use in their academic work. It was our intention to unveil opportunities and topics to which students previously had no access and to raise questions about students' perceptions of the "completeness" implied by the electronic resources with which they are most familiar. At the completion of the unit, we hoped students would be equipped to locate and investigate items of interest in the collections, describe the collections' limitations and constraints, make arguments about the significance of the item they had selected as their springboard, and produce work in response to those arguments.

The unit was comprised of two assignments that we explored and supported through with five distinct phases playing out over a five-week period. The first assignment was for each student to select, examine, research, and report on a single item chosen from special collections, investigating its origins, production, and circulation, positioning it within the DIY ethos. Students were then to produce multiple copies of a zine that, in some way, responded to the original item they chose. The first phase of the unit was an introductory visit to special collections led by the curator, followed by a workshop on search and discovery techniques from the subject specialist librarian the next week. A binding workshop and investigation of artists' books led by our library's expert in preservation and book arts coincided with the point in the unit where students began their zine production. Students presented their research on the special collections items they selected toward the end of the unit, and, finally, returned to the library to hold a public "Zine Fest" in which they shared and read from their zine projects at the unit's conclusion.

Session One: Introducing Students to Participatory Culture and Radical Collections

In the first library visit, the curator selected an array of rare and unique publications from the library's special collections—ranging from an abolitionist newspaper of the 1830s to mimeographed poetry journals from the 1960s—which students were encouraged to think of as a springboard from which they could contextualize their own publications. The students also learned to think about materiality as information—learning to handle, examine, and investigate the traces of a publication's production. Committed to diverging from the traditional modes of special collections instruction—the "one-off" presentation of highlights from the collections without engaging in dialogue with the students—the subject specialist librarian and the curator allowed students to handle and explore the materials themselves at their own pace while the instructor conveyed to them that special collections would be a recurring site for the class meetings and individual research.

The furniture in the seminar room was rearranged into four groupings of tables upon which materials were placed. The entire class was walked through the four groupings of materials as the curator demonstrated proper handling techniques; gave some contextual information on the items; and asked the students questions about what they noticed in terms of design, writing styles, format, and so on. Emphasis was placed on getting the students to critically compare these historical print forms with the contemporary media landscape familiar to them. After about 30 minutes of group discussion and modeling proper handling, the students were then let loose to move around the room individually and to handle, read, and discuss the materials amongst themselves. At the conclusion of the session, the instructor called on the students to point out things that had sparked their interest and share any ideas or questions that had been generated by the session.

The goals of this session were to get students to take ownership of the research process, to develop self-efficacy in the special collections environment, and to introduce them to our holdings that embody the DIY ethos that students would be using in their projects. To maximize the time spent on these goals, we deliberately did not instruct students in how to use the catalog and finding aids to locate materials during this session. After the session, the materials were placed on reserve in the special collections reading room and students were given instructions about how to return to special collections to view these and other items as the assignment required.

Session Two: Interrogating the Tools of Discovery

In the week following the visit to special collections, the subject specialist librarian met with students for a workshop on how to locate materials using our catalog, finding aids, and other tools. The goals of this session were to give students "permission" to seek items that were both personally interesting that reflected some aspect of the DIY ethos. The subject specialist emphasized the importance of spending time searching—viewing searching as invention—and advocated multiple visits to the reading room to contemplate multiple items. Along with the traditional approaches to demonstrating how one may search the catalog and finding aids, the subject specialist librarian emphasized what those tools *are* and *are intended to do,* positioning them in contrast to the full-text databases and web-based tools to which students were accustomed. The group engaged in active consideration of the descriptive and interpretive work of the catalogers and archivists who build and maintain these tools and examined the boundaries of how they represent items like those they had handled in the previous class session.

The subject specialist invited students to think of searching not as a means of locating an item but of exploring and understanding the finding aids, and in turn, the limitations and possibilities of the archive. He led the students through an activity in which they looked critically at how our systems of discovery represent and provide access to special collections materials. Students were asked the question "What are the ways the 'do-it-yourself' ethos is expressed in the language of the finding aids?" and brainstormed keywords reflective of the trappings of DIY publications as they might be described by the archivists and catalogers who maintain these tools. From there, students were expected to search the catalog and finding aids, request items of interest, and visit the reading room to view them. Additionally, the session briefly covered tools for locating additional scholarly and popular materials to help contextualize the people, events, and phenomena students uncovered in their searching. Students were encouraged to seek the assistance of the subject specialist librarian, the reading room staff, and the curator for assistance as they worked with their items and prepared their reports.

Session Three: Learning from Blank Books

The next phase in the process was intended to help students connect the special collections materials they were researching with their own production of publications, scheduled to begin the following week. We welcomed students back to the library, where they participated in a booklet binding workshop and brief survey of binding techniques led by our library's expert in preservation and book arts. This workshop focused on the techniques, processes, and demands involved in producing multiple copies of printed materials. The goal of this session was to acquaint students with book-production methodologies and to place their own zine production in conversation with the publications in the library's holdings. Each student constructed a simple booklet using a three-hole pamphlet stitch and handled artists' books from the collection showcasing different binding techniques. During the workshop students were asked to consider the intellectual and manual labor their zines might demand and were given tips for working with print materials.

Session Four: Becoming Experts and Sharing Knowledge

After two weeks of in-class, hands-on zine workshops led by the course instructor, students returned to the library during the final week of the unit to present their research on their chosen item in special collections. The instructor asked students to make arguments in their research reports based on the following prompt:

> As you investigate its history, you might consider the items'—
>
> - Origin: Who produced it? Why? How did it come to exist? To what degree was the idea original? Challenging? Political?
> - Production: How was it made? What materials and why? Who was involved at each step? Why this format? What were the obstacles?
> - Circulation: How did it move from production to consumption? Was it sold? Traded? Borrowed? Mailed? Smuggled?

- Conflicts: How was the publication challenged? From the inside and the outside?
- Audience: Who read or experienced it and why? What communities did it shape or divide?
- Significance: What is the historical relevance of this item? Why does SU house it? Who cares about it and why?[37]

The results were surprising and instructive. Not only did the students locate materials in the special collections that the subject librarian and the curator were not aware of and which had rarely, if ever, been accessed by researchers before, but the students' selections also offered productive "misreadings" of special collections materials. For example, one student, who had previously been in the armed forces, selected the underground punk magazine *Search and Destroy*, not because of any personal interest in the subject headings under which the magazine is catalogued: "Punk rock music—Periodicals" and "New wave music—Periodicals." He selected the magazine because of the meaning of "search and destroy" as a military strategy that connected with his particular life experiences. Another student selected a small handmade booklet containing handwritten poems as his example of DIY publishing, despite the fact that the book was not actually published. His selection of it, therefore, points to the seeming "publicness" of library materials to researchers accessing them through public media, like online finding aids, regardless of whether the items are actually published. The student presentations suggest that we should think of our collection materials not "only from the standpoint of subject related evidence or documentation," as Peter Carini has argued, but "as materials that lend themselves to the teaching of research skills."[38]

Session Five: Putting Print Communities on Public Display

On the final day of the unit, students gathered in the library to host a "Zine Fest," which they planned and promoted on campus and via social media. Members of the public, undergraduate and graduate students, faculty, and library staff were welcomed to the event, which featured a station for each student to display copies of his or her zine, with many available for sale or trade. Students were available to answer questions about their zines and engage with the audience, and several students read publicly from their written work. Students' zines were wide-ranging in their coverage and approach, but some aspect of each student's zine—its form, its content, its aesthetic considerations, its method of production, its intended audience—recalled or responded to the special collections item he or she chose to research the previous week. Additionally, many zines also incorporated techniques students witnessed and engaged with during the artists' books and pamphlet binding workshop. Examples include a mimeograph-inspired pamphlet of printed appropriations of well-known Internet memes rewritten to reflect student life on our campus, a mash-up between a historical family scrapbook and late night text messages sent by fraternity brothers, a comic/fanzine placing science fiction characters from different generations in dialogue, and a satirical remix of an early 19th-century newspaper.

Discussion

This collaboration was especially fruitful and satisfying for us as information professionals in how it presented the library as a site of sustained, social, organic, and productive inquiry that would not be possible anywhere else on campus. Additionally, bringing students into the library on so many occasions exposed them to the functional diversity of the library's staff, highlighting the work of curators, collections development librarians, reference librarians, preservation and conservation librarians, catalogers, archivists, and more. Most exciting, however, was seeing the students become truly, independently interested. We saw them equip themselves to discover special collections materials that addressed their own interests and eventually take ownership of the library as a space where they could think, explore, create, and present their work.

We know that undergraduate students often find it difficult to think about the sources they are using in context—to acknowledge that this information exists within and reveals networks of connections among people, publications, ideas, and time periods. It is clear that students can come to assignments with wildly varying levels of epistemological sophistication, experience, and comfort with regard to information, and we view the introduction of special collections materials as an opportunity to reshape and renegotiate, as a group, student beliefs about the information landscape. Moreover, students often struggle with subtle differences among genres and formats that are sometimes muted when information is accessed through only electronic means. The manner in which deep engagement with local archives and print materials uncovers the boundaries, limits, and interpretations buried within our search interfaces provides students the opportunity to think critically and reflectively about these tools.

This collaboration took place during the pilot stage of this new course, and the writing program has chosen to repeat the class in the coming academic year, complete with our library-based project. The instructor observed that when students engaged in the zine assignment, "they feel a certain ownership and pride that simply doesn't occur with the traditional term paper or even their own blogs."[39] That this ownership and pride came about through an assignment that could not have been completed without deep connection with our library collections and with our librarians underscores criticisms of the "one-off" intervention of traditional library instruction and special collections visits. We found the same enthusiasm in our own experience—the curator and subject specialist librarian found this project to be much more satisfying than the typical class visit thanks to the sustained interaction and the acknowledgment that we were helping students to develop skills and concepts with benefits beyond merely completing another assignment.

We have come to view undergraduate research and instruction in special collections as an integral part of information literacy in that it enables students to consider the tactile connections, contrasts, and surprises among the diverse array of information available to them. We believe that the defamiliarization with what can be a "source" at the heart of this assignment allowed us to step back and examine students' (and our own) assumptions about how we should think about and search for information. Furthermore, engagement with rare printed materials and the ways in which they are represented and accessed complicates the traditional process of finding sources. Searching, in this regard, is a means of finding individual sources, a way to acquaint oneself with the limitations and affordances of systems we use and a means of considering what may be hidden or what is not there at all. We believe this encourages critical, transferable approaches to using all electronic sources in that it demonstrates that completeness can be an illusion and draws attention to the shared contexts of materials, not just the strings of words they happen to contain.

We spent considerably more time on this collaboration than we do with most classes, mostly due to our excitement at the chance to have such deep curricular involvement and because the subject matter of the course was of shared interest. We must admit that this approach is not necessarily scalable in the sense that a prepackaged drop-in session would be, but we feel that is was the slower pace, not necessarily the amount of time spent on this collaboration, that made it satisfying and effective. It is the sustained class activity within the library that we feel was the most important part of our approach, and we believe there are many ways to encourage and coordinate such activity. Because students returned to the library not only to conduct their research but also to share and present their ideas and work, we feel that their anxiety and tendency to rely on sheer convenience in finding sources was diminished.

In this process, as a librarian and a curator, our personal convictions and scholarly interpretations of the materials informed our obligation to help make the archive more than a repository but an active public space of debate and dissent that openly and critically includes our position as well as the position of others. Through the approach described in this chapter, we were able to shift student attention and raise questions about the origins, production, audiences, and purposes of rare materials in a way that extends beyond the unit assignments. In this way, the archive can become a site where histories can be continually engaged, reinterpreted, debated, and revisited. If we can create meaningful experiences for students which present our libraries as environments dedicated to these processes, students will be much better equipped to make sophisticated choices about the information they use in their work, academic and otherwise.

Notes

1.   Gloria J. Leckie, "Desperately Seeking Citations: Uncovering Faculty Assumptions about the Undergraduate Research Process," *The Journal of Academic Librarianship* 22, no. 3 (1996): 201–08. Ethelene Whitmire found in 2004 that students were more comfortable with straightforward web resources and regularly confused modes of searching among different tools (i.e., OPAC and journal indexes), and they were also unable to make sound quality judgments about the sources they chose: "The Relationship between Undergraduates' Epistemological Beliefs, Reflective Judgment, and Their Information-Seeking Behavior," *Information Processing and Management* 40, no. 1 (2004): 97–111.

2.   Lea Currie et al., "Undergraduate Search Strategies and Evaluation Criteria: Searching for Credible Sources," *New Library World* 111, no. 3-4 (2010): 113–24.

3.   Hannah Gascho Rempel, Stefanie Buck, and Anne-Marie Deitering, "Examining Student Research Choices and Processes in a Disintermediated Searching Environment," *Portal: Libraries and the Academy* 13, no. 4 (2013): 363–84.

4.   Daqing He et al., found that undergraduate students made choices among a variety of different tools in academic tasks based on their own personal expectations and past experiences: "Undergraduate Students' Interaction with Online Information Resources in Their Academic Tasks: A Comparative Study," *Aslib Proceedings* 64, no. 6 (2012): 615–40. These findings are echoed by Lynn Connaway, Timothy J. Dickey, and Marie L. Radford's article citing

convenience, which is influenced by both familiarity and time available, as a critical factor in information seeking, especially among the millennials who make up the bulk of the populations completing the traditional research assignments in academic libraries: "'If It Is Too Inconvenient, I'm Not Going After It:' Convenience as a Critical Factor in Information-Seeking Behaviors," *Library and Information Science Research* 33, no. 3 (2011): 179–90. Nigel Ford, David Miller, and Nicola Moss do more to uncover the effects of individual differences on students' information seeking, identifying cognitive style, gender, age, study approach, and self-efficacy as contributing factors: "The Role of Individual Differences in Internet Searching: An Empirical Study," *Journal of the American Society for Information Science and Technology* 52, no. 12 (2001): 1049–66. Ethelene Whitmire's work linking epistemological beliefs to Carol Kuhlthau's information seeking process (ISP) found that student performance at different stages of the ISP was affected by the sophistication of the students' epistemological beliefs: "Epistemological Beliefs and the Information-Seeking Behavior of Undergraduates," *Library and Information Science Research* 25, no. 2 (2003): 127–142. Jannica Heinström recently found that personality type plays a factor in approaches to information seeking and that under stressful or uncomfortable circumstances, students' approaches may shift: "Fast Surfing, Broad Scanning, and Deep Diving: The Influence of Personality and Study Approach on Students' Information-Seeking Behavior," *Journal of Documentation* 61, no. 2 (2005): 228–47.

5.   Rempel, Buck, and Deitering, "Examining Student Research Choices and Processes," 381. This runs counter to Connaway, Dickey, and Radford's suggestion that, in the interest of convenience and saving users' time, libraries should concentrate on providing an experience "more like that available on the web:" "'If It Is Too Inconvenient, I'm Not Going After It,'" 187.

6.   Joanne Archer, Ann M. Hanlon, and Jennie A. Levine, "Investigating Primary Source Literacy," *The Journal of Academic Librarianship* 35, no. 5 (2009): 410–20.

7.   David Nicholas et al., "Student Digital Information-Seeking Behaviour in Context," *Journal of Documentation* 65, no. 1 (2009): 129.

8.   Currie et al., "Undergraduate Search Strategies and Evaluation Criteria," 123.

9.   Sonia Bodi, "How Do We Bridge the Gap between What We Teach and What They Do? Some Thoughts on the Place of Questions in the Process of Research," *The Journal of Academic Librarianship* 28, no. 3 (2002): 109–14.

10.   Susan M. Frey, "Facilitating Critical Thinking and Self-Reflection: Instructional Strategies for Strengthening Students' Online Research Skills," *Indiana Libraries* 30, no. 1 (2011): 49–56.

11.   Robert Detmering and Anna Marie Johnson, "'Research Papers Have Always Seemed Very Daunting:' Information *Literacy Narratives and the Student Research Experience," Portal: Libraries and the Academy* 12, no. 1 (2012): 14.

12.   Van E. Hillard, "Information Literacy as Situated Literacy," in *Teaching Literary Research: Challenges in a Changing Environment,* ed. Kathleen A. Johnson and Steve R. Harris (Chicago: Association of College and Research Libraries, 2009), 11–22.

13.   Jennifer L. Bonnet et al., "The Apprentice Researcher: Using Undergraduate Researchers' Personal Essays to Shape Instruction and Services," *Portal: Libraries and the Academy* 13, no. 1 (2013): 37–59.

14.   Albert Bandura, *Social Learning Theory (Englewood Cliffs, NJ: Prentice Hall, 1977).*

15.   Matthew S. Eastin and Robert LaRose, "Internet Self-Efficacy and the Psychology of the Digital Divide," *Journal of Computer-Mediated Communication* 6, no. 1 (2000): 0.

16.   Bonnet et al., "The Apprentice Researcher," 49.

17.   Adeyinka Tella, "Correlates of Undergraduates' Information-Seeking Behavior," *College and Undergraduate Libraries* 16, no. 1 (2009): 14.

18. Steven Escar Smith, "From 'Treasure Room' to 'School Room:' Special Collections and Education," *RBM: A Journal of Rare Books, Manuscripts, and Cultural Heritage* 7, no. 1 (Spring 2006): 33.

19. Ibid.

20. Ibid., 32

21. Adam Berenbak et al., *Special Collections Engagement* (Washington, DC: Association of Research Libraries, 2010), 16.

22. Scott Carlson, "Special Effects," *The Chronicle of Higher Education*, June 17, 2005, http://chronicle.com/article/Special-Effects/18436.

23. Matthew C. Reynolds, "Lay of the Land: The State of Bibliographic Instruction Efforts in ARL Special Collections Libraries," *RBM: A Journal of Rare Books, Manuscripts, and Cultural Heritage* 13, no. 1 (2012): 25.

24. Anne Bahde, "Taking the Show on the Road: Special Collection Instruction in the Campus Collection," *RBM: A Journal of Rare Books, Manuscripts, and Cultural Heritage* 12, no. 2 (2011): 75.

25. Bianca Falbo, "Teaching from the Archives," *RBM: A Journal of Rare Books, Manuscripts, and Cultural Heritage* 1, no. 1 (2000): 34.

26. Ibid.

27. Magia G. Krause, "'It Makes History Alive for Them:' The Role of Archivists and Special Collections Librarians in Instructing Undergraduates," *The Journal of Academic Librarianship* 36, no. 5 (2010): 401.

28. Bahde, "Taking the Show on the Road," 87.

29. There are additional factors that complicate the picture. For example, scholars and librarians are careful to point out the increased security and safety risks for collection materials that accompany increased outreach and instruction (see Bahde; Reynolds; and Allen). Another factor is the debate around faculty status for librarians. As Reynolds writes, "a lack of tenure status may also suggest a reason that many academic faculty members are not more involved in bringing students into the libraries for instruction: They may see librarians as information providers rather than teaching professionals" (Reynolds, "Lay of the Land," 35).

30. Susan M. Allen, "Rare Books and the College Library: Current Practices in Marrying Undergraduates to Special Collections," *Rare Books and Manuscripts Librarianship* 13, no. 2 (1999): 110–19.

31. Ibid., 110.

32. Ibid., 118.

33. Elizabeth Yakel, "Information Literacy for Primary Sources: Creating a New Paradigm for Archival Researcher Education," *OCLC Systems and Services: International Digital Library Perspectives* 20, no. 2 (2004): 63.

34. Ibid.

35. Stephen Duncombe, *Notes from Underground: Zines and the Politics of Alternative Culture* (New York: Verso, 1997), 3.

36. Ibid., 2.

37. Jason Luther, "Unit 1: Tactile Proof," WRT 200: D.I.Y. Publishing, accessed August 19, 2014, http://courses.jasonluther.net/diy/?page_id=7.

38. Peter Carini, "Archivists as Educators: Integrating Primary Sources into the Curriculum," *Journal of Archival Organization* 7, no. 1-2 (2009): 45.

39. Jason Luther, "Using Zines in the Classroom," *HASTAC: Jason Luther's Blog (blog)*, January 28, 2014, http://www.hastac.org/blogs/taxomania/2014/01/28/using-zines-classroom.

CHAPTER 19

Witnessing the World:
Journalism, Skepticism, and Information Literacy

Laura Saunders

Given the vital role mass media in disseminating timely information, offering checks on governmental abuse, and promoting an informed citizenry capable of exercising their rights in a participatory democracy, it is critical that college students learn about these outlets so that they can become effective consumers of news information. But to what extent are our students being taught how to access, evaluate, and understand this kind of information? Do faculty instructors and librarians address mass media sources or media literacy concepts in their teaching? Little research exists addressing these questions, but discussions within the literature of higher education and library science suggests that media literacy is not receiving widespread or consistent attention.

Hans C. Schmidt found that, although most faculty members agreed media literacy is important for their students, most did not address it within their own courses.[1] After reviewing two national reports on the state of media literacy in higher education, Paul Mihalidis concludes that there is a lack of awareness and understanding surrounding media literacy and that since the term was introduced, the US has lagged behind other countries in implementing a curriculum that addresses it.[2] Mihalidis finds "vague and somewhat disparate understandings of what media literacy education is and how it functions in a university classroom" and suggests that the adoption of media literacy into the curriculum has been "constrained."[3] Likewise, librarians appear to be less likely to address news outlets than other, more scholarly sources in their library instruction sessions. In a recent survey, 39.1 percent of librarians indicate that they address non peer-reviewed sources like newspapers in their sessions. However, when asked to rate the amount of time devoted to various information literacy topics, the plurality of respondents (14.6 percent) indicated that they spend the least time on that topic and 13.5 percent stated they do not cover the topic at all.[4]

The Case for Media Literacy

Media permeates every aspect of our lives, and as such, people need to develop the skills and competencies to interact with the information they receive from these many outlets on a continuous basis. On a broad level, mass media plays an important role in participatory government, based on the philosophy that citizens need to be well informed in order to form opinions, make decisions, and otherwise fully participate in their own government. By investigating and reporting on political and government activities in an objective manner, and thereby providing citizens with information and a forum for public discourse on policy issues, journalism and news reporting are central to the functioning of a democracy.[5] Sometimes referred to as the fourth estate, mass media and journalism are seen as a potential check on the excesses or abuse of government by investigating and reporting on those excesses and abuses.[6]

However, media consumers need to be critically evaluative of information and its sources to determine what is trustworthy and what, ultimately, to believe. Mass media outlets tend to focus on current events and report on stories as they unfold. They lack the time and distance to offer a "long view" of events, and when stories are being covered in the moment, pieces of information may get reported that will later be shown to be inaccurate. The Newtown shootings at the Sandy Hook Elementary School in 2012 offer a grim example of just such misinformation, including reports that the shooter's mother was a teacher and was one of the victims at the school.[7]

While such mistakes are usually corrected, there is a difference between correcting text and correcting the information that someone has already absorbed. Indeed, misinformation and inaccurate reporting can have lasting and detrimental effects on the public. For instance, John M. Budd, Zach C. Coble, and Katherine M. Anderson found that researchers continue to cite scientific and medical journal articles even after they have been retracted, thereby perpetuating the incorrect information.[8] Such practices can contribute to the continued influence effect, whereby people continue to believe the information they received first, even after they have been presented with the corrected version.[9] One method for combating the effects of misinformation is to teach people to evaluate the information and its sources as they receive it, in other words to be skeptical of information, which can reduce people's susceptibility to misinformation and lead to more accurate understandings.[10]

Media literacy, a set of competencies related to but distinct from information literacy, can nurture these skills in students and make them less vulnerable to media bias.[11] The Partnership for 21st Century Skills identifies media literacy as an essential competency for students to master.[12] Sonia Livingstone argues its importance, suggesting "the promise of media literacy, surely, is it can form part of a strategy to reposition the media user—from passive to active, from recipient to participant, from consumer to citizen."[13] Similarly, Mary Lou Galician contends that Americans are largely illiterate with regard to media and strongly asserts "it is high time that we make the research, teaching, and practice of *media literacy as a lifelong endeavor* a personal and national priority in our mediated global village."[14] The rest of this chapter offers a brief overview of the possible place of news sources and media literacy in the curriculum, along with suggestions for librarians and faculty to integrate media literacy into their instruction.

Defining Media Literacy

Before faculty and library instructors can move forward to integrate media literacy into their teaching, they need to agree on a common definition and learning goals on which to focus. The Partnership for 21st Century Skills defines media literacy as students

- understand[ing] both how and why media messages are constructed and for what purposes;
- examin[ing] how individuals interpret messages differently, how

values and points of view are included or excluded, and how media can influence beliefs and behaviors; [and]

- apply[ing] a fundamental understanding of the ethical/legal issues surrounding the access and use of media.[15]

The Kaiser Family Foundation draws on the National Leadership Conference on Media Literacy to define the concept as "the ability to access, analyze, evaluate, and produce communication in a variety of forms."[16] Finally, Livingstone lays out a comprehensive definition centered on the core areas of access, analysis, evaluation, and content creation.[17] Librarians will readily see the overlap with the definition of information literacy created by the Association of College and Research Libraries (ACRL), which similarly focuses on issues of location, access, and evaluation of information.[18]

Areas of Knowledge and Competence

In addition to defining the concepts, instructors need to determine learning outcomes, or what they want students to know, understand, and be able to do as a result of their interaction with mass media outlets. While the specific outcomes will vary depending upon the particular courses, departments, and individual instructors, there are certain areas that are likely to be common across different areas. As noted above, evaluation of media information and sources is crucial, and indeed a recent survey of faculty from several different disciplines indicates that they are concerned with students' ability to uncover bias and evaluate the credibility and authority of information. Further, many faculty members identified the teaching of evaluation of information as a role librarians could play, using their expertise to help students sift through results and dig deeper into source material.[19] One interviewee described this process as turning students into skeptics.

Production Cycle

In order to evaluate media outlets, students should be familiar with the publication and information life cycles of the different news sources and formats. For instance, they should understand the difference between a news stories that are fact-checked, produced, and disseminated through a journalistic process as opposed to opinion pieces, commentary, or content created in social media that often bypasses these processes. Students should question how each type of production or creation cycle affects the story. On the one hand, produced news pieces have been through an editorial process that is meant to ensure a certain level of quality and accuracy. On the other hand, the production cycle might slow down reporting in some cases, and by necessity media outlets have to make choices about what stories to report, meaning some stories go untold. Similarly, students must learn the difference between current news that is reported as it unfolds as opposed to investigative journalism that might be built on weeks or even years of research and the processes that support each. Even the word "research" as it is applied to journalism and mass media is problematic as it differs from scientific research. Students must understand what journalistic research is; what it entails; and how to assess whether a journalist has been thorough, unbiased, and ethical in his or her research.

Authority

Related to how a journalist researches and builds a story is the question of authority. Traditional approaches to evaluating authority tend to focus on author credentials. Instructors often tell students to look for signs of authority such as the degrees that the writer holds, former publications, or other outward signs of expertise within the field. However, when the writer is a journalist or staff writer, whose academic training might not reflect the content area on which they are reporting, how should a student proceed? Often, once students learn about peer review and the basics of authority evaluation, they might be likely to simply exclude news media sources from their searches as untrustworthy, and indeed, they are often at least subtly encouraged in this practice by librarians who focus almost exclusively on peer-reviewed sources when teaching searching. Amy K. Hofer, Lori Townsend, and Korey Brunetti suggest teaching authority as something that is both constructed and contextual.[20] In other words, what constitutes authority can vary based on format, sources, research processes, and so on. Although this approach is more complex, it allows students to engage with a wider range of resources and move beyond the "checklist" approach to assessing authority.

Bias

Bias is always a concern when evaluating information and sources, and the intricacies of authority and production in news media can make it especially difficult to assess. One issue that is of concern to many news consumers is the issue of media ownership and consolidation. Most of the mainstream media outlets are for-profit entities often dependent on advertising dollars and therefore might be pressured by the interests and opinions of their owners and advertisers. Students need to be aware that when editors make decisions as to what is "newsworthy," or what to include and exclude in terms of news stories, as well as how to report those stories, their decisions can be influenced by their larger organization. Another issue is the consumer-driven nature of many media outlets. In an effort to keep listeners and readers, some outlets might pander to their audience and provide them with stories or slants that support their particular worldview.[21] Various news outlets accuse each other of having biases, and many conservatives broadly paint the media as having a liberal bias overall. News consumers must question the purpose, sources, and audience of the story to determine whether bias exists.

Visual Content

Unlike scholarly journal articles, news sources and mass media information often contains a strong visual element such as photographs, maps, or videos. Decoding visual information requires a different set of skills from those needed to evaluate textual information. In fact, some proponents argue that visual literacy comprises yet another, separate literacy.[22] ACRL defines visual literacy as the ability to "understand and analyze the contextual, cultural, ethical, aesthetic, intellectual, and technical components involved in the production and use of visual materials."[23] These competencies include the ability to understand the physical and content aspects of images and the elements of production and to distinguish between originals and reproductions. Like textual information, visual images are meant to convey meaning and may be manipulated, distorted, or misrepresented. Students and information consumers need to develop the specific skills necessary to make sense of, interpret, and evaluate such imagery.

Mass Media and the Curriculum: Approaches and Ideas

There are many ways that news sources can be integrated into courses and curricula for a rich learning experience. To begin with, it is worth considering that news stories can be used as both primary and secondary sources, depending on the context. For instance, interviewees in the study of faculty perspectives on information literacy offered examples of news stories in both roles. A biology professor described using media outlets, such as the BBC or CNN, to introduce certain stories to her classes, and then having them discuss media coverage of scientific stories and what is represented well and what is not. Another interviewee asserted that anthropologists use newspapers to keep current, and this instructor likes to have students read current news articles with the perspective of an anthropologist to discern what the stories reveal about the society in which they are printed. This anthropological use of newspapers begins to move from news as a secondary source to news as a primary source. Other disciplines went even further with the concept. A political science professor discussed having students use historical newspapers as primary sources to understand the thoughts, opinions, and reactions of people at the time.[24] In each case, whether as a primary or a secondary source, news stories are providing students and media consumers with a particular lens onto the world. With practice the students can begin to understand how that lens was constructed and by whom and how the lens then colors the particular picture of the world it is representing. Following are some specific ideas for lessons on news media.

Content Analysis

In January 2013, the author worked with faculty members from computer science and communications in an interdisciplinary team involved in teaching an undergraduate course on analyzing news media. The course was an experiential learning seminar, in which students were faced with the current issues and challenges surrounding mass media, including consolidation, bias, and audience-driven programming, and tasked with developing solutions to these problems. Before students could delve into the issues, it was necessary for them to understand how news media outlets operate and to develop and practice their media literacy skills. The faculty members chose content analysis as a methodology for examining and evaluating news. More than just a close reading, content analysis is a rigorous and systematic examination of resources, including its origins, authors, and intentions.[25] Practitioners must consider and question each aspect of the resource and look for repetition or patterns across resources. In addition to quantitative counts of words or images, researchers might use contextual clues to make qualitative judgments about aspects like tone, emphasis, and attitude. For instance, researchers might try trying to gauge whether the source has a bias toward immigration reform by the use of terms such as "illegal immigrant" versus "illegal alien" versus "undocumented worker." They could look for other contextual clues as well, such as whether accompanying pictures and captions focus on, for instance, groups of families or fences and barbed wire. Readers could also examine the amount of text devoted to numbers of undocumented workers and the cost of illegal immigration compared to the amount of text focused on the effect on families or success stories.

In the above course, students were introduced to the methodology through an in-class demonstration followed by a series of individual and group activities. To begin with, the instructors displayed a series of publicly available images from magazine covers to demonstrate how content analysis could be used to assess the portrayal of women in men's magazines. In this example, the instructors focused on visual analysis, using cover photos from *Esquire* magazine. Photos were displayed on-screen, and the class worked together to analyze aspects of the image, including facial expression, type of clothing (or lack thereof), setting, props, and so on to set up a codebook. (A sample of the codebook is included in Appendix 19A.) Students noted patterns such as the number of models wearing underwear or bikinis as opposed to those wearing dresses or business attire; the number of models smiling, pouting, having parted lips, or biting something; and the number of models standing, sitting, squatting, or lying down with descriptions on how their arms were positioned. Finally, the class looked at the completed codebook and discussed what inferences or conclusions might be drawn from the data.

Students were then assigned a series of images to code on their own using the existing codebook. During the next class session, it was revealed that groups of students had been assigned the same set of images. Students then met with their groups where they compared their coding and discussed discrepancies. Finally, students were placed into different groups and given several weeks to locate news stories on a specific topic, develop a codebook, and code the stories. By the end of these activities, students demonstrated increased ability and confidence in analyzing news stories and images in a critically evaluative manner.

Checklists and SMELL Tests

As described above, content analysis is an intensive process and could take more than a one-shot session to carry out. However, other frameworks exist for teaching critical evaluation of information and sources that lend themselves to one-shot sessions. For instance, the Kaiser Family Foundation offers a set of generic questions that could be applied to nearly any news information source or format:

- Who created this message and why are they sending it? Who owns and profits from it?
- What techniques are used to attract and hold attention?
- What lifestyles, values, and points of view are represented in this message?
- What is omitted from this message? Why is it left out?
- How might different people interpret this message?[26]

John McManus, a journalist, professor, and founder of a consumer report for news sources in California, developed what he refers to as the SMELL test. Like the questions from the Kaiser Foundation, this framework offers a checklist of points and questions packaged around a conveniently memorable acronym:

S stands for Source: Who is providing the information?

M is for Motivation: Why are they telling me this?

E represents Evidence: What evidence is provided for generalizations?

L is for Logic: Do the facts logically compel the conclusions?

L is for Left Out: What's missing that might change our interpretation of the information?[27]

Even in a one-shot session, instructors could introduce these questions and have students apply them to various news stories in class then encourage them to return to those questions each time they encounter new stories or information. (Appendix 19B offers some sample activities for longer sessions.)

Conclusion: A Call to Action

For many librarians and faculty the case for media literacy might seem obvious. The challenge is to underscore that students are not learning these skills simply to meet the demands of an assignment or a course. Rather, critical consumption of information is an essential skill for success beyond school, in both their personal and professional lives. By teaching them information and media literacy skills, we are giving them the necessary tools to succeed in an information economy. By teaching them to be critical and even skeptical of the information they receive, we are arming students to protect themselves against the continued influence effect and to base their opinions, beliefs, and decisions on reliable information.

Further, however, we are sensitizing students to the broader social justice implications of information access and information literacy in society. James H. Kuklinksi et al. contend that factual information is the currency of a democracy, and citizens must have access to credible and authoritative information to support their decisions.[28] Similarly, the American Library Association asserts that information literacy is "central to the practice of democracy" and suggests that the ability to access, evaluate, and interpret information can allow people to improve socioeconomic imbalances, sentiments that have been echoed more recently in the Alexandria Proclamation, which asserts information literacy is a basic human right.[29] Through information literacy education, we can alert students to inequities in access to and understanding of information as well as the detrimental effects that such inequities can have in terms of depriving people of the ability to make sound decisions. Once students have gained this understanding, they might not only guard against their own vulnerability to misinformation and propaganda but work to facilitate access and understanding for others. As Heidi L.M. Jacobs reminds us, "The work we do is part of a broader educative project that works to empower individuals both locally and globally."[30]

We are bombarded with media stories every day, whether through more traditional news sources or through newer media. As pressure mounts for outlets to get news out fast, fewer stories are subjected to the rigorous fact-checking that might have been assumed at one time. At the same time, because of the quick turnaround on news stories, they are often the first contact that students and the general public have with new information. If students are not given the tools to critically evaluate the news they receive, they are at greater risk of basing decisions and beliefs on inaccurate information and of falling prey to the continued influence effect. While most educators seem to acknowledge the importance of media literacy, it is unclear the extent to which it is being addressed in any systematic way within higher education curricula. By ignoring or superficially covering news media in library instruction sessions and in the larger curriculum, we are failing to acknowledge the prevalence and influence of these outlets, and we are doing our students a disservice. Rather, we should find ways to incorporate news media as part of a larger framework of information literacy. As information specialists, librarians may be in a unique role to promote the integration of media literacy on their campuses by emphasizing the critical role it plays not only in students' educational success but to their personal and professional success beyond their education.

Appendix 19A: Sample of Codebook for *Esquire* Magazine Covers

Image Number		Image 1	Image 2
Gender	Male		
	Female	X	X
Clothing	Sports attire		
	Swimwear	X	
	Suit/Business Attire		
	Underwear		X
	Naked/Covered by towel/sheet/etc		
Facial Expression	Smiling	X	X
	Lips parted		
	Licking lips		
	Laughing		
	Eating/licking food		

Appendix 19B: Sample Media Literacy Activities

If instructors have more time, they might consider building sessions or assignments around the following ideas:

- Have students review a single news story from multiple outlets, including some considered liberal and conservative as well as outlets from different geographic regions inside and outside the US. In addition to analyzing the internal content of an individual story, students can look for patterns and differences across the sources and determine whether the portrayal of the story is consistent, and if not, whether they can determine what factors might be influencing the portrayal. For instance, students could review different coverage of the Trayvon Martin story, specifically of George Zimmerman's trial and acquittal. Are there differences in the way "liberal" and "conservative" outlets such as MSNBC and Fox News cover the story? In what ways is the coverage consistent, and in what ways is it different? Are there differences in how various geographic regions cover the story? In particular, are there differences in states that are pro-gun or have "stand your ground" laws compared to those that do not? Have students look for patterns in how the Zimmerman and Martin are portrayed and what words are used to describe or refer to them. How does the mainstream media coverage compare to social media reports? Are certain outlets leaving out or glossing over some points? How does that affect the story? Is that evidence of bias?

- Have students trace the evolution of a story over time. For instance, have them follow the story of the Boston Marathon bombing. What is the first or earliest mention of the bombing? What "facts" are being reported in the early stories? How does later coverage compare to early coverage in terms of tone as well as specific details and facts? Does the amount or tone of coverage vary by geographic region? Have them compare the early news stories and details about the suspect to the later cover story in *Rolling Stone* magazine.[31] Does the lapse of time seem to affect the story? How does time and distance affect the tone of a story, if at all? (*Rolling Stone* was accused of being sensationalist and insensitive in running that cover story.) Have students weigh in on those accusations based on their content analysis and comparison to other coverage. How does the depth and breadth of the *Rolling Stone* article vary from the earlier news coverage? Explain how the type of journalism and story plays into these differences. Many of the stories offer "facts" about the events, the victims, and/or the suspects. Where did the reporters get their information? Does it seem reliable? Why or why not?

- Marshall McLuhan famously said, "The medium is the message."[32] Ask students to explain what that means in their own words and give examples from mass media that illustrate their point. Next, have students look at the coverage of the same story in several different formats, including audio, video, photographs, and text. For instance, have them examine Miley Cyrus' 2013 Video Music Awards performance and reaction to it in various formats. How do their reactions to and understanding of the story change with the different formats, if at all? Is the message affected by the format? How so? Does one format seem more effective? Why? Have them analyze several sources that offer negative and positive reviews of the performance. Are there any patterns as to who is critical and who is supportive? Why might that be? Is that evidence of bias?

- Have students trace the evolution of a story that has been shown to be distorted or false such as the toppling of the Saddam Hussein statue in Firdos Square (where original pictures were angled to make the crowd look larger and more engaged than it actually was), the story linking the MMR vaccine to autism, or reports of weapons of mass destruction in Iraq. Begin by having students look at the contemporary pictures or reports as primary documents. What are they saying? What was the reaction? Next have them trace the changes in the story and look at the contrasting developments. What has changed with regard to the original story? Why did the original story change—was it bias, misinformation, falsifying information, poor research, etc.? Has the opinion or reaction changed along with the story? Is there evidence of the continued influence effect?

Notes

1.   Hans C. Schmidt, "Essential but Problematic: Faculty Perceptions of Media Literacy Education at the University Level," *Qualitative Research Reports in Communications* 13, no. 1 (2012): 10–20.

2.   Paul Mihalidis, "Are We Speaking the Same Language? Assessing the State of Media Literacy in US Higher Education," *Simile 8, no. 4 (2008): 1–14.*

3.   Ibid., 1.

4.   Findings of this study reported in Laura Saunders, "Culture and Collaboration: Fostering Integration of Information Literacy by Speaking the Language of Faculty," in *Imagine, Innovate, Inspire: The Proceedings of the ACRL 2013 Conference,* ed. Dawn Mueller (Chicago: Association of College and Research Libraries, 2013), 137–47, http://www.ala.org/acrl/sites/ala.org.acrl/files/content/conferences/confsandpreconfs/2013/papers/Saunders_Culture.pdf.

5.   *Encyclopedia of International Media and Communications,* s.v. "democracy and the media."

6.   "Amid Criticism, Support for Media's 'Watchdog' Role Stands Out," Pew Research Center for the People and the Press, last modified August 8, 2013, accessed August 19, 2014, http://www.people-press.org/2013/08/08/amid-criticism-support-for-medias-watchdog-role-stands-out/.

7.   Ron Miller, "Journalistic Responsibility in the Digital Age," *EContent* 36, no. 2 (2013): 32, http://www.econtentmag.com/Articles/Column/Media-Redux/Journalistic-Responsibility-in-the-Digital-Age-88024.htm.

8.   John M. Budd, Zach C. Coble, and Katherine M. Anderson, "Retracted Publications in Biomedicine: Cause for Concern," in *A Declaration of Interdependence: The Proceedings of the ACRL 2011 Conference,* ed. Dawn Mueller (Chicago: Association of College and Research Libraries, 2011), 390–95, http://www.ala.org/acrl/sites/ala.org.acrl/files/content/conferences/confsandpreconfs/national/2011/papers/retracted_publicatio.pdf.

9.   Ulrich K.H. Ecker et al., "Correcting False Information in Memory: Manipulating the Strength of Misinformation Encoding and Its Retraction," *Psychonomic Bulletin Review 18, no. 3 (2011): 570–78.*

10.   Stephan Lewandowsky et al., "Misinformation and Its Correction: Continued Influence and Successful Debiasing," *Psychological Science in the Public Interest* 13, no. 3 (2012): 106–31.

11.   Elisah Babad, Eyal Peer, and Renee Hobbs, "The Effect of Media Literacy Education on Susceptibility to Media Bias" (paper, International Communication Association Annual Meeting, Chicago, IL May 21–25, 2009).

12.   "Media Literacy," *Partnership for 21st Century Skills,* accessed August 19, 2014,

13.   Sonia Livingstone, "What Is Media Literacy?" *Intermedia 32, no. 3 (2004): 18–20.*

14.   Mary Lou Galician, "Introduction: High Time for Dis-Illusioning Ourselves and Our Media; Media Literacy in the 21st Century," *The American Behavioral Scientist* 48, no. 1 (2004): 8.

15.   "Media Literacy," *Partnership for 21st Century Skills.*

16.   "Media Literacy," Henry J. Kaiser Family Foundation, accessed September 3, 2013, http://kaiserfamilyfoundation.files.wordpress.com/2013/01/key-facts-media-literacy.pdf.

17.   Sonia Livingstone, "Media Literacy and the Challenge of New Information and Communication Technologies," *The Communication Review 7, no. 1 (2004): 3–14.*

18.   Association of College and Research Libraries, *Information Literacy Competency Standards for Higher Education,* accessed September 3, 2013, http://www.ala.org/acrl/standards/informationliteracycompetency.

19.   Laura Saunders, "Faculty Perspectives on Information Literacy as a Student Learning Outcome," *The Journal of Academic Librarianship* 38, no. 4 (2012): 226–36.

20.   Amy R. Hofer, Lori Townsend, and Korey Brunetti, "Troublesome Concepts and Information Literacy: Investigating Threshold Concepts for IL Instruction," *Portal: Libraries and the Academy* 12, no. 4 (2012): 387–405.

21.   John McManus, "Don't Be Fooled: Use the SMELL Test to Separate Fact from Fiction Online," Mediashift, last modified February 7, 2013, http://www.pbs.org/mediashift/2013/02/

dont-be-fooled-use-the-smell-test-to-separate-fact-from-fiction-online038.

22. Michael Griffin, "Visual Competence and Media Literacy: Can One Exist without the Other?" *Visual Studies* 23, no. 2 (2008): 113–29.

23. "ACRL Visual Literacy Competency Standards for Higher Education: Visual Literacy Defined," Association of College and Research Libraries, last modified October 2011, accessed September 1, 2014, http://www.ala.org/acrl/standards/visualliteracy.

24. From interview notes taken for Saunders, "Faculty Perspectives."

25. "Content Analysis," Writing @ CSU: The Writing Studio, accessed September 4, 2013, http://writing.colostate.edu/guides/guide.cfm?guideid=61.

26. "Media Literacy," Henry J. Kaiser Family Foundation.

27. McManus, "Don't Be Fooled."

28. James H. Kuklinksi et al., "Misinformation and the Currency of Democratic Citizenship," *The Journal of Politics 62, no. 3 (2000): 790–816.*

29. American Library Association, Presidential Committee on Information Literacy: Final Report, accessed February 13, 2014, http://www.ala.org/acrl/publications/whitepapers/presidential; Alexandria Proclamation on Information Literacy and Lifelong Learning," United Nations Educational, Scientific, and Cultural Organization, accessed February 15, 2014, http://portal.unesco.org/ci/en/ev.php-URL_ID=20891&URL_DO=DO_TOPIC&URL_SECTION=201.html.

30. Heidi L.M. Jacobs, "Information Literacy and Reflective Pedagogical Praxis," *The Journal of Academic Librarianship* 34, no. 3 (2008): 261.

31. Janet Reitman, "Jahar's World," *Rolling Stone*, July 17, 2013, http://www.rollingstone.com/culture/news/jahars-world-20130717.

32. Marshall McLuhan, *Understanding Media: The Extensions of Man* (Boston: MIT Press, 1994), 7.

About the Authors

Editors

Heather Jagman is the coordinator of reference, instruction, and academic engagement and the subject liaison to the Theatre School at DePaul University Library in Chicago, Illinois. She was an ERIAL Project participant and a 2013 ACRL IMLS Assessment in Action grant recipient. She is particularly interested in information literacy and library user behavior.

Troy A. Swanson is the teaching and learning librarian and the library department chair at Moraine Valley Community College in Palos Hills, Illinois, where he is also the president of the Moraine Valley Faculty Association. Troy is the author of the book *Managing Social Media in Libraries: Finding Collaboration, Coordination, and Focus* and coauthor of the textbook *Why White Rice? Thinking through Writing.* He has published on social media, website usability, and information literacy. Troy is also a contributor to the Tame the Web blog.

Contributors

Andrew D. Asher is the assessment librarian at Indiana University Bloomington, where he leads the libraries' qualitative and quantitative assessment programs and conducts research on the information practices of students and faculty. Andrew's most recent projects have examined how "discovery" search tools influence undergraduates' research processes and how university researchers manage, utilize, and preserve their research data. Andrew holds a PhD in sociocultural anthropology from the University of Illinois at Urbana-Champaign and has written and presented widely on using ethnography in academic libraries, including the coedited volume *College Libraries and Student Cultures*.

William B. Badke is associate librarian for Associated Canadian Theological Schools and Information Literacy at Trinity Western University, Langley, British Columbia, Canada. He is author of *Research Strategies: Finding Your Way through the Information Fog* and *Teaching Research Processes: The Faculty Role in the Development of Skilled Student Researchers*; he also authors the Infolit Land column for *Online Searcher*. As a frequent writer in the field of information literacy, his main concerns are students becoming highly developed users of information for problem solving and the advancement of knowledge. He holds two master's degrees in theological studies as well as a MLS.

Anne C. Barnhart is the head of instructional services at the University of West Georgia, where she oversees reference, instruction, and the liaison program. Her research interests include interview techniques, library management, library's strategic political alignment, and professional development for recent library graduates. She is also interested in pursuing Scholarship of Teaching and Learning projects, including explorations of "vulnerability" in the learning experience and what she likes to think of as "mixed-media pedagogy." Prior to being at the University of West Georgia, she was the librarian for Latin American and Iberian studies, Chicana/o studies, and religious studies at the University of California, Santa Barbara. Anne also teaches as an adjunct instructor for University of Illinois at Urbana-Champaign's Graduate School of Library and Information Sciences in their LEEP program.

Patricia Brown is a reference librarian at Louisiana State University Eunice. Before her recent entry into librarianship, she earned a PhD in English literature from LSU, taught at several colleges in the South, and wrote about Renaissance drama. Her current project, "Beyond Recreational Literacy," involves a local high school dual-enrollment English course. In addition to her library work, she freelances as an editor and writes poetry.

Ashley Cole is a reference and instruction librarian at Eastern Kentucky University, specializing in student engagement and the first-year experience. In this role, Ashley collaborates with formal and informal undergraduate campus communities to develop, implement, and assess services and programs aimed at improving student success. Along with a BA from EKU, she also holds a MLIS from the University of Kentucky.

Jessica Critten received her MLIS and MA in interdisciplinary humanities from Florida State University. Her research interests include the cultural and ideological dimensions of information literacy, critical information literacy, and media studies. She has presented extensively about teaching and learning at the state, national, and international level. Jessica currently works as assistant professor and first-year programs librarian at the University of West Georgia.

Joe Eshleman has been the instruction librarian at Johnson and Wales University Library-Charlotte since 2008. He completed the Association of College and Research Libraries' Immersion program in 2009. He has presented on numerous occasions including the American Library Association Conference, the Lilly Education Conference, and the Teaching Professor Technology Conference. Joe is a coauthor of the book *Fundamentals for the Academic Liaison.*

Barbara Fister is a professor and academic librarian at Gustavus Adolphus College in St. Peter, Minnesota. She is the author of *Third World Women's Literatures: A Dictionary and Guide to Materials in English,* many articles and book chapters, and writes for *Inside Higher Ed* and *Library Journal.*

Deana Greenfield is an instructional systems designer who specializes in training others on educational technology. Formerly an assistant professor at National Louis University, she developed and taught courses in digital information literacy. She earned a MLIS from the University of Illinois at Urbana-Champaign and a MA degree in English from Northwestern University. She is currently the chair of the American Library Association Spectrum Scholarship Program.

Rebecca Halpern is the social work librarian for the University of Southern California's online MSW program, where she works to embed information literacy into the MSW curriculum. Rebecca's research interests include adult learning theories, online pedagogy, and re-imagining what it means when we say "information literacy instruction." Rebecca received her MIS from the University of Texas at Austin. When she isn't working as a librarian, she loves answering pub trivia, spending quality time with quality television, and exploring Los Angeles by bike.

Alison Hicks (http://alisonhicks.weebly.com) is the romance language librarian at the University of Colorado Boulder. After graduating from the University of St Andrews, Scotland with a MA in French and Spanish, Alison worked in Buenos Aires, Argentina before completing her MSIS from the University of Texas at Austin. Her research interests include studying critical information literacies and modern languages; changing practices of digital scholarship; and building community through participatory culture. Originally from the UK, she is fluent in French and Spanish and loves to ski, skate, and hike.

While in graduate school at UCLA, **Lisa Lepore** cofounded a reading program in a juvenile hall in Los Angeles, and she continues to advocate for reading in her current position as library director and a member of the faculty at Antioch University Los Angeles. Lisa is presently examining the closings of libraries in public schools throughout California and the deleterious effect that is having on book and reading culture.

Alison M. Lewis is an associate teaching professor at Drexel University, where she teaches a variety of graduate-level courses in the MLIS degree program. She received her MLS degree from Florida State University and her PhD from Temple University. She is the chief acquisitions editor for Library Juice Press and serves as the executive director of the Beta Phi Mu Honor Society.

Brad Marcum is the distance and online education program officer at Eastern Kentucky University Libraries (EKU) in Richmond, Kentucky. Brad has worked in libraries since 1998. Brad splits his time between working with EKU's regional campuses and online students and faculty and is an active conference presenter and author on distance librarianship issues. He received his MLS from the University of Kentucky in 2003 and has worked in distance education since then.

Beth McDonough has almost two decades of experience teaching information literacy. Beth is the coauthor of *The One-Shot Library Instruction Survival Guide* and co-teaches online professional development classes for the American

Library Association on the same topic. She holds a MLIS from the University of North Carolina at Greensboro and an EdD in leadership of curriculum and instruction from Western Carolina University. Her dissertation focused on critical information literacy from a practitioner perspective. She was formerly a National Board certified teacher in school library media and currently works as a research and instruction librarian for education at Western Carolina University.

MaryBeth Meszaros is an instructional services librarian at Monmouth University. She holds a PhD in English from University of Pennsylvania and a MLIS from Drexel University. Her book, *The Gothic Impulse in Contemporary Drama,* reflects her research interest in theater and drama—an interest she continues to pursue as a librarian. She serves as a member of the editorial board of *Communications in Information Literacy* and has published articles on postmodern drama, information literacy, and the research behavior of theater practitioners and scholars. A veteran of the first-year composition classroom, she likes to explore the reading-writing-information literacy nexus as well as faculty-librarian relationships.

Willie Miller is a librarian at Indiana University-Purdue University Indianapolis University Library, where he serves as subject liaison to the School of Informatics and Computing and the School of Journalism. In addition, Willie leads the library's campus outreach group, which develops outreach programming and media to promote library services to students, faculty, and staff. His research interests focus on library outreach, instructional technology, and library instruction. Willie is a 2010 graduate of the Indiana University School of Library and Information Science, an Indiana's Librarians Leading in Diversity Scholar, and a 2012 American Library Association Emerging Leader.

Rob Morrison is an associate professor at National Louis University and is serving as interim dean of Library and Learning Support in 2014. He has published on distance learning library services, information literacy, and critical pedagogy. His dissertation focused on the role of culture in information literacy. He earned a doctorate in adult and continuing education from National Louis University, a MLIS from Simmons College, and a BA from Syracuse University.

Lucy Mulroney is curator of special collections at Syracuse University Libraries' Special Collections Research Center with a courtesy appointment in the Department of Art and Music Histories. She received her PhD in visual and cultural studies at the University of Rochester and is currently completing a book on the publications of Andy Warhol. Her writing has appeared in *Grey Room, Photography and Culture,* and McSweeney's *The Believer.* Most recently, she curated the exhibition Strange Victories: *Grove Press 1951–1985* and co-organized the symposium "Positions of Dissent" at Syracuse University.

Trenia Napier is the research coordinator for the Noel Studio for Academic Creativity and a reference and instruction librarian at Eastern Kentucky University (EKU). In her dual position, Trenia collaborates efforts between the Noel Studio, EKU Libraries, and the larger university community to develop services and resources that reflect the synergistic relationship between research and written and oral communications.

Julie Obst is a librarian with Central Piedmont Community College (CPCC), where she's been working in library services since 2007. In her current role as an e-learning librarian, she's expanded the library's e-learning services to include in-person practice sessions for new and popular databases accompanied by online components for distance students. She has also co-created the embedded extension service, which places UNC Greensboro library science students as embedded librarians in select CPCC English and business courses.

Amy Pajewski is a reference and instruction librarian at West Texas A&M University, where she provides leadership in campus outreach and emerging technologies in the classroom. She is nearing completion of her MA in English literature, focusing on western eco-literature, and is a poetry editor for *Sundog Lit.* Her work has appeared in numerous literary journals, and she serves on the editorial committee for Open Library of Humanities. Amy holds a MLS from Clarion University of Pennsylvania as well as a BA in English from Millersville University. She is also a graduate of the Harvard Graduate School's Leadership Institute for Academic Librarians, class of 2013.

Stephen A. Sanders is the Library Science 102 coordinator at Southeastern Louisiana University in Hammond. This one-hour information literacy course is required in majors as diverse as nursing and history and graduates over 1200 students per year. Stephen is a veteran, having served in both Afghanistan and Iraq as an Army chaplain. His research interests include faculty input into course assessment and the philosophical foundations of bibliographic instruction.

Laura Saunders is an assistant professor at Simmons College Graduate School of Library and Information Science, where she teaches in the areas of user instruction, reference, intellectual freedom, and academic libraries. Her research interests include information literacy, assessment, and social justice aspects of information access and literacy. Laura has a PhD and MLIS, both from Simmons College, and a BA in English literature and Italian from Boston University.

Craig Schroer is the systems librarian at the University of West Georgia. He holds a MLIS from the University of Texas at Austin, where he worked as an area studies librarian for 20 years. Outside of systems-related work he also teaches a for-credit course in library research and information literacy. His research interests focus primarily on pedagogy, in particular, teaching "real-world" critical thinking skills and assessment of the contribution of libraries to the mission of higher education. He is presently serving as chair of the library assessment task force reporting to the University System of Georgia's Regents Academic Committee on Libraries.

Daniel Von Holten teaches professional writing at Kansas State University. His research interests include collaborative writing, teaching research skills, and English language learners. He received his MA in rhetoric and composition from the University of Akron and a BA from Trine University.

Nicole Walls is an assistant professor of English at West Texas A&M University (WTAMU). She teaches first-year and advanced composition, advanced grammar, creative nonfiction, and a graduate seminar in composition theory and pedagogy. She plays an active role in resource development and curriculum design for WTAMU's Office of Writing Programs and serves as an advisor to instructors and teaching assistants of basic writing. Her research areas include the role of critical writing pedagogy within an educational system under national revision, US participation in global education development, and international language politics. Nicole holds a BA in literature/writing from UC San Diego and a PhD in English from the University of Illinois at Urbana-Champaign.

Lane Wilkinson is lead instruction librarian at the University of Tennessee at Chattanooga and formerly a philosophy instructor at several metropolitan Detroit universities. His research interests include social epistemology, testimony, professional ethics, and information literacy. Lane frequently writes about these and other issues on his blog Sense and Reference (http://senseandreference. wordpress.com). He holds a MLIS and a MA in philosophy, both from Wayne State University.

Patrick Williams is an associate librarian and subject specialist for English, linguistics, and communication and rhetorical studies at the Syracuse University Libraries. He holds a BA in English from the University of North Carolina at Greensboro and a MS and PhD in information studies from the University of Texas at Austin. His research interests include digital humanities, social interaction in reading and writing environments, and information literacy.

Brian W. Young is an engineering reference librarian and assistant professor at the University of Mississippi, where he serves as the library's liaison to the School of Engineering and teaches information literacy. Brian's research interests include information literacy, library user experience, and engineering resource use. Brian holds a MLS from the University of North Carolina at Chapel Hill and a BS from Clemson University.

INDEX